MUZZLELOADER MAGAZINE'S

THE BOOK OF
BUCKSKINNING III

Edited by

WILLIAM H. SCURLOCK

REBEL PUBLISHING COMPANY, INC./TEXARKANA, TEXAS

EDITORIAL STAFF

EDITOR:
William H. Scurlock

ASSOCIATE EDITOR:
Mary Frances Scurlock

GRAPHIC DESIGN:
William H. Scurlock
David Wright

COVER PHOTOGRAPHY:
David Damer

PUBLISHER:
Oran Scurlock, Jr.

ABOUT THE COVERS

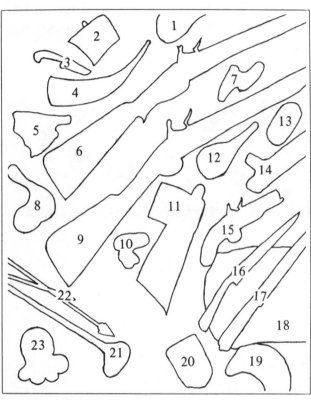

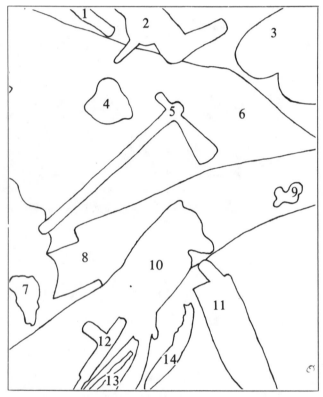

FRONT COVER: *(1) Wooden noggin... Oran Scurlock (2) Rum horn . . . David Wright (3) Patch knife . . . Hoppy Hopkins (4) Powder horn... David Wright (5) Bullet molds (6) Virginia style rifle . . . Hershel House (7) Shot Flasks . . . Original English (8) Crow beads . . . Original, ca. 1840 (9) Fowling piece . . . G. L. Jones (10) Flint & steel (11) Western knife sheath... David & Diane Chambers (12) Shot flask . . . Original English (13) Tobacco box... Tedd Cash (14) Clay pipes (15) English pocket pistol... Original by Bond (16) Rifleman's knife... Hershel House (17) Rifleman's knife... Paul Young (18) Indian saddle bag . . . Deborah Hohn (19) Shell gorget (20) Beaded pouch... Betty Walker (21) War club... Jim Hamm (22) Arrows . . . Jim Hamm (23) Jefferson peace medal & coins of the period*

BACK COVER: *(1) Beaver castor container... David Wright (2) Hand forged beaver trap... Original (3) Floral beaded moccasins (4) Quilled mirror case (5) Tomahawk head forged from gun barrel (6) Crow style war shirt... Steve Laughbaum & Donna Hamm (7) Indian neck amulet... Robert Guion (8) Plains rifle in blanket case (9) Original period coins (10) Indian pipe bag ... Jim & Donna Hamm (11) Indian knife case . . . Gary Johnson (12) Plains style pipe (13) Beaded pipe tamper (14) Bear jaw handled knife*

Contents

DEDICATION

*This book is affectionately dedicated
to the memory of our friend and colleague,
Pat Tearney, who left us too soon.*

HISTORIC GUNS & TODAY'S MAKERS

BY DAVID WRIGHT

"I CONSIDER MYSELF FORTUNATE that I can combine my career with my deep rooted interest in muzzle loading guns and American history," says David Wright, well known painter of the American frontier. Wright's life began in the small Kentucky town of Rosine in 1942 and the majority of his years since then have been spent living in rural communities in Kentucky and Tennessee.

"I can remember even before I started to grade school, shooting the guns of my grandfather and other relatives, of hunting and running the woods with my brothers and cousins, so I reckon I've always had an interest and love for guns and the outdoors. I bought my first muzzle loading gun when I was nineteen and have been shooting and hunting with them for the last twenty-four years."

In 1962 Wright began his art career after two years of art school and in 1973 joined Gray Stone Press, a limited edition print publisher. Today editions of his prints of mountain men and the American frontier are sold out upon release.

So why is an artist writing about muzzle loading gun makers? Wright explains, "I've always viewed muzzle loading gun making as an art. I enjoy any opportunity to promote the arts, whether two dimensional or three dimensional, so I welcome this chance to showcase the work of some of the fine gun makers of the country." His writings have appeared in *Muzzleloader, Muzzle Blasts, Dixie Gunworks Black Powder Annual*, and *The Book of Buckskinning*.

David Wright has been included in *Who's Who In American Art, Contemporary Western Artists* published by Southwest Art Publishing Co., and a host of other publications. He is a member of The Tennessee Longhunters, American Mountain Men, NRA, and the NMLRA. He lives in Cross Plains, Tennessee with his wife Charlotte, his daughter, Shannon, and son, Shawn.

"Here we found several large bands of Buffaloe we went to a small spring and encamped. I now prepared my self for the first time in my life to kill meat for my supper with a Rifle. I had an elegant one but had little experience in useing it. I however approached the band of Buffaloe crawling on my hands and knees within about 80 yards of them then raised my body erect took aim and shot at a Bull: at the crack of the gun the Buffaloe all ran off excepting the Bull which I had wounded, I then reloaded and shot as fast as I could untill I had driven 25 bullets at, in and about him which was all that I had in my bullet pouch whilst the Bull still stood apparently riveted to the spot I watched him anxiously for half an hour in hopes of seeing him fall, but to no purpose, I was obliged to give it up as a bad job."

SO stated Osborne Russell in 1834. I've always liked that excerpt, not because it shows an apparent inefficiency in either the gun or the hunter to bring down the game but because of the candor of the author. Too bad Russell didn't tell us a little more about the gun that he used, other than it was an "elegant one," because it might have helped us to understand why "25 bullets at, in and about" a buffalo didn't bring it down.

Of course, by Russell's own statement, he was a greenhorn, just beginning his career as a mountain man. Since this was the first time he had ever tried to make meat with a rifle, it is entirely possible that at 80 yards very few of those 25 bullets actually hit the buffalo. Other contemporary accounts, such as that of Ashley in 1823, testify that the guns of the day were plenty efficient to bring down a buffalo at a very long range, assuming that the proper caliber was used. Ashley's rifle had a 42" barrel and shot a 1 oz. ball (about .66 cal.).[2]

Today, the buckskinner recreating a certain period in history has a wide variety of muzzle loading firearms from which to choose to fit his purposes, whether his interests are buckskinning, military re-enacting, or hunting. He can choose from the mass produced, factory made guns, or from semi-custom guns produced in the smaller shops, or from those firearms built by custom makers for the individual customer.

Although the different models of factory made firearms are endless (and many function very well), most are not authentic reproductions of the guns of the 18th and 19th centuries. So, for the person who wants an authentic period firearm, the custom gun maker provides the best solution.

It seems plausible that a man in the 18th and 19th centuries leaving the settlements for the frontier, as Charlie Hanson very aptly puts it, "carried the best gun he could find. It was his companion, his protector, and his commissary. If it ever failed him, he might not come back."[3]

As early immigrants came to America, many brought their firearms with them from their homelands: the short barreled "Jaeger" hunting rifles from Germany and the fine single and double barreled rifles and fowlers from England and France. But the Indian trade and a new country full of game made it worthwhile to ship firearms to America for sale and trade.

During the 1700s many "Fusil de Chasse" or "Hunting Guns" were shipped to New France for use by the coureurs de bois, voyageurs, and Indians. Most were made at the Tulle Arms Manufactory in France and had 44 inch 28 gauge barrels, with walnut full stocks deeply curved at the butt. These fusils were iron mounted, light, rugged, and easy to handle in the woods. Close copies of the Tulle Fusil de Chasse are being produced today by at least three arms companies.

The lightweight and inexpensive smoothbore seemed to be a favorite among some western frontiersmen. It loaded easily and fired ball or shot thus making it an attractive piece to the Indian as well. But the all-time favorite was the Northwest gun, and the fact that it stayed in production until late in the nineteenth century attests to its popularity all through the fur trade and following years. These popular guns came in barrel lengths of 36, 42, and 48 inches with bore sizes of from 16 ga. through 28 ga. The 24 ga. appears to have been the most popular. The oversized trigger guard and the dragon side plate were two easily recognized characteristics of the Northwest gun. Thousands of these fusils, or "Hudson's Bay fukes" as they were sometimes called, were imported mostly from England by the Hudson's Bay Company and by various American fur trading companies for trade with the Indians and for use by company employees as well. American makers, beginning with Deringer in 1816,[4] finally began producing these guns.

The smoothbore musket played a more important part in the settling of America than many people realize. The three wars fought on American soil against England and France brought many thousands of military arms into this country. These, along with military arms produced locally, fell into civilian hands to be used for hunting, as well as in defense against marauding Indians. During the French & Indian War, France equipped many of her soldiers with the M1734 French Marine musket made at Tulle. The French & Indian War and the American Revolution brought into this country numbers of French Charleville muskets and the English Brown Bess, two rugged arms built to function regardless of abuse. Certainly many of these, not to mention American-made military arms, fell into civilian use at the close of the wars. For example, Manuel Lisa reportedly carried a Brown Bess made in 1740 when he went up the Missouri River in 1807.[5]

When American gun makers began building what eventually became known as the Pennsylvania rifle (after the War of 1812 to be referred to as the Kentucky rifle), they built a gun that saw extensive use during the 18th and 19th centuries. Utilized in both the northern and southern colonies before the Revolution, the earlier rifles were full stocked, mostly in plain maple, with a wide butt, octagon barrel, brass furniture, and either a sliding wood patchbox or a simple brass one. The weapon's graceful lines, combined with a long accurate rifled barrel of generally .45 to .52 caliber, made the Kentucky rifle a favorite with

A Tulle "fusil de chasse" or hunting gun made at the armory at Tulle in France and shipped to Canada during the 18th century. Courtesy of The Museum of the Fur Trade

backwoodsmen, longhunters, and gentlemen hunters as well.

Although not built as a military arm, these "rifle-guns" earned their place in history during the Revolutionary War by their influence in the formation of rifle companies such as Daniel Morgan's Riflemen. In a letter to Morgan dated June 3rd, 1777, General Washington set the tone of one method in which he expected to utilize Morgan's shirtmen:

A German artist's version of the American rifleman at the time of the Revolution. They are shown clothed in fringed hunting frocks and overalls. It's interesting to note that the riflemen are shown bearded and armed, not with rifles, but with bayonetted muskets.

"... It occurs to me that, if you were to dress a company or two of true woodsmen in the Indian style, and let them make the attack with screaming and yelling, as the Indians do, it would have very good consequences, especially if as little as possible were said or known of the matter beforehand."[6]

The feats of long range sniping with the weapons were respected by the British, and the important part the rifle played in carrying the day at Cowpens and King's Mountain is history.

Meanwhile, at the same time the Kentucky rifle was in its "Golden Age," a new breed of rifle makers in the Southern highlands began to produce a distinctive "Southern" Kentucky rifle. These variants were still long barreled, full stocked guns but plainer in ornamentation. Iron mountings were common and early rifles were of heavy calibers for bear hunting and Indian fighting. In later years the calibers became smaller for use on deer and squirrels. Some guns still carried patchboxes but a great many had a tallow hole drilled in the stock to store tallow

In the last quarter of the 18th century the Pennsylvania rifle reached its "Golden Age" of craftsmanship and ornamentation. Rifles were embellished with rococo relief carving and silver inlays of wire and sheet to enhance the long graceful stocks. Among such craftsmen whose names are famous today to collectors and students of the Kentucky rifle are Jacob Dickert, Frederick Sell, John Armstrong, A. Verner, John and Herman Rupp, and J. P. Beck.

for greasing patches.

As the tide of explorers, hunters, and settlers poured over the Appalachian Mountain chain these long barreled rifles went with them to the frontier regions of Kentucky, Tennessee, and the Ohio and Illinois country. Whereas before only builders of the Northern and Southern coastal states turned out guns, now makers from the Western states of Kentucky and Tennessee were building to fill the need. The Bean family from eastern Tennessee was a prolific

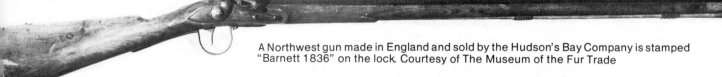

A Northwest gun made in England and sold by the Hudson's Bay Company is stamped "Barnett 1836" on the lock. Courtesy of The Museum of the Fur Trade

group of rifle builders that built "Tennessee" and mountain rifles for a number of years.

As exploration pushed on across the Mississippi River and headed for the Rocky Mountains many Southern guns were taken along. The heavy bores and plain strong stocks of the guns suited the needs of the mountain men.

In 1803 when Meriwether Lewis and William Clark were organizing their expedition to the Pacific Coast, Lewis wrote to President Jefferson on April 20, that "my rifles, tomahawks and knives are preparing at Harpers Ferry, and are already in a state of readiness that leaves me little doubt of their being in readiness in due time."[7]

It has been assumed by many authorities (and doubted by others) that the "Corps of Discovery" carried the U.S. Model 1803 Harpers Ferry rifled musket. The 1803 was definitely in early production at the time of their departure in 1804, and since the expedition members did carry *rifles* specifically made for them at the Harpers Ferry Armory, the weapons could well have been the Model 1803. This was the first regulation U.S. rifle and the expedition presented a prime opportunity for testing the firearm under adverse and unique conditions. This new rifle was half stocked with a 33" octagon-to-round .54 caliber barrel. The mountings were brass and the rifle

carried an iron underrib with the first ramrod pipe belled to receive the iron ramrod easier. During the fifteen years this model was in production, a total of 19,726 U.S. Rifles, Model 1803, are accounted for in the U.S. Ordnance records.[8]

The U. S. government had been giving guns as treaty settlements and annuities for years and as the fur trade moved up the Missouri River, government factory posts were built to help regulate the Indian trade. These posts were stocked with a variety of firearms to sell to the Indians, the biggest sellers being the Northwest guns. A check of the inventories of some of these posts show that sometime around the early 1800s the factory outposts began stocking *rifles* for trade with the Indians. Among the contractors who made rifles for the Indian trade were Jacob Dickert, Peter Gonter, Henry Leman, and John Joseph Henry, all from Pennsylvania. Of all the builders who supplied trade rifles to the government and the fur companies, the firms of J. Henry and H. E. Leman stand out.

The characteristics of the trade rifle were barrel lengths of 36 to 42 inches in calibers of .45 to .54. They were usually plain, although some rifles were styled after the Kentucky and were mounted in brass or iron. J. Henry

This fanciful old wood engraving shows members of the Lewis and Clark expedition shooting Grizzly bears. Mentioned several times in the Captains' journals, encountering the "great white bears" provided some exciting and challenging moments for the men of the party. Note the sailing sloop on the river at left. The artist has undoubtedly taken license with history.

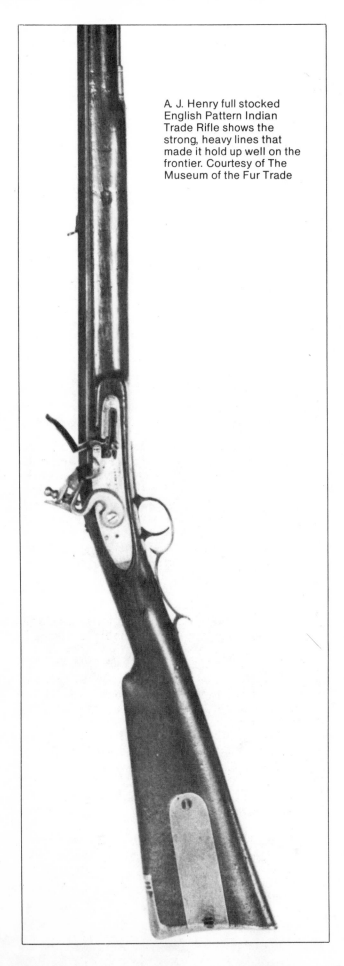

A. J. Henry full stocked English Pattern Indian Trade Rifle shows the strong, heavy lines that made it hold up well on the frontier. Courtesy of The Museum of the Fur Trade

introduced the popular "Lancaster" pattern which was styled after the Lancaster County rifles of Pennsylvania. A short time later he began building the English Pattern Indian trade rifle which became his biggest selling Indian rifle throughout the fur trade. It was a well built gun with a full stock of walnut and a 42 to 44 inch octagon barrel. It came brass mounted and carried a 6" flint lock and a British military style patchbox. The American Fur Company first ordered this rifle in 1826 and, by the date of its final order in 1842, a total of 710 rifles had been ordered from Henry.[9] During the 1830s Henry also built the New English or "scroll guard" pattern and some steel mounted Kentucky styled rifles but the Lancaster and the English Pattern were the two most popular models. These guns were probably the work horses of the fur brigades in the '30s. Today's mountain man would certainly be authentic if equipped with one of these.

Another gunsmith, H. E. Leman of Lancaster, Pennsylvania, was a prolific supplier of Indian trade rifles. Active from 1834 until the 1880s, his company began supplying both flint lock and percussion arms to the government and fur trade companies in 1837. The characteristics of his Indian rifles were short heavy barrels inletted into strong, plain, full stocks. The calibers ranged from .45 to .60 and some of his guns carried brass cap boxes and were artificially striped to look like curly maple.

Being the jumping off place for brigades going to the Rockies, the arms trade flourished in St. Louis. The firm of Jake and Sam Hawken emerged as one of the more well known gunsmiths in this river city. It is known that the two Hawken brothers were operating there in the '20s, because Sam stated later in life that William Ashley carried one of his finer rifles when he went to the mountains in '23.[11] (This was the one that Ashley used to make an extremely long kill on a buffalo.) The earliest clearly documented rifle order, however, dated from 1831. The rifle was sold to Peter Sarpy for twenty-eight dollars.[10] The Hawken brothers' production was small, probably under a hundred guns a year but during the '30s and '40s they had developed a reputation among mountain men for making one of the finest rifles of the day. Their guns had distinct Southern influences. Always mounted in iron, they had heavy barrels with big calibers — .50 to .54 being the most common. Most all had a "scroll" type trigger guard, some being flat to the wrist and others more rounded. (One surviving rifle has a "pinched" scroll guard with Virginia influences.) They were generally stocked in plain maple. (Another existing full stock rifle has a tallow hole in the stock, a definite Southern characteristic.) The Hawken brothers' shop built both full and half stocked rifles with full stock barrels seldom being over 40". They definitely built guns with flint locks although none are known to survive in that condition today.

The classic half stock percussion rifle that became popular with the mountain man during the 1840s and the following years — that model we refer to today as the "Hawken Rocky Mountain Rifle" — was iron mounted, stocked in plain maple, with a heavy barrel of 30-36 inches. It was almost always bored .50 to .54 caliber and had a patent hooked breech. The forestock was double keyed to the barrel, and it had double set triggers and the scroll type trigger guard. This particular rifle was con-

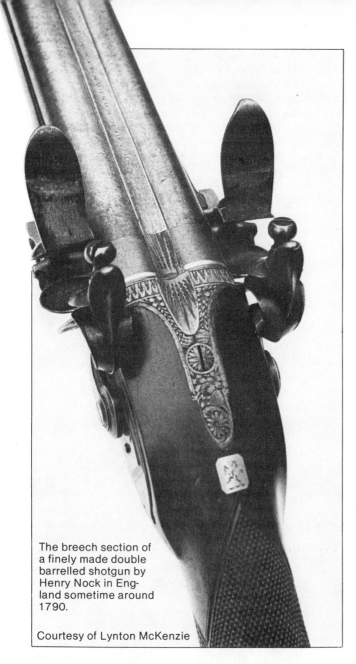

The breech section of a finely made double barrelled shotgun by Henry Nock in England sometime around 1790.

Courtesy of Lynton McKenzie

June 18, 1823— W. H. Savage announces the sale of the stock of the Office of Indian Trade factory at Prairie du Chien, including "Rifles of different kinds, some very elegant; shotguns . . ."

June 2, 1834— J. R. Stanford — "English shotguns, 2 cases, containing 25 each, some of them very good."

Aug. 29, 1834— C. Redon—"French and English fowling pieces, single and double barrels . . ."

Nov. 14, 1834— Bentzen & Kloppenburg - "25 pieces English, French and German double and single barrel guns and rifles."

Jan. 11, 1837— Meade & Adriance — "a few elegant Damascus twist, London double barrel guns, in Mahogany cases; also a large assortment of fine & common double and single barrel guns."[12]

The history of the long guns of America has only been briefly touched upon here, primarily to provide background for the following pages outlining some of today's builders' works. For a more thorough coverage of the guns of the American frontier I suggest reading Charles Hanson's excellent chapter "The Guns" in *The Book of Buckskinning.*

For the buckskinner who wishes to acquire a firearm of historical background, and who wants to feel comfortable knowing that the gun he or she purchases will be authentically correct for the period which is portrayed, the following pages showcase some of the country's finest makers. Not all of the firearms pictured are fancy art pieces, just as all of the guns carried by our forefathers were not fancy art pieces, but all the firearms shown have a solid foundation in the background of our nation's history.

NOTES

[1] Osborne Russell, *Journal of a Trapper (1834-1843)* (Lincoln, Ne.: University of Nebraska Press, 1965), P. 5.

[2] Charles E. Hanson, Jr., *The Hawken Rifle: Its Place in History* (Chadron, Ne.: The Fur Press, 1979), p. 11.

[3] Charles E. Hanson, Jr., "The Guns," in *The Book of Buckskinning,* ed. William H. Scurlock (Texarkana, Tx.: Rebel Publishing Co., Inc., 1980), p. 80.

[4] Hanson, "The Guns", p. 86.

[5] John G. W. Dillin, *The Kentucky Rifle* (Washington, D.C.: The National Rifle Association of America, 1924), p. 15.

[6] Joe D. Huddleston, *Colonial Riflemen in the American Revolution* (York, Pa.: George Shumway Publisher, 1978), p. 37.

[7] Stuart E. Brown, *The Guns of Harpers Ferry* (Berryville, Va.: Virginia Book Company, 1968), p. 30.

[8] L. D. Satterlee, *A Catalog of Firearms for the Collector* (Detroit, Mi.: 1939), p. .

[9] Hanson, *The Hawken Rifle,* p. 67.

[10] *Ibid.,* p. 31.

[11] *Ibid.,* p. 11.

[12] *Ibid.,* pp. 73-74.

sidered fairly expensive in its day, but even at that time some fancy rifles of this model Hawken were built stocked with finely curled maple wood and included patchboxes and engraving.

Fowlers and double barreled shotguns always had their place in the gun trade too. The wealthy preferred their finely crafted English guns by the Mantons, Durs Egg, and H. Nock, but to fill the need, fowlers and shotguns were imported from continental Europe as well. The double barreled shotgun in plainer versions, too, showed up on the frontier throughout the nineteenth century. The Hudson's Bay Company still sold *flint* shotguns as late as 1860 and the percussion well on into the twentieth century. The men of the Rocky Mountains armed themselves with shotguns as evidenced in the writings of Jim Beckwourth, Josiah Gregg, Joe Meek, and others. The fur companies bought them in quantities, and a look at the number of advertisements that ran in the newspapers will show that there was a healthy demand for the American product as well as the imported guns. Here are just a few ads which ran in the *Missouri Republican:*

Interest in muzzle loading firearms came early to Kit Ravenshear. While he was a student at Feltonfleet Prep School, he fully restored a boxlock pistol to working order, part of which involved making up a hand filed cock. His age . . . 13! Interest in firearms remained with Kit throughout Prep School and on into college while he studied engineering and law at Brighton and London University.

While in the Army in 1949 and 1950 Second Lieutenant Ravenshear served as a Weapons Training Officer in the Queen's Own Cameron Highlanders stationed in Tripoli, North Africa. (Later, in 1960-63, he served as a 1st Lieutenant with the Argyll and Sutherland Highlanders in Scotland.)

For several years following his discharge from the Army, Kit farmed in Scotland, served on the police force in Suffolk, England, and eventually wound up back in Scotland working as a salesman.

All the while he was pursuing these professions he functioned as a part-time gunsmith until 1962. It was this year that a move from Scotland to England placed Kit in charge of an old established gun business, Normans of Farmlingham. This move established the direction in which Kit's life was to develop in the years following.

As owner of Normans, Kit built an enviable reputation for his restoration work and in 1963 he was admitted as "Master Gunmaker" in the Gunmakers Association of Great Britain. He was a pioneer in the use of investment casting for the production of quality antique gun parts and eventually developed a worldwide market for his castings.

In 1971 his talents and special services took him to Canada and two years later to the United States where he has since settled in rural Pennsylvania. In 1973 Kit was engaged by Parks Canada as arms consultant and supplier for the Fortress of Louisbourg Rebuilding Program which resulted in the research and re-creation of the French Marine and Colonial Musket. Other research and implementation contracts have included such museums and historic sites as Fort Michilimackinac, Fort Conde, The Valley Forge Museum, Old Sturbridge Village, The National Park Service, and others.

Kit admits his "first loves" are the 18th century European Military firearms. The creation of Museum Services, Inc., through which are offered authentic reproductions of these and English sporting guns, has been the culmination of a lifetime of work.

At present Kit's company, Museum Services, produces authentic copies of at least 10 French and British military long arms and pistols, and British sporting guns. Extensive research has gone into the production of each piece and close attention to quality is always foremost. Firearms are offered completed and as component parts. Write to Kit Ravenshear, Museum Services, Inc., Ashland, PA 17921, (717) 875-3369.

KIT RAVENSHEAR
BORN: SURREY, ENGLAND
JUNE 13, 1930

TYPES OF FIREARMS OFFERED: *A wide variety of early French and English military muskets, German Jaeger rifles, English rifles and fowlers, French and English pistols*

M 1734 TULLE FRENCH MARINE MUSKET
SPECIFICATIONS:
WOOD: *European Walnut*
BARREL: *Getz, octagon-to-round*
BBL LENGTH: *44"*
CALIBER: *.66 (smoothbore)*
LOCK: *Flint*
TRIGGER: *Single, standard military style*
FURNITURE: *Iron*
KIT OFFERED: *Yes*

KIT RAVENSHEAR

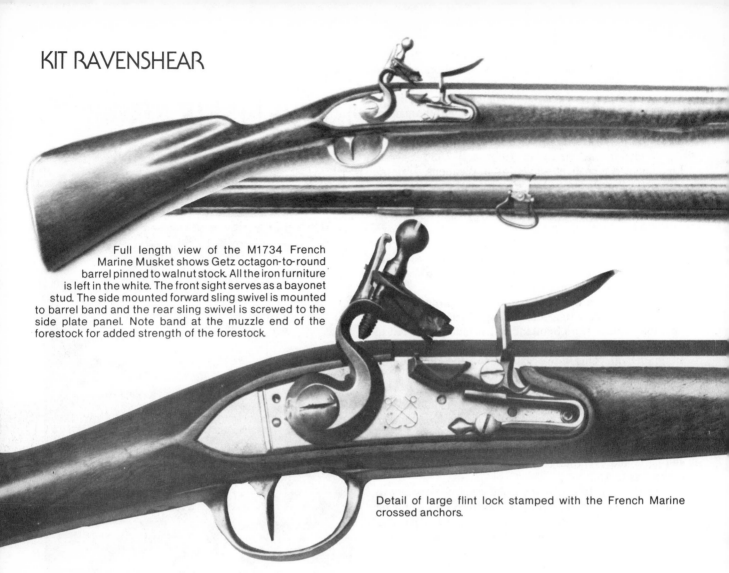

Full length view of the M1734 French Marine Musket shows Getz octagon-to-round barrel pinned to walnut stock. All the iron furniture is left in the white. The front sight serves as a bayonet stud. The side mounted forward sling swivel is mounted to barrel band and the rear sling swivel is screwed to the side plate panel. Note band at the muzzle end of the forestock for added strength of the forestock.

Detail of large flint lock stamped with the French Marine crossed anchors.

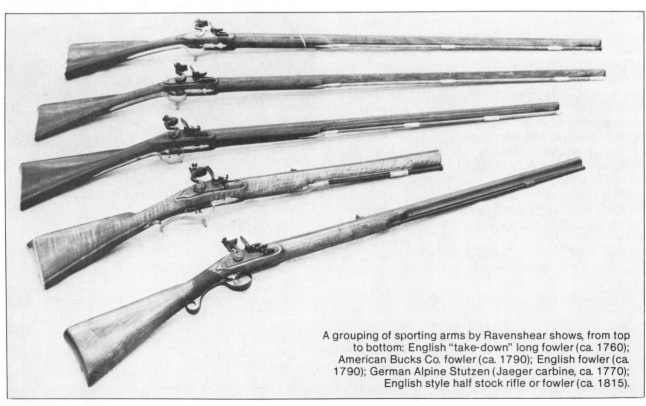

A grouping of sporting arms by Ravenshear shows, from top to bottom: English "take-down" long fowler (ca. 1760); American Bucks Co. fowler (ca. 1790); English fowler (ca. 1790); German Alpine Stutzen (Jaeger carbine, ca. 1770); English style half stock rifle or fowler (ca. 1815).

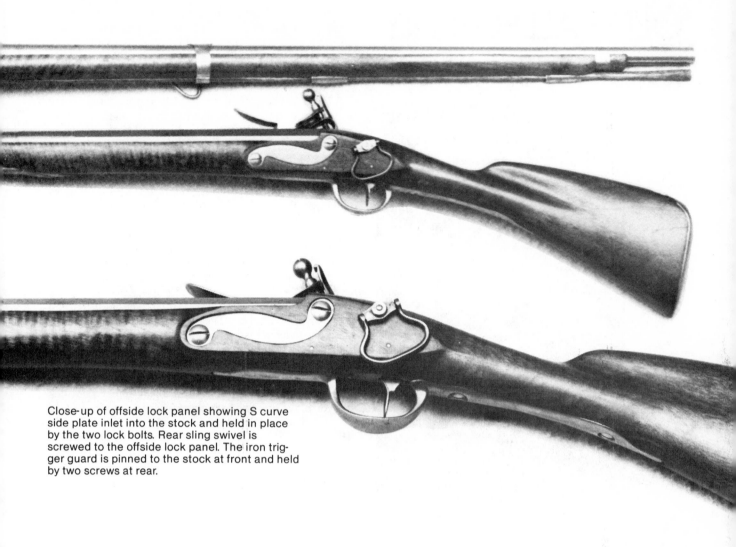

Close-up of offside lock panel showing S curve side plate inlet into the stock and held in place by the two lock bolts. Rear sling swivel is screwed to the offside lock panel. The iron trigger guard is pinned to the stock at front and held by two screws at rear.

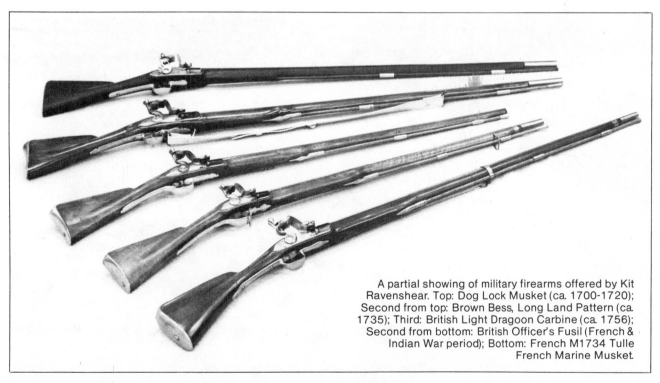

A partial showing of military firearms offered by Kit Ravenshear. Top: Dog Lock Musket (ca. 1700-1720); Second from top: Brown Bess, Long Land Pattern (ca. 1735); Third: British Light Dragoon Carbine (ca. 1756); Second from bottom: British Officer's Fusil (French & Indian War period); Bottom: French M1734 Tulle French Marine Musket.

OLDE ALLEGHENY TRADING COMPANY

BEGUN: PITTSBURGH, PENNSYLVANIA 1983

Brian McCarthy, president of Olde Allegheny Trading Co. has been involved in shooting and building muzzle loading guns for a number of years. Hailing from the Hudson River Valley of upstate New York, Brian's interest in the French & Indian War was nurtured by living close to many of the war's historical sites.

His avid involvement in F & I War re-enactments led Brian to feel there was a need for a reproduction of an authentic pre-Revolution period smoothbore, hence in 1983, the rebirth of the French Tulle "Fusil de Chasse." Until 1983 there were several copies of British arms on the market that could be used by persons interested in the American pre-Revolutionary War period, but for those interested in the French arms, other than individual custom builders, only Kit Ravenshear was offering a French gun; the M1734 French Marine musket.

Brian McCarthy feels his Tulle Fusil de Chasse fits the needs of F & I War re-enactors, courier du bois, and all others who are looking for an authentic smoothbore of the period.

The fusil or "hunting gun" is offered as a finished gun or as a 98% inletted kit. The 42" 20 ga. octagon-to-round smoothbore barrel is inlet and pinned into a plain maple full length stock. Optional stocks of fancy maple, walnut, and cherry are offered.

The large flintlock by Gene Davis features a fly in the tumbler and comes with a lifetime guarantee. The lock plate displays the Tulle touchmark.

Brian McCarthy is a life member of the NMLRA, NRA, Pennsylvania Gun Collectors Association, Pennsylvania Longhunters Association, and the NAPR.

A catalog describing the Tulle "Fusil de Chasse" and other products is available by writing to: Olde Allegheny Trading Co., 128 23rd Street, Pittsburgh, PA 15215, (412) 782-2990.

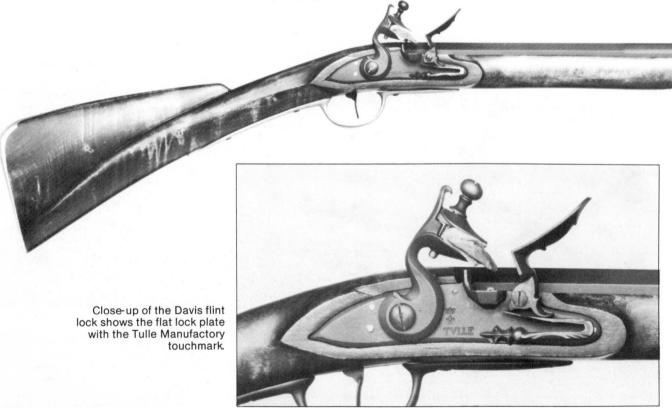

Close-up of the Davis flint lock shows the flat lock plate with the Tulle Manufactory touchmark.

13

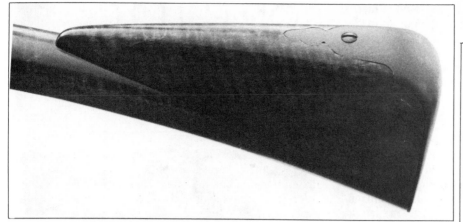

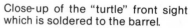

Top view shows a beefy butt stock with a French styled finial on this iron butt plate.

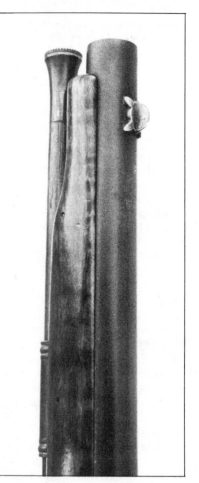

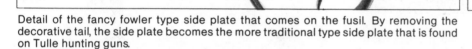

Detail of the fancy fowler type side plate that comes on the fusil. By removing the decorative tail, the side plate becomes the more traditional type side plate that is found on Tulle hunting guns.

Full length view of the Tulle Fusil de Chasse shows the French style butt stock and full stocked octagon-to-round barrel. The barrel is pinned to the stock. With a fowler appearance, the Fusil sports a brass butt plate, trigger guard, and three ramrod pipes. The gun can be purchased with either brass or iron furniture.

Like the originals the trigger guard is not inlet into the wood but is fastened to the stock with a forward pin and two rear screws.

TYPES OF FIREARMS OFFERED:
Tulle Fusil de Chasse

SPECIFICATIONS:
WOOD: *Plain Maple - Optional, curly Maple, Walnut, Cherry*
BARREL: *Octagon-to-round, smoothbore*
BBL LENGTH: *42"*
CALIBER: *20 Ga. (.630 cal.)*
LOCK: *Flint by Gene Davis*
TRIGGER: *Single*
FURNITURE: *Brass or Iron*
KIT OFFERED: *Yes*

RON EHLERT
BORN: ADRIAN, MICHIGAN
JULY 3, 1947

Raised around Adrian, Michigan, Ron Ehlert's younger days were always filled with outdoor sports — snow and water skiing, scuba diving, horseback riding, camping, and, of course, hunting and fishing.

Completing high school, Ron attended Ferris State College at Big Rapids, Michigan and obtained an associate degree in technical illustration. In 1969 he was drafted into the U.S. Army and was stationed at Fort Bragg, North Carolina as an illustrator until his discharge. Returning to civilian life in 1971, Ron picked up where he had left off and worked the next several years as an illustrator for Ford Motor Company's Engineering Center in Dearborn and later as a project engineer for various companies.

Along about 1976 Ron purchased a Thompson/Center Hawken Rifle kit and assembled it. Even then, he felt the urge to add his own personal touch, so he customized the rifle to make it different from all the other T/Cs. However, it was three years before Ron actually built his first "scratch" rifle. With guidance and help from friends, Homer Dangler and Tom La Goe, Ron built a rifle that could have been considered from the North Carolina school of gun building. He has been building guns ever since, going full time in 1984.

Ron will build any style gun — from smoothbores to Tennessees — a customer may prefer as long as it is within the traditional schools, but his personal preferences are the rifles from Bucks County, Pennsylvania. For individuality he prefers to make his own patchboxes for his rifles and modifies the outward appearance of the locks he uses. He insists on using quality components in his guns, preferring to use Getz barrels, Siler and Allen locks, and Cain and Davis triggers.

Many of his relief carved guns will exhibit silver wire inlay — a feature Ron particularly enjoys doing. Though he states that he likes building the decorative, relief carved rifles, he also likes to build a Hawken, or plain gun every so often. He feels that variety helps keep him in tune to design and simplicity of lines in a rifle.

The enjoyment of buckskinning comes naturally to Ron because of his interest in history. Since he was a child he has been interested in the history of the American frontier period and he feels being a rifle builder, for him, goes hand-in-hand with his interest in buckskinning. Most intriguing to Ron are the years of exploration west of the Appalachian Mountains during the 18th century. Being a resident of Tennessee he researches the lives of explorers and trappers of this region. Names of lesser known longhunters such as Spencer, Bledsoe, Boren, and others have become true life figures to Ron because they were the ones who trod the country where Ron now resides.

Living in a log house of his own building in Hickman County, Tennessee, Ron is still an active hunter, though all his hunting today is done with a flint lock rifle of his own making. He has taken deer as well as small game with the gun. He feels that actively using a muzzle loading gun for hunting and target shooting helps keep him in touch with building a gun that is useful as well as pretty. He belongs to the NMLRA, Tennessee Longhunters, and American Mountain Men.

For more information, Ron Ehlert can be contacted by dropping him a line at Rt. 1, Box 156 A, Duck River, TN 38454. No catalog is available.

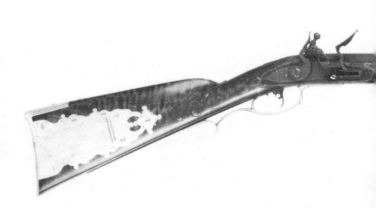

Close up of the relief and incised carved C-scroll on the buttstock.

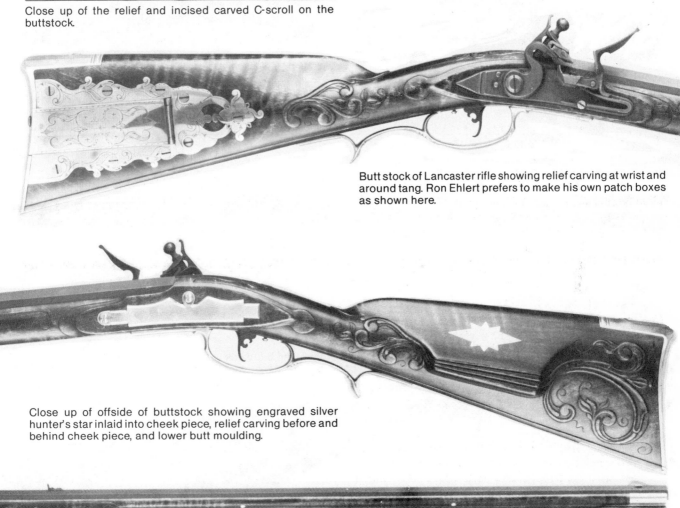

Butt stock of Lancaster rifle showing relief carving at wrist and around tang. Ron Ehlert prefers to make his own patch boxes as shown here.

Close up of offside of buttstock showing engraved silver hunter's star inlaid into cheek piece, relief carving before and behind cheek piece, and lower butt moulding.

Brass mounted Lancaster full stock rifle based on one by J. P. Beck. Stocked in curly maple with a 42" Green River .45 cal. barrel, it features a handmade patch box, relief carving, Siler lock, and engraving.

RON EHLERT

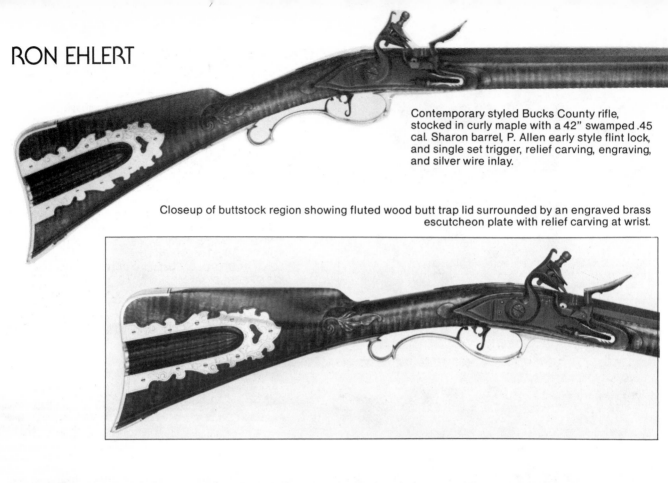

Contemporary styled Bucks County rifle, stocked in curly maple with a 42" swamped .45 cal. Sharon barrel, P. Allen early style flint lock, and single set trigger, relief carving, engraving, and silver wire inlay.

Closeup of buttstock region showing fluted wood butt trap lid surrounded by an engraved brass escutcheon plate with relief carving at wrist.

A left-hand Bucks Co. styled brass mounted fullstock rifle. Stocked in curly maple, it features a 38" swamped Getz .50 cal. barrel, Siler lock, single set trigger, relief carving, and brass and silver wire inlays.

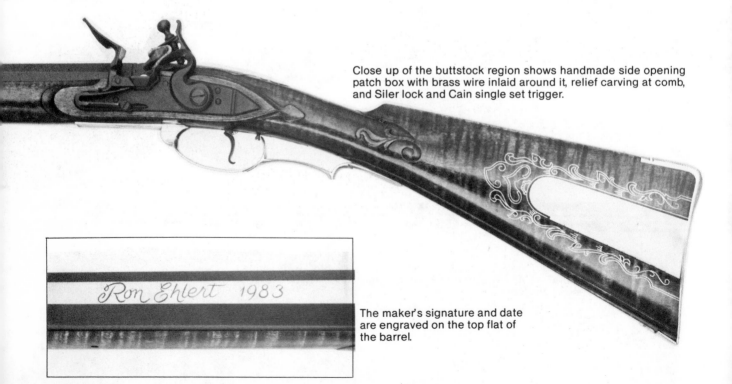

Close up of the buttstock region shows handmade side opening patch box with brass wire inlaid around it, relief carving at comb, and Siler lock and Cain single set trigger.

The maker's signature and date are engraved on the top flat of the barrel.

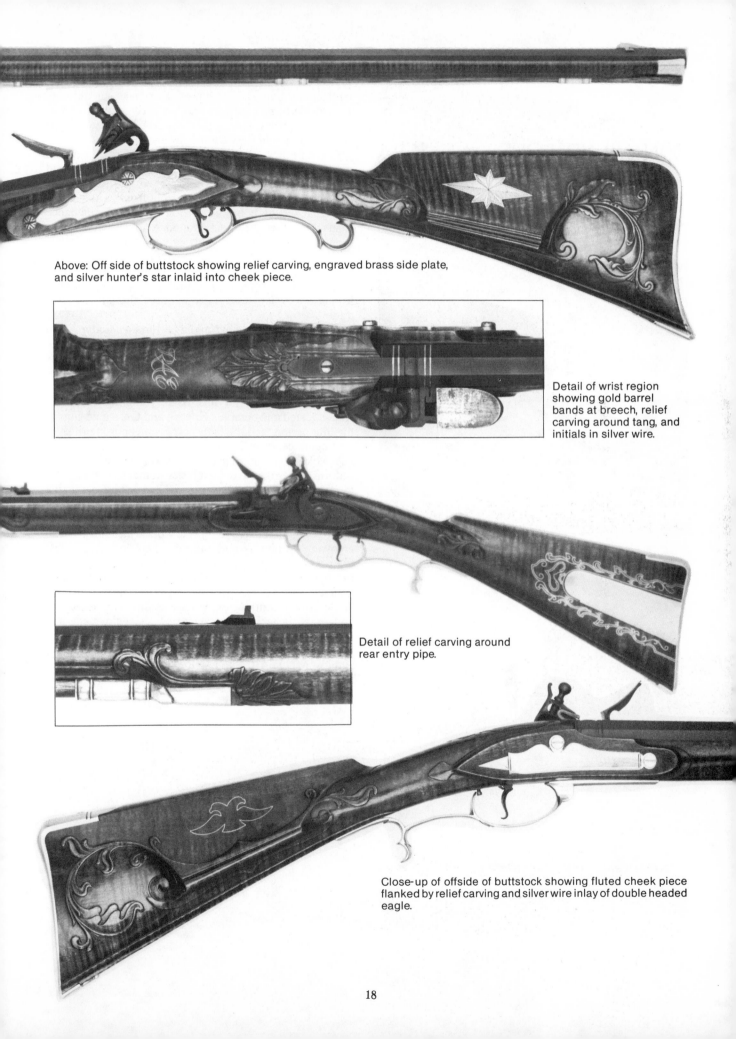

Above: Off side of buttstock showing relief carving, engraved brass side plate, and silver hunter's star inlaid into cheek piece.

Detail of wrist region showing gold barrel bands at breech, relief carving around tang, and initials in silver wire.

Detail of relief carving around rear entry pipe.

Close-up of offside of buttstock showing fluted cheek piece flanked by relief carving and silver wire inlay of double headed eagle.

MICHAEL C. HAYES

BORN: MINNEAPOLIS, MINNESOTA SEPTEMBER 8, 1950

Michael's first encounter with a muzzle loading rifle came at age 24. While visiting Mr. Gurney Fern, a distant relative in northern Minnesota, he dropped by the old gentleman's bait shop. Gurney Fern was an old-time muzzle loading enthusiast and an early builder of traditional longrifles. During this visit Mr. Fern took him to his workshop and showed him around.

Mr. Fern was testing a newly finished rifle prior to a shooting match to be held the next day. Michael enjoyed shooting this longrifle which prompted him to build his own gun. After building only two rifles from scratch parts, he recognized this hobby as a serious interest. He has since changed his lifestyle to accommodate this disciplined art form and eventually ended his career in auto parts sales, having served as manager of a major auto parts store and motorcycle parts dealership. He removed himself from metropolitan Minneapolis and moved to northern Minnesota, where today he practices the gun building trade.

Mike began his gun building efforts by studying and emulating the work of traditional American longrifle makers. Rifles built by Herman and John Rupp served as an inspiration, and Michael truly loves the subtle variations in American longrifle schools of style.

More recently he has begun building the more sophisticated and complex English and Germanic guns of the flint period, and the later percussion sporting rifles of nineteenth century England.

Mike continues to improve his work in technique and artform. He strives to delight his customers and his goal is to make each gun a unique piece. His guns are enjoyable acquisitions, as they hold many tiny details that are often noticed only after a long while of study. He encourages other potential makers to try this work which has been so enjoyable to him — and cautions them to have modest financial expectations. The most satisfying part, according to Mike, is to have designed and built a rifle that pleases yourself and others. Mike expects the demand for best grade work to continue to increase as shooters, collectors, and enthusiasts become aware of the enjoyment and investment value of fine guns.

Write to Michael C. Hayes, Rt. 3, Box 123, Park Rapids, MN 56470. No catalog is available.

Lock detail of the Allentown rifle, shown on the following pages, displays the handmade lock plate fitted with Siler parts. The lock was polished to a satin sheen, and finished to a dull patina. The handmade scroll style trigger is typical of this school.

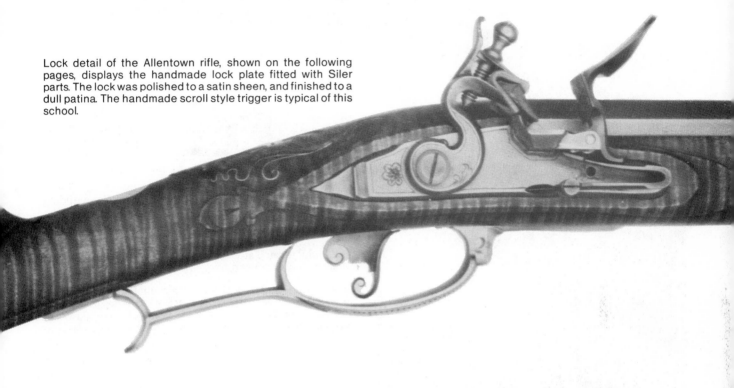

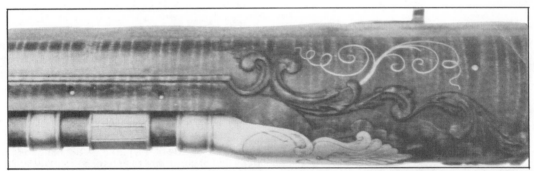

Close-up of the entry pipe detail shows the unique ramrod entry pipe, made in one piece, and double pinned to the stock. Raised carving and silver wire accent the finial design of the entry pipe tang.

The signature of Michael Hayes, found on the top flat of the octagon barrel, between the breech and the rear sight.

TYPES OF FIREARMS OFFERED:
Pennsylvania Rifles, fowlers and shotguns

SPECIFICATIONS:
WOOD: *Maple, Walnut*
BARREL: *Getz*
BBL LENGTH: *Customer's preference*
CALIBER: *Customer's preference*
LOCK: *Flint by Siler*
TRIGGERS: *Single or double set*
FURNITURE: *Iron or brass*
LENGTH OF PULL: *Customer's preference*

KIT OFFERED: *No*

MICHAEL C HAYES

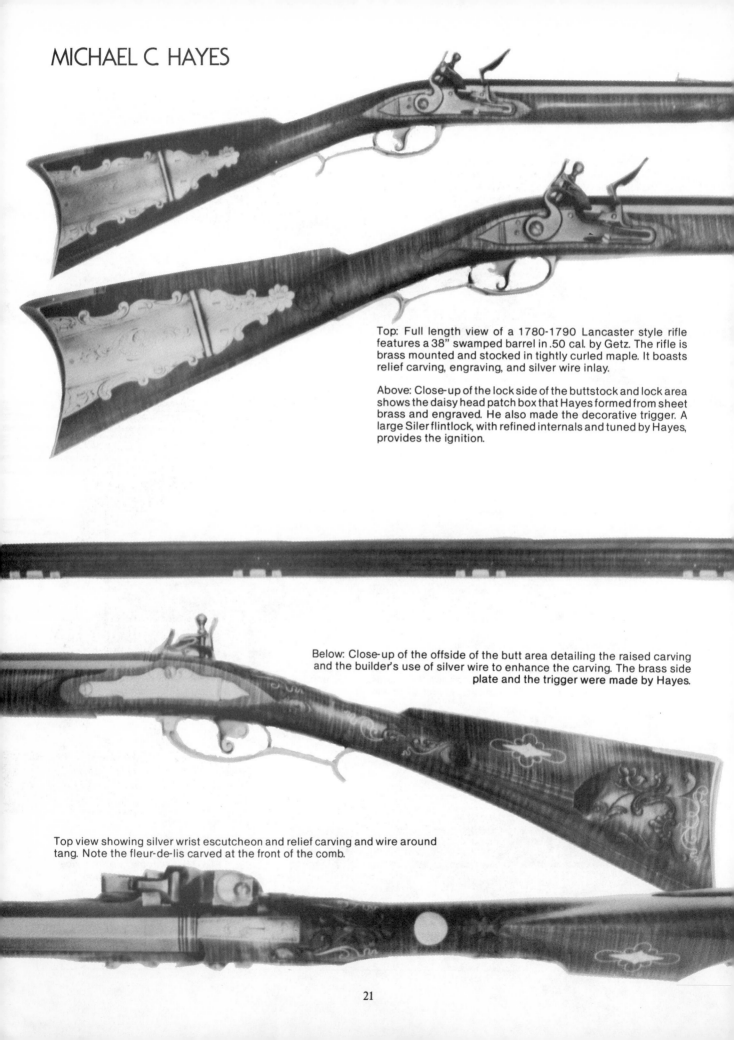

Top: Full length view of a 1780-1790 Lancaster style rifle features a 38" swamped barrel in .50 cal. by Getz. The rifle is brass mounted and stocked in tightly curled maple. It boasts relief carving, engraving, and silver wire inlay.

Above: Close-up of the lock side of the buttstock and lock area shows the daisy head patch box that Hayes formed from sheet brass and engraved. He also made the decorative trigger. A large Siler flintlock, with refined internals and tuned by Hayes, provides the ignition.

Below: Close-up of the offside of the butt area detailing the raised carving and the builder's use of silver wire to enhance the carving. The brass side plate and the trigger were made by Hayes.

Top view showing silver wrist escutcheon and relief carving and wire around tang. Note the fleur-de-lis carved at the front of the comb.

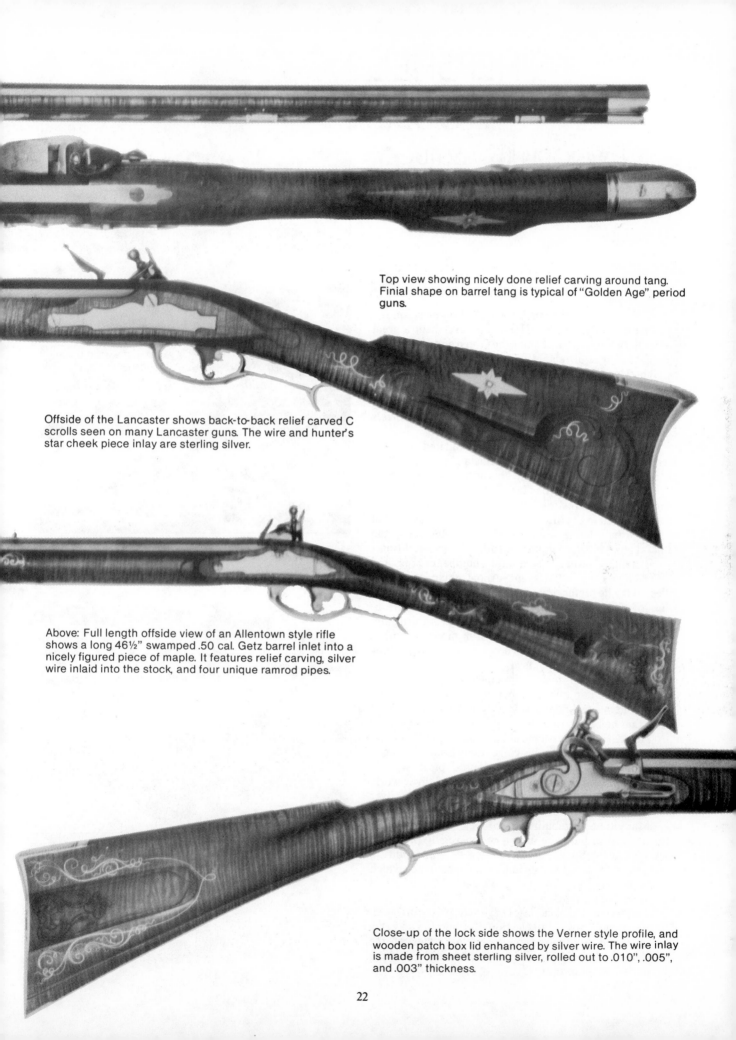

Top view showing nicely done relief carving around tang. Finial shape on barrel tang is typical of "Golden Age" period guns.

Offside of the Lancaster shows back-to-back relief carved C scrolls seen on many Lancaster guns. The wire and hunter's star cheek piece inlay are sterling silver.

Above: Full length offside view of an Allentown style rifle shows a long 46½" swamped .50 cal. Getz barrel inlet into a nicely figured piece of maple. It features relief carving, silver wire inlaid into the stock, and four unique ramrod pipes.

Close-up of the lock side shows the Verner style profile, and wooden patch box lid enhanced by silver wire. The wire inlay is made from sheet sterling silver, rolled out to .010", .005", and .003" thickness.

HERSHEL HOUSE

BORN: WOODBURY, KENTUCKY
JULY 4, 1941

Growing up in the small town of Woodbury on the Green River in Kentucky, Hershel House spent a great deal of his younger years fishing the Green and running the woods hunting squirrels by day and 'coons and 'possums by night. He recalls that his love of early American history was instilled in him at an early age by his grandfather Hershel Finney who spent hours telling stories to young Hershel when he didn't have the boy out hunting squirrels and 'possums.

In 1956 Hershel found a delapidated original Kentucky rifle in a barn and he painstakingly pieced the old squirrel rifle back together. This began a romance with the Kentucky rifle that has lasted 'til this day. His part-time building and restoring of guns was interrupted by a four year hitch in the Marine Corps in the early 1960s but after returning home from the Marines, Hershel began building and restoring muzzle loading firearms full time.

Through the years he has built a number of brass and iron mounted Kentuckies and Appalachian Mountain rifles. today he prefers to build the iron mounted Southern rifles of the type carried by the longhunters and frontiersmen of the 1750-1790s period. These guns are usually stocked in curly maple or walnut, iron mounted with a wooden or two piece iron patch box and most always show a small amount of silver inlay.

A wide butted stock complemented by a swamped barrel results in an attractive but well balanced gun that goes to a man's shoulder easily and comfortably. Hershel states that he builds rifles for people who will use them.

Hershel has quite a hand at blacksmithing and always forges his iron mounts for his guns. Many times his forged butt plates, trigger guards, and ramrod pipes will be tastefully dressed up with a small amount of silver work, and his guns usually have a large engraved silver thumbpiece at the wrist.

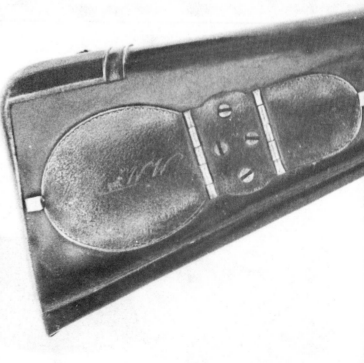

Many times a rebuilt original lock will show up on Hershel's rifles but if he uses a commercially produced lock he prefers Siler. Almost always he will modify a commercial lock to give it an individual appearance which is one of the things which gives each House gun a uniqueness of its own.

Today, if asked what styles of guns he prefers to build, Hershel responds with a selection of several: The early iron mounted Southern rifles, the plain rifles of the Appalachian and eastern Tennessee Mountains, and the flint period Virginia squirrel rifles of 1810-1830s.

Fame has come along with the work for Hershel. In addition to the multitude of articles written about him in various publications and newspapers through the years, he was featured on a segment of Sports Afield, an outdoor television show hosted by Grits Gresham in 1978.

Foxfire V, one of the *Foxfire* series of books edited by Elliot Wiggington and devoted to recording the old ways of the people of the Appalachian Mountains, featured Hershel as one of several muzzle loading rifle builders. A whole segment showed how Hershel went about building a rifle.

More recently, he has received a grant from the National Endowment of the Arts to teach an apprentice the art of muzzle loading rifle building. This government program was originated for craftsmen to teach apprentices to carry on the endangered traditional folk crafts, many of which have all but died out in our country until a revival in recent years. Mel Hankla of Jamestown, Kentucky was Hershel's apprentice.

Hershel has since been nominated for the National Heritage Fellowship Award of which there are only sixteen awarded each year. Should he receive this honor, the rifle which was built under the auspices of the grant will be exhibited in the Smithsonian Institution — a giant step in the art of muzzle loading rifle building.

Hershel House can be reached at Rt. 3, Woodbury, KY 47761. No catalog is available.

TYPES OF FIREARMS OFFERED: *Iron mounted Southern Rifles, North Carolina, Virginia style rifles, fowlers, Southern pistols*

SPECIFICATIONS:
WOOD: *Maple, walnut*
BARREL: *Getz, Douglas, Green Mountain*
BBL LENGTH: *37" to 48"*
CALIBER: *.45 to .60*
LOCK: *Siler, own manufacture*
TRIGGER: *Single, Double set by Davis or own manufacture*
FURNITURE: *Iron*
LENGTH OF PULL: *Customer's preference*
KIT OFFERED: *No*

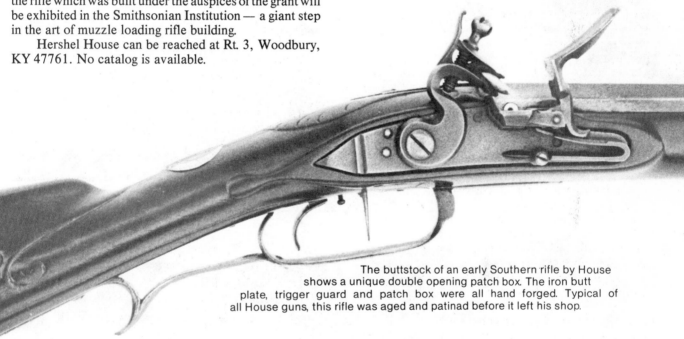

The buttstock of an early Southern rifle by House shows a unique double opening patch box. The iron butt plate, trigger guard and patch box were all hand forged. Typical of all House guns, this rifle was aged and patinad before it left his shop.

A familiar sight on House rifles; the H. House signature engraved in script on the top barrel flat. Occasionally the signature will be engraved into a silver panel inlaid into the barrel.

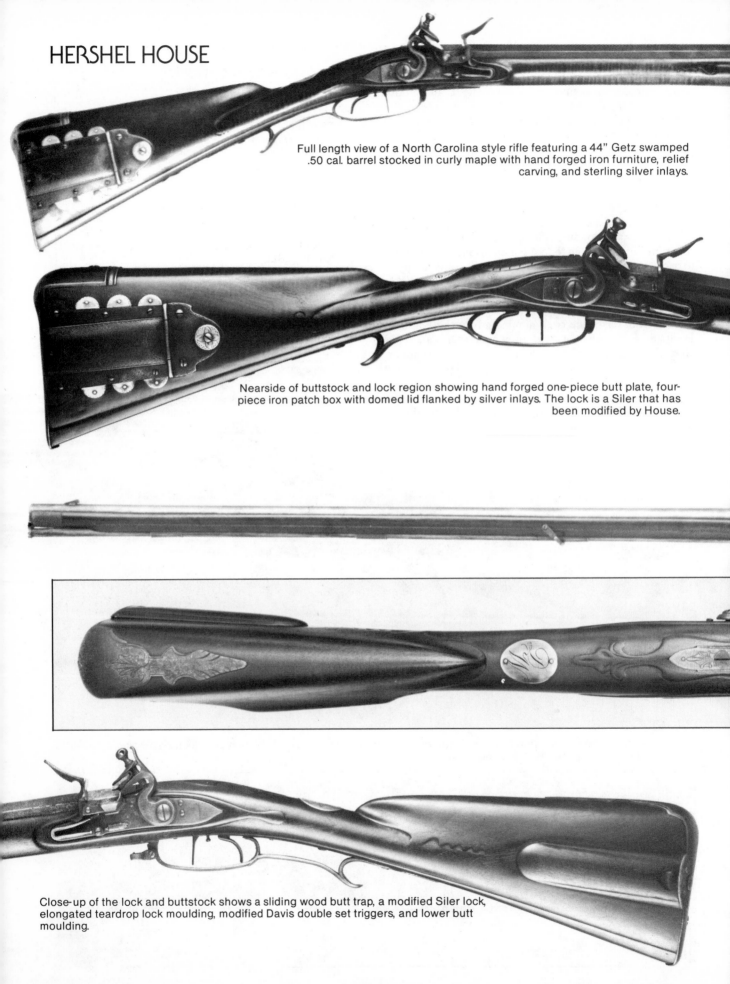

HERSHEL HOUSE

Full length view of a North Carolina style rifle featuring a 44" Getz swamped .50 cal. barrel stocked in curly maple with hand forged iron furniture, relief carving, and sterling silver inlays.

Nearside of buttstock and lock region showing hand forged one-piece butt plate, four-piece iron patch box with domed lid flanked by silver inlays. The lock is a Siler that has been modified by House.

Close-up of the lock and buttstock shows a sliding wood butt trap, a modified Siler lock, elongated teardrop lock moulding, modified Davis double set triggers, and lower butt moulding.

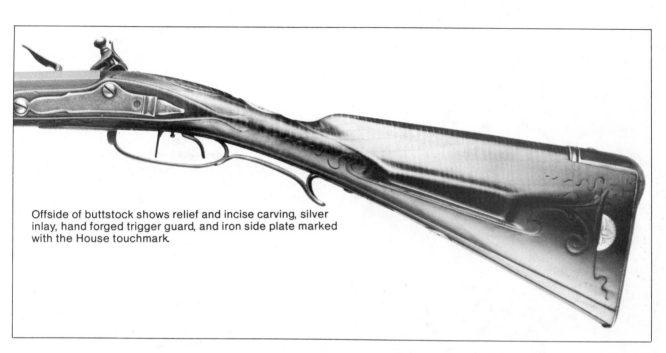

Offside of buttstock shows relief and incise carving, silver inlay, hand forged trigger guard, and iron side plate marked with the House touchmark.

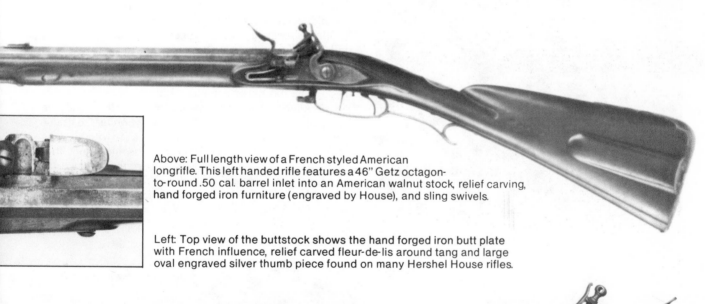

Above: Full length view of a French styled American longrifle. This left handed rifle features a 46" Getz octagon-to-round .50 cal. barrel inlet into an American walnut stock, relief carving, hand forged iron furniture (engraved by House), and sling swivels.

Left: Top view of the buttstock shows the hand forged iron butt plate with French influence, relief carved fleur-de-lis around tang and large oval engraved silver thumb piece found on many Hershel House rifles.

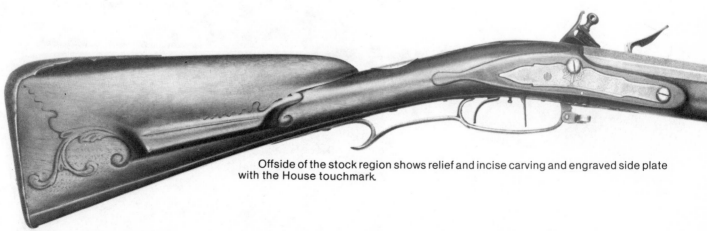

Offside of the stock region shows relief and incise carving and engraved side plate with the House touchmark.

STEPHEN H. DAVIS
BORN: EVANSVILLE, INDIANA
OCTOBER 27, 1946

Steve Davis will tell you he was born into a hunting family and grew up close to Sturgis, Kentucky. As he recalls, he spent a great many days in the fields and woods being taught to hunt by his father and grandfather. Because of this, his interest in guns goes back as far as he can remember and was always natural to him to have a few shotguns and rifles around the house.

After graduation from high school, Steve joined the Air Force and became a sentry dog handler. He and his dog were shipped to Viet Nam in 1966 where they spent the next year patrolling the outer perimeter of the unit's base at Phu Cat. With his combat experience behind him, Steve returned to the States in 1967 and received his discharge from the Air Force. He then attended the University of Kentucky, graduating with a degree in forestry. Seeking a job working out of doors, he moved to Tennessee and went to work for the federal government in strip mine reclamation.

In 1972 Steve met a friend who squirrel hunted with a percussion rifle. Steve tried hunting with it, liked the challenge, and bought himself a cheap muzzle loading rifle. Before long he found that the gun was incapable of shooting the way he felt it should, so he built one from scratch. He sold that one, built another and continued in this manner until 1982 when he quit his job with the government and began building guns full time.

In 1974 Steve met Hershel House and began a friendship that lasts to this day. During the past ten years Steve has visited with Hershel as often as possible, hunted with him, and learned from Hershel the tricks of the trade in building muzzle loading firearms. Steve credits Hershel as having been a strong influence on him in his gun building. The guns that Steve prefers to build are iron mounted "Southern transition" rifles and Virginia squirrel rifles. He forges all of his own iron hardware for his guns. Though he has never completely built a lock, he almost always alters the outside appearance (as well as tunes the internals) of the commercial flint locks he prefers to use — Siler and Long locks. He seeks individuality with his guns whether it's in a handmade patch box or some quaint little characteristic he adopted from some original rifle.

Like many muzzle loading rifle builders, Steve expresses a strong interest in American history, particularly the French and Indian War and the mid 1700s

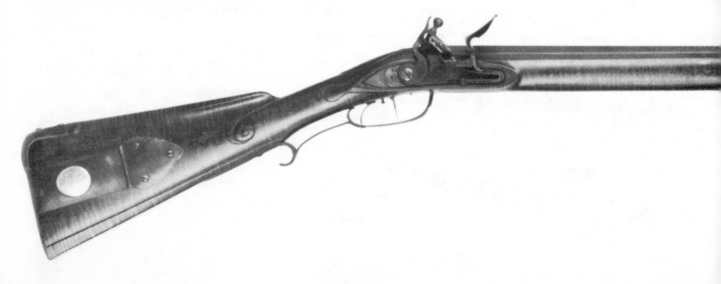

period of the longhunters' explorations into what is now Kentucky and Tennessee. Considering his interest in frontier history, buckskinning comes naturally to Steve. He prefers to portray the character of the longhunter and when time permits, he enjoys taking cross country survival trips, living off the land with the same tools and accoutrements available in the 1760s.

Today Steve Davis lives in Hickman County, Tennessee with his wife, Paulette, and son, Jacob, where he continues to build muzzle loading firearms on order. He can be reached by dropping him a line at P. O. Box 265, Centerville, TN 37033. No catalog is available.

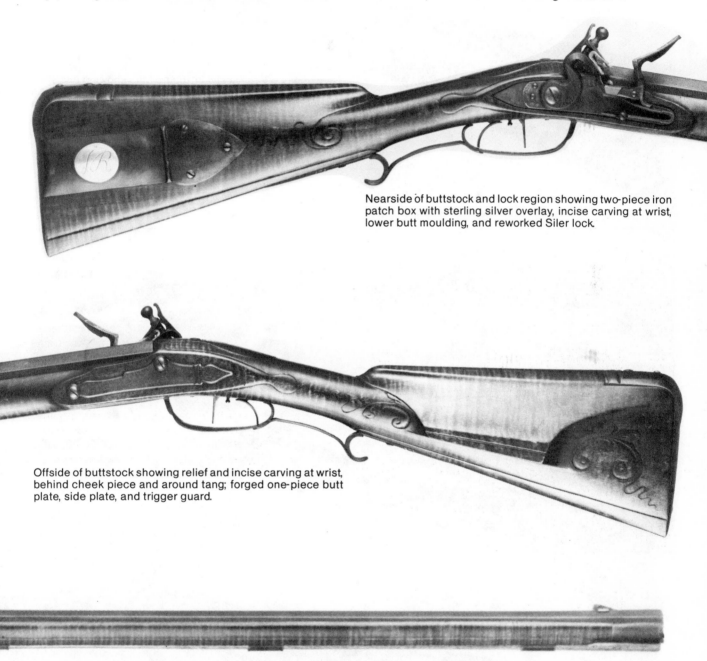

Nearside of buttstock and lock region showing two-piece iron patch box with sterling silver overlay, incise carving at wrist, lower butt moulding, and reworked Siler lock.

Offside of buttstock showing relief and incise carving at wrist, behind cheek piece and around tang; forged one-piece butt plate, side plate, and trigger guard.

Full length view of an early Southern styled rifle featuring a swamped .50 cal. Getz barrel stocked in curly maple with hand forged iron furniture. This rifle features a beefy buttstock with a fluted comb.

STEPHEN H. DAVIS

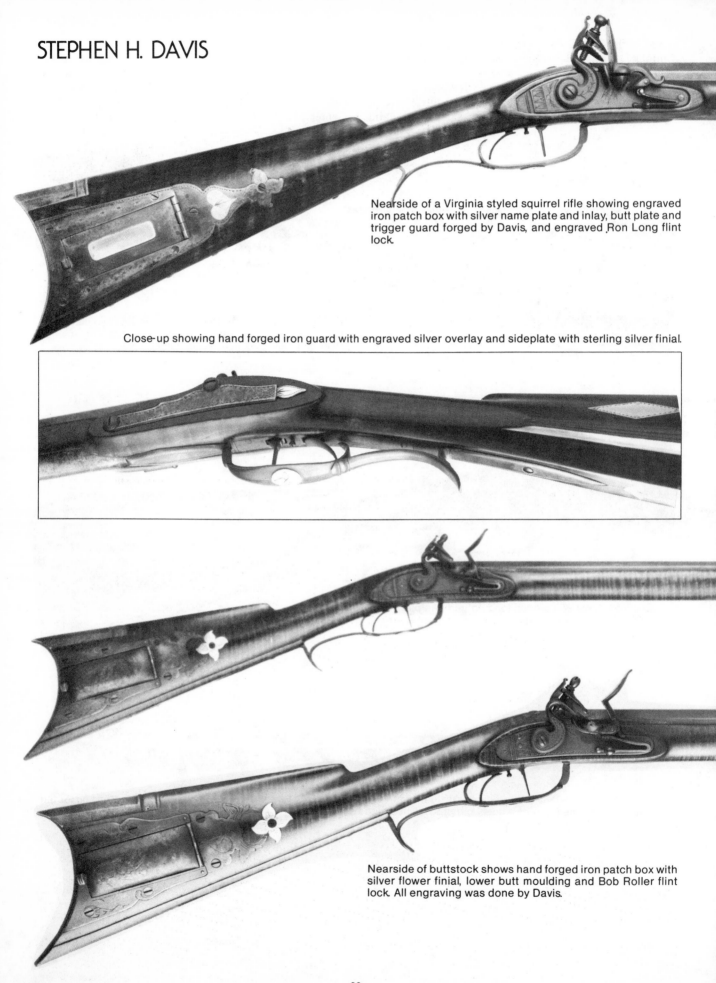

Nearside of a Virginia styled squirrel rifle showing engraved iron patch box with silver name plate and inlay, butt plate and trigger guard forged by Davis, and engraved Ron Long flint lock.

Close-up showing hand forged iron guard with engraved silver overlay and sideplate with sterling silver finial.

Nearside of buttstock shows hand forged iron patch box with silver flower finial, lower butt moulding and Bob Roller flint lock. All engraving was done by Davis.

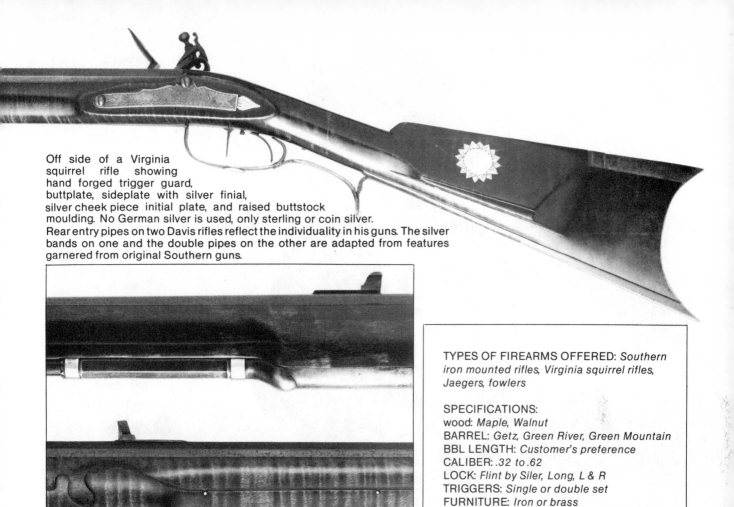

Off side of a Virginia
squirrel rifle showing
hand forged trigger guard,
buttplate, sideplate with silver finial,
silver cheek piece initial plate, and raised buttstock
moulding. No German silver is used, only sterling or coin silver.
Rear entry pipes on two Davis rifles reflect the individuality in his guns. The silver
bands on one and the double pipes on the other are adapted from features
garnered from original Southern guns.

TYPES OF FIREARMS OFFERED: *Southern iron mounted rifles, Virginia squirrel rifles, Jaegers, fowlers*

SPECIFICATIONS:
wood: *Maple, Walnut*
BARREL: *Getz, Green River, Green Mountain*
BBL LENGTH: *Customer's preference*
CALIBER: *.32 to .62*
LOCK: *Flint by Siler, Long, L & R*
TRIGGERS: *Single or double set*
FURNITURE: *Iron or brass*
LENGTH OF PULL: *Customer's preference*
KIT OFFERED: *No*

Full length view of a late flint period, iron mounted rifle in the Southwest Virginia style. It features a 38" Getz swamped .32 cal. barrel stocked in curly maple. Sterling silver overlays grace the hand forged patch box, ramrod pipes, trigger guard, and side plate.

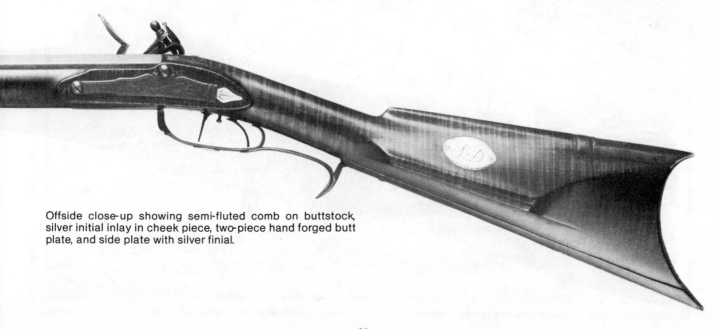

Offside close-up showing semi-fluted comb on buttstock, silver initial inlay in cheek piece, two-piece hand forged butt plate, and side plate with silver finial.

BRUCE LePAGE

BORN: MINNEAPOLIS, MINNESOTA
APRIL 14, 1946

Bruce LePage grew up in the country around Waverly, Minnesota. During high school, while in shop class, he built a muzzle loading pistol as a shop project. He was coached by a fine gunsmith from a nearby town and under his guidance he learned the first lessons about building muzzle loading guns, including the lock for his first gun. So it was while in high school that Bruce became a black powder shooter.

Upon graduation from high school Bruce spent the next eight years pursuing his MFA degree at the University of Wisconsin. His areas of interest were in art metal, and specifically in iron forging and blacksmithing.

In 1975 Bruce settled down and got married and together his wife and he started a business of making and selling crafts. His wife is a potter and his specialty was forging decorative wrought iron articles. One of his pieces was selected for a show sponsored by the Smithsonian Institute and in 1980 he was chosen, along with ten other Americans, to represent the United States at the first World Blacksmithing Convention held at Hereford, England. While there he demonstrated his engraving techniques on forged iron. Since then he has conducted workshops on forging, engraving, and gunsmithing at various schools throughout the country.

As his blacksmithing business grew, he developed his skills at gun building and, as the demand grew, he found himself devoting full time to his gun making. His knowledge and skill at smithing and engraving have added great dimension to Bruce's ability to turn out finely built firearms. He enjoys building several styles of guns, including Pennsylvania rifles and fowlers, English fullstock and half stock rifles and shotguns, German style flint rifles, and modern percussion firearms. He often makes the hardware for his firearms because he still enjoys working at the forge, and occasionally he will build a lock if there's not a good commercial lock available for the style of gun he's building. All commercial locks that he does use are completely tuned and polished inside.

After nine years of being in the business of building muzzle loading firearms Bruce sees himself as a New Wave gun maker, interpreting and building upon tradition. Bruce LePage may be reached at Route 1, Belleville, Wisconsin 53508. No catalog is available.

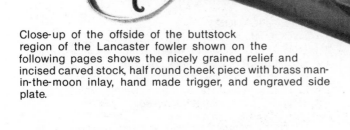

Close-up of the offside of the buttstock region of the Lancaster fowler shown on the following pages shows the nicely grained relief and incised carved stock, half round cheek piece with brass man-in-the-moon inlay, hand made trigger, and engraved side plate.

BRUCE LePAGE

Close-up of the lock region shows the L & R flintlock, engraved by LePage, wrist checkering, and forged scroll guard.

Floral engraving accentuates the bow of the trigger guard on the Lancaster fowler.

TYPES OF FIREARMS OFFERED: *English fowlers and double barreled shotguns, American Pennsylvania Rifles, German Jaeger rifles.*

SPECIFICATIONS:
WOOD: *Maple, Walnut*
BARREL: *Getz, Mellot, Green River, Bill Large*
BBL LENGTH: *Customer's preference*
CALIBER: *Customer's preference*
LOCK: *Flint by L & R, Siler and own manufacture*
TRIGGER: *Single and double set*
FURNITURE: *Iron and brass*
LENGTH OF PULL: *Customer's preference*
KIT OFFERED: *No*

Full length view of an American Lancaster style fowler stocked in curly maple. The barrel was made by Getz in 20 ga. and 36" in length, octagon-to round tapered with a slight flare at the muzzle. This smoothbore features engraved brass furniture and a Siler flint lock.

Full view of an 1800 period English half stock shotgun featuring a 30" 12 ga. Mellot barrel inlet into a piece of California walnut Mounted in iron forged by LePage, all furniture is temper blued.

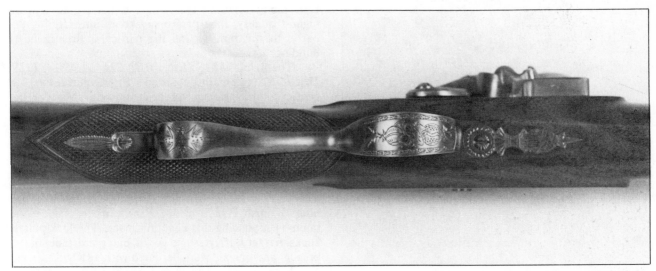

Above: Bottom view shows English style trigger guard made and engraved by Le-Page.

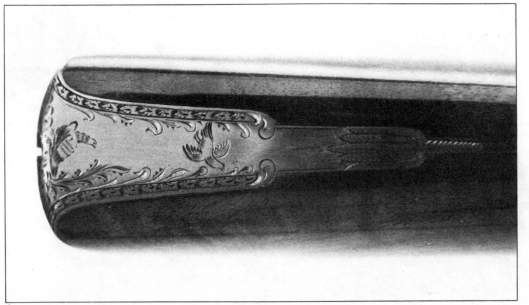

Left: Close-up of the finely engraved butt plate. All engraving was done in the traditional English style.

MIKE EHINGER
BORN: FORT WAYNE, INDIANA
OCTOBER 20, 1942

Mike grew up in Fort Wayne leading what he terms a fairly average life. Upon graduating from high school he joined the Army and served the majority of his three years at Fort Bragg with the 82nd Airborne. After service he returned to Fort Wayne for two years, then moved to North Carolina where he met his wife, Becky.

While still in the Army, Mike began building muzzle loading rifles part time in 1962. Formerly a carpenter by trade and also a self taught machinist, Mike followed various styles of longrifles in his building. Since 1981 he has devoted himself full time to gun building and arms restoration.

Attracted by the wide spectrum and variation of styles while studying photos of European arms, Mike built his first European gun in 1980.

Utilizing American walnut, usually cut from a stump by himself, he incorporates the more artistic features of the European style into his fowlers and doubles. Rust blued barrels and handmade locks polished bright are usually offset by baroque carving tastefully complemented with gold and silver wire inlaid into the stock.

Considering that all parts and furniture (less the barrels) are handmade by Mike, it's not unusual for him to have 350-500 hours wrapped up in one of his firearms. Even though he doesn't make his own barrels, he buys the highest quality, then puts many hours into refining the barrel to suit himself and the particular firearm he is building.

The book, *MASTER FRENCH GUNSMITHS' DESIGNS* (originally published in France during the 17th century), furnishes much of the incentive for Mike's relief carving and wire inlay designs. One of the book's drawings is the basis for a large elaborately pierced sterling silver wrist medallion. Chisled in high relief, the form of a satyr graces the wrist of one of his Parisian fowlers.

A French double utilizing Getz custom milled and turned barrels set into a burled walnut relief carved stock with sterling silver wire inlays required more than 700 hours to finish. Handmade locks and furniture added to the hours in producing this beautiful piece. The lock plates, cocks, frizzens, triggers and guard, butt plate, tang, barrel breech, and muzzle were bordered with 18K gold wire.

More recently, Mike has begun building fine English

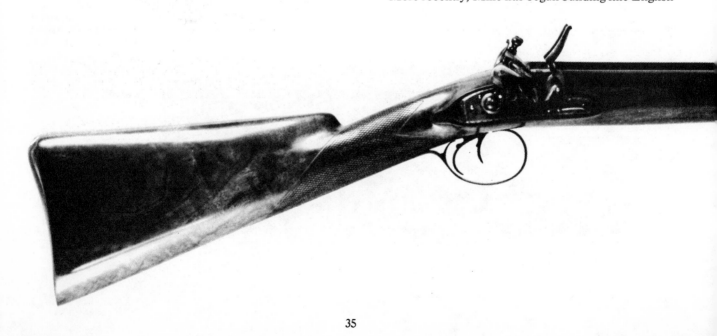

flint doubles in the London style of the early 19th century. Now using English walnut, his own handmade waterproof locks and barrels with recessed breeches display the same quality as all his firearms show. Additionally, these arms can be had cased in Honduras mahogany with the traditional accoutrements.

Though Mike Ehinger prefers building the fine doubles of the London and European styles he still enjoys building the higher quality English and European rifles and pistols.

Mike can be reached at Rt. 1, Box 293D, Stedman, NC 28391. No catalog is available.

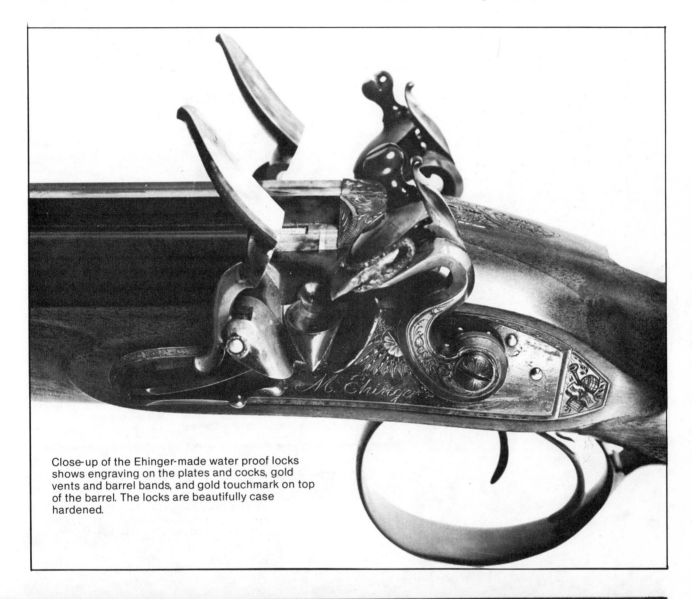

Close-up of the Ehinger-made water proof locks shows engraving on the plates and cocks, gold vents and barrel bands, and gold touchmark on top of the barrel. The locks are beautifully case hardened.

Full length view of an English early 19th century double flint fowler in 12 gauge. Showing features adherent to H. Nock and the Mantons, the simple clean lines, oversize trigger bow, and checkering set this double in a class of its own.

MIKE EHINGER

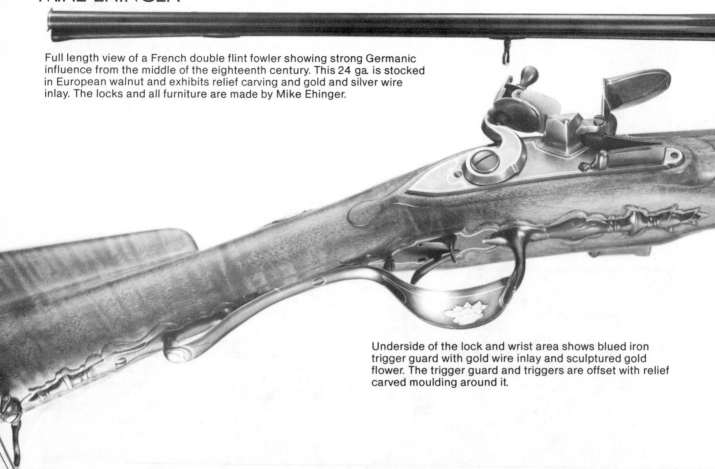

Full length view of a French double flint fowler showing strong Germanic influence from the middle of the eighteenth century. This 24 ga. is stocked in European walnut and exhibits relief carving and gold and silver wire inlay. The locks and all furniture are made by Mike Ehinger.

Underside of the lock and wrist area shows blued iron trigger guard with gold wire inlay and sculptured gold flower. The trigger guard and triggers are offset with relief carved moulding around it.

Upon request, Mike Ehinger will case his firearms with all accessories.

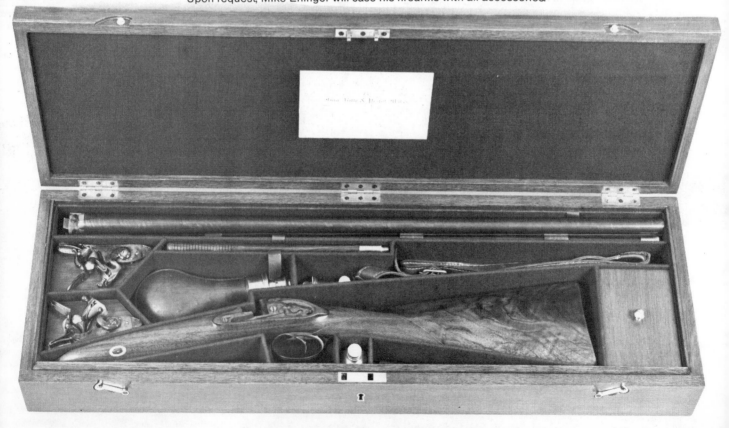

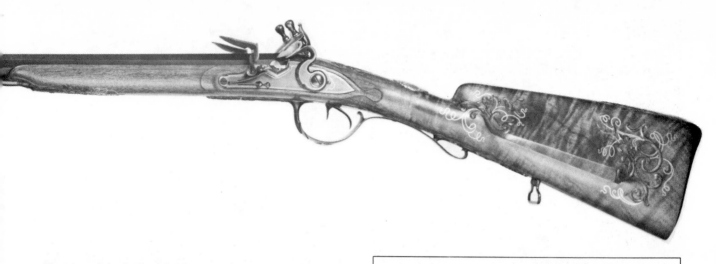

Close-up of the lock and wrist area shows a pair of Ehinger-made locks inlaid with gold wire, relief carving around tang and at comb, silver wire inlay, and a sculptured silver wrist medallion. All steel components are rust blued.

TYPES OF FIREARMS OFFERED: *London style early 19th century double barrel flint fowlers, French and other European single and double barrel fowlers.*

SPECIFICATIONS:
WOOD: *European walnut*
BARRELS: *Modern blanks reworked and choked to customer's specifications.*
BBL LENGTH: *Customer's preference*
CALIBER: *12 Ga. to 24 Ga.*
LOCK: *Flint by own manufacture*
TRIGGERS: *Double by own manufacture*
FURNITURE: *Iron*
LENGTH OF PULL: *Customer's preference*
KITS OFFERED: *No*

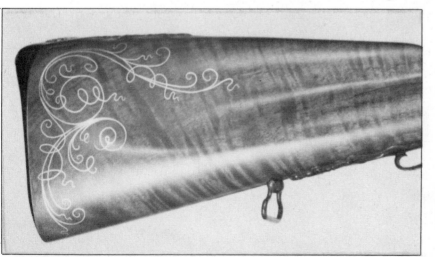

Close-up of well designed and executed silver wire inlay on the butt stock of the French fowling piece.

The fun of shooting well made muzzleloading firearms is a year-round activity as shown by this longhunter in the "dead of winter" shooting his copy of a Jacob Dickert long-rifle.

ROBERT "CURLY" GOSTOMSKI

BORN: DAYTON, OHIO
JUNE 5, 1915

At age 14 young Curly Gostomski left school to "see the world." And that he did, traveling around the United States working at a succession of jobs that, if nothing else, "built experience." These included slinging hash and washing dishes, tending bar, working the harvest fields, and driving trucks and mules. (For a brief but exciting time, he claims to have driven trucks for rum runners.) His restive travels at one time took him to Poland, the native homeland of his parents.

In 1933 Curly began a six year apprenticeship to a machinist which has led him to a 50 year career in the tool and die business. While working in Wisconsin in 1952 Curly met and two years later married Irma White. Today Irma is a very active partner in their business.

During these earlier days, having had an interest in guns, Curly acquired his first muzzle loading firearm in a trade to an "old Swede in La Crosse, Wisconsin." Being a machinist he had made parts for his own modern guns for years. For this antique gun he first made a new lock, then a new stock and finally bought a new barrel. He claims to have learned a great deal, in more ways than one, in rebuilding that old gun, but without realizing it at the time, the seeds had been planted that would eventually lead to his current career and business, North Star Enterprises.

North Star had its beginnings about 20 years ago. When the tool business was experiencing a mild recession, Curly and an out-of-work friend decided to make some muzzle loading gun parts, starting with triggers. What emerged was the North Star Trigger and North Star Enterprises.

Fifteen years ago Curly bought his first trade gun. Unknown at the time, it was a rare "Chief's Grade" smoothbore. With the purchase of this gun his interest in trade guns grew and after much research, North Star introduced the first replica Northwest trade gun. These guns are authentic copies patterned after the early "Barnetts" and "Wheelers" of the 1790-1830 period. Today, in addition to their line of quality parts, North Star offers, in both kit and finished form, a right and left hand version of the Northwest gun and a "Chief's Grade Trade Gun." These guns are stocked in walnut and are available in 20 and 24 ga. and three different barrel lengths. A "blanket" trade gun kit is also available in 20 ga. with an 18 inch barrel.

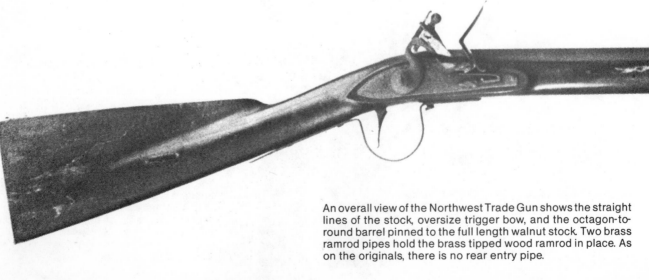

An overall view of the Northwest Trade Gun shows the straight lines of the stock, oversize trigger bow, and the octagon-to-round barrel pinned to the full length walnut stock. Two brass ramrod pipes hold the brass tipped wood ramrod in place. As on the originals, there is no rear entry pipe.

The fancier "Chief's Grade" smoothbore is patterned after an original British fowler such as those presented to Indian chiefs during the War of 1812. It features a smaller trigger guard and a silver escutcheon at the wrist.

In 1985 North Star will introduce in kit form an authentic replica of a French "Fusil Fin." Stocked in walnut with brass hardware it will be offered in 12, 20, and 24 ga. in three different barrel lengths. As Curly points out, this gun will definitely fill a need for those buckskinners who are looking for something different but authentic.

An avid buckskinner, Curly makes most of the major rendezvous around the country and admits to making 32 in one year. Asked about hunting, he shows confidence in his own guns by having brought down two buffalo with them.

His interest in buckskinning and his passion for the past, particularly the fur trade era has led Robert "Curly" Gostomski to a fun filled but most interesting career. He's a life member of the NMLRA and NRA.

For a catalog write North Star Enterprises, 2401 Guernsey Dell Ave., P. O. Box 234, Dayton, Ohio 45404.

TYPES OF FIREARMS OFFERED: *North West Trade Gun, Chief's Grade Trade Gun, French "Fusil Fin"*

NORTH WEST TRADE GUN
SPECIFICATIONS:
WOOD: *Walnut*
BARREL: *Octagon-to-round, smooth bore*
BBL LENGTH: *18", 30", 36", 41"*
CALIBER: *12 Ga., 20 Ga., 24 Ga. (smooth bore)*
LOCK: *Flint by North Star*
TRIGGER: *Single*
FURNITURE: *Iron, Brass*
KIT OFFERED: *Yes*

Close-up of the lock region shows the large flint lock by North Star stamped with the sitting fox in a circle. The trigger guard is screwed from the bottom up through the stock and the tang. This was a common procedure on earlier guns.

Right: A buttplate of flat iron (or brass) bent over for the heel and nailed to the stock was traditional for Northwest guns.

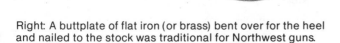

Close-up of the brass serpent side plate, the beaver tail lock panel, and the raised moulding around the tang.

42

DON "PAPPY" HORNE
BORN: WORCESTER, MASSACHUSETTS 1928

Don Horne grew up on a small farm in rural New England. He states that the old ways were instilled in him at an early age and that the only guns on the place were original muzzleloaders which were used regularly to put meat on the table. Being introduced to muzzle loading at this early age in life motivated Don toward a growing interest in colonial antiques and firearms which has continued to this day.

A student of history and particularly the Lewis and Clark Corps of Discovery's Expedition to the Pacific coast and back from 1804-1806, Don developed an interest in the 1803 Harpers Ferry rifled musket. By the early 1960s his interest in the rifle had led Don to search out and examine at least 30 original Harpers Ferrys. With his notes, specifications, measurements, etc., he built his first Harpers Ferry making all the components, less the barrel, by hand. Requests from friends for Don to build them a copy of the Harpers Ferry prompted Don to feel that perhaps the time for an authentic copy of the 1803 was at hand. Through Roy Keeler, castings from original furniture were obtained. Barrels were made by Bill Large. Don's son, Bruce, made up the master lock which was cast by Gene Davis. Each gun is built one at a time paying strict attention to detail and dimensions. Today, Don is still building the Harpers Ferry and offers the rifles on order.

As a gun builder, he will craft other firearms for customers and has built early French fusils, fowlers, and Kentuckies.

Don Horne has enjoyed buckskinning for years and attends rendezvous whenever possible, but running a full time black powder shop, aptly named "Pappy's Place", and building guns, keeps Don and his family busy at home most of the time. He states that he hasn't been able to get out and rendezvous as much lately as he would like to.

Organizationally, Don belongs to the NMLRA, NAPR, and holds the degree of Greybeard in the American Mountain Men.

Don Horne can be contacted by writing him at Pappy's Place, R.R. 2, Box 127, Lovington, Illinois 61937. No catalog is available.

Full length view of the 1803 Harpers Ferry Rifled Musket. The walnut stock is held to the barrel by one key and the iron ramrod is held in position by two iron ramrod pipes attached to the underrib. The first pipe is flared to accept the ramrod easier.

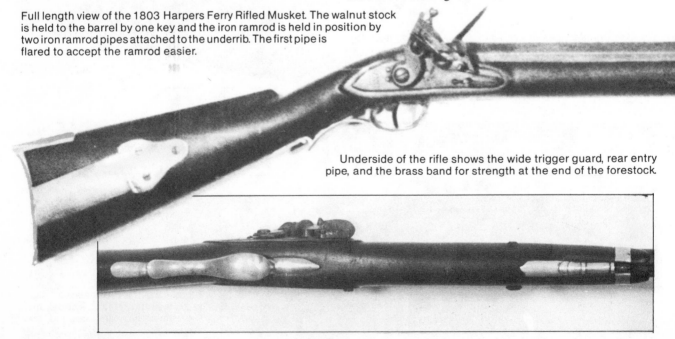

Underside of the rifle shows the wide trigger guard, rear entry pipe, and the brass band for strength at the end of the forestock.

Close-up of the buttstock showing the two-piece patch box which is opened by a push button release at the top of the butt plate. The thick wrist beefs up this rifle for service.

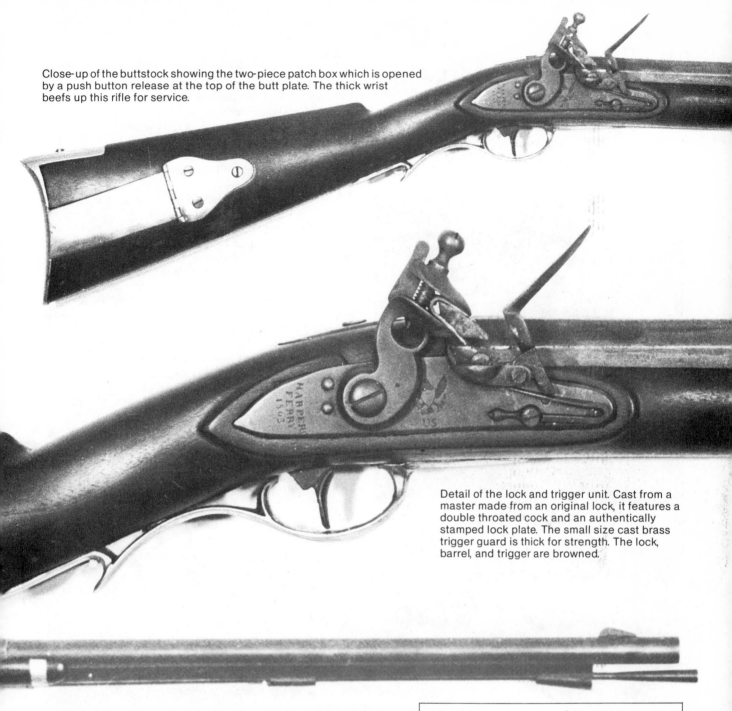

Detail of the lock and trigger unit. Cast from a master made from an original lock, it features a double throated cock and an authentically stamped lock plate. The small size cast brass trigger guard is thick for strength. The lock, barrel, and trigger are browned.

Offside of the lock region shows the brass military style side plate inlet flush with the stock.

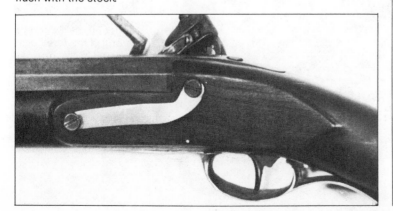

TYPES OF FIREARMS OFFERED:
*1803 Harpers Ferry,
Pennsylvania rifles, French fusils, fowlers*

1803 HARPERS FERRY RIFLED MUSKET
SPECIFICATIONS:
WOOD: *Walnut*
BARREL: *Getz, octagon-to-round*
BBL LENGTH: *33"*
CALIBER: *.54 rifled*
LOCK: *Flint by own manufacture*
TRIGGER: *Single*
FURNITURE: *Brass*
LENGTH OF PULL: *Customer's preference*
KIT OFFERED: *No*

FRED JOHNSON
BORN: MURRAY, KENTUCKY
DECEMBER 2, 1949

Brought up in Detroit, Michigan, Fred Johnson's main interests while in high school were sports, debating, and history. For a while he attended Southern Illinois University in Carbondale, later transferring to Western University in Macomb, Illinois where he graduated in 1972 with a B.A. in political science.

With his college education behind him, Fred returned to his home in Detroit and worked for a year in the auto industry. Not satisfied with this type work, he relocated to a dude ranch in Michigan and the next year was spent living in a wall tent and lean-to during which time his interest in American history resurfaced.

The closeness to nature in which he lived during this time in his life motivated him to study American Indian religion, which he feels has influenced his life ever since. Along about this time he was introduced to the sport of muzzle loading which he says (unknown to him at the time) greatly influenced the turn his life was to take in the years to come.

A short visit to Montana in 1974, then back to Macomb to work for the Burlington-Northern Railroad brought Fred to meet George Potter, muzzle loading rifle builder, and Barry Anderson, horn and pouch maker, both of whom encouraged him to continue his interest in the history of the American fur trade.

By 1976 Fred was back in Montana again, on the West Fork of the Bitterroot River, working for the railroad. Because of his love for the outdoors and respect for the Indians' earlier way of life, Fred spent four of the next five winters living in a tipi.

During this time his passion for Western fur trade history grew and his interest in muzzle loading firearms expanded. With the arrival in the Bitterroots of Phil

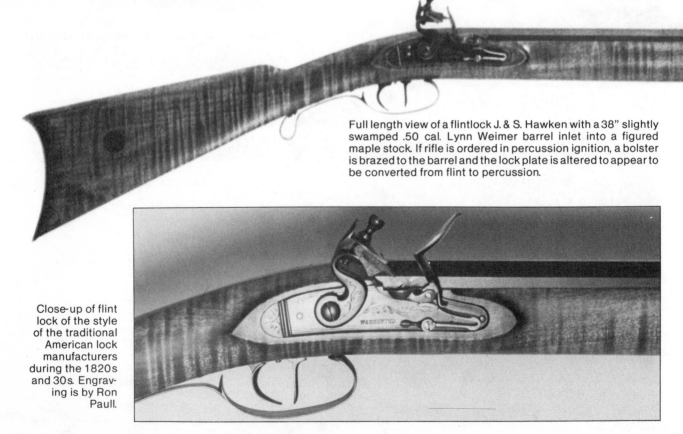

Full length view of a flintlock J. & S. Hawken with a 38" slightly swamped .50 cal. Lynn Weimer barrel inlet into a figured maple stock. If rifle is ordered in percussion ignition, a bolster is brazed to the barrel and the lock plate is altered to appear to be converted from flint to percussion.

Close-up of flint lock of the style of the traditional American lock manufacturers during the 1820s and 30s. Engraving is by Ron Paull.

"Bluejacket" Sanders in 1976 and Ron Paull in 1977, both excellent rifle builders, Fred's interest in gun building began to take serious root. Their influence had a tremendous effect on him and he started riflesmithing with Ron Paull in 1978, eventually going full time with Bluejacket in 1981.

During these same years his continuing quest for knowledge about the fur trade brought him in contact with buckskinning where he met and developed a close friendship with noted western author and history buff, Terry Johnston. With Terry's encouragement Fred occasionally does some writing on firearms history of the fur trade period.

Several years ago Fred met Dr. Edward Kollar who at that time owned an original full stocked J & S Hawken rifle. Though converted to percussion many knowledgeable firearms buffs felt this gun had originally been of flint ignition. Fred was so intrigued with this gun and its strong "Tennessee" influence, with its slightly swamped barrel and grease hole in the stock, that he photographed it and wrote down all specific information and dimensions. Since then he has built a close copy of the rifle and plans to build more in the future.

Presently, Fred is building guns with Ron Paull and though still in the Bitterroot Mountains, he now lives in a cabin instead of a tipi. He builds authentic copies of the muzzle loading rifles, pistols, smoothbores, and axes used during the fur trade period. However, he claims his most enjoyable gun to build is a good authentic full stocked Hawken rifle based on the original gun owned by Dr. Kollar.

Fred Johnson can be contacted by writing to him at P. O. Box 1390, Hamilton, Montana 59840. No catalog.

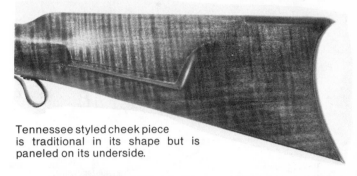

Tennessee styled cheek piece is traditional in its shape but is paneled on its underside.

Close-up of two-piece iron nose cap attached to stock with a copper rivet. Ramrod pipes are sculptured with rings at each end.

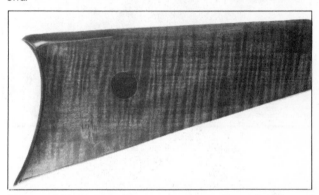

Close-up of buttstock shows copper brazed two-piece forged butt plate and Tennessee style grease hole.

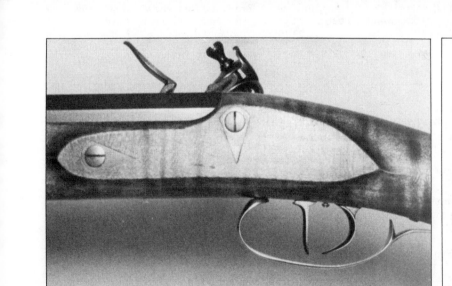

Close-up of offside of the lock panel showing the Tennessee style lock bolt inlays, the sculptured Hawken triggers, and hand forged Virginia style iron trigger guard secured at the rear by a copper rivet.

TYPES OF FIREARMS OFFERED: *Full stock J. & S. Hawken, firearms of the fur trade, fowlers*

J. & S. HAWKEN
SPECIFICATIONS:
WOOD: *Walnut, Maple*
BARREL: *By Lynn Weimer, swamped*
BBL LENGTH: *38" (Customer's preference)*
CALIBER: *.50, .54*
LOCK: *Flint, by Ron Long (Percussion optional, converted from flint)*
TRIGGERS: *Double action, double set*
FURNITURE: *Iron, forged*
LENGTH OF PULL: *Customer's preference*
KIT OFFERED: *No*

RON F. PAULL
BORN: RUTLAND, VERMONT
JULY 18, 1946

At age eight, Ron Paull began his interest in shooting sports when he received an air rifle by promising his parents he would be "good as gold" — a promise he admits he had trouble keeping. By age twelve he had joined the local YMCA and entered the juniors' rifle and air rifle marksmanship courses. By 15 he had earned his distinguished marksmanship award and began shooting competitively in the New England states, qualifying for the New England Gallery Championships three years in a row.

During the American Civil War Centennial (1961-65) Ron had his introduction to muzzle loading firearms by joining a re-enactment group patterned after Berdan's 1st U.S. Sharpshooters, Co. E, which was originally a target rifle company.

His love for historical muzzle loading arms grew to more than just a hobby when Ron went to work as a rifle smith for Green River Rifle Works in Roosevelt, Utah. GRRW was known for the fine copies of Hawken and Leman rifles they produced. Ron learned the trade well and three years later, in 1977, he left Green River, moved to Hamilton, Montana, and established his own custom gun shop. Since that date, he has built muzzle loading firearms full time, taking off each fall when he can to guide for Ken Alleman's black powder hunts in the Bitterroot Mountains. Ron states he does this "to keep fit as you don't get much exercise building guns."

Ron builds a variety of custom guns on order, ranging from plain mountain rifles, to fancy relief carved Ken-

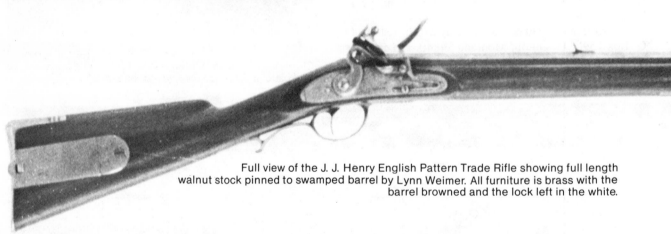

Full view of the J. J. Henry English Pattern Trade Rifle showing full length walnut stock pinned to swamped barrel by Lynn Weimer. All furniture is brass with the barrel browned and the lock left in the white.

TYPES OF FIREARMS OFFERED: *J. J. Henry English Pattern Trade Rifle, American firearms of the fur trade, English sporting rifles and fowlers*

J. J. HENRY ENGLISH PATTERN RIFLE
SPECIFICATIONS:
WOOD: *American walnut*
BARREL: *By Lynn Weimer, octagon, swamped*
BBL LENGTH: *42½"*
CALIBER: *.54*
LOCK: *Flint by own manufacture.*
　　　(Percussion optional, converted from flint)
TRIGGER: *Single*
FURNITURE: *Brass*
LENGTH OF PULL: *Customer preference*
KIT OFFERED: *No*

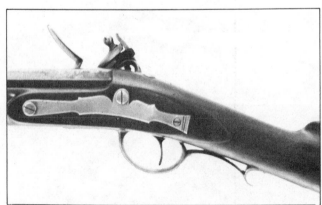

The wrist area is heavy, both in height and thickness. The brass side plate is of Lancaster style, one of the many blends of American/English characteristics of this piece.

tuckies as well as high quality English and European arms, cased if the customer desires. Recently he has been accepted into the American Custom Gun Makers Guild.

One gun in particular holds a certain fascination for Ron and that gun is the J. Henry English Pattern rifle, a firearm produced in the Henry shop in Boulton, Pennsylvania from approximately 1827 to 1850. His interest in the English Pattern rifle began when he saw his first one at Charlie Hanson's Museum of the Fur Trade in Chadron, Nebraska. Upon learning from Charlie that a great number of these guns went west during the fur trade era, Ron decided it would be a very appropriate gun for the buckskinner who wanted an authentic firearm of the 1830-50 time span — a weapon documented to have been shipped west by the American Fur Co. as early as 1827.

Ron embarked upon building himself an exact copy of the Henry rifle and, finding no parts available, he had to produce them himself. Building over-sized masters (to allow for shrinkage in casting) with exacting details of the original parts, Ron has finally produced a high quality copy of the lock, butt plate, trigger guard, and other furniture of the Henry rifle. Following strict dimensions of the original rifle, Ron has built a fine copy of the J. Henry English Pattern trade rifle. For the past several years he has been building this unique gun on order.

Ron Paull may be reached at N.W. 1132 Wildflower Road, Hamilton, MT 59840. Brochure is available upon request.

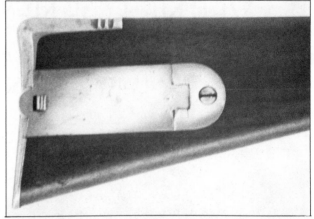

The brass butt plate and patch box are solid, simple, and functional. Note the sculptured fore end of the butt plate.

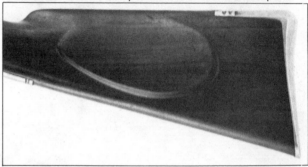

The cheek piece of the J. Henry is oval shaped, which is typically English. The bottom of the butt stock is rounded as are military rifles and muskets.

Ron Paull's copy of the original lock is true to the most minute detail. The lock is large with the plate a full six inches in length. The frizzen is fitted with a roller and the internals are heavy for durability. Like the originals, the lock is left in the white and the plate is stamped "J. J. HENRY BOULTON."

VERNE FORNES
BORN: LISBON, NORTH DAKOTA
JANUARY 20, 1963

Verne Fornes' youth was spent growing up on a farm near Kathryn, North Dakota. Much of his spare time was spent in the fields and woods hunting whitetails and other game so Verne's familiarity with firearms was taken as an everyday part of life. It wasn't, however, until after graduation from high school that he was introduced to muzzle loading guns. By a friend, he was shown several muzzle loading rifles built by Ron Paull of Montana. Verne's interest was piqued enough by the artistry and craftsmanship in these guns to seriously consider looking into a career of gun building and smithing. A phone call to Ron Paull to inquire into the whereabouts of such a school resulted in an invitation out to Montana to discuss an apprenticeship to Ron. Both men must have liked what they saw because by the fall of 1982 Verne Fornes became an apprentice gun builder to Ron Paull.

Verne's interest in American history, coupled with the association of folks who share a mutual interest in the fur trade era of 1810-1840 has led Verne to particularly enjoy building guns of that period. His favorite is the full stock rifle built by H. E. Leman for trade to the Indians. The simple, straightforward lines of the gun, coupled with the historical background of the Leman trade rifle, hold a fascination for Verne that causes him to continue to enjoy building authentic copies of trade rifles.

Today he is in his third year as an apprentice to Ron Paull but his workmanship strikes one as being that of a far more experienced builder. His future plans consist of continuing his study of early rifle construction and expanding his knowledge of the historic aspects of muzzle loading firearms — and, of course, building more guns.

Verne Fornes can be reached at N. W. 1132 Wildflower Road, Hamilton, Montana 59840. He has no catalog available.

Full length view of Leman full stock Indian Trade Rifle with flint ignition. Stocked in walnut, it features brass furniture, simple lines, and a single trigger. The barrel is pinned to the stock.

TYPES OF FIREARMS OFFERED: *H. E. Leman Trade Rifle*

SPECIFICATIONS:
WOOD: *American walnut, maple*
BARREL: *Montana Barrel Co., Lynn Weimer*
BBL LENGTH: *28"-42" Customer's preference*
CALIBER: *.32 to .62*
LOCK: *Flint or percussion; Siler, Long or own manufacture*
TRIGGER: *Single or double set*
FURNITURE: *Brass*
LENGTH OF PULL: *Customer preference*
KIT OFFERED: *No*

Close-up of the lock area showing lock, single trigger, and brass guard which is pinned to the stock. The lock, barrel, and trigger are browned.

Offside of butt region shows clean lines of the stock contour, the cheek piece, and lock bolts with inletted escutcheons.

THE HAWKEN SHOP

REOPENED: ST. LOUIS, MISSOURI

The history of the famed St. Louis gun makers, Jake and Sam Hawken, has been widely published in recent years. Almost everyone with an interest knows that they produced the widely acclaimed "Rocky Mountain Rifle" the classic half stock "Hawken," a name that became synonymous with quality.

After Jake's death in 1849, Sam carried on the shop until the early 1860s when the Hawken ownership passed into the hands of gunbuilder J. P. Gemmer. Gemmer continued producing guns until 1915 when he closed the shop.

Early in the 1960s at the sale of the Gemmer estate in St. Louis, Art Ressel came into possession of the remnants of the Hawken-Gemmer gunshop. Art, with the acquisition of the Hawken-Gemmer artifacts and with the encouragement and endorsement of the Hawken heirs "reopened" the Hawken Shop in St. Louis.

Art, an antique arms appraiser and collector (who at one time has owned as many as 14 original Hawken rifles), decided that the Hawken Shop would begin producing the classic Hawken half stock rifle again.

Believing that there is only one way to do it and that's to do it right and that "close doesn't count" when reproducing an exact copy, Art set about to produce an authentically correct Hawken. Using original guns from his collection he made molds from the original parts and had well known barrel maker, Bill Large, duplicate the tapered, 7 groove barrel with one twist in 48 inches.

The locks were cast from an original on a deluxe S. Hawken rifle and features a fly in the tumbler. Attention to minute detail, such as the ¼ inch taper from front to rear of the lock plate area from side to side, slotted barrel keys, patent hooked breech, buckhorn rear sight, and a front sight of a German silver blade set in a copper base, will be some of the things that will please the person who wants a truly authentic copy of a classic Hawken rifle.

Though in the past completed guns have been built on order, presently the Hawken Shop offers the S. Hawken half stock rifle in kit or component form only. Offered in .54 cal. percussion, the kit comes 95% inletted with a detailed set of plans. Fancy grades of wood are available. According to Art, no expense has been spared to make this rifle the best and only true copy of the classic "Hawken" on the market today.

More information may be obtained by writing The Hawken Shop, 3028 N. Lindbergh Blvd., St. Ann, MO 63074. The "Classic" brochure is available for $3.00.

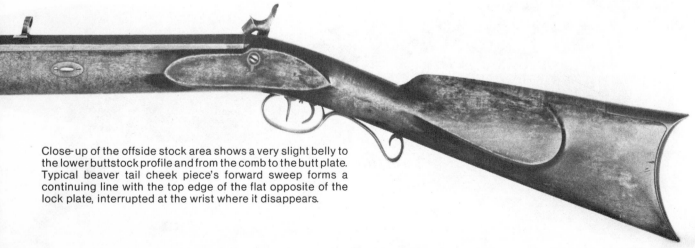

Close-up of the offside stock area shows a very slight belly to the lower buttstock profile and from the comb to the butt plate. Typical beaver tail cheek piece's forward sweep forms a continuing line with the top edge of the flat opposite of the lock plate, interrupted at the wrist where it disappears.

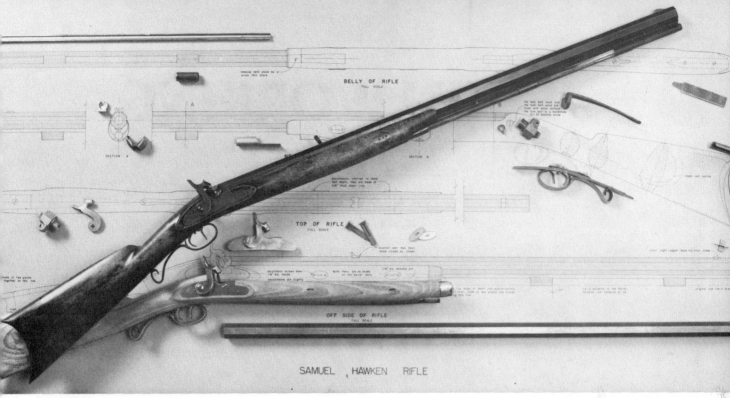

SAMUEL HAWKEN RIFLE

Full length view of the "classic" S. Hawken Plains Rifle shows the traditional lines of the typical half stock Hawken rifles. The plain maple stock holds a 34" Bill Large .54 cal. barrel tapered 1⅛" to 1". Since the rifle is offered in component form only, the 95% inlet stock comes with all components needed plus a well drawn set of plans.

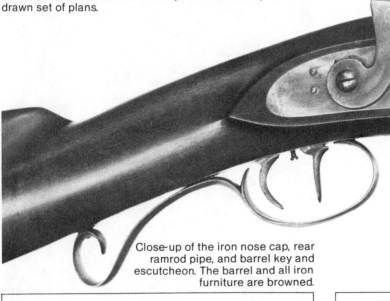

Close-up of the lock area shows the double pointed lock moulding, percussion lock manufactured by the Hawken Shop, and double set triggers and scroll trigger guard cast from originals by The Hawken Shop.

Close-up of the iron nose cap, rear ramrod pipe, and barrel key and escutcheon. The barrel and all iron furniture are browned.

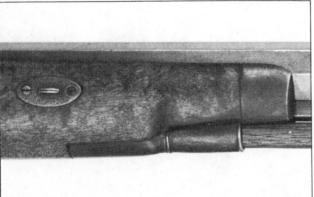

TYPES OF FIREARMS OFFERED: *S. Hawken Plains Rifle*

SPECIFICATIONS:
WOOD: *Maple (fancy grades are available)*
BARREL: *By Bill Large, 1" straight or 1⅛" to 1" tapered*
BBL LENGTH: *34"*
CALIBER: *.54*
LOCK: *Percussion by The Hawken Shop*
TRIGGERS: *Double set, double action by The Hawken Shop*
FURNITURE: *Iron*
LENGTH OF PULL: *Customer's preference*
KIT OFFERED: *Yes*

QUILLWORKING

BY CATHY SMITH

THE FIRST WOMAN TO RIDE into an American Mountain Man rendezvous was Cathy Smith. It was July 1981 when she and a brigade of AMM members rode over the High Uintahs of Utah to the Henry's Fork Rendezvous. That's Henry's Fork of the Green and the site of the original 1824 gathering. To re-enact history, to really live and feel the part, so as to know it personally, was the purpose of this expedition, and that's how Cathy approaches life in general.

She lives with her 12 year old daughter on a ranch in the Black Hills of South Dakota, and perhaps it was this sacred land and its harsh demands that influenced her destiny. Cathy has spent a lifetime in the study and production of 18th and 19th century North American Indian art forms. Her business, Medicine Mountain Trading Co., was founded in 1974 as a center for that activity. She learned quillwork and more than that: the traditional Lakota lifeways and spiritual values from relatives on the reservations of South Dakota. In keeping with her quest for "real" life experience, Cathy started at the beginning by apprenticing to a traditional Lakota elder, a process which became a lifelong commitment and responsibility.

This in turn led to years of research and study in this country and abroad, the collection and restoration of artifacts, and a desire to preserve these sometimes obscure American Indian art forms, using traditional tools, techniques, and materials. To serve those interested in "living history" has also been a goal of hers, as is dispelling some of the stereotypes and distorted perceptions arising from the "Myth of the West."

Through Medicine Mountain Trading Co., Cathy has been creating clothing and accoutrements, weapons and tools, and beadwork and quillwork, on a commission basis for collectors, museums, galleries, and buckskinners. She is also well known on the Western Rendezvous and Indian art circuits. She has modeled for Western artists and is a serious black powder shooter as well, with interests in muzzle-loading and cartridge guns.

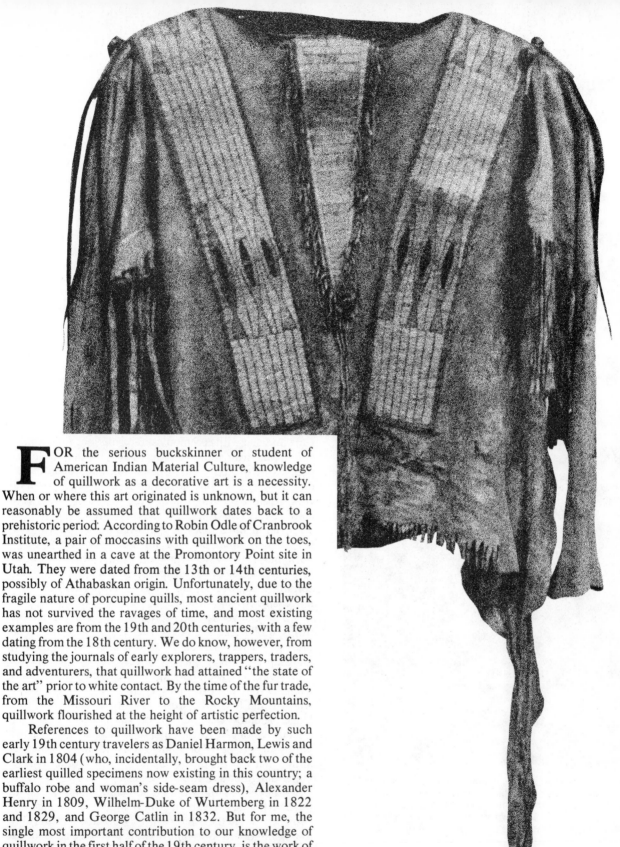

FOR the serious buckskinner or student of American Indian Material Culture, knowledge of quillwork as a decorative art is a necessity. When or where this art originated is unknown, but it can reasonably be assumed that quillwork dates back to a prehistoric period. According to Robin Odle of Cranbrook Institute, a pair of moccasins with quillwork on the toes, was unearthed in a cave at the Promontory Point site in Utah. They were dated from the 13th or 14th centuries, possibly of Athabaskan origin. Unfortunately, due to the fragile nature of porcupine quills, most ancient quillwork has not survived the ravages of time, and most existing examples are from the 19th and 20th centuries, with a few dating from the 18th century. We do know, however, from studying the journals of early explorers, trappers, traders, and adventurers, that quillwork had attained "the state of the art" prior to white contact. By the time of the fur trade, from the Missouri River to the Rocky Mountains, quillwork flourished at the height of artistic perfection.

References to quillwork have been made by such early 19th century travelers as Daniel Harmon, Lewis and Clark in 1804 (who, incidentally, brought back two of the earliest quilled specimens now existing in this country; a buffalo robe and woman's side-seam dress), Alexander Henry in 1809, Wilhelm-Duke of Wurtemberg in 1822 and 1829, and George Catlin in 1832. But for me, the single most important contribution to our knowledge of quillwork in the first half of the 19th century, is the work of Prince Maximilian von Wied and Karl Bodmer in 1835. For those of you unfamiliar with this work, I highly recommend that you take a look at *People of the First Man, The Firsthand Account of Prince Maximilian's Expedition Up the Missouri River, 1833-34.* Bodmer's watercolors, contained therein, are particularly important. The near photographic quality of Bodmer's work allows us to pick out minute details of costumes and accoutrements,

PLATE 2: Arapahoe quilled cradle ornament, ca. mid-19th century. Symbolizes the makers' prayers for a long life and health to the child. Ornament was kept as a protective amulet after the cradle was outgrown. Items of this nature could only be made by a member of the prestigious women's craft guild.

quillwork colors and stitching techniques, that may serve as an indispensable source of reference for the quillwork of the fur trade era.

THE TRADITIONS

Most Plains tribes had a tradition of mythology to explain the origin of quillwork. I think that this is important to mention here, in order to place quillwork in the proper perspective, especially for those of you who wish to pursue the art. The Blackfoot maintain that the "Thunder Beings" brought the porcupine and taught the use of quills to the people. The Cheyennes learned the sacred art from "Buffalo Wife" and founded a quillworker's guild based upon her instructions. The Sioux were taught by "Double Woman," a being who appeared in a vision as a human, but disappeared as a deer; and anyone who dreams of her is considered "wakan" and unexcelled in quillwork. People were often afraid of Double Woman Dreamers, as they were able to possess any man who stood near them. (This is according to James Walker's Oglala informants.) They were sometimes thought of as crazy, but they were very skillful and industrious, they did much quillwork, and were also capable of working like a man.

Though the traditions of origin may differ, most Plains tribes considered quillwork a holy or sacred art and surrounded it with ceremony and regulation. This concept still holds true today among many of the traditional peoples of the Northern Plains. For the contemporary quillworker, it is valuable to approach the craft within this context, for as we appropriate the sacred arts of another culture, it is important to do so with sensitivity.

Among the Blackfoot, quillwork was the province of a few women, members of a quillworkers' society. Before beginning to work they prayed, painted their hands and faces to prevent blindness and swollen hands, and wore a certain protective amulet. The first item quilled, often moccasins, was given to the spirits.

The Cheyenne had, perhaps, the most rigidly controlled quillworkers' guild. To belong was a mark of social prestige. Their standards of membership and workmanship are still religiously adhered to by the surviving "traditionals." Membership varied from ten to thirty women, from the post-pubescent to the elderly. No woman who wished to do the work could be excluded from the lodge. Members could not be selected by those who already belonged to the organization. Membership was purely on the basis of ability. It could not be inherited, although it was the duty of the Cheyenne mother to instill in her daughter a desire to belong.

Cheyenne guild work could be done only during the daylight hours, from about eight A.M. until noon, and from two until four in the afternoon. To work at other times was to risk blindness. Summer was the preferred season. The work done by the guild could only be done in fulfillment of a vow: It might be vowed, as was the Sun Dance, to cure the illness of a relative; or for an easy childbirth; or as a marriage gift for a relative; or for personal health and longevity.

A woman who wished to apprentice with the guild went first to the head woman and made a vow to do a certain type of quillwork. Four types of work might be done by guild members: quilled tipi linings, tipis, pillows,

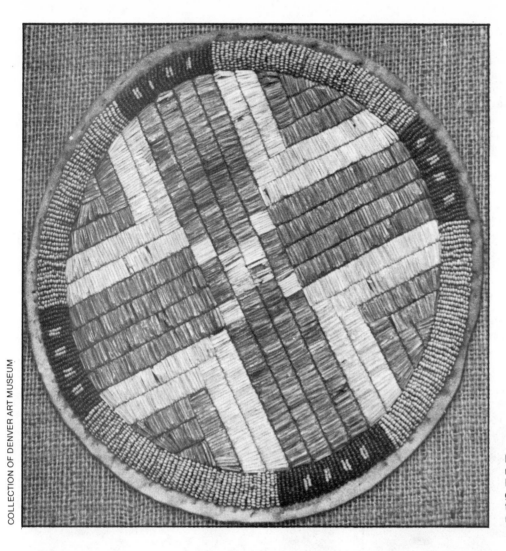

PLATE 3: Central Plains tipi rosette, ca. mid-19th century. Representative of quillworkers' guild work. Design represents the Four Directions giving the rosette a sacred nature.

or robes; all women's articles. On the appointed day, the members gathered at the home of the vower, each dressed in her best, and with faces painted in a specific manner. The head woman then conducted the vowing ceremony, using specific prayers and medicine bundles. The pattern for the vowed work was marked and four sinew strands must be quilled up at that time. Once the work was begun for the day, the woman could not leave her place until noon. Absolute attention must be given to the work at hand. All men and children were rigidly excluded from seeing or touching the work in progress. Two possible fates might befall a man who violated the rules of the guild, either by touching the uncompleted work, seeing it, or learning of the ceremonies: He might be gored to death by a bull or he might become deaf. Examples have been related of each of these.

While she was working, a vower might not have sexual relations, nor could she work on sacred quillwork during menstruation or pregnancy. When the vowed work was finished it was ceremoniously examined and displayed by the guild and a feast was held. At this time the head woman was paid by the vower: She was given the dishes and cooking utensils from the feast, as well as an entire new outfit of clothing and a horse. Once a vow was made to complete a certain quilled project, it *must* be completed, and in a reasonable length of time, or harm

(even death) would come to the vower and the recipient of the vow.

The quillworking regulations of the *Sioux* are much less restrictive, at least as far as I have been able to ascertain from living informants. Quilling was looked upon as being the highest attainment in the female arts and most young women were expected to learn it from their mothers. Quill designs were considered personal property and *not copied,* for they were dreamed and only the dreamer could claim ownership. On regular occasions, women met to exhibit their work and show how they did it. A feast was held and gifts were presented to those who showed excellence in workmanship. The meeting was called by an old woman, a leader in the craft, and was a holy occasion. A "quilling count" was made by each woman and displayed just as a man displayed his war honors.

Today, to learn quillwork one must seek out an elderly woman of excellent reputation and take her four offerings to solicit her help. This should be done even if one happens to be a self-taught quiller, as quillwork is "wakan" or sacred and offerings must be made appropriately to insure the safety of the quillworker and the longevity and soundness of the work itself.

I have had the good fortune to live near the Sioux and have access to this information for my own apprenticeship. I have found that it helps immensely with the work and adds another dimension to the process that is missing in "how-to" manuals. Further, I would recommend that any serious quillworker find a way to apprentice with a knowledgeable person, even if only to give the proper offerings. It is also a good idea to give away one's first piece of quillwork as a sign of thanksgiving, respect, and sincerity.

One last item of consideration, as far as tradition goes: Where do the *men* fit in? Traditionally, they don't! Men did not do quillwork or beadwork in the old days, unless of course they were a "winkte," a male who adopted the feminine role. Dressed as women and following the feminine pursuits of tanning and quilling, they lived in their own tipis at the edge of the camp circle. Winktes generally excelled in this work and were possibly supernaturally inspired. Pieces produced by them were highly desirable, entirely marketable, and often cherished. Today, many, if not most of the best craftworkers are men, Indian and non-Indian alike; winkte and non-winkte. And now that I'm treading on thin ice, at least with a couple of male quillworkers who happen to be friends of mine, I will leave the resolution of this question to the reader, and move on to the less controversial porcupine.

THE QUILLS

Quills were probably as desirable a trade item in the 1800s as they are becoming now. The porcupine is widely distributed across the northern part of our continent, however, many of the native peoples who practiced quillwork lived outside its habitat.

PLATE 5: Brulé Sioux fan handle, ca. mid 19th century. A superbly executed floral design using very fine quills.

PLATE 4: Sioux cradle board cover, ca. 1870. Also representative of guild work. Elaborate pattern with aniline dyes.

Porcupines, fortunately for contemporary quill-workers, are not an endangered species. In fact, a prime source of quills today is the "road-kill," depending of course, upon whether you live in a rural area and the strength of your stomach. I obtain my quills from a trapper who finds porcupines a nuisance in his coyote sets, and from shooting the varmints in my own barnyard. I have found the easiest method for dealing with porcupines is to skin the carcass (preferably before the bloating stage) and flesh the hide, rubbing a good amount of borax into it. I then stack the dry hides up for future use. Ten to twelve hides are usually enough for a good winter's work, while one good hide will probably suffice the beginner. Another point worth mentioning: If the porcupine is fresh, the meat makes an excellent stew, in fact the roasted tail is considered a delicacy by my Sioux relatives.

I've heard stories of various ways to obtain quills without killing the porcupine; such as hitting them with styrofoam or foam rubber or throwing a blanket over them. These methods are not very realistic considering that the few quills obtained would be the short, thick ones from the tail or lower back and mostly unsuitable for good quill-work. If all else fails, porcupine hides and/or plucked quills may be purchased from several trading companies. I would recommend that you purchase whole hides rather than plucked quills, as the latter are fairly expensive and most often not the appropriate size.

QUILL PREPARATION

Quills can quite easily be plucked from the dried porcupine hide. Cut a 1" wide strip from the hide with a sharp knife and soak it in warm water for an hour or so. By bending the now pliable strip of hide over thumb and forefinger, the quills will separate, and can be plucked and sorted out simultaneously, leaving the guard hairs behind. The best quills are those along the flanks, neck and upper back. They are usually no thicker than 1/16" and from 1 to 2" in length. These quills can generally be used for all the quillwork techniques and are the best for quill wrapping.

The very fine quills, which are overgrown guard hairs, usually found on the edge of the flanks, should be separated out for use in quill plaiting. Larger quills, up to 3/16" in diameter, found in the greatest number on a hide, can be used for quill embroidery when covering fairly large areas such as blanket strips, shirt and legging strips. Any quill larger than this is generally too inflexible for the manipulation required to produce fine work. Avoid the temptation to use those long, thick quills. The length gained does not make up for the difficulty you'll experience in folding them. Also, disregard any quill under 1" in length.

Once the quills are plucked and sorted, they must be washed thoroughly in hot water with any mild soap. A teaspoon of clorox can be added to the water for disinfecting purposes if desired. Be careful not to use too much because it can cause the quills to become brittle. Washing removes the natural grease from the quills so that the dye can penetrate evenly.

DYEING THE QUILLS

"Knowledge of the materials and techniques used by the American Indians to dye porcupine quills is very scarce. Quilling and dyeing were the work of women, and womens' societies often kept the secrets of these arts only for the initiated. Transmitted only by oral tradition, knowledge was passed from mother to daughter, or from master artist to apprentice. Much of what was once known has been lost in time and disuse. That which has survived is jealously guarded by the people who inherited it or earned it."*

The majority of pre-1850 quillwork was dyed with native dyes. The people in different regions of the country used whatever was available to them locally or through trade from neighboring regions. Since plants and minerals vary greatly from one area to the next, a great number of

---

* *This material on natural dyes has been contributed in part by Blue Laslow, White River, Arizona. Blue is one of the current experts on natural dyes and dyeing methods for porcupine quills. He is currently writing a book on the subject.*

them could have been used to produce the same or similar colors.

Frances Densmore compiled a list of colors and dye sources in 1927, from the Chippewa of the Great Lakes region. The colors were red, brownish-black, yellow, and purple-blue. Red was obtained from puccoon root, bloodroot, and wild plum. Black was found in various mixtures of the bark of burr oak, butternut, alder, dogwood, and hazelnut. Yellow was produced from alder (inner bark), sumac stalk, gold-thread root, and shredded inner root of bloodroot. Blue was found in rotted maple wood, mordanted with grin stone dust.

The Western Plains were not as rich in dye vegetation as was the more humid Great Lakes region. The three major colors found in surviving specimens of pre-1850 Plains quillwork are yellow, orangish-red, and brown-black, with a limited amount of bluish-green and bluish-purple. Undyed, white quills were used as background in the majority of the quillwork, with yellow being the next most commonly used background.

Yellow was produced from wild sunflower, cone flower petals, and fox moss from pine trees in the Black Hills. I have also produced a pale lemon yellow from onion skins. Orangish-red in various intensities was made from buffalo berries, dock root, mountain mahogany root, and inner bark of the hemlock. Brownish-black could be obtained from wild grapes and the green hulls of walnuts, the latter obtained in trade. Maidenhair fern stems were often substituted for quills when black was the desired color.

Blue is a questionable color. Orchard maintains that blue dye was unknown, at least among the Dakota Sioux. However, bluish-green quills, much faded, can be seen on many old Plains specimens. Pale blue was extracted from trade wool by boiling it with the quills, but I doubt that much of this valuable material was actually sacrificed in this way. Indigo, the best natural source of blue dye was common to the Southwest, but I have not found documentation of its use on the Northern Plains.

Clues to old dye sources can be found in the folklore of any given area, in old trade manifests, anthropological reports, and dye books for spinners and weavers. For those of you who wish to experiment with natural dyes, these are the places to start. I have found that the majority of dye recipes that I use for dyeing wool (I am also a weaver) do not work on quills. Either the color doesn't penetrate the quill or it is not color-fast on quills.

Blue Laslow recommends two methods for trying potential dyes on quills: fermentation and decoction (or simmering in water). Fermentation is the process of simply covering the dye vegetation with water and leaving it in a warm place. If the water becomes colored, it is poured over the quills and left until they are infused with color several days or weeks later. Decoction involves placing the dye material in a clean cotton bag and simmering it with the quills until they take up the color. Be careful not to boil the quills or they will become too brittle to use. Enamel or non-reacting pots must be used, as iron, aluminum, and copper will react with certain dyes, changing the color or dulling it.

PLATE 6: Detail pf Assiniboin shirt, style is ca. 1830. Note the quilled target, dyed with natural dyes and pony bead accents. Shirt made by Lance Grabowski, quillwork by Blue Laslow.

Using a mordant in the dye bath will often help to increase the color intensity or set the color. Mordants are minerals or tannin-rich plants, such as alum, copper sulfate, and ferrous sulfate. Alum is commonly found in natural mineral deposits and white clays. Ferrous sulfate as a mordant can be obtained simply by using an iron pot.

Not all colors obtained from natural materials are color fast, especially those obtained from berries, fruits, and vegetables. So be sure to test your dyed quills in bright sunlight for fading. The pH of the water will also influence the dye; rainwater is the preferable source.

You may not recreate exactly the same colors that were used in early quillwork, but then again, you might. Remember, the pre-1850 quill colors were basically white, yellow, brownish-black, and red-orange, with limited amounts of bluish shades. The majority of this quillwork was done in combinations of only two or three and sometimes four colors. The designs were usually contrasting color blocks or bands on a lighter background.

Aniline dyes were invented around 1850 and appeared on the northern Plains as early as 1855. The first documented evidence of this fact will appear in James Hanson's work on the G.K. Warren collection, due to be published sometime in 1985. Lt. G. K. Warren, a U.S. topographer in a campaign against the Sioux in 1855, obtained a major collection of Sioux artifacts from the Battle of Ash Hollow. Among the items presented to the Smithsonian were fourteen bladder bags of quills. An .analysis of the quills found them all to be dyed with commercial dyes, three of which were aniline. All major colors were observed, including a green made from a mixture of blue and yellow. 1855 might seem rather early for aniline dyes to be found on the Plains, however, it must be remembered that there were twelve trading posts within 100 miles of the Black Hills at that time.

Commercial dyes, such as Rit, may be used in place of natural dyes in contemporary quillwork. With careful mixing of colors, the dyer can come close to approximating the old colors. I would recommend that you do your museum research first, looking closely at the old colors on original pieces and then never use Rit straight out of the box. Mix the colors to dull them a bit; commercial dyes can be almost fluorescent in hue at times.

PLATE 7: Bladder bag quill container and umbilical fetish, Sioux, ca. mid-19th century.

THE QUILLWORKER'S
TOOLS AND MATERIALS

The traditional tool kit contained a bladder bag of quills, a bone marker, an awl, knife, sinew, possibly a quill flattener (made of bone, antler, or later, iron), and buckskin or rawhide. Today's tools would more likely include a colored pencil, scissors, needles and thread, beeswax, an awl, and a flattener.

The bone marker or pencil is used to mark the stitching guidelines for quill embroidery. The bone edge or an awl can also be used to incise the guidelines into the leather, which sometimes helps to keep the lanes of quillwork straighter. I find that a hard, wax, colored pencil, finely sharpened and in a color close to that of the buckskin works well. It gives a clean, semi-incised line to follow, without the smudging of graphite or the indelible traces of ball point pen. These guidelines will be important, as maintaining straight, even lanes of embroidery is usually the biggest difficulty facing the novice.

Stitches were done by making an awl hole through the top surface of the leather, not by piercing entirely through the skin from back to front. The stiff end of the sinew thread was then threaded through the hole before it closed up. This method is not as painstaking as it might seem, once a bit of practice is acquired. The sinew holds the quills firmer and for a much longer period of time than does thread. (This becomes apparent when we examine very old specimens.) It is not inappropriate to use needle and thread, however. Most contemporary quillers use them. I like to use the finest needle possible, a size #12 sharp, short beading needle. It carries a fine thread easily through the leather, leaving scarcely a hole or thread to be seen between the quills. Cotton or linen thread is preferable to nylon or artificial sinew for the sake of authenticity and waxing the thread keeps the stitches tighter.

The awl will be helpful as a guide for folding the quills over and for tucking in spliced ends.

The quill flattener is used when the work is finished to press and flatten the quills after they've been sewn down. It is not used to flatten each quill individually prior to use. The flattener I was taught to use by the Sioux is a large "S" shaped piece of iron, 12 to 14" in length, which is heated and then used to press the quillwork. A damp towel is placed between the hot iron and the quills.

The choice of leather is one of the most important considerations in the production of a fine piece of quill embroidery. Brain tanned hides usually of buffalo or moose were originally used. These are still the best choices and smoked hides are even better. A leather with body, minimum stretch and a firm surface is desirable. Buckskin or elk can certainly be used if it is not too stretchy. (Smoking the hide will often shrink some of the stretch out of it and give it extra body.) If you are making a quill ornamented garment, the quillwork is almost always done on a separate piece of leather first, and then buckskin for the garment itself and the old, smoked tipi tops for the quillwork base. I personally prefer smoked moose hide for quilling. Although it has become quite expensive, it is the easiest and best to quill on and the end result is well worth the price. If cost is a problem, the next choice would be "commercial brain tanned" hides. Some of these hides look and work as well as pure brain tanned. I would not recommend regular commercially tanned hides at all. The leather fibers are usually broken instead of stretched (as they are in brain tan) and stitches will be more likely to pop loose unless they penetrate fully through the hide. Further, they are usually too stretchy, tough to get a needle through, and as far as authenticity goes, commercial leather just doesn't make it.

Rawhide is another necessary material which is used for quill wrapping, especially for pipebag slats, armbands, tipi ties and the like. (Birchbark was sometimes used in this respect.) A flat, even surface of consistent thickness is called for here. Thin buffalo (a heifer hide is ideal) or elk rawhide is appropriate. Deer or antelope can be used if it is not too thin. Cow or preferably calf rawhide can also be used, although it is tougher to cut and tends to be stiffer, having more glue in the hide. Be careful to avoid scars or skinning cuts, as the rawhide is weakened in these spots. If the rawhide is too thin, the moisture of the dampened quills will cause it to twist and warp. If it is too thick, it is difficult to cut with an even edge, resulting in uneven and sloppy wrapping.

Having the tools and materials assembled, the quills sorted for size and dyed, the next step is to soak and flatten them. Clip off the follicle end of the quill, (to let the air out) and the tip of the black barb. (I leave the barb end intact for quill wrapping, but remove it for cleaner embroidery work.) Place as many quills in your mouth, follicle end first, as you can reasonably hold. In a few minutes the quills will be pliable enough to flatten. Pull a quill out of your mouth, grasp the barb end tightly between your front teeth and flatten it by pinching it between thumbnail and index finger and pulling along the length of the quill.

Quills can be soaked in water and flattened with an awl handle or the back of a spoon if desired. However, there is a reason for using one's mouth. Saliva somehow always gives the quills the proper pliability, without brittleness, perhaps due to its enzyme content. It also conveys part of the spirit of the artist into the work (according to the Lakota) and it is definitely easier to manipulate quills with the teeth. I have tried time and again to keep the quills out of my mouth, and invariably they find

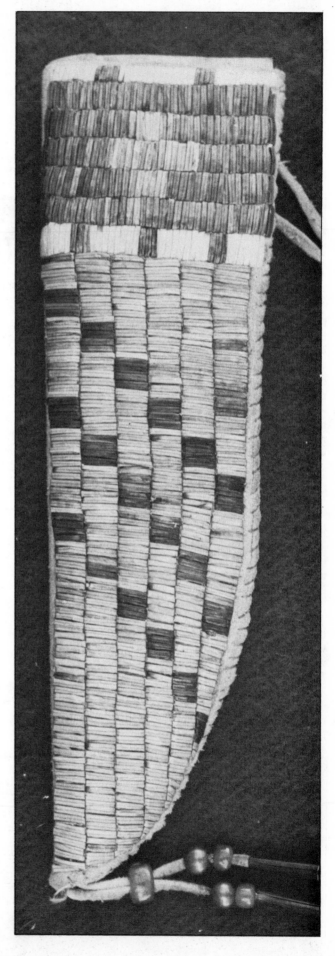

PLATE 8: Central Plains style woman's knife sheath in parallel fold embroidery technique. Made by the author.

PLATE 9: Quilled feather strip, front and back views. Made by the author.

their way back. If you choose to soak your quills in water, be careful not to leave them too long, (fifteen minutes or so), as the white, pithy lining will soften and be extruded as you flatten the quill. For quill wrapping on rawhide, be careful not to have the quills or the fingertips too wet, as the rawhide will begin to soften and warp.

One last thought pertaining to tools: If it is not apparent by now, thumbnails are a prerequisite to the manipulation of quills. So stop biting your nails, you're going to need them.

THE TECHNIQUES

Quillwork may be divided into four basic techniques: wrapping, sewing or embroidery, plaiting, and weaving. The item to be decorated usually determined the technique used. Within each major technique area there are innumerable variations, based upon the skill and ingenuity of the quiller.

As space does not permit the inclusion of a detailed "how-to" manual in this work, I am going to outline the basic techniques and merely present a few of the many variations. I would refer the serious student to the basic work on the subject, William Orchard's, *Technique of Porcupine Quill Decoration Among the Indians of North America.* Gary Johnson, noted contemporary quiller, also did an excellent series of articles in *Muzzleloader* magazine, Sept./Oct. '81 to Nov./Dec. '82 issues. Carrie

Lyford's, *Quill and Beadwork of the Western Sioux* may also be helpful.

QUILL WRAPPING

Quill wrapping is the easiest technique to master and as it has many applications, this is the logical place to start. The most obvious use of the wrapping technique is on the rawhide slats of pipebag bottoms, arm bands, hair ornaments, and feather strips. Tipi ties, various quill-wrapped thongs, wrapped hair locks, pipe tampers, and thin pipe stems are all made with variations of this technique.

A quilled feather strip is a good beginning project to learn the wrapping technique. This is a thin strip of quilled rawhide tied to the feather shaft with sinew. Feathers, decorated in this manner were used in bonnets, as hair ornaments, in eagle feather fans, etc. **Plate 9** shows front and back sides of a feather strip.

To begin: Cut a piece of flat, thin rawhide the length of your feather shaft (not counting the feather quill which projects beyond the feathers themselves.) This should be approximately ¼" wide and can be tapered as is the feather shaft. Pierce two small awl holes in each end of the strip to facilitate attachment to the feather. See **Figure 1**.

I almost always flatten the quills prior to wrapping, although it is not necessary to do so. **Figure 2** illustrates the steps involved in this technique. Each quill is knotted

FIGURE 1

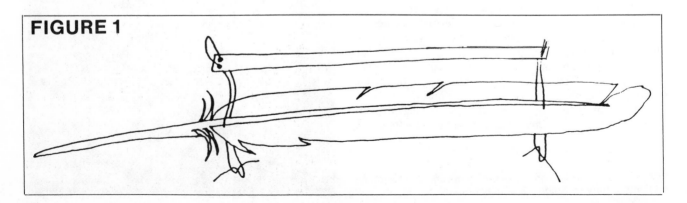

FIGURE 2

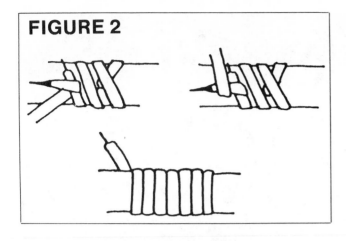

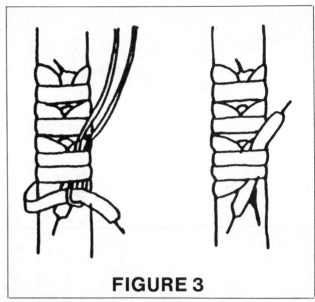

FIGURE 3

PLATE 10: Eastern Sioux quill wrapped pipestems, ca. mid-19th century. Note unusual design obtained from addition of a separate quill woven over and under the quill wraps.

into the previous one and always on the same side of the rawhide slat. Start just below your attachment holes, laying the quills in, barbed end up, making sure that you pull them very tight, while holding the knotted end down with your thumbnail. If the quills are fairly long, it is possible to get two or three wraps before splicing on another. Sometimes the quill will only be long enough for one wrap or you may want to change colors. Stripes or blocks of color are the only patterns possible, unless a separate quill is woven over and under the wraps on the front side of the strip. **Plate 10** shows a pipestem quilled in this way.

Tying off the last quill is shown in **Figure 3**. Use a fairly long quill for the last one, and with a piece of sinew, lay a loop on the last splice. Wrap the final quill over it at least two times, then catch the end of the quill in the loop and pull it up beneath the last few wraps and clip off the exposed end. The strip is now ready to be tied, through the awl holes, to the feather shaft. Use sinew for this, as it will show on the front of the strip.

Pipebag bottoms and armbands are made with this same wrapping method, the only difference being the rawhide base. Instead of using separate strips, one piece of rawhide is used, with slits cut into it. Pipebag slats, as shown in **Plate 11,** were characteristic of most Plains

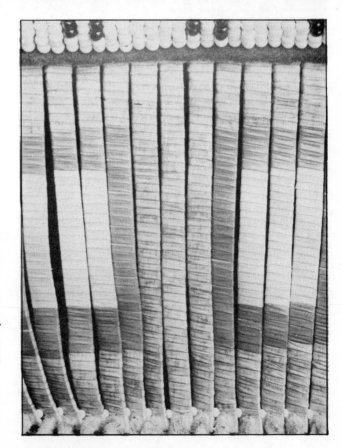

PLATE 11: Detail of quill wrapped rawhide slats on pipe bag bottom. Made by the author.

PLATE 12: Detail of Upper Missouri shirt showing quill wrapped fringe on shirt bib and hair locks. Made by Medicine Mountain Trading Co.

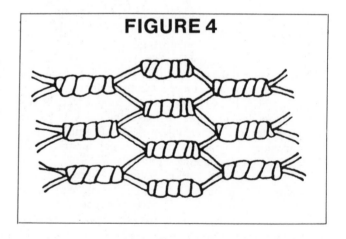

FIGURE 4

tribes—Sioux, Cheyenne, Arapahoe, Gros Ventre, Shoshone, Assiniboin, and occasionally Crow, though seldom Blackfoot. Patterns for pre-1840 quill wrapping are generally simple geometrics (rectangles and squares, bands and stripes) in three or four basic colors.

VARIATIONS IN WRAPPING

Buckskin fringes on bags, coats, dresses, shirts, and leggings were often quill wrapped in pairs for an inch or two. Hair locks and buckskin thongs were also wrapped in this way, although these tend to become round (instead of flat) in the process, and thus have no definite front and back sides. **Plate 12**, a detail of an early Upper Missouri society shirt shows wrapped fringe on the shirt bib.

Netted fringe was seen among the Great Lakes tribes, Plains Cree, and Metis. This is wrapping pairs of buckskin fringe for a distance and then alternating the pairs, to give a net effect. **Figure 4.**

Still another form of wrapping was done on thin, round pipe stems, club handles, pipe tampers, whistles, or any object whose circumference did not exceed the length of one quill. **Figure 5.** A sinew thread is wrapped around the object and tied. The loose end is stretched down the length of the object and again tied off. This becomes the **stationary** thread about which the quills are fastened. The

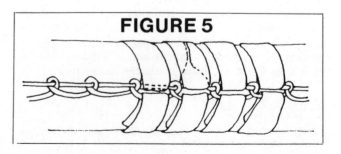

FIGURE 5

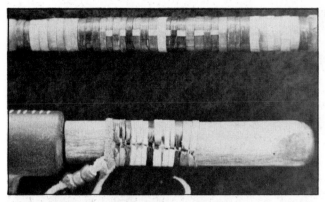

PLATE 13: Detail of quill wrapping on pipe tamper and the reverse side of this technique on a small pipe stem. Made by Medicine Mountain Trading Co.

barb end of the quill is tucked under this thread, the quill folded back over itself, passed around the object, and finally, half-hitched back to the stationary thread. This procedure is repeated, with one quill completing one wrap, down the length of the object, ending at the point at which the stationary thread is tied off. **Plate 13** illustrates the front and back sides of this technique.

Quill wrapped horsehair was a method used to make rosettes or shirt and legging strips, by *very* skillful early quillworkers on the northern Plains. The technique involves wrapping, coiling, and sewing. Quills were wrapped around two bunches of horsehair and stitched down to the backing between the hanks. The stitches are pulled so tight that they become concealed. **Figure 6** shows this advanced technique. It has been used to form wide bands of eight or more, laid lengthwise side by side. **Plate 14** illustrates this technique used to make the strips on an 1840 Nez Perce shirt. Quill wrapped horsehair has been collected from the Upper Missouri and Sioux tribes as well.

A final thought on wrapping is directed towards the quill wrapped hatbands and medicine wheels, so often seen at rendezvous. I have to agree with Gary Johnson's statement (*Muzzleloader*, Nov./Dec. '81) that they are questionable items prior to 1850. Further, I would agree that it is inappropriate to use medicine wheels as ornamentation on bags and garments in the place of

PLATE 14: Detail of Nez Perce shirt, ca. 1840. The strips are quill wrapped horsehair. Quill colors are red and yellow on a white background. Note pony bead edging in blue and white.

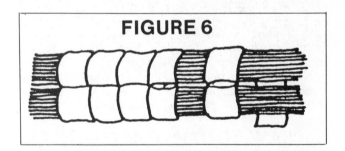

FIGURE 6

PLATE 15: Quill wrapped hat band and arm bands backed with buffalo hide. Made by the author.

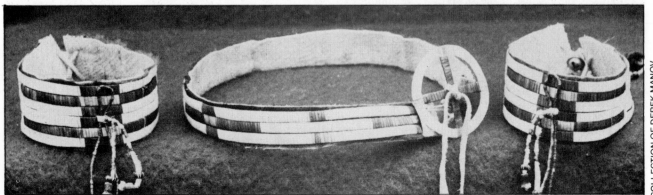

PLATE 16: Detail of sawtooth embroidery on a belt bag. Made by the author.

embroidered rosettes or to attach quilled rawhide slats to objects which were traditionally embroidered (knife sheaths, shirt strips, pouches, etc.). **Plate 15**.

QUILL EMBROIDERY

Orchard, in his previously mentioned book, identified three types of stitches used in early quill embroidery: the spot stitch (A), backstitch (B), and loopstitch (C), as illustrated in **Figure 7**. I generally use the backstitch, although some circumstances call for backstitch on one side of the quill and spot stitch on the opposite side. Each quillworker has to develop a stitching technique that works for him. This will come with practice and experience. For embroidery, quills should have both ends clipped, be *very* pliable, and flattened perfectly. The work has a neater appearance if the quills are all of the same width; and remember, the quill itself is never pierced with needle or awl because it will split. Stitches are done over the quill.

SAW-TOOTH OR ZIG-ZAG EMBROIDERY

This is the easiest of the sewn-down techniques to master and probably the most commonly used. This technique can be used on almost any item, geometric or floral pattern, although blanket strips, rosettes, and other wide bands were most often done in the parallel-fold technique. Refer to **Figure 8**.

Begin by drawing guidelines on the buckskin, ½" to ¼" apart. Large areas to be covered had wider lanes, small areas, narrower lanes. With awl and sinew or needle and thread, stitch the follicle end of the quill down on one side of the guideline. Bend the quill over the sinew thread, along the line, and stitch it in place along the opposite line with a second thread. Continue to fold the quill back and forth, stitching it down each time, until you're ready to splice in a new one. Slip the new quill under the old one, clip off any excess on the old quill, fold both over as one, and the old quill end will disappear under the new. When the final stitch is reached, the quill must be folded over the needle and the end tucked back under the stitch. **Plate 16** illustrates saw-tooth embroidery.

PARALLEL-FOLD EMBROIDERY

This technique resembles quill wrapping in final appearance. It is a bit more difficult to manipulate, but historically, one of the most common, especially when wide bands or large areas were to be covered. It was also used to execute floral designs.

Figure 9 shows this stitch. Begin with very damp quills, just as in saw-tooth style. Sew down the follicle end of the quill, bend it over the stitch to the opposite guideline. At this point fold the quill over your awl or needle point, pass the thread under the fold and stitch. Repeat this procedure of sewing down flat on one line and folding the quill over on the opposite line until a new quill is needed. Remember, the same side of the quill *is* always uppermost.

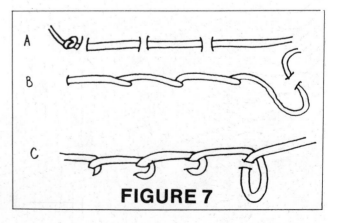

FIGURE 7

67

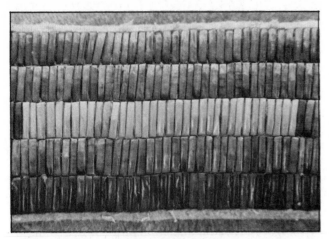

PLATE 17: Detail of parallel fold embroidery on shirt strips. Made by Medicine Mountain Trading Co.

Splice in the same way as described for saw-tooth embroidery.

It requires some practice and a lot of patience to achieve flat, even work with crisp edges. I was told to do quill embroidery at least one hour per day to keep the "touch" in my fingertips. **Plates 17** and **18** are examples of the parallel-fold technique.

The parallel-fold allows for square and rectangular design elements, while the saw-tooth produces triangular or stepped-side rectangles. Saw-tooth also has more of a texture to the finished look, while parallel lies flat. It can easily be seen from the parallel technique how lazy stitch beadwork originated.

VARIATIONS IN EMBROIDERY

There are many variations of the two techniques described above involving multiple quills or contrasting colored quills.

Figure 10: One Thread Embroidery (**Plate 19**) was often used to cover a seam and was popular among the Plains Cree, Metis, and Great Lakes peoples for making a

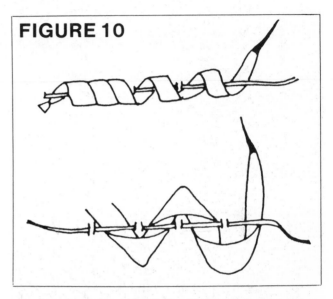

FIGURE 10

PLATE 18: Detail of parallel fold embroidery in floral style from a Brulé Sioux vest, ca. late 19th century.

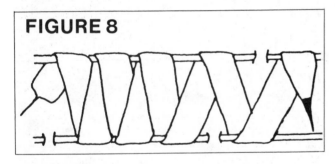

FIGURE 8

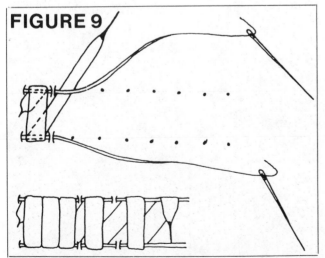

FIGURE 9

PLATE 19: Detail of one-thread embroidery in flower stems from bag made by Medicine Mountain Trading Co.

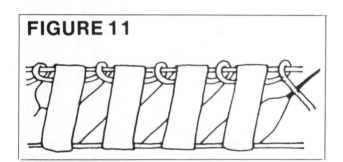

FIGURE 11

delicate or curving line in floral patterns. Rarely used by the Sioux, this is a parallel wrap technique using spot stitch. Two variations are shown.

Figure 11: Parallel fold technique with addition of a third thread. This extra thread runs across the surface of the leather along the top of the row. The other thread on top is sewn as in simple parallel style except that it passes under and over the third thread, forming a loop between each quill.

This technique is often seen on tipi bags decorated with many narrow rows of quillwork set an inch or so apart. **Plate 20.** The reason for this third thread is unclear. Perhaps it helps to keep a single row of embroidery straight and even, or that it gives the edge of the lane more depth.

Figure 12: A variation of Saw-tooth style with two quills of different colors superimposed and treated as if they were a single quill. The result is diagonals of alternating color. The moccasins in **Plate 21** illustrate this stitch in the outermost row of the rosettes on their toes.

Figure 13: The two quill diamond is a more complex technique of the parallel fold style, involving two separate quills started on opposite sides of the lane and crossed over and under each other. **Plate 22.**

Figure 14: A variation of the previous technique, using quills of contrasting colors. This technique was found on Upper Missouri work (Mandan, Hidatsa), Sioux, Plains Cree, and Iowa.

PLATE 20: Cheyenne tipi bag illustrating parallel fold, three- thread technique, ca. mid-19th century.

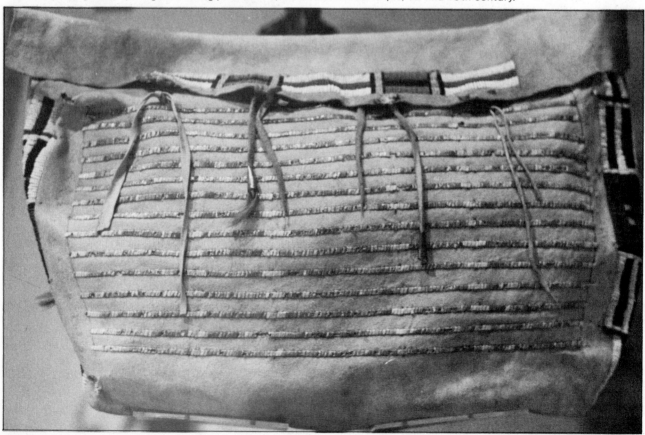

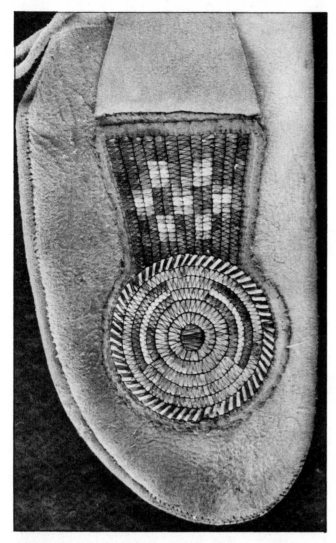

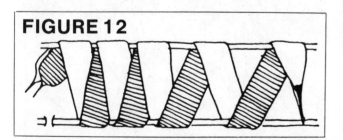

PLATE 21: Mandan moccasin rosette. Note sawtooth embroidery with two contrasting colors in outermost row. (Brown, white, pale blue, and red/orange) Made by the author.

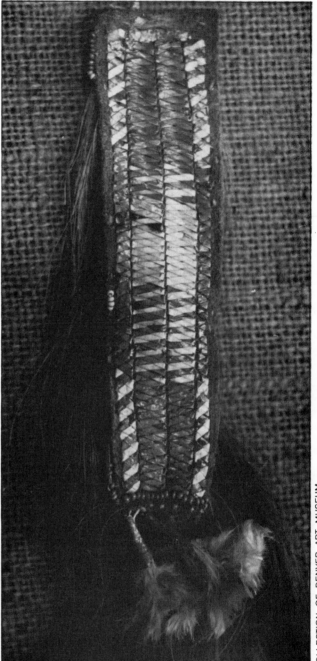

PLATE 22: Detail of Sioux hair ornament, ca. 1840, illustrating two-quill diamond embroidery.

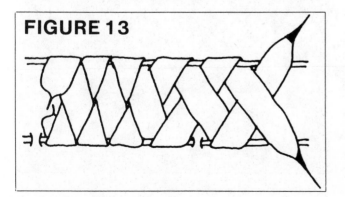

FIGURE 12

FIGURE 13

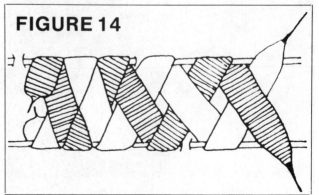

FIGURE 14

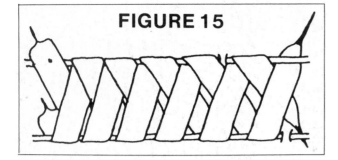

FIGURE 15

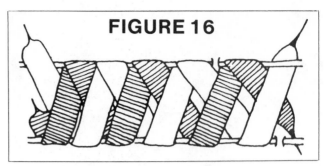

FIGURE 16

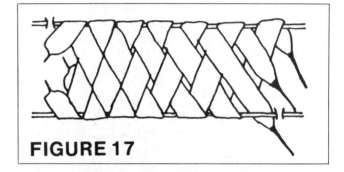

FIGURE 17

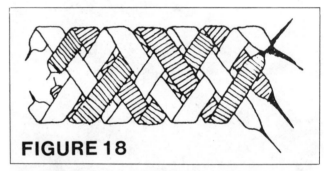

FIGURE 18

Figure 15: The two quill triangle pattern is an adaptation of the Saw-tooth technique, except that the diagonal crossings are extended and two quills alternately overlap at the crossings.

Figure 16: Variation of the two quill triangle with contrasting colors.

Figure 17: The three quill double diamond style is an extension of the two quill diamond with the addition of another quill. More variation can be attained by using different colored quills.

Figure 18: The four quill diamond, with two contrasting colored quills.

Figure 19: The multi-quill or plait-like technique. Here, quills are interwoven using parallel technique, spot stitched. New quills are spliced into the center of the design with a third thread. This technique was used on shirt and legging strips and for covering large areas up to 10" in width. It was a favorite of Mandan and Hidatsa quillers and probably originated on the Upper Missouri. See **Plate 23.**

Figure 20: The multi-quill checker-weave has spot stitching to secure the edges. I have seen this on Upper Missouri knife sheaths.

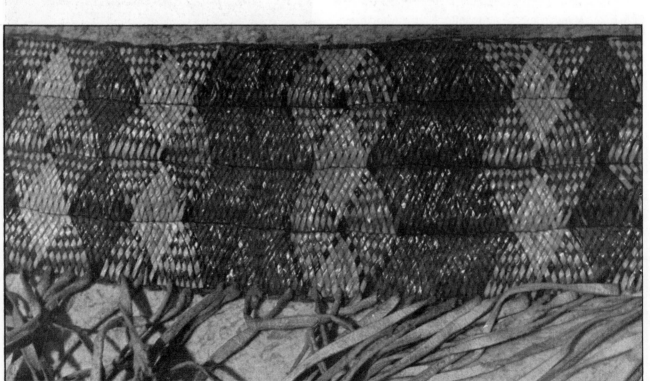

PLATE 23: Detail of Upper Missouri (Arikara) shirt strip illustrating multi-quill embroidery.

QUILL PLAITING

Plaiting is the extremely delicate work you saved your finest quills for. (Remember the quills that look like thick guard hairs?) Usually applied to pipe stems, plaiting must be done with these "hair-like" quills to look as it should. Larger quills make for "lumpy" plaiting.

The object that will be wrapped with plaiting must be at hand; the plaiting is attached to it as the work progresses. Begin by preparing two sinew threads, as long as possible. Tie them to a small stick, sit on the ground, and holding this stick between your toes or stuck inside your moccasin, stretch the sinew threads tightly and tie them to the pipestem lying on your lap. Proceed as shown in **Figure 21.** Roll the completed plaiting around the pipestem each time three inches or so is completed, and work your pattern design in as you go. Traditionally, pipestems had very elaborate patterns of geometric and pictographic figures.

It is sometimes beneficial to cover the stem with thin buckskin prior to plaiting because this cushions the plaiting and keeps it from slipping on the stem. When the plaiting is completed, tie the sinew threads off on the stem and tuck them under the last wrap. **Plate 24** is an example of very fine plaiting on a Lakota pipestem, circa 1830.

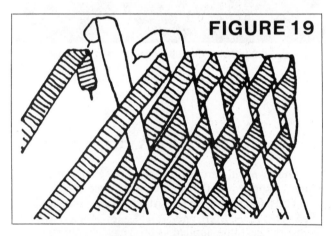

FIGURE 19

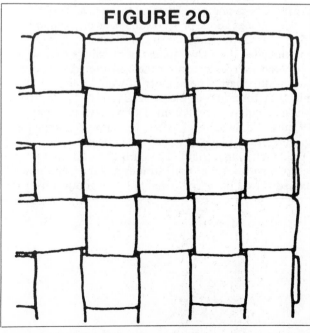

FIGURE 20

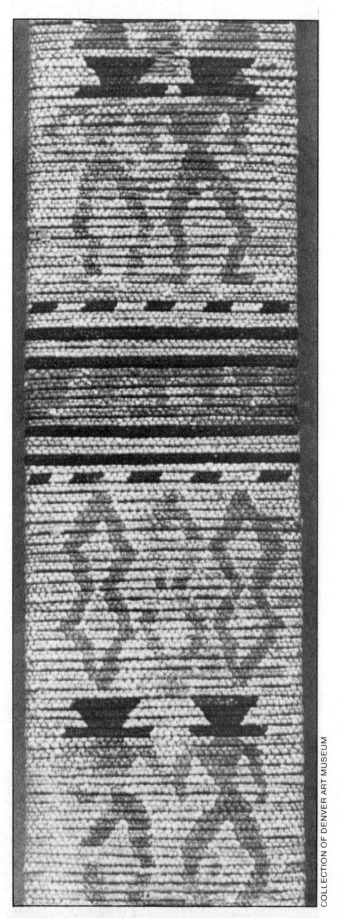

PLATE 24: Detail of very fine plaiting on a Lakota pipestem, ca. 1830.

72

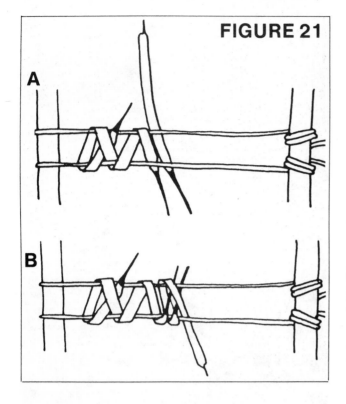

FIGURE 21

A

B

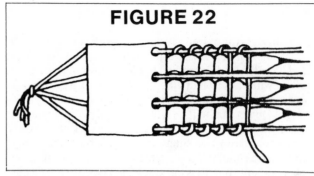

FIGURE 22

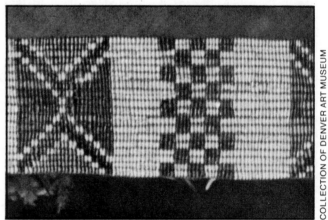

PLATE 26: Detail of quill woven strip in progress.

PLATE 25: Bow loom for quill weaving.

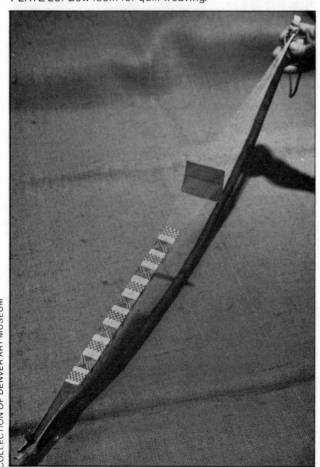

QUILL WEAVING

Quill weaving produces a band of geometric pattern which is applied to the article being decorated. It was frequently found among the Athabaskans, Plains Cree, Ojibwa, Iroquois, Meti, and Great Lakes peoples. Woven quillwork was often applied to browbands on horse gear, panels of bags and pouches, and to coats and shirts.

Weaving is done on a bow loom, as pictured in **Plate 25**. Sinew warp strands are stretched the length of the bow and threaded through a spacer of birchbark or rawhide. This spacer serves to position the warp threads exactly one quill width apart. The number of warp strands is determined by the width of the project. (A 1¼" wide strip of weaving requires a minimum of 20 warp strands and thus, 19 quill widths across.) After the warp is stretched and spacers are in place, a weft strand (sinew) is tied to the outside left warp strand. The barb end of a quill is now inserted between two warp strands and the weft thread is passed across the warp. The quill is bent down over the

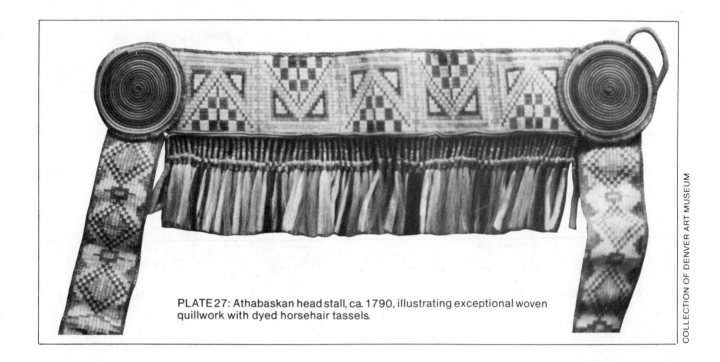

PLATE 27: Athabaskan head stall, ca. 1790, illustrating exceptional woven quillwork with dyed horsehair tassels.

weft which is then passed across the underside of the warp. The quill is then bent back upwards around the weft and back to the top of the warp. This is repeated with a quill between each warp strand, splicing in color changes as needed until the desired length is achieved. The ends of the quills are left hanging down below the warp and when finished are cut off close to the weave. The strip is then cut off the loom and lined with a backing or appliqued to another object. **Figure 22** illustrates weaving. **Plates 26** and **27** picture a strip in progress on a loom and a brow band of Athabaskan origin (perhaps as early as the late 1700s.)

PUTTING IT ALL TOGETHER

Once all the techniques have been mastered, the contemporary quillworker is faced with the problem of putting it all together. What colors and designs to use, what techniques were used where and by what tribes and in what time period? The meticulous, labor-intensive nature of quillwork demands that one not waste precious time by producing a piece that is out of context, inappropriately decorated, or not correct to the period. As this work is aimed primarily at the buckskinner, we must concern ourselves with basically pre-1850 quillwork and specifically pre-1840.

When I began the photographic research for this chapter, I was told by several authorities on American Indian art, to "Give it up!" Pre-1840 specimens of quillwork in this country are too few and far between. They were correct. So please forgive the inclusion of many photographs of later period quillwork in this chapter. It became necessary to use them in order to illustrate the techniques sufficiently.

In spite of this, the best research avenues available to the serious enthusiast are the artifact collections of our museums. To study first hand the original works, their colors, and design elements is worth a dozen books on the subject. Unfortunately, the majority of the pre-1850 artifacts are in museums in Europe. I visited a good number of them in 1980, and the collections are truly worthy of the trip. If the opportunity ever presents itself, go have a look!

SPECIAL SECTION!

Turn to pages X and XI of the special color photo section for more on quillwork.

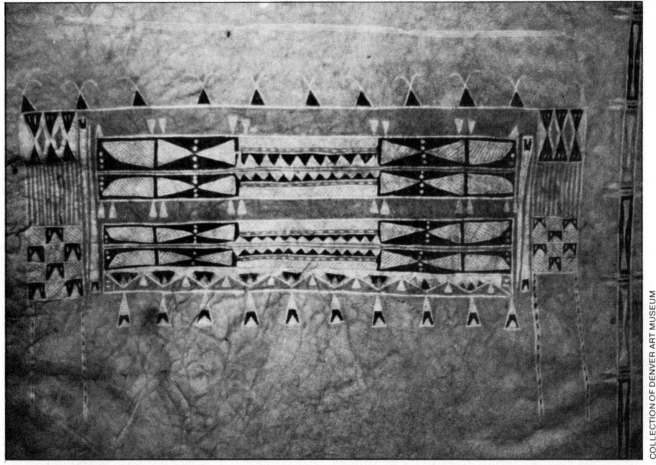

PLATE 28: Detail of Arapahoe "box and border" painted buffalo robe. Note painted designs of isosceles triangles.

STYLES AND DESIGNS

Prior to 1800, designs used in quillwork were predominantly geometric. According to John Ewers, many quillwork designs were a direct carryover from early painted patterns on robes, skins, and parfleche. The feather or Blackbonnet element frequently used by the Sioux and the parallel horizontal stripes of the Blackfoot became consistently used quill designs. Elements of box and border robe painting can be seen in many quilled patterns. See **Plate 28** and **29**. From this I think it is safe to say that quill designs can be interpolated, by the contemporary quiller, from those seen on early painted specimens.

The differentiation between definite tribal styles in quill or beadwork cannot actually be made until the seed-bead era, well after 1850. Prior to this time, only regional styles can be differentiated: The Upper Missouri style, including Mandan, Hidatsa, and Crow; the Central Plains style of Sioux, Cheyenne, and Arapahoe; The Plateau areas of Blackfoot, Nez Perce, and Sarcee; The Great Lakes and eastern groups of Iroquois, Seneca, Ojibwa, Menomini, and some Eastern Cree; The Prairie Tribes of Potawatomi, Winnebago, Iowa, Ponca, Oto, and Kansa; and the northern extension of the Great Lakes types, the Metis, Athabaskan and Plains Cree.

The Great Lakes peoples employed the double-curve motif in early quill embroidery, as well as in moose hair embroidery. This is generally thought to be due to the influence of early white contact. Their pre-contact work was geometric though, weaving particularly, and often on black dyed buckskin. The thunderbird and underwater panther motifs in quillwork were limited to the Great Lakes region. They also developed floral designs in quills at a much earlier date than did the Plains groups. (Most floral styles in Plains work are dated after 1850.) Beads were also available to the eastern tribes before they appeared on the Plains. (Possibly as early as 1640 among the Iroquois.) **Figure 23** diagrams a few Great Lakes quill designs.

Quillwork flourished among the northern groups until hides began to be replaced by stroud cloth. It was geometric: Straight lines, rectangles and triangles, usually against a white or light blue background. Quilled garters, knife sheaths hung from a thong about the neck, quill wrapped fringe and thongs, netted fringes, and the famous Metis coat are all part of this northern tradition. There was a predominant use of bilaterally symmetrical patterns in asymmetrical compositions on such objects as pouches, pipe bags, bandoleers, and moccasins. Representation was also made of the "lifeline" and kidneys in the pictographic quillwork of animal spirits or human figures.

FIGURE 23.

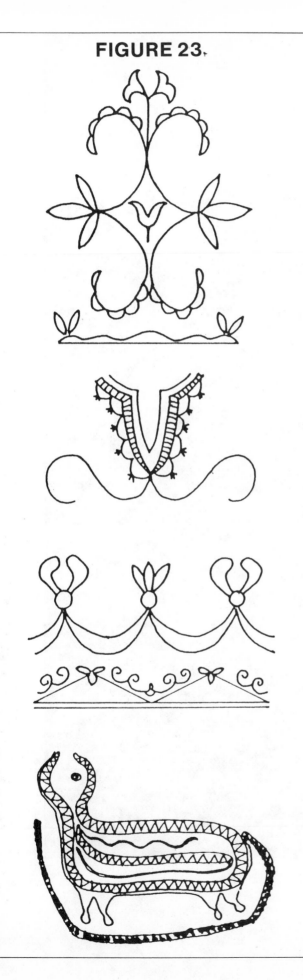

PLATE 29: Detail of Santee quilled ornament shows the vertical isosceles triangles, elements adapted from early painting designs on robes.

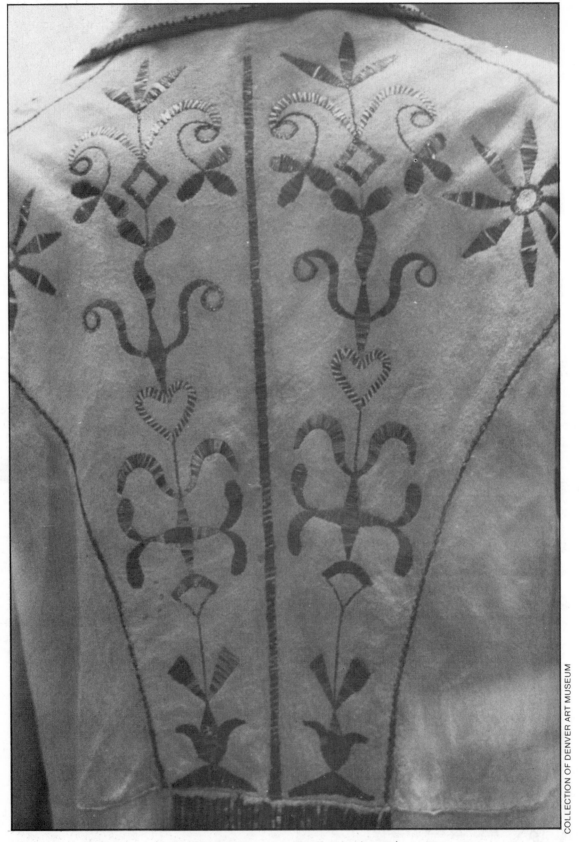

PLATE 30: Metis' coat - detail on back panel.

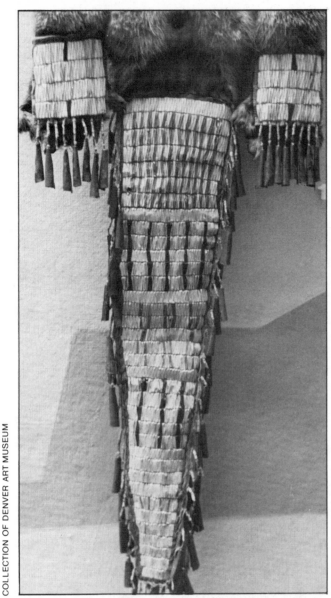

PLATE 31: Detail of quilled tail section of Omaha otterskin bag, ca. 1820. Such bags were used in "shell society" as containers for sacred objects. Quill colors are dark brown, yellow, and rust on white background.

The side seam dress, with its long quill-wrapped fringes is characteristic of the western Cree of this northern region. The Athabaskans excelled in woven quillwork and later moose hair embroidery. Floral designs are generally thought to have been brought to them by the Cree.

Quillwork was on the decline by 1850, but the distinct floral style of the Red River Metis, beginning as early as 1800, had spread to the Ojibwa and Cree, the Assiniboin and eastern Sioux, and subsequently to Blackfoot. It is interesting that among the western Plains tribes, these floral designs were applied mainly to the same items the Metis specialized in: horse gear, coats, pouches, and moccasins.

On the western Plains, prior to 1850, quill orna- mentation is much more difficult to differentiate, even among the regional groups. The trading network focused around the Upper Missouri villages of the Mandan, Hidatsa, and Arikara, allowed for extensive intertribal contact. Furthermore, the peace established between those traditional enemies, the Sioux and Crow, from approximately 1851-1857, provided for flourishing trade. Ted Brasser is quoted as saying, "Teton Sioux painted robes were popular among the Crow who traded their own decorated clothing to the Hidatsa and Mandan. Mandan-Hidatsa quillworked costumes were highly prized by the Cree and Assiniboin, and Assiniboin beaded moccasins found eager customers among Blackfeet women. Richly decorated clothing was made in great quantities by the Red River Metis for trade with all tribes on the northern and central Plains."

Quillwork was practiced to some extent by all of the western Plains groups. Shirt and legging strips worked in geometrics, plaited pipestems, and quilled rawhide pipebag slats were fairly common to all regions. There were, however, some areas of differentiation:

Upper Missouri:

Sometimes referred to as "The Paris of the Prairies", this region was the heart of artistic accomplishment on the Plains. Known for their splendid quilled shirts, rosettes, and plait-like, multi-quill embroidering, the Mandan-Hidatsa were the fashion leaders of the day.

Central Plains:

The Sioux accomplished the most quillwork of any tribe on the Plains, with geometric designs pre-dominating, and floral work developing around the 1870s. A large portion of Sioux work done after this time was aimed at the tourist trade and so patterns and colors adapted accordingly.

The Sioux quilled almost everything imaginable. Designs based on units of narrow bands, in com-binations of stripes, bars, squares, rectangles, tri-angles, and circles, were used on pipebags, garments, cradleboards, tipi storage bags, saddleblankets, headstalls, vests, robes, and any other item of everyday use.

Cheyenne and Arapahoe quillwork is much more scarce, but was mainly geometric in design and from what we know of the Cheyenne guilds, superbly crafted.

Plateau groups:

Blackfoot quillwork was relatively uncomplicated, with a limited number of techniques in use: Single thread, wrapping, and simple bands. Designs were usually trapezoidal patterns built up from many small squares. See **Plate 14**, an exception to this idea.

Prairie groups:

The Prairie group was producing curvilinear and floral work sometime before 1840 and rather quickly gave up quillwork in favor of beads. See **Plate 30**.

BEADS IN CONJUNCTION WITH QUILLWORK

This leads us to the appearance of pony beads used in conjunction with quillwork. Pony beads came into use on the Plains in the early 1800s. By the 1830s, as can be seen in Bodmer's paintings, blue and white pony beads were much in vogue, mainly as trim or border for quilled designs. Seed beads were already in use by the eastern and Great Lakes groups at this time, but they did not get west of the Missouri River much before the mid-1840s.

It is, therefore, appropriate to incorporate pony beads into your western fur trade quilled items, but please remember that the predominant colors available were pony trader blue, white, black, and a limited amount of transparent cranberry red or white-lined rose, with an even smaller amount of greasy yellow. Eastern quillwork was accented mainly with white seed and pony beads. **Plates 6** and **12** illustrate the use of accent beadwork.

Plate 31, a Crow strike-a-light bag, fully pony beaded in blue, white, and black, is included here to illustrate the replacement of quills with beads. Note the geometric design and layout of lanes, which are highly reminiscent of earlier quillwork.

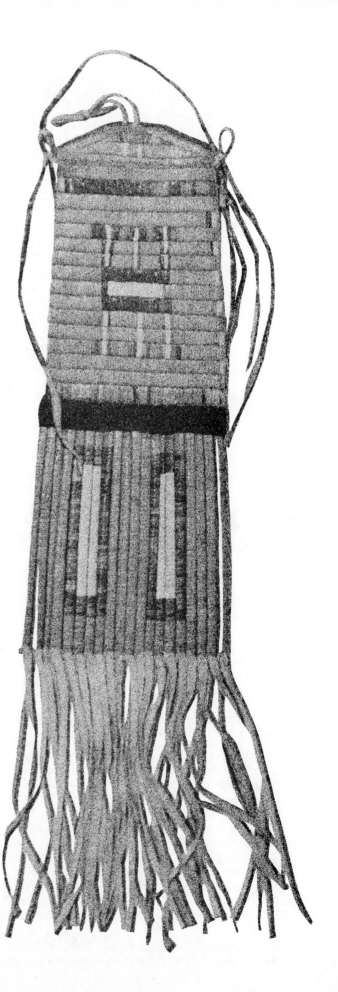

PLATE 32: Crow strike-a-light bag, fully pony beaded in blue, white and black, demonstrates transition from quillwork to beadwork. Made by Gary Johnson.

79

ACKNOWLEDGEMENTS

Special thanks to Stan Dolega for the line illustrations and the entire photographic body of this work; to Richard Conn, Curator of American Indian Art, Denver Art Museum, for his kindness in providing access to the museum's quillwork collections; to Blue Laslow for her work on natural dyes; and to my daughter and friends whose patience and encouragement got me through the typing.

WORKS CONSULTED

Bebbington, Julia M. Quillwork of the Plains. Ottawa: Glenbow Museum, National Museums of Canada, 1983.

Brasser, Ted J. Bo Jou, Neejee! Ottawa: National Museum of Man, National Museums of Canada, 1976.

Densmore, Francis. "Chippewa Customs." Bureau of American Ethnology Bulletin 86. Washington, D. C.: 1929.

Ewers, John C. Plains Indian Painting, A Description of an Aboriginal American Art. Stanford University Press, 1939.

Grinnell, George B. The Cheyenne Indians. Vol. 1. New Haven: Yale University Press, 1923.

Harmon, Daniel W. Sixteen Years in the Indian Country. W. Kaye Lamb, Toronto: Macmillan, 1957.

Hassrick, Royal B. The Sioux. Norman: University of Oklahoma Press, 1964.

Johnson, Gary. "Plains Indian Art of the Fur Trade Era, Part I." Muzzleloader, 8 (Sept./Oct. 1981), 49-53.
　　"Plains Indian Art of the Fur Trade Era, Part II." Muzzleloader, 8 (Nov./Dec. 1981), 55-60.

　　"Plains Indian Art of the Fur Trade Era, Part III." Muzzleloader, 9 (Mar./Apr. 1982), 51-57.
　　"Plains Indian Art of the Fur Trade Era, Part IV." Muzzleloader, 9 (Nov./Dec. 1982), 40-45.

Lyford, Carrie A. "Quill and Beadwork of the Western Sioux." Indian Handicraft Pamphlet 1. Washington, D.C.: U.S. Bureau of Indian Affairs, 1940.

Marriott, Alice. The Trade Guild of the Southern Cheyenne Women. Indian Arts and Crafts Board, U.S. Dept. of Interior: Oklahoma Anthropological Society, 1937.

Odle, Robin. "Quill and Moosehair Work in the Great Lakes Region." In Indian Art of the Great Lakes. Flint, Mich.: Flint Institute of Arts, 1973.

Orchard, William C. The Technique of Porcupine Quill Decoration Among the Indians of North America. New York: 1916.

Thomas, Davis, and Karin Ronnefeldt, eds. People of the First Man. New York: Promontory Press, 1982.

Walker, James R. Lakota Belief and Ritual. University of Nebraska Press, 1980.

BRAIN TANNING BUCKSKIN

BY BRUCE SCHWAEGEL

BRUCE SCHWAEGEL'S INTEREST IN muzzle-loading and buckskinning began simultaneously when he purchased his first muzzle loading rifle, a flintlock, in 1975. Since then, he has built several muzzle loading guns, an 18 foot tipi, and has become an accomplished beadworker, hornsmith, tanner, and horseman.

Bruce has always had an interest in the outdoors, shooting, and American history, particularly the fur trade. "Buckskinning," he says, "is a natural extension for people with these interests, provides a creative outlet for building functionally beautiful objects, and develops an appreciation of the survival skills and life of early American frontiersmen."

Bruce lives in Texas with his wife, Sally, and two children, Brian and Robert. Bruce is a graduate of Washington University in St. Louis, and is employed as a telecommunications market analyst by AT&T. He is a life member of the NRA as well as a member of the NMLRA, serves on the board of directors of the Dallas Muzzle Loading Gun Club, and is a member of the Silver Creek Skinners and the Texas Association of Buckskinners. He also lectures on Native American Crafts and Fur Trade History.

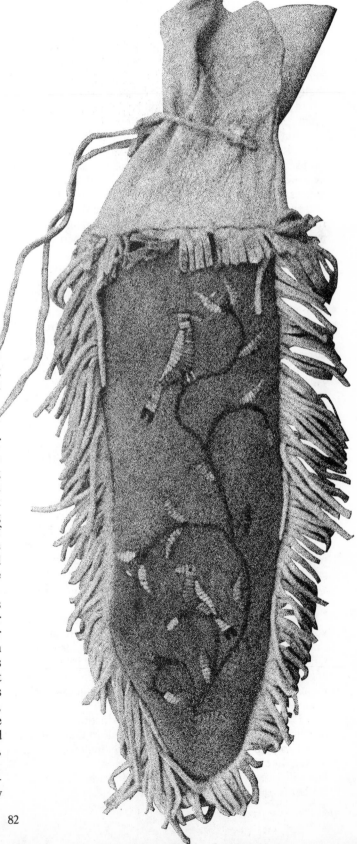

IN this chapter we are going to discuss how to make the buckskinner's most valuable resource for clothing and gear: leather. Without it we wouldn't have shirts, moccasins, dresses, leggings, hunting bags, rifle scabbards, or any of the hundreds of items that are so necessary for our comfort and well being.

In *The Book of Buckskinning II,* Pat Tearney's excellent chapter titled "Working With Leather" describes Indian or hand tanned buckskin as "the best kind of leather for frontier type of clothing." Furthermore, he states that "this is the kind of leather found in all existing clothing of frontier origin." The frontiersman of the east and west wore buckskin not only because it was convenient to his way of life, but it was simply better than anything else. It could be argued that he had little other choice of materials, but the applicability of buckskin for wilderness apparel cannot seriously be questioned when hand tanned in the Native American manner. Let's look at some of the reasons for this.

Commercially processed leather when worn as clothing next to the skin is hot and clammy in the summer and cold in the winter. A brain tanned deerskin on the other hand is as cool as a cotton flannel shirt or a pair of denim jeans and warm in the winter even when wet. This is because of its porosity. The only lubricant used, except when tanning a very heavy hide such as a cow or buffalo, is brains. The brains are so effective that very little is needed, and they dry out leaving no clammy oils or fats to clog the pores of the finished product. In addition, brain tanned fibers are not tumbled or broken as in commercial hides, but loosened, so that there is a lot of air space.

Despite its porosity and flannel-like softness, brain-tanned buckskin is far stronger than a commercially

Hides, as the skins of large animals such as cows, bulls, and buffalo are called, are the best suited for items like moccasin soles, knife sheaths, shields, parfleches, and harness leather. Smaller animals, such as sheep, goats, calves, deer, and elk furnish what are classed as skins. In this chapter we will discuss the processing of elk and deer skins for buckskin, even though I may use the terms "hide" and "skin" interchangeably.

Skins from deer and elk make the best clothing and they are easy to obtain. Besides downing your own deer, friends who hunt are a great source of hides. In addition, during hunting season you might check local meat processors, local stores that do their own butchering, or any other place that might receive deer hides. Also, don't overlook hunters' camps. Many hunters skin their deer in camp and discard the hides. With a little ingenuity and timing, this can be a good source of inexpensive hides. Hides from hunters are generally available for about two dollars apiece.

Most areas also have commercial hide buyers who purchase from large butcher shops. These products are then resold to tanneries, rendering plants, etc., for a very large profit. Hides are available from these companies for about four dollars each.

The advantage of dealing with commercial buyers is that you have a large selection of hides to choose from. Be *extremely* selective. Usually, larger hides produce thicker buckskin. Smaller skins are therefore better for lightweight shirts and dresses. Larger hides are best for winter shirts, coats, pants, and moccasins.

It goes without saying that if you wish to make the best buckskin, you must have good hides to start with. The most proficient and experienced tanner cannot make good leather from skins that are badly damaged or poorly trimmed.

The main thing to watch for when selecting hides is "score marks." These are places where the skinning knife cut the hides from the flesh side. A few light scores are acceptable. Scores that slice almost all of the way through to where the hair follicles show, are certain to tear through in the buckskin process. I have spent as long as a day sewing up small tears on a hide that was improperly skinned. Believe me, once you have spent ten hours on a hide bringing it through the process, it is very disappointing to spend a day sewing scores that could have been avoided by being more selective. The neck and flank areas of the hide are where scores occur most frequently.

Bullet holes are also a problem. Size and location are the key. Select hides with as few and as small holes as possible. Avoid hides with cannon-sized holes in the center of the hide. Don't worry about flesh or fat left on the hide. Any vestiges of flesh can easily be removed with the bar flesher described in the section on fleshing.

In skinning a deer, or any other animal, it is best to use a knife as little as possible. "Fist" the hide off. This means pulling the hide off with one hand while pressing between the hide and flesh with the other hand. This avoids most scoring. When obtaining hides from a meat locker in a chilled state, it is necessary to use the knife more frequently. If this is necessary, keep the blade of the knife turned slightly away from the skin to avoid cutting it, and

tanned leather of similar thickness. This is because the chemicals used to soften a commercially tanned hide also tend to weaken it. Since brain tanned buckskin is not chemically altered in the traditional sense, "tanning" is really not an accurate description of the Indian process. More properly, buckskin is conditioned, manipulated and often referred to as "dressed."

But this is only part of the story. Smoked buckskin will dry soft after wetting. The smoke which permeates the skin's pores and fibers acts as an anti-bacterial agent. The skin actually resists harmful bacterial build-up, which causes odor in cotton and other clothing materials. For this reason, buckskins can and were worn virtually all of the time, with no bad effects. My current set of skins are four and one-half years old and have never been washed, except for an unscheduled swim while watering my horse, and being caught in downpours a few times. They are quite clean inside and out from an occasional brushing with sandstone and still retain their built-in smoky aroma. Try that with Levis, or for that matter, commercial leather.

Brain tanning is fast and safe! A fleshed hide that has been dried on its frame by Saturday morning can easily be completely tanned and ready to smoke by Sunday evening. Compare that with Salt-Acid tanning or the Alum-Salt tanning methods, which take approximately one to two weeks, and involve the use and disposal of either caustic or acid solutions.

Another reason why I believe many buckskinners tan is ideological and personal. It is our desire to be independent, and to experience and appreciate real and natural wilderness values, to enjoy a life style, if only for a short time, that is slower paced and closer to nature than the rampant commercialism and hustle of modern society.

The methods that I will describe in this chapter will enable you to make good, tough, serviceable buckskin. They are the results of eight years of experimentation, research, and exchanging of notes with others. Reasonably good success should result from the very first effort, even if you are a beginner, *providing that you carefully follow each step of the process as described.*

If you have never tanned before, I would suggest that you read this chapter entirely through first. Then on your first few hides, stick closely to the techniques set forth here. Once you have a feel for what the hide should look like at each stage of the process, you can try varying methods. Ease, speed, and perfection of the finished buckskin will come with experience.

I am sure that the tanned buckskin that you will produce will dwarf to insignificance the effort that you put forth to obtain your hide and dress it. After making, seeing, feeling, smelling, and wearing your brain tanned buckskin, you will agree with me that commercially tanned chemical leather is a waste of buckskin.

Without rawhide and leather, we wouldn't have much gear. Various articles created from rawhide and brain tanned skins are shown here on a brain tanned buffalo robe.

use the knife only when necessary. I like to lay my knife down after making the initial cuts to avoid overuse, to free both hands, and to decrease the possibility of an accident. Most modern day hunters prefer to skin from just below the hock and to cut the neck skin from just below the ears. A fresh hide may easily be skinned to the hooves, and I would encourage you to do so if you are doing your own skinning. This option is usually not available when obtaining hides from packing plants, since the legs are often removed before the hide is skinned from the deer.

If at all possible, obtain fresh, unsalted hides. Salted hides are very hard on tools. Besides creating rust, salt tends to dull scraper blades and makes poor rawhide. If you are in a situation where you must use salt, apply it liberally — one pound of salt per pound of hide. If several hides are to be cured, pile them one on top of another, always hair side down, with their heads at one end. In piling hides, do not drag them across a stack of salted ones, as this creates unsalted spots and spoiled hides.

The brine from a stack of hides treated in this manner must be diverted away from the stack or the lower hides will spoil. This is most easily accomplished by stacking the hides on a wooden pallet.

If the hides have been properly salted, they will become firm and stiff and are called "salt firm" or "salt hard." This generally requires six to fourteen days. Hides cured in this manner can safely be kept until spring without deterioration.

Hides that have been salted must be thoroughly rinsed in several changes of water, fleshed, and then rinsed again before taking them through the buckskin process.

The easiest and most efficient way to store skins is to "flesh" and dry them. Fleshing is the process by which all fat and meat are removed from the hide and is best done as soon as possible. This is the method that I use to store all skins that I am going to use for buckskin. Drying is superior to salt-curing hides because dried hides take less space, are not as messy, keep longer (years), and seem to make better buckskin.

To "flint dry" hides simply flesh and lightly tack them, flesh side out, to a large flat surface such as a barn or shed wall, stockade fence or even a sheet of plywood. Since I usually have a large number of skins to dry, I like to use an electric staple gun with ½" staples to do this. The electric gun is fast, can be operated with one hand, and leaves about ¼" of staple protruding above the surface of the skin for easy removal. If you only have one or two fresh hides and want to take them through the brain tanning process, they may be fleshed and laced directly into their frames in preparation for scraping.

In a primitive situation, simply drape the fleshed hide over the limb of a tree, bush, or lay on dry ground. Hides dried in these unsecured methods will shrink, be more awkward to handle and require more storage space. In addition, the edges will tend to curl and remain moist. These moist protected crannies will attract flies and their eggs. To prevent edge-curling, rub dry dirt, sawdust or similar moisture absorbing material into these edges. Small sticks may also be used to help hold these edges open.

Always keep an unfleshed hide cool, preferably on ice, and out of the sun or it will become "grease burnt." The term grease-burnt refers to fat that has melted into the skin and weakened it. While not evident at the time, the oil will deteriorate the skin structure, so that later, in the vigorous, softening process, the skin will disintegrate into a buckskin that resembles a large slice of swiss cheese! When drying hides, I take one other precaution against grease-burning; I always dry my fleshed skins in the shade.

After drying hides, it is a good practice to lightly spray them on both sides with an insecticide containing diazinon. This will kill any ticks on the hide, and also prevent carrion beetles from attacking the hair and hide in warm weather.

When your hides are completely dry, they will be very thin and flat. At this point I mark each skin, in pencil, on the flesh side, with the year that it was collected. In the event that all of my skins aren't tanned by the following deer season, this will enable me to use my oldest skins first. I roll several hides together (eight to ten) and drop these into two heavy-duty, large plastic trash bags. Into the center of each roll, I drop a box of moth balls with three-sided tabs cut into the box, so that it can "breathe," to further discourage insects. Two more heavy-duty bags, one slipped into the other, are then pulled over the remaining open end of the bundle, and the entire package securely tied with string. All dried hides must be kept in a dry, sheltered area such as your garage. Hides, properly stored in this manner, will last years.

Photo showing various tools used in the brain tanning process. Left to right: steel fleshing bar, staker, sanding rocks, whetstone and knives, wood and elk handled scrapers, and a canon bone flesher. See text for descriptions and uses for each tool.

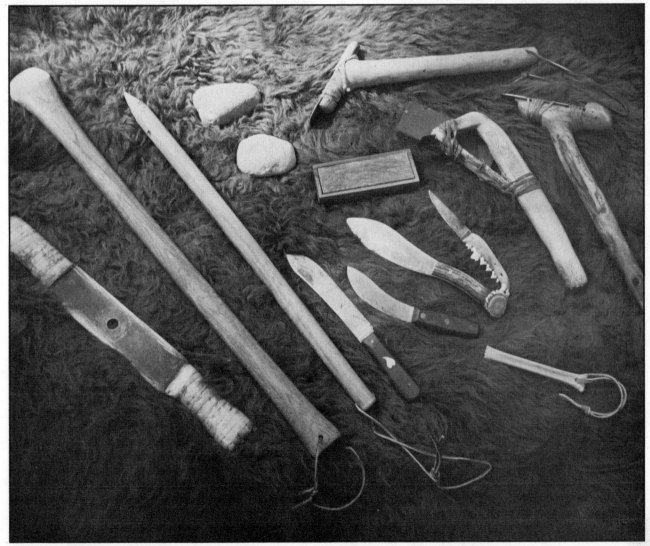

If drying is not possible where you live, the next best method is freezing. Simply flesh each hide and fold into a square, squeezing as much air out as possible. Wrap each hide in freezer paper and a small plastic trash can liner or place each folded skin in two small plastic liners, squeeze out as much air as possible, seal, and freeze. Fleshed hides preserved in this manner will be good for one year. This is an excellent method for furs that cannot be tanned immediately.

OBTAINING BRAINS

Wherever you finally end up in your search for hides, don't forget brains. There is an old saying that "each animal has just enough brains to tan its own hide." I always use about one pound of brains per deerskin or two small deerskins to one beef brain. For large deerhides, I usually use one beef brain or two deer brains, because the buckskin seems to soften more if I use a generous amount of brains. Any brains will work in this process — sheep, goat, cow, deer, hog, etc. Most of the time, however, you will find that hides are much easier to obtain than brains.

Since brains are edible, they are sometimes available in the meat section of the grocery store or from local butcher shops in many parts of the country. They are usually packaged in small plastic tubs near the livers and gizzards. Here in Texas, the only brains that I *occasionally* see in the store are pork brains. The supply is very inconsistent and unreliable. Beef brains in our area and many other parts of the country are simply not available. Apparently, from the sketchy information that I have been able to gather, there seems to be an abundance of state and federal government regulations regarding the butchering, processing and sale of brains that results in this inconvenience.

Although brains are oftentimes not available from the grocery store, they are available in the form of deer brains from all of the above mentioned sources of deer hides during the hunting season. Since any kind of brains will work, I have found my best non-hunting season source to be pork and beef brains from local slaughter houses. If you are willing to cut your own brains from the heads, a slaughter house will usually give you the brains. This is easily accomplished by hack-sawing through most of the back of the skull and prying it open with a small hatchet or tomahawk. Spoon out the brain and place it in a large plastic bucket or plastic bag to take home (yuck — I'm glad that's over). When you get home with your fresh stash of brains, drop each one into its own individual zip-lock bag to freeze for future use. If you don't have a freezer, or, in a survival situation, brains may be sliced to a ½" thickness and sun dried for future use. To reconstitute, the dried pieces are soaked in a small amount of water. Personally I find this aspect of brain tanning the least enjoyable.

To minimize the inconvenience of obtaining brains, I usually ask the butcher shop to save unwanted deer heads for me for a few weeks during the hunting season. If obtaining cow or pork brains, I wait until a "killing" day to visit the slaughterhouse. After about a half-hour of "extracting," you will begin to ignore the unpleasant aspects of this endeavor, and become quite proficient at it.

I can usually obtain a year's supply of brains in two visits. If all of this seems like a lot of trouble, let me assure you that it is well worth the effort. I have tried all sorts of concoctions that were supposed to be good substitutes for brains. The resulting buckskin was not as soft, thick, or white as the brain-conditioned skin.

FLESHING TOOLS — HOW TO MAKE AND USE THEM

The first of these tools that we must construct is the *fleshing beam.* The best fleshing beam is made from a cottonwood or willow log that is five to six feet in length and six to twelve inches in diameter. I prefer aged cottonwood for my beams, because it does not split or splinter. My first fleshing beam was constructed using a pine 2 X 12 that I belt sanded round on one side. After tanning my first two skins, subsequent hides developed little pin-head sized thin spots that later developed into actual holes when breaking the hide. At first, I thought that I was dry-scraping my skins incorrectly. I ruined two skins before I realized that the problem was not my scraping technique but my fleshing beam. Repeated wettings of the pine beam by water-soaked hides had caused thousands of tiny whiskers or splinters to form on the beam. The pine worked fine for fleshing skins because the hair, still intact, cushioned the skin for the beam. After dry-scraping the hair, I like to resoak the skin and remove any remaining membrane from the flesh side with the bar flesher and beaming log. Since the hair was no longer on the skin to serve as a cushion, the bar flesher pushed the tiny splinters on the log through the skin, creating the pin holes. Two ruined skins and twenty hours of work later, I realized that pine was a poor choice for my beaming log. Choose seasoned dead wood for your log, or cut your logs from a living tree and season with the bark on the log, off of the ground, and in a shaded, sheltered area to avoid splitting. In a pinch, any rounded smooth surface will work (canoe bottom, oil drum, etc.); however, a wooden fleshing beam works best, because it has a little "give."

In my sketch (Figure 1), I have drawn several different varieties of fleshing beams, however, my favorite is the waist beam. With the waist beam, the skin is draped over the working end and is held in place by leaning against it with your hips or thigh as you work. Since the fleshing motion is a downward push away from you, the waist beam affords the best leverage and is the easiest to use.

Under the perspective drawing of the waist beam, I have included a front and side view of the leg assembly, including dimensions. The legs are assembled using wood screws and waterproof glue. The upper ends of the legs are rounded to avoid damaging skins. The cottonwood beaming log itself is carefully notched on the underside to form a tight friction-fit when the leg assembly is driven into the notch. This feature enables the fleshing beam to be easily disassembled for travel and storage.

When cutting your cottonwood log, you may want to cut two so that you can construct the upright beam. To use the upright beam, lean it against a wall, tree, or other stationary object. The skin is held in place between the top of the beam and the surface against which the beam leans. The fleshing motion is a downward pull if you are using the bar flesher made of steel, or, a downward stabbing motion if using the canon bone flesher. (See Figure 1.)

Once again, I prefer the waist beam, because, for me it is more efficient and requires less effort, but occasionally, I like to switch between the two styles of beams when doing a large number of hides. This enables you to use different muscle groups, and therefore is less tiring.

Some of the most common tools found at archeological sites worldwide are bone and stone scrapers for fleshing hides. The canon bone flesher (the long bone nearest the hoof in the lower legs of deer, elk, bison, moose, etc.) is one of the most common (Figure 2). To make such a flesher, simply cut the cleaned bone on a bevel at its lower end just above the joint. Tiny sharp teeth are then filed into the chisel-shaped end. A buckskin loop is tied or run through a hole drilled at the top of the tool for a wrist brace. The canon bone flesher is used in a stabbing, scraping motion to remove fat and flesh from the hide. It may be used with hides that have been pegged to the ground, stretched in a frame, or draped over a fleshing beam.

The fastest, most efficient fleshing tool that I use and prefer is the "bar flesher" (Figure 2). This tool is easily manufactured from either a 16 to 18 inch length of automobile leaf spring, or a lawnmower blade. Since the edges of your steel will probably be slightly rounded, grind them square with a bench grinder, and then drawfile, so that the resulting surface is 90 degrees to the remaining two larger surfaces. Since it is neither desirable or necessary for the resulting edges to be sharp, dull these corners slightly by rubbing them with 4-0 steel wool. To finish your tool, wrap about four inches of each end with cloth to form hand grips.

The bar flesher is used with the waist beam and is held in a horizontal position, but tilted back slightly, so that only one of the squared edges is pushed along the hide. With forward and downward pressure against the hide, the bar flesher will easily remove flesh and fat from most skins. Start in the center of the hide and work toward the edges, rotating the hide in a circle and covering every square inch of the skin with the flesher. As the squared edge of the flesher bites into the flesh and fat, it will tend to stretch the

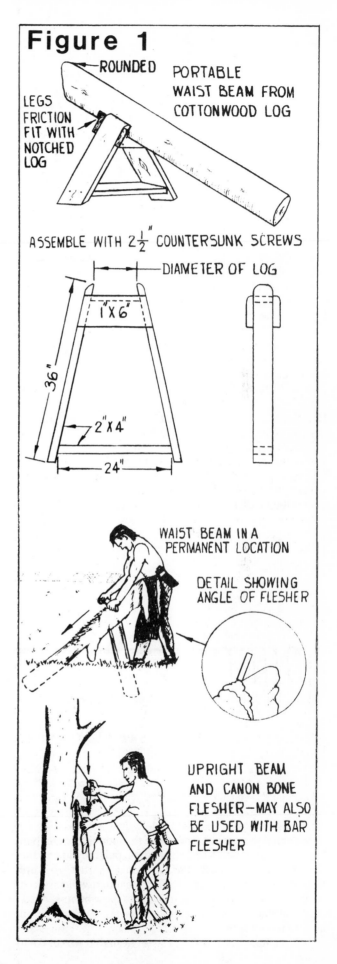

Figure 1

ROUNDED
PORTABLE WAIST BEAM FROM COTTONWOOD LOG
LEGS FRICTION FIT WITH NOTCHED LOG

ASSEMBLE WITH 2½" COUNTERSUNK SCREWS
DIAMETER OF LOG
1"X6"
36"
2"X4"
24"

WAIST BEAM IN A PERMANENT LOCATION
DETAIL SHOWING ANGLE OF FLESHER

UPRIGHT BEAM AND CANON BONE FLESHER—MAY ALSO BE USED WITH BAR FLESHER

Figure 2

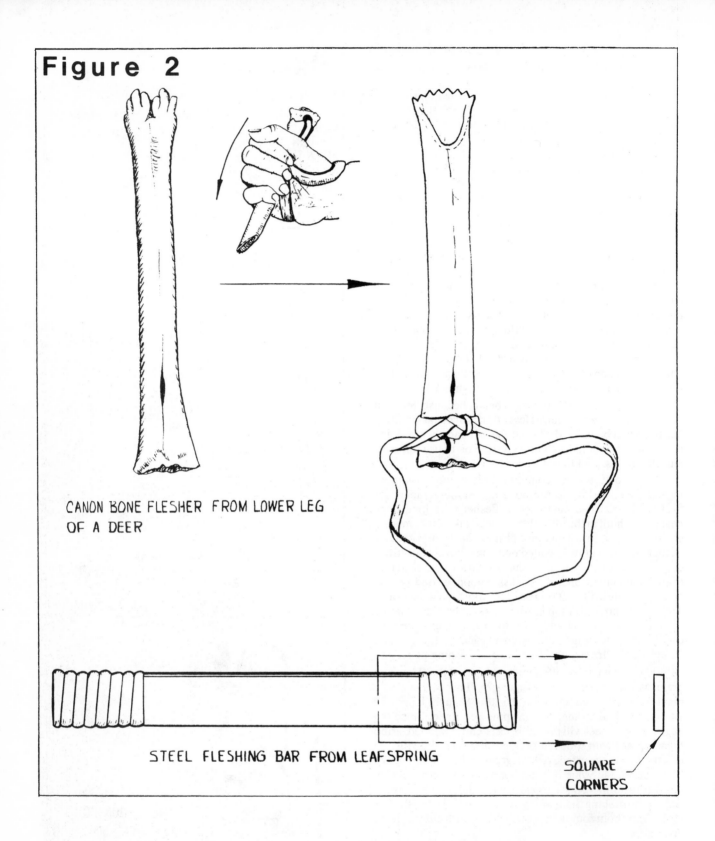

CANON BONE FLESHER FROM LOWER LEG OF A DEER

STEEL FLESHING BAR FROM LEAFSPRING

SQUARE CORNERS

hide behind the flesher, and cause the hide to bunch up in front of the flesher. When this occurs, pull the hide up the fleshing beam to keep the area smooth that you are fleshing. Failure to observe this precaution will result in large holes as the flesher pushes across these bumps. Also, don't let the tool slip sideways, as this will result in additional holes in your skin.

If the hide becomes dry as you flesh it, it will make it difficult to work with. Always remoisten dry areas with water and, if still tough, resoak the entire hide until it is thoroughly saturated. Sometimes very dry meat may take several days to soak up.

Another thing to watch for when fleshing hides are score marks. These roughly parallel cuts on the flesh side, resulting from careless skinning, can tear through in the fleshing process. When you encounter these (hopefully

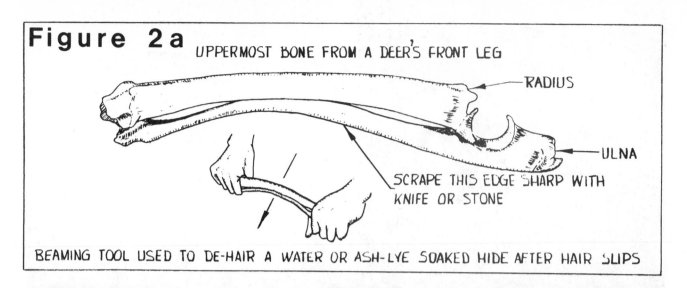

Figure 2a

UPPERMOST BONE FROM A DEER'S FRONT LEG

RADIUS

ULNA

SCRAPE THIS EDGE SHARP WITH KNIFE OR STONE

BEAMING TOOL USED TO DE-HAIR A WATER OR ASH-LYE SOAKED HIDE AFTER HAIR SLIPS

Don Heit is shown fleshing a deer skin using a cottonwood waist beam and a steel bar flesher. Note how the skin is held in place by leaning against it with the hips.

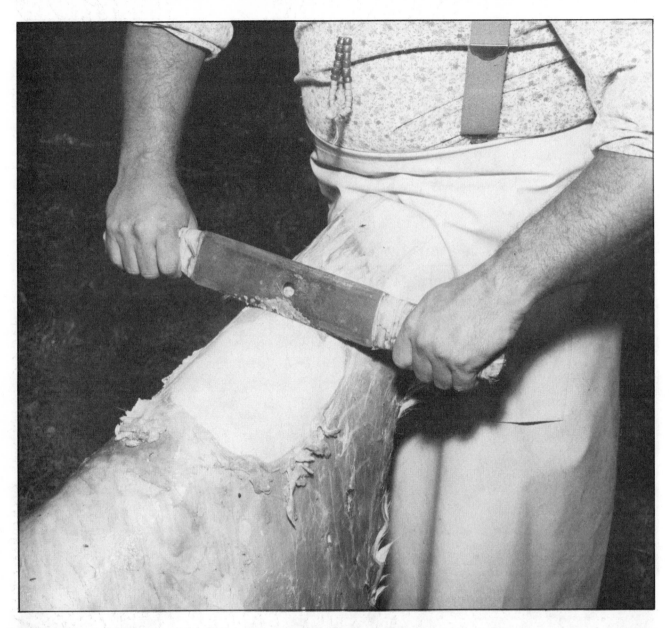

Fleshing using a waist beam and a bar flesher. Note the angle of the bar flesher to the skin and how its square edge is used to push flesh and fat off of the skin.

there aren't many), the direction of your bar flesher must be changed to a stroke that is parallel to the thin areas formed by the scoring. Fleshing across scores will result in a deepening of the cuts and will create holes.

Fleshing is probably the messiest step in the tanning process; you will therefore need a plastic apron so that when you lean against the fleshing beam, you will not get blood, grease, dirt, and water on your pants. Plastic from a painter's drop cloth or a ground cloth used for camping works fine and can simply be tucked into the waistband of your pants. If you plan on doing several hides, I believe a heavy rubber butcher's apron, from a professional butcher's supply house, is a very worthwhile invest-ment.

When you finish fleshing your skin, there are several options available to the tanner. The skin may be folded, sealed in a heavy plastic garbage sack, and frozen for future use. If care is taken to eliminate as much air as

possible from the sack, to prevent freezer burn, a skin may be kept for as long as one year. When you are ready to tan your hide, just take it out of the freezer and drop it into a garbage can full of water, weighing it down with bricks or rocks until it is pliable. If this is done in the evening, the skin will be ready for the next step by morning.

The second option available is drying. If you have several skins of deer-size or smaller, and want to preserve them for future use, simply tack them to a flat surface, in the shade, flesh side out, using staples or wire-nails (see the section on Selection and Care of Skins).

Our third option, after fleshing, is to thoroughly rewet the skin, and dry it in a frame for the next step in the brain tanning process. This, of course, requires the construction of one or more frames.

BUILDING HIDE FRAMES

Almost any reasonably straight, sturdy wood will make good hide frames, but my favorite wood is pine. My current set of frames for tanning deer skins is made from the large ends of tipi poles that I replaced because they were not straight enough to suit me, or because the smaller ends were broken off too short. If you live in a logging area, oftentimes slash piles are a good source of raw material, or, simply cut fresh poles.

Squared lumber may also be used for frames, but should be of 2X4 dimensions or larger for deerskins. For heavier hides, such as cattle or bison, 2X8 or 2X10 boards make the best frames. In either case, boards should be paired together, and securely joined at the corners to construct frames of double thickness. Failure to do this, when using lumber, will result in warped, wobbly, and twisted frames. Frames must be constructed sturdily. A hide in a wobbly frame that is not square is difficult to work. Save yourself a lot of trouble; build good frames!

When building your first frame, it is a good idea to build it around your largest hide. A frame with inside dimension of roughly four and one-half feet wide by five and one-half feet high is large enough to accommodate most average size deerskins or small elk hides. My frames for large deer hides measure five and one-half feet by six and one-half feet on the inside.

Hides should fit snugly in their frames. A small hide in a large frame is unstable, uses much rope, and is difficult to scrape.

The best frames are made from dry, seasoned, and peeled wood. When obtaining poles, cut them about two and one-half feet longer than the inside dimension, so that the corners can overlap and form one foot legs for the frame to stand on. The legs raise the poles off of the ground, making stretching, scraping, and staking much easier.

For sturdy corners that will not twist or slip, I notch my poles so that they interlock closely (see Figure 3). In addition, I either nail or peg the corners and then lash them with rope or wet rawhide. If your frame is correctly made, it will not sway or wobble.

Although Figure 3 shows several types of frames, I prefer individual, portable frames. Stationary frames can't be rotated, turned over, or moved into sun, shade, or out of the rain.

STRETCHING ON THE FRAME FOR SCRAPING

To successfully stretch a skin, it must be thoroughly wet. If you have just finished fleshing a fresh hide, adequate wetting may be assured by soaking it in *cool* water for about twelve hours.

Always soak your skins and hides in a wood or plastic container. Do not use a metal one. If you are stretching a skin that was previously fleshed and dried, it usually requires forty-eight hours of soaking to eliminate all of the dry spots. *Never soak a hide in hot water;* it will cook and pull apart like wet tissue paper.

After soaking, I usually use heavyweight baling twine to frame a hide, however, any natural fiber rope that is less than one-quarter inch in diameter will work. I prefer natural fiber twine over most of the synthetics, especially nylon, because the knots seem to hold better.

Lay your frame down on a large, clean, flat surface. Cut sixteen to twenty pieces of twine about nine feet long and tie the end of each piece to the frame, using a square knot, every one to one and one-half feet. The use of short lengths makes it easy to evenly position the skin in the frame, and, should one or more slits in the skin rip out, eliminates the need to retighten the entire skin. With all of your ropes in place, you are now ready to mount your thoroughly soaked skin in the frame.

Figure 3

NOTCH POLES ONE FOOT FROM EACH END SO THAT THEY INTERLOCK. LASH WITH WET RAWHIDE OR ROPE.

VARIOUS METHODS OF ERECTING HIDE FRAMES

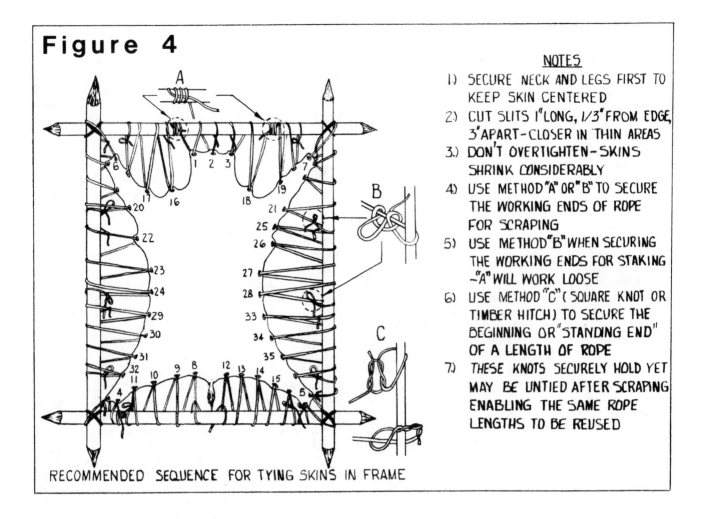

Figure 4

A

B

C

1.) SECURE NECK AND LEGS FIRST TO KEEP SKIN CENTERED
2.) CUT SLITS 1"LONG, 1/3"FROM EDGE, 3"APART-CLOSER IN THIN AREAS
3.) DON'T OVERTIGHTEN—SKINS SHRINK CONSIDERABLY
4.) USE METHOD"A"OR"B"TO SECURE THE WORKING ENDS OF ROPE FOR SCRAPING
5.) USE METHOD"B"WHEN SECURING THE WORKING ENDS FOR STAKING —"A"WILL WORK LOOSE
6.) USE METHOD"C"(SQUARE KNOT OR TIMBER HITCH) TO SECURE THE BEGINNING OR"STANDING END" OF A LENGTH OF ROPE
7.) THESE KNOTS SECURELY HOLD YET MAY BE UNTIED AFTER SCRAPING ENABLING THE SAME ROPE LENGTHS TO BE REUSED

RECOMMENDED SEQUENCE FOR TYING SKINS IN FRAME

Spread your hide, *hair side down*, on the flat surface in the center of your frame. Stretch it out as symmetrically as possible, eliminating any curled edges. Using a *very sharp* knife with a pointed, thin blade, cut one inch long slits about one-third of an inch in, and parallel to the edge of the skin. Cut these slits about three to four inches apart, making them slightly closer together in the rump and tail area, since the skin is weaker there and rips more easily.

Begin by tying the neck to the frame first. Work from the center of the neck outward toward the front legs. Pass your twine through the hide from the flesh side to the hair side and around the frame to the next hole. When coming to the end of a length of rope, use two half hitches so the rope can easily be untied to take up additional slack or to remove the skin from the frame. (See Figure 4).

Make your next ties in the bottom corners of the frame, being careful to keep the skin perfectly centered. Finish centering the hide by securing the front two legs to the top corner of the frame. Finally, make a tie on one side (belly of the skin) and then the other, alternating ties so as to keep the skin centered and symmetrical in the frame. Cinch each tie enough to remove the slack from the skin, but do not attempt to make the skin drum tight because it will shrink and tighten considerably as it dries. This is very important in the weak flank and tail area since these will tear if they are tied too tightly.

When finished, examine the edges of your skin carefully; there should be no loose or sagging areas. If you locate an edge that is not tight, it may be necessary to add another slit and tie to eliminate the sag.

A freshly framed hide will always dry most evenly in the shade. If you dry your hide in the sun, thinner areas such as the flank and belly will dry faster than the center of the hide where it is the thickest. The resulting wrinkles will make the hide much harder to scrape. In addition, temperature changes from day to night will cause a skin to expand and contract, and after several days the skin will become slack in the frame. It is therefore a good practice to scrape skins as soon as they dry in the frame.

MAKING A HIDE SCRAPER

The hide scraper, or "wahintke" (Figure 5) is the single most important tool in the dry-scrape buckskin process. Besides its primary function, that of removing the hair and outer epidermal layer of skin from the hide, it is also used in the staking process to help soften the hide, and can be used as a flesher. Its construction is very simple as it consists of only two parts, the handle and the blade.

Pre-Columbian scrapers were constructed using bone or chipped stone blades. However, as soon as steel became available, it was universally adopted as the scraper blade material of choice. Since good hide scrapers are time

Figure 5

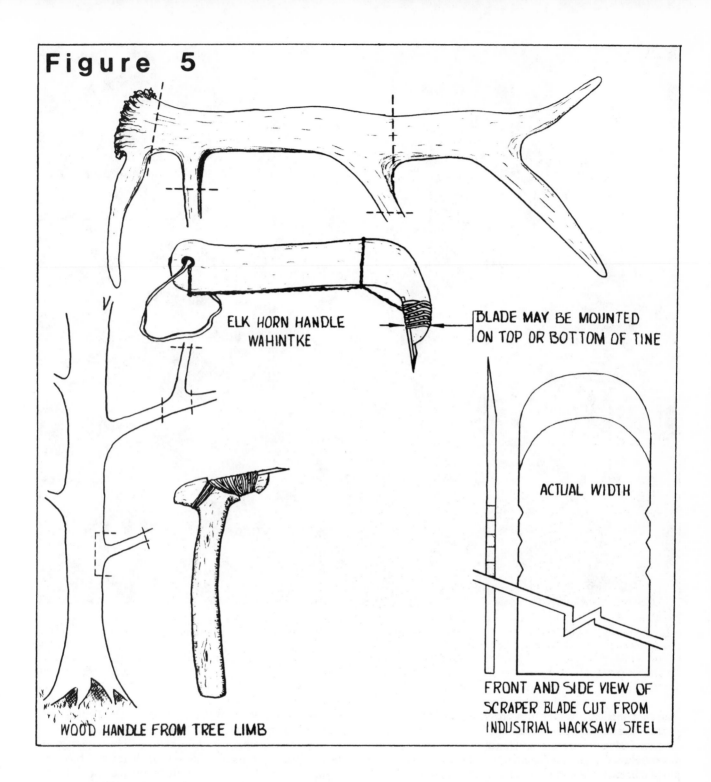

ELK HORN HANDLE
WAHINTKE

BLADE MAY BE MOUNTED
ON TOP OR BOTTOM OF TINE

ACTUAL WIDTH

WOOD HANDLE FROM TREE LIMB

FRONT AND SIDE VIEW OF
SCRAPER BLADE CUT FROM
INDUSTRIAL HACKSAW STEEL

saving devices and a joy to use (poorly made scrapers are just the opposite), they were handed down from one generation of tanners to another. As a result, there are many good examples of old scrapers still in use today and in museums.

Almost any flat piece of steel of one-quarter inch or less in thickness and one to two inches wide by three to six inches in length will make a *workable* scraper blade. To make a *good* scraper blade that doesn't require constant sharpening and holds a razor-sharp edge, we need a very tough and extremely hard steel that contains some tungsten. Sections from old circular saw blades, industrial

PHOTO BY DON HEIT

Close up photo showing clockwise from the top: elk handled scraper with a file-steel blade, canon bone flesher (from a deer leg), wood handled scraper with a hacksaw-steel blade, wood staker with 1½ inch head, wood handled scraper with a wood-plane blade, and wood staker with a 3 inch head.

hacksaw blades, and old files provide the best steel, are readily available, and inexpensive. Old leaf springs also make suitable scrapers, but will not hold a sharp enough edge unless drawn and rehardened. My favorite scraper that I currently use is made from a worn industrial hacksaw blade that I obtained from a local machine shop.

Use an electric bench grinder to carefully shape the blade to resemble my illustration in Figure 5. Hold the steel in your fingertips so that you can feel it heating. When the steel becomes uncomfortable to touch, quench it in a bucket of cold water. Never allow the steel to become too hot, especially the thin beveled edge, or it will "burn". Burning causes the steel to turn blue or black and destroys its ability to hold a sharp edge. To finish the cutting edge of your blade, clamp it in a vise to hold it steady, and final hone its edge with oilstones.

Your finished blade will take about one or two hours to make. It should have a rounded cutting edge without

corners as viewed from the top, and is sharpened on a single bevel as viewed from the side (Figure 5).

The proper length for your blade will be the length of the front of the handle, plus one inch for the blade to extend. To avoid getting your blade too short, build your handle before cutting the already ground blade to its finished length.

The handle of your blade should be constructed of either hardwood or antler. If you choose wood for your handle, use the hardest, densest wood that grows in your area. My wooden handled scrapers are made of osage orange. Yew, service berry, and mountain mahogany are also very good. Oak and juniper make serviceable scrapers, but are lighter and therefore do not work as well.

Use dead, seasoned, wood for your handles whenever possible, since wood shrinks considerably as it dries and tends to crack. Handles may also be cut "green" in

95

January and February when the sap is down. If the cut surfaces are painted and the wood allowed to dry slowly, indoors, with the bark on, it will not crack. This usually requires about six months. Several coatings of linseed oil, tung oil, or hot animal grease on your finished handles will also help prevent cracking. Cut your handles about two inches in diameter and about two feet in length. Keep in mind that your handle will be considerably smaller in diameter after peeling and final sanding. If your handle is too small in diameter, it will be difficult to comfortably grip; it will be too light and will be tiring to use. The finished length of most of my scraper handles is about twelve inches, however, this is strictly a matter of preference.

The best material to fashion scraper blade handles from is elk antler that is two inches or greater in diameter. This was the favorite material of Native Americans for scraper handles. The blade may be lashed, beveled side up, to the tine nearest the head or to the tine nearest the fork in the branches as illustrated in Figure 5.

Before making any hacksaw cuts, carefully examine the antler tines nearest the fork and the head to determine which tine will make the best anchoring point for the blade. The ideal tine is only slightly narrower than the blade. In addition, grasp the antler with your dominant hand from each of the two ends to determine the end that provides the most comfortable grip; this end should become the lower end of the scraper handle.

Whether you choose wood or antler for your handle, the best method of securing the blade is with long buckskin (brain tanned) or rawhide bindings. This way the blade can easily be removed from the handle if major reshaping becomes necessary.

A wood handled scraper in various stages of manufacture.

DRY SCRAPING THE HIDE TO DEHAIR

At this point in the buckskin process, you should have a rounded, well shaped, razor sharp blade that is lashed to a smooth, comfortable handle, and a fleshed hide that has been evenly stretched and dried in a frame. If your scraper blade is not razor sharp, now is the time to put that finishing edge on it with medium and fine grade oilstones. Always sharpen the blade by pushing the stone against the edge of the blade. After *lightly* sharpening the beveled side of the blade, stone the flat underside of the blade just enough to remove the jagged edge curl. In addition to preventing you from fully sharpening the blade, the jagged edges will gouge and tear the hide. After stoning my scrapers, I always strop the blades with a heavy piece of smooth leather glued grain (smooth) side up to a block of wood. The leather is oiled with Neatsfoot oil and then rubbed with a piece of jeweler's rouge. When stropping, draw the leather away from the edge of the blade instead of toward the blade as is done in sharpening. Stropping both sides of the blade will greatly increase your scraping time between major sharpenings. In addition, when your blade begins to dull, you can usually bring the blade's finished edge back by simply stropping. This normally works twice before another major sharpening with the oilstones is required.

Before you begin scraping the hide, examine it from the flesh side first. Using a very sharp knife or your scraper, *carefully* trim the hair away from the edges of any holes in

the skin. It is also a good idea to note any scored areas on the hide. As in the fleshing procedure, scraping should be done with the direction of the scores and not across them. If your tools are sharp, very little pressure will be required to shave the hair around these areas.

With the fragile areas clearly marked, lean your frame against a good solid object, such as a wall or a couple of trees. Since we will start our scraping in the neck area, position the skin so that you can comfortably reach the front legs and neck. This may require that you position the frame on its side with the neck to your left. Never use a box or pedestal in an attempt to reach some distant part of the skin because a fall with a scraper may poke a hole in your hide!

Dry-scraping to remove the hair and the epidermis (grain) of the skin.

To achieve the best stability and control with your scraper, grip it with one hand down low near the end of the handle and place your other hand around the top where the blade is lashed. The scraping motion should always follow the direction that the hair naturally lays. A good analogy to remember until you get the feel of the tool is that of an airplane practicing takeoffs and landings. That is, the scraping motion begins with the blade in motion before reaching the area being scraped, making contact with the skin in the center of its arc. Pressure on the tool is increased as the blade planes the hair and outer epidermal layer of skin off of the hide. As the blade nears the end of the stroke, pressure is gradually decreased on the tool, and it is lifted from the hide, completing the arc. (See Figure 6.) Both arms are used to evenly "pull" the scraper over the hide, the entire stroke taking only about a second.

While scraping, frequently clean the tip of the scraper blade of hair and shaving that accumulate on it by gently brushing the beveled edge of the blade lightly against the hide as you are lifting the scraper to make the next stroke. This will enable you to scrape faster and more efficiently because the blade will get a better "bite" on each pass.

One of the most common causes of popping through the skin is failure to maintain a 90 degree angle with the hide. Don't allow the blade to angle into the hide at the end of your strokes or to move sideways or it will slice through.

Continue scraping in overlapping but parallel strokes until you have cleared an area that is about one foot square. Examine the area carefully, and you will notice greyish streaks or peppery looking areas; these are hair follicles. Beneath those is a yellowish layer, having a smooth texture. Both of these layers must carefully be scraped off before proceeding to the next one foot square area. When the area in which you are working has been properly scraped, it will be an eggshell white color, and will have a slightly fuzzy texture, unless it is adjacent to a bullet hole or in some other way has become bloodstained.

On most hides, the grain is thickest in the neck and down the center of the back, and thinner in the rump and belly areas. Legs are the most difficult areas of all to successfully scrape since they seem to be almost all grain! Oftentimes, when scraping thick-grained areas, a washboard effect develops on the surface of the skin. If your hide starts to washboard, scrape with the ridges shearing them off. Never scrape across a washboard or your blade will pop through the hide. Since washboarding is generally caused by a dull scraper, immediately re-sharpen your blade before correcting the washboard.

Remember those holes and scores that we trimmed the hair from when we started? Scrape delicately around these areas, carefully removing the grain down to the fuzzy white dermis. When scraping over scores, keep in mind that the grain (epidermal layer) may be the only layer holding the skin together. When this is the case, don't try to remove all of the grain; it's better to leave some grain than to pop through the skin with your scraper.

Another potential problem area when scraping is scarring along the shoulders, back, and rump areas caused by barbed wire, thorns, brush, etc. When encountering these, don't try to scrape across them or your blade will pop through the hide. Carefully scrape scars lengthwise, but like scores, if the grain appears to be the only material

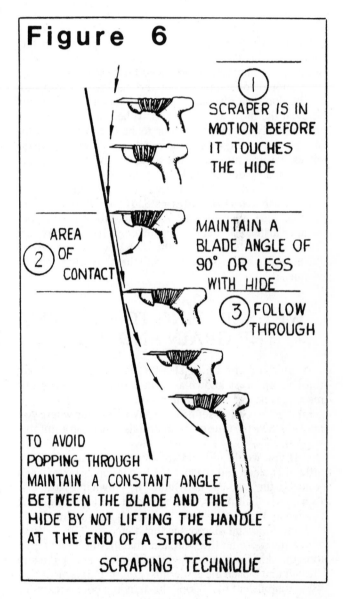

Figure 6

1 SCRAPER IS IN MOTION BEFORE IT TOUCHES THE HIDE

2 AREA OF CONTACT

MAINTAIN A BLADE ANGLE OF 90° OR LESS WITH HIDE

3 FOLLOW THROUGH

TO AVOID POPPING THROUGH MAINTAIN A CONSTANT ANGLE BETWEEN THE BLADE AND THE HIDE BY NOT LIFTING THE HANDLE AT THE END OF A STROKE

SCRAPING TECHNIQUE

holding the hide together, don't try to remove it. The very narrow strip of grain, usually only a sixteenth of an inch or less in width, does not detract from the appearance of the hide and is much more desirable than a large tear.

Continue scraping the skin, one square foot at a time, until you have removed the hair and grain from the entire hide.

Inadequate removal of the grain is second only to inadequate removal of the membrane as the leading cause of failure to fluff and thicken the skin during the staking process. On the other hand, excessive scraping into the white layer will cause scraper furrows and uneven thickness in your finished buckskin, so try to stop scraping when you reach the white dermis layer.

When you have finished scraping the hide, reexamine it carefully for insufficiently scraped areas. If you would like to soften the edges of the skin, including the tie holes, now is the time to resharpen your scraper to a *very fine edge,* and to *gently* scrape any last vestiges of grain and hair from these areas. These softened holes and uneven edges with occasional tufts of hair, particularly on the lower legs, are characteristics found in almost all examples of early Native American clothing. I believe that this detail adds a lot to the appearance of a garment and further separates true, hand-worked, traditional, brain tan leather from any commercially produced product.

Should you happen to pop through the skin with your blade, don't get discouraged. This happens occasionally to even the most accomplished. When this occurs, stop immediately. Reexamine your technique. Is your blade sharp? Are you drinking too much beer? Are you using excessive pressure in a thin area, or are you failing to maintain a 90 degree angle or less between the bottom of the blade and the hide? Are you scraping at right angles to scars, washboards, or scores instead of parallel with them? Is your hide grease-burnt? Are you stabbing with your scraper instead of making long, even, controlled strokes? These cuts, as well as any other holes, will be mended in the next step of the process so well that they will barely be visible.

WET SCRAPING TO REMOVE THE GRAIN AND HAIR

Hair and grain may also be removed from the skin through a process known as "wet-scrape." Although this method is not as thorough in removing the grain as "dry-scraping," it is very useful in a survival situation where you may not have the time or the materials to fashion a suitable scraper.

If you would like to experiment with this method a little, first clean and sharpen the upper bone from a deer's front leg; the "radius" and "ulna" as shown in Figure 2 A. In a survival situation, this bone and the lower leg bone flesher in Figure 2 are the only tools required to flesh, dehair, grain, and membrane the skin.

After fleshing the skin and shaping the radius-ulna tool, the skin must be soaked in water long enough to slip the hair and loosen the epidermis (grain). This is most easily accomplished by staking the skin in a cold stream for several days, or by soaking the skin in a plastic container such as a trash barrel. If you use a trash barrel or other container, the water must be changed at least twice daily or the skin will begin to rot.

The grain and hair may also be loosened with a lye solution. This is made by combining a 3 gallon bucket of hardwood ashes and a bucket and one-half of boiling water, or by using commercial lye that has been diluted with water to the same strength used to make soap (solution will float an egg). The skin is soaked in the solution until the toughest grainy area (usually the neck) can be scraped off with your thumbnail.

In another variation of the lye method, simply cover

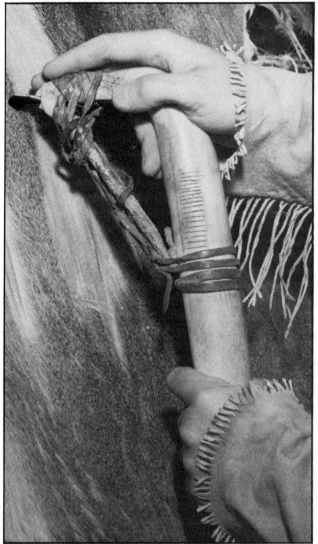

PHOTO BY DON HEIT

Close-up of dry-scraping with an old, original, elk horn scraper, equipped with a file-steel blade. Note that a 90 degree angle or less is maintained between the blade and the skin.

the hair side of a fleshed skin with about three inches of hardwood ashes, pour enough soft, cold, water on the ash to form a paste, and then work it into the hair using the hands. The wood ash-pasted skin is folded with the hair sides touching, rolled into a bundle, and stored in a warm place until the hair can easily be slipped using the ulna-radius tool. The main drawback to this method is that it does not remove the grain.

After employing one of the above methods to loosen the grain, use the radius-ulna scraper in the same manner as the bar flesher (Figures 1 and 2A) to slip the hair and grain. Following graining, any skins that have been soaked in one of the lye solutions, or wood ash-pasted, must be thoroughly rinsed in several changes of water to prevent damage to the skin fibers.

In summary, since wet-scraping does not always completely remove the grain, I prefer dry-scraping all of my skins. A dry scraped skin has a nicer finished grain

99

surface, softens easier, and smokes more thoroughly than its wet scraped counterpart. However, this is just my personal preference based on my successes and failures with each method.

After scraping, many people suggest that you flip your frame over and scrape any remaining membrane from the flesh side. I believe that this is not only time consuming, but ineffective. The membrane is very hard, tough, and slick. This makes it very difficult for the scraper to get a good bite. In addition, the color and texture differences between adequately and inadequately scraped areas is not as apparent as it was on the grain side. The result of dry-scraping off the membrane is usually an excessively thinned hide. For this reason, I have incorporated the following method of removing the membrane in my buckskin process to assure successful softening.

REMOVING THE MEMBRANE

Unlace your skin from the frame and soak it in cool water until it is thoroughly saturated. This usually only takes about two or three hours since the grain has now been removed. After soaking for about one hour, pull and stretch the skin to help the water penetrate the less permeable areas. When the skin is sufficiently soaked, it will be snow white in color (except for blood stains), and not have any amber or grey colored dry areas.

Previously, in the fleshing process, there was hair on one side of the skin. While it prevented us from removing *all* of the membrane, it also protected the hide from any irregularities in the beaming log. therefore, run your hand over the surface of the beaming log to assure its smoothness. If you have any nicks, splinters, whiskers or other irregularities in your log, eliminate them now or they will make holes in the skin.

The procedure for membraning is exactly the same as for fleshing. Remove your thoroughly soaked skin from the water and lay it flesh side up on the beam. Work carefully with the fleshing bar, maintaining the correct angle, to systematically cover every square inch of the hide. Since the hair has been removed, the skin is much more delicate. Don't use any more pressure than is necessary to push off the membrane, or allow the blade to bounce over the "slack" area that always forms in front of it. Keep the hide as smooth as possible on the log by pulling the uppermost end of the hide toward you. The fleshing bar will "slicker" or squeegee water from the hide as you use it, making the areas covered a greyish color and easy to identify.

Membraning should always be done in the shade, or the sun will cause the skin to dry, making the membrane impossible to remove. Should your hide start to dry, resoak it for a few minutes before resuming the membraning process.

If you want to soften the edges of your hide, including the area around the tie holes, make sure that you remove all of the membrane adhering to the perimeter of the skin. This is often best accomplished by scraping parallel along the hide's edges. In addition, it is not a bad idea to gently go over the edges of any holes or cuts to remove any remaining tissue or these areas will not stretch and soften after they are mended in the staking process.

If I have the time, I usually turn my hide over and use the flesher to rescrape the edges of the hide, holes, cuts, and grainy areas that were inadequately scraped.

As I mentioned previously in the section on scraping, *failure to adequately remove all of the membrane is the leading cause of stiff areas in finished buckskin.*

MENDING HOLES AND CUTS

The best time to mend any holes in the skin is immediately after membraning, while the skin is still damp. If the hide has started to dry in some of its thinner areas, especially around the holes, I rinse and stretch the skin by hand in fresh water before mending. If the area being mended is kept damp, your needle will make smaller holes, resulting in a neater, stronger repair.

I always mend skins from the flesh side. This makes the repair almost invisible from the grain side, and protects the stitch from wear. Fold the skin so that the edges of the hole touch and sew them closed, using a simple overhand "whip" stitch. If the hole has any irregular edges, it's a good idea to trim them off with a sharp knife, so that the seam lays as flat as possible. In addition, double tie each end of the thread with two knots, so that the knots don't pull through the skin during the staking process or come untied.

In a primitive or survival situation, sinew and an awl would be used to perform this task. For practical reasons, however, I have found that the best thread to use is "J. & P. Coats Dual Duty Plus" in either the white or beige color. This is a cotton covered polyester button and carpet thread. Unlike the pure synthetic threads, such as nylon, it will not enlarge your holes because of its cotton covering. In addition, the cotton smokes very nicely, and therefore matches the finished hide.

The thread is most easily pulled through the skin if a *small* "Glover's" instead of a "Sharps" needle is used. Glover's needles are available from Tandy Leather Co. stores located nationwide, or from any of the larger suppliers advertising in black powder magazines.

Besides mending holes in your skin, examine it carefully for scored areas that you think will break through during the vigorous staking process. If you do a thorough job of mending your holes, you will not only have a more attractive finished product, but a more usable one that will stretch evenly and more closely resemble its original wearer.

The skin is now ready for braining. If several hours or days are going to elapse before you can go on, store the skin in a plastic bag in the refrigerator to prevent spoilage. For longer periods of time, the skin should be dried.

BRAINING

When I first started brain tanning, I had an abundance of skins, but could not obtain brains from local stores to make my dressing solution. In my search for a substitute, I found and tried a recipe that dated back to pioneer times called "tawing."

In this process, a bar of homemade lye soap or Fels-Naptha soap is shaved or grated into a pot containing about three quarts of hot water. Add about eight ounces of Lexol or pure Neatsfoot oil (never use Neatsfoot oil compound) and simmer. Don't allow the mixture to boil, or the resulting suds will drown you! This amount of tanning solution is enough for an average size deer hide.

Before using, allow the solution to cool enough that you can comfortably place your hand in it; if the solution is hot enough to cook your hide, it will also cook the deer's.

I used tawing on my first four skins to soften them, however, they never turned out as soft, thick, or velvety as with brains. Since then, I have discovered that the real secret of good buckskin is the brains. No oils or soaps are as effective in softening and thickening the buckskin. The brains also lightly bleach or whiten the hide. If you pursue the sources that I outlined in the section titled Obtaining Brains, I am certain that you will have no problems keeping yourself adequately supplied in brains.

In historic times, or in a survival situation, the brains were usually cleaned of any blood, and mashed or beaten into a paste, which was rubbed into both sides of the skin with the hands or smooth stones. This procedure was almost always preceded by a thorough washing to remove any loose bits of flesh or fat and a wringing procedure that squeezed out as much water as possible, leaving the fine fibers of the hide damp and open to soak up the brain dressing. The freshly brained hide was then rolled up and placed in a warm location that was secure from animals for several hours or even overnight to allow the dressing to thoroughly penetrate the skin. After braining, the skin was wrung out to eliminate all of the excess moisture and then stretched and worked until it was completely soft and dry.

If the brains were not going to be used immediately, they were lightly boiled and spread to dry in the sun, then mixed with dried moss and further dried so that they would not spoil before they were needed. To reconstitute, the dried brains were simply soaked in a small amount of water.

I believe that the best way to brain a hide is to soak it in a slurry of brains overnight. To make your slurry, first thaw one cow brain (or one pound of any other animal's brain) for two small to medium deer skins. For very large skins, use one brain per skin. If you are braining three to five skins at the same time, you will need to thaw three cow brains for five deer hides. If you are using deer brains, use one and one-half brains per hide or supplement one deer brain per deer skin with a few tablespoons of pure Neatsfoot oil or Lexol. Dump the thawed brains into an electric blender, hit the liquify button and presto, you have a thick, pink "brainshake." Blend this glop until the brain is totally liquified. When the brain is thoroughly liquified, fill the blender to the top with boiling water and reblend.

I usually dump the brain slurry into a pan at this point and cook it for about fifteen minutes, bringing it to a slow boil for about three to five minutes. While it is not necessary to cook the brains at all, it has been my experience that the brains don't seem to spoil as quickly if they are. Some tanners also believe that the uncooked fats and oils in the brains are capable of grease-burning the skin like fat that is not fleshed from a fresh skin. I have successfully dressed skins with both cooked and raw brains with no discernible difference in the finished product. However, I usually cook the brains because it seems to result in a better smelling skin.

After preparing your solution, pour it into a plastic bucket. Stir in enough cold water to make approximately one gallon of liquid or enough to cover all of the skins that you are going to soak. When the mixture has cooled to a temperature that is comfortable to your hand, work each skin in the sudsy liquid, making certain that the solution comes in contact with all parts of the skins. Rub each skin between your hands, pulling and stretching all of its areas to assure good penetration.

When you are satisfied that the skins have been thoroughly saturated, lay a couple of bricks or rocks on them so that they stay submerged in the liquid. I usually do this in the evening and soak the skins overnight. This assures complete penetration of all areas of the skins.

After the skins are removed from the brain solution (or unrolled after the mashed brains have had time to penetrate), you can proceed in several different ways. I usually remove any skins that I am not going to work that same day from the solution, and drape them over a clothesline, in the sun, until they are baked completely dry. The sun drying further assures complete penetration of the oils into the skin, and is particularly effective in a survival situation where the hides are pasted on both sides with mashed brains. Since our skins have been soaked overnight, drying is not necessary; it merely provides a convenient way to store skins that are not going to be worked that same day. Dried, brained skins are very attractive to insects and must be carefully protected in plastic bags until they are ready to use. To soften a brained and dried skin, simply soak it in water until it is again pliable, then wring it out in preparation for the staking process.

Let us return, however, to the skin that is taken directly from the brain solution. It must be thoroughly wrung out to eliminate any excess moisture.

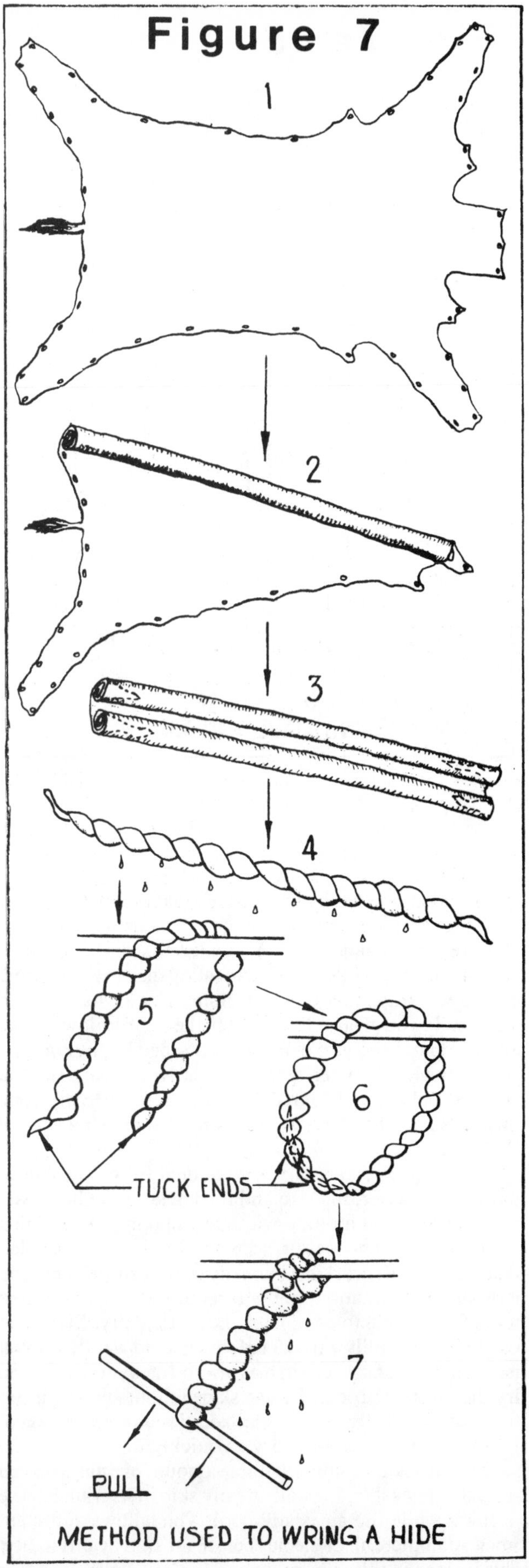

Figure 7

METHOD USED TO WRING A HIDE

WRINGING

Wringing is the important preparatory step to "staking" (working the hide soft). It is also employed by some tanners prior to the braining procedure to stretch the fibers and to open the pores of the skin to assure thorough penetration of the brains. If you are soaking the skin overnight in a slurry, wringing (before braining) is not necessary. If you mash and rub the brains into the skin, as in the survival situation discussed previously, I recommend wringing before and after braining, as well as sun drying the skin to assure complete penetration of the conditioning oils.

Wringing serves two important functions when employed following the braining procedure: It facilitates softening by stretching the fibers of the skin, and it reduces excess moisture to a very low level, thereby greatly shortening the length of time needed to work the hides dry.

A good buckskin that is not grease-burnt, over-scraped, or badly scored, will withstand a vigorous wringing with no damage. Occasionally a few thin areas or poorly mended holes will tear open, but these areas would have probably torn in the staking process anyway. When this occurs, simply mend the holes as you did following membraning.

There are as many different variations in wringing techniques as there are in brain tanning buckskin. The procedure that I use and teach is as follows (see Figure 7): 1) Spread the damp skin, grain or hair side up, on a clean flat place (grass, concrete, tarp, etc.). 2) Beginning at a front or rear leg, fold in the uneven edges and tightly roll the skin, on a diagonal, from front leg to the opposite rear leg. 3) Do the same with the other side of the skin, forming two parallel rolls shaped like a scroll. 4) Step on one end of the scroll and twist it several turns. 5) Pick up both ends of the now twisted skin and loop it around a smooth stationary bar such as a tree limb. 6) Work each of the loose ends into one another forming a continuous twisted skin loop around the stationary bar. 7) Insert a smooth sturdy stick, such as your staker, through the loop and begin to twist. As the skin begins to "knot up", pull on the twisting stick, keeping the skin taut, but being careful not to pull the tucked ends of the loop apart. When the skin finally "knots up" and can be twisted no tighter, fasten the twisting-stick by tying, or hooking it under the stationary cross-bar that the skin is twisted on. If the skin has been properly scraped and membraned, water and air bubbles will squeeze through all visible surfaces of the skin. When the water dropping slows or ceases, blot the skin with an old towel. Untwist the skin to step 6 (see Figure 7), the skin loop, and rotate the loop one-quarter turn around the stationary bar to change the stress points, and retwist as before, but in the opposite direction.

After wringing the skin, it must be untwisted, un-rolled, and hand-stretched to its original shape in preparation for tying in the frame.

If the skin is properly wrung, it will have a very uniform level of dampness. Any areas that are still wet will appear bluish or grey in color. This may indicate overlooked grain or membrane or uneven wringing. Blot these areas with your towel and work them extra hard during the staking process to assure softness.

If you are working the skin on a very hot and dry day, try to leave more moisture in the skin to give you time to tie it into the frame. Likewise, in a more humid or cool situation, wring your hide out as dry as possible, but without allowing it to become stiff or dry to the touch (sandy in texture). These factors, like scraping, membraning and many others in the buckskin process, are evaluations that you, the tanner must make based on your environment and the characteristics of the skin that you are working. The process is a very forgiving one that allows a lot of room for error.

With the skin thoroughly brained and wrung, the skin may be refrigerated for up to two days, frozen, or tied in the frame and staked.

STAKING

There are two basic methods that are generally used to work a skin soft and dry: 1) hand-pulling over a rope loop, and 2) in a frame using stakers. Each method has its advantages and disadvantages, however, I prefer the frame because it stretches the skin more evenly, and results in a larger finished product. A staker worked skin is of more uniform thickness and lays flat when removed from the frame, because of the even tension that the frame's ties exert on the skin's edges. This is a tremendous advantage when making pants or other items of clothing that require a pattern. The hand-pulled skin, on the other hand, will tend to stretch and thin more in the edges, and less in the center, than a frame-worked skin. Since the center area of the hand-pulled skin tends to not fully stretch, and the edges tend to over-stretch, pattern pieces cut from the pulled skin don't hold their planned shape. For these reasons, I prefer to frame and stake my skins until they are completely dry. I then use the pulling technique to buff both sides of the skin after it is removed from the frame, and to work any slightly stiff or damp areas that may still remain.

The specialized tools used in this process are very easy to construct. In Figure 8, I have drawn a picture of some stakers that took approximately twenty minutes each to shape. The largest of these was constructed from a hickory double-bladed axe handle, and has a chisel shaped head that is three inches wide. The smaller wood staker was made from a hickory maul or sledge handle, has the same shaped head, but is only about one and one-half inches wide. The large staker is used on the main body of the skin, while the smaller size staker is good for manipulating the skin between the ties and in areas that are too confining for the large staker, such as the legs.

Stakers may also be fashioned from antler, wooden canoe paddles, or any kind of wood that is dense, fine-grained, and not inherently rough or splintery. Woods having these characteristics include dogwood, serviceberry, yew, chokecherry, juniper, and ash.

The most important part of the staker is the head. Make sure that the round-cornered, chisel shaped head is very smooth and polished. In addition, it should have a smooth, comfortable handle that won't splinter or blister the user's hands. This is why I prefer laquered, ready made axe and maul handles for the construction of this very important tool; the only work required is the shaping and polishing of the head.

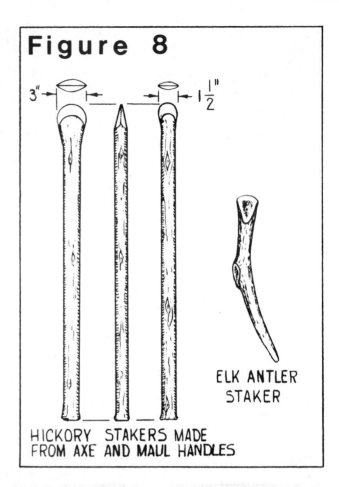

Figure 8

3" ← → 1½"

ELK ANTLER
STAKER

HICKORY STAKERS MADE
FROM AXE AND MAUL HANDLES

In addition to the two sizes of stakers, you will need your hide scraper (resharpen before starting), a knife, some pieces of sandstone or pumice that have rounded corners, or, if you have trouble locating these in your area, sandpaper wrapped around a sanding block with rounded corners. If you would like to buff the skin following the staking operation, you will need a braided ½" nylon rope that is about eight to ten feet in length. Never use a twisted rope as I did on the first skin that I pulled, the rope untwisted, pinched the skin, and tore a six inch hole in one of its edges!

Staking time can vary a great deal from one skin to another. Weather, the size and thickness of the hide, and even your mental attitude will affect staking time. If you have a choice, choose a warm sunny day and a shaded location to start working the skin. This will provide you with an ideal situation that will require only about three hours for the skin to completely be worked dry. Skins can also be successfully worked indoors in cold weather if you use a direct heat source such as a wood stove to warm and dry the air in the room. I stake skins indoors each winter; however, it usually requires an additional hour or two of time since the skins don't dry as quickly.

Because of the unpredictable amount of time required to stake a buckskin, I usually tie my skin in its frame in the morning while the air is still cool. This allows sufficient time to complete all of the ties before the skin begins to dry. This is done in the same manner as before, hair side down

Guy Cowden is shown in the final stages of staking a buckskin. Note the amount of force that is used to push and rub the staker across the skin as well as the stretchy quality of the finished buckskin.

Another view of the staking process which shows the overall set-up of the frame with the hide laced to it.

PHOTO BY DON HEIT

(if your frame is on the floor), neck first, then the front legs, sides, etc. Keep your skin symmetrical in the frame and use knots that will not come untied during the vigorous staking process, such as the square knot or the double half hitch shown in Figure 4B and 4C. *Do not overstretch the skin in the frame.* Tighten the ties only enough to take the slack out of the skin, so that when the frame is stood in an upright position, before working it, the skin does not sag. Never use the friction tie shown in Figure 4A when staking, because it will work loose as the skin begins to stretch and loosen in the frame.

Observe the skin as you are tying it into the frame. If you notice areas that are turning whiter in color, especially in the thin belly, groin or flank areas, work them briefly but rapidly, then complete the remaining ties as quickly as possible. The most effective way to work a small area like this is to place the palm of one hand against the front of the skin and the palm of the other against the back. Press both

105

hands together so that the hide is clamped between them. Move your hands up, down, and in a circular motion such that it stretches, pulls, whitens, and softens the skin in the area around your hand. Use this effective but simple technique not only on the rapidly drying spots when tying the skin in the frame, but also later, on as much of the skin as you can reach, before you begin staking.

Another technique that is very good utilizes the thin piece of metal out of the blinders on an old horse harness or a large metal cooking spoon. To use the tool, place it on the front side and fit it into the palm of your other hand which is on the back side of the skin. Now pull hard, going over the rapidly drying spot several times before finishing your ties. This method is also very useful to stretch and soften the edges between the ties.

When the skin is completely laced in the frame, you are ready to begin staking. If you haven't done so already, begin the staking procedure by using the palm-to-palm technique to work as much of the outer edge of the skin as you can reach. In addition, as one of the preliminary procedures, poke the skin all over with the tip of one of your stakers. Begin by depressing the skin only two or three inches. As you continue poking the skin, you will notice a much larger area stretching around the area where you push, and you can increase the amount of pressure that you exert with the staker. It should take about ten or fifteen minutes of poking and the palm-to-palm technique for the skin to loosen and sag considerably in the frame. This is desirable and indicates that the fibers are becoming stronger and more elastic as the skin dries. When this occurs, do not retighten the ties unless some of the key ties rip out, or, unless the skin stretches so much that it is losing its natural shape. The slack allows the skin to stretch and then rebound with each push of the staker. This rebounding is necessary for the skin to become thick, soft, and strong.

When the whole skin is loose and stretched, and the tip of the staker slides easily and smoothly along the surface of the skin (too much surface moisture causes the staker to move in a jerking fashion), it is ready to stake. This must be done in a *systematic* manner that covers the *entire skin* on *both sides*. Don't rub the staker back and forth, but apply pressure in long downward strokes, working from the center of the skin toward the edges. rotate the frame on each of its four sides as you stake not only to facilitate reaching all areas of the skin, but also to encourage even drying. When one side has been completely and systematically covered, turn the frame over and work the back side of the skin in the same manner. Always spend equal amounts of time on both sides of the skin; this stretches the fibers in as many different directions as possible and results in a superior finish on both sides.

As the skin dries, it will become noticeably stronger, enabling you to substantially increase the amount of pressure that you exert on the skin with the staker. Areas that are not drying as rapidly as the rest of the skin will be blue-gray in color and feel slippery when you slide over them with the staker. This indicates either a grainy or membrany spot. Use your sanding rocks, sanding block, or your hide scraper (wahintke) to go over these spots. In addition, use your sandstone or sanding block to go over both sides of the skin as you stake it. This will result in a nicer finish on each side, and enable moisture to evaporate faster from the skin.

Don't decrease your staking efforts until the entire skin feels warm to the touch (hold the skin against your face). If there are any areas that still feel damp and cool, continue to work them with the staker, and if they appear to have any grain or membrane, with the sandstone and scraper. Really stretch and distend the skin with your bodyweight when you reach this point. Since ninety percent or more of the skin is softened and dry, move your frame into the sun to finish staking. Work like your life depended on softening every square inch of the skin until no cool, damp feeling spots remain.

I dry my skins totally in the frame using these techniques. If any ties tear out that I think will change the natural shape of the skin, I retie them immediately, and continue staking. When the skin is totally dry, I remove it from the frame by cutting the twine that holds it in the frame, and lightly buff it on both sides with rope (see photo on page 109).

In aboriginal America, this rope was usually a piece of braided sinew. The rope I use, however, is a ten foot long piece of one-half inch braided nylon that will not unwind and pinch the skin. It is secured at each end to a tree so that the working area between the two knots is about six feet long. The rope is tied as securely and as taut as possible since it stretches and sags with use. I rotate the skin as I work each side until the entire skin is buffed on both sides.

If any spots remain slightly stiff or crinkle when bent, they were not worked enough. Lightly sand these areas and rework them on the rope; they usually soften with reworking or with use, after the buckskin is worn as clothing.

If the grain and membrane have been completely and thoroughly removed, and if the skin is continuously, systematically, and completely worked over both sides, even the edges will soften. If the entire skin is stiff, you should probably resoak it in the brain water with your next dry-scraped skin and rework it as before. I have been very lucky and have never had to work a skin more than once (fingers crossed). However, I believe that the most common cause of having to work a skin more than once (assuming the skin was properly dry-scraped and membraned) is a rest break to eat lunch or to drink a beer after the brained and wrung skin is in its frame. If you would like to take a five or ten minute break, do so only toward the end of staking, when the skin is almost completely dry, and with your frame in a shaded location.

SMOKING

Brain tanned buckskin is naturally white, and if it gets wet, will dry stiff. A smoked skin, however, is easily resoftened, even after repeated wettings, by simply shaking and lightly working it with your hands. This is because the water resistant pitch in the smoke penetrates and coats the skin's fibers, thus preventing them from adhering to each other when they become wet.

Smoking also has many other advantages: 1. It increases the strength of the buckskin, making it two or three times stronger than an unsmoked skin. 2. Smoking discourages clothes moths, crickets, and other insects that attack other natural fabrics such as wool. 3. Smoking is a long lasting bacteria killing agent that preserves the leather from deterioration. 4. Depending on the type of fuel used, smoking gives the skin a very nice aroma and a beautiful brown or gold color.

To prepare a single skin for smoking, fold it lengthwise, flesh side out, along the backbone line, and sew it into a bag, working from the top of the neck to the end of the rear legs (leave the bottom open). This is easily and quickly accomplished using a three-cornered glover's needle and button and carpet thread to make one-half inch overhand (whip) stitches. This can also be done by stapling the edges together.

If you have two skins of similar size and thickness, you can save time and achieve the same color on each skin by sewing or stapling them into a single bag. When you do this, work from the neck of the skins down one side to the end of the hind legs, then, starting again at the neck, sew the other side closed.

Always sew your hides into bags with the grain sides facing each other, to the inside of the bag. By sewing the skin inside out, the less permeable grain side is smoked first, when the smoke is the thickest.

Indians usually dug a small pit, built a fire in the pit to produce hot coals, added their smoking material to the coals, and then pegged the skin bag, which was suspended from a tripod framework, directly to the ground around the pit. Since the bottom edge of the skin was touching the ground, it oftentimes did not smoke evenly. In addition, the skin was very close to the heat source, and had to be carefully watched to prevent heat damage. (See Figure 9.) Oftentimes, to avoid this danger, the skin was staked several feet from the fire pit, and a tunnel in the earth was used to carry and to cool the smoke to the skin.

To assure that I only smoke the skin and not burn it, I reserve the above "stake-to-the-ground" method for primitive or survival situations only. To more efficiently smoke a skin, it should be positioned as far away from the heat source as possible. This is most easily accomplished with the use of an inexpensive steel garbage can that has the bottom cut out. In Figure 9, I have drawn a picture of such a set up. It consists of a tripod over a small pit that is approximately one foot wide and twelve to sixteen inches deep. There is a draft hole that is located one to one and one-half feet from the top edge and intersects with the bottom of the pit. This draft hole enables the coals in the bottom of the hole to breathe and can easily be punched in the ground with a smooth steel or hardwood rod. The garbage can is positioned around the hole with its largest end to the ground.

Before suspending the skin from the tripod, I always

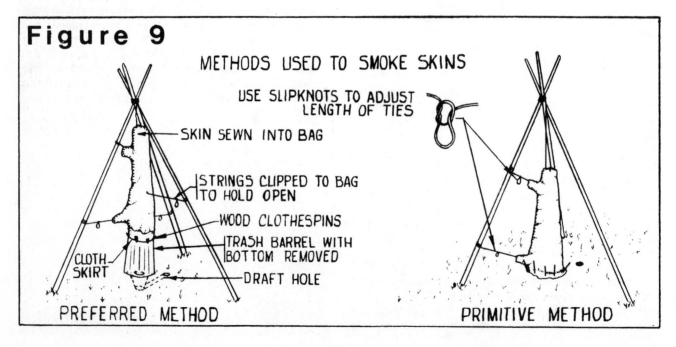

Figure 9

METHODS USED TO SMOKE SKINS

USE SLIPKNOTS TO ADJUST LENGTH OF TIES

SKIN SEWN INTO BAG

STRINGS CLIPPED TO BAG TO HOLD OPEN

WOOD CLOTHESPINS

TRASH BARREL WITH BOTTOM REMOVED

CLOTH SKIRT

DRAFT HOLE

PREFERRED METHOD

PRIMITIVE METHOD

Skin being prepared for smoking, using the author's preferred method - a cloth "skirt" sewn to the open end of the buckskin bag, and a steel garbage can with the bottom removed. This method helps prevent the skin from scorching and permits the skin's edges to be more evenly smoked.

Guy Cowden (left) and the author (right) pegging a skin to the ground for smoking. While this method is very effective, it must be closely watched to prevent the skin from scorching.

108

Before and after smoking, skins should be buffed on each side using a braided rope to give both sides a more consistent texture.

sew or staple a cloth "skirt" (from an old bedsheet, pillowcase or towel) that is about one or two feet in length to the bottom edge of the skin. This "skirt" enables you to smoke the entire edge of the skin irrespective of how uneven it may be. In addition, it further raises the skin above the heat source, and prevents the edge of the buckskin from touching the hot steel can.

I always suspend my skin from the tripod, using the same rope that is used to tie the tripod together. I tie or pin (using a large safety pin) the neck of the skin to the rope. This enables me to adjust the height of the skin, so that the cloth skirt just slips over the rim of the can where I clothespin it in place. (Always use *wooden* clothespins as the plastic ones tend to warp.)

I use small twigs that I push through the seams in the bag to hold it open. This enables the smoke to reach all of the bag's surfaces. In addition, I tie three pieces of string with alligator-clip electrical connectors on their ends to each of the tripod poles. These are clipped to the skin wherever needed to help hold the bag open. Both the clips and the sticks must be moved periodically to prevent tiny unsmoked spots from forming where the object is touching the skin.

If there are any unrepaired holes in the bag, plug them with a clean, white rag or a piece of toilet paper. As the smoking progresses, you can check the color of the skin by pulling out these plugs and looking at the color of them.

I always build my coal producing fire with seasoned hickory or oak, although any wood that produces a long lasting bed of coals is fine. When I have several inches of hot coals in the pit, and the skin in place but suspended safely to the side, I drop several handfuls of smoking material on the hot coals, and quickly position the skin on the barrel.

Lift the "skirt" occasionally and place your hand in the smoke; you should be able to hold your hand in it indefinitely without getting burnt. If it feels uncomfortably hot to your hand, it is also too hot for the buckskin. Cover your draft hole, add more smoking material to the coals, and feel the smoke again. The objective is to produce thick, billowy smoke that is cool enough that it will not burn the buckskin. In addition, always listen to your fire; it should make no sounds. If you hear a crackling noise, it is an indication of heat and flames; feel the smoke, and be prepared to jerk your skin away from the fire immediately.

My favorite smoking material is rotten, slightly damp, cottonwood that crumbles in my hands. It is abundant in river bottoms, easy to collect, has a great smell, and produces a beautiful golden brown color. Rotten, damp, ponderosa pine, douglas fir, and oak are also good choices. Green willow leaves, sagebrush, and juniper are also good. The list is almost limitless since the only requirements are that it smells good, smokes profusely, and produces a nice color.

Avoid smoking skins on windy days. The wind fans your fire, making it difficult to control, and blows the skin around, causing it to smoke unevenly.

I always smoke the grain side first until it turns a dark brown and the color begins to penetrate through. I then turn the skin inside out and continue smoking until the flesh side is almost as dark as the grain side. This usually takes several hours if done with slightly damp rotten wood or green leaves. I prefer the rotten wood to be damp because the steam that is formed penetrates the skin faster, produces more smoke, and is less likely to burst into flames than dry material.

Once the skin is completely smoked, seal it in a bag overnight to set the smoke. Lightly buff both sides of the skin the following day with a rope loop, to eliminate any moisture left from smoking and to fluff it up.

BUCKSKIN CARE

After a day of normal wear in dry weather, about all that is required to clean your buckskin is a small clothes brush. If your skins get muddy, scrape or rub them clean with a rounded piece of sandstone or with your knife.

Smoked skins may be washed just as you would wool, in lukewarm (not hot) soapsuds. I usually use about one-fourth to one-third of a bar of Fels Naptha soap, homemade lye soap, or saddle soap dissolved in water. If the buckskin has been previously washed several times, I add about six tablespoons of pure Neatsfoot oil (never use Neatsfoot oil compound) or Lexol to the sudsy mixture.

After thoroughly washing and rinsing the buckskin, I squeeze or wring the water out by hand, stretch and pull the article back into its original shape, and then blot it between a couple of towels. Since the damp skin will assume the shape of any object that it is placed on, spread it out flat, turning it occasionally until it is almost dry or drape it over a smooth, round object outside where the air can circulate around it. When the article is still slightly damp, rub, shake, and pull it briskly all over. Repeat this periodically until the buckskin completely dries, or, if it is an article of clothing, put the garment on and wear it until it dries.

After many washings, your skins will become a light tan color as the smoke is washed from the hide. When this occurs, simply give them another smoke job to restore their original color or to make them match any newer garments that you have made.

If you have an electric or gas clothes dryer that can be set to blow cool air (never dry your skins in a hot clothes dryer — they'll shrink about four sizes!), smoked or unsmoked skins can effortlessly be further suppled after first working them by hand. This method works even better if you throw several blocks of wood or baseballs in with the buckskin. The tumbling action of the dryer, combined with the blocks, does a very good job of finishing your skins.

CONCLUSION

The system that I have described in this chapter may seem a bit complicated, however, in practice it is very simple. It employs techniques that have been in use for thousands of years on the North American Continent. These techniques, unlike many of the highly specialized skills that existed, were practiced by members of nearly every Native American family. This fact alone demonstrates that the average person is capable of producing good serviceable buckskin, providing he or she has the desire to do so.

There are very few feelings of pride that will outweigh the completion of your first brain-tanned skin. I have tried, I hope successfully, to provide you with a detailed description of the methods that I currently employ, so that I may share that success with you.

TRADE BEADS

BY JEFF HENGESBAUGH

JEFF WAS RAISED WITH HISTORY. The first house he remembers had been built by a surveyor sent to Ohio, then called the Western Reserve, by George Washington. All the upstairs windows were gunports, and the Indian was a legend on those "dark and bloody grounds."

He moved to Arizona in the third grade and met the real thing, two Yauqi Indian boys. Their tribe had recently been driven out of Mexico, and they camped within a drum beat of Jeff's home. Jeff received his first strand of beads from them, seeds so to speak, that would grow into years of studying, collecting, and researching trade beads. It was a natural blend of passions: fur trade history and trade beads. Somewhere along the way they became one and the same.

First published under the title of "Saigon Journals" during the Vietnam War, Jeff worked for newspapers, wrote a few screenplays, and is working on a book about his experiences in the new wild west. His last creative effort was a Mountain Man Musical entitled "WAGH!" in pre-production in Salt Lake. Because of his somewhat mobile status, he has been given the official title of "Roving Ambassador" for the American Mountain Men.

IT looked like a piece of the sky had fallen. A brilliant blue bead, about the size of a pea, lay in the sand among the creosote bushes and cactus. Heat waves danced and lizards scurried over the bottom lands of the great Salt River, an historic trade route through the deserts of the Southwest. The bead disappeared into a little boy's pocket, its alluring power still awesome, its destiny renewed.

Years would pass before I heard of fiery furnaces and sailing ships, of world conquest and cultural clashes. It was an incredible story that created my blue bead and carried it across continents and centuries until it was abandoned in the shifting sands of Arizona. And that is what this chapter is about.

Trade Bead has become a common term among people who enjoy, study, and relive frontier history of North America. The trade bead has accompanied that history every step of the way. However, more common are questions concerning the manufacturing, distribution, identification, age, and value of those beads. These questions are a few I've set out to answer.

Ed Seaton moves through camp with his wares on his arm. A time honored method for displaying and selling beads.

115

MANUFACTURING

Most trade beads are made of glass. Glass is primarily a mixture of quartz sand, soda, and lime that melts together at high temperatures. Beadmakers subjected glass to two basic methods of manufacture, the Drawn Method and the Wire Wound Method.

DRAWN METHOD

A glass maker dipped a hollow pipe into a melting pot, gathering a glob of molten glass, and blew enough air into it to create a "pear-shaped" bubble. A co-worker stuck a pipe with a small plate attached to the end of this bubble. The glass blower handed his pipe to a third worker and watched the two men run full speed in opposite directions, stretching the bubble into a tube up to 150 feet in length before it cooled. The air pocket created by the blower, though much smaller due to elongation, remained the same the entire length. The tube was cut into manageable sections, and these in turn were cut into smaller tube or cane beads.

There were a few interesting things that could happen to the "pear-shaped" bubble before it was drawn. It could be layered, inlaid, marved, and twisted to produce a wide variety of beads.

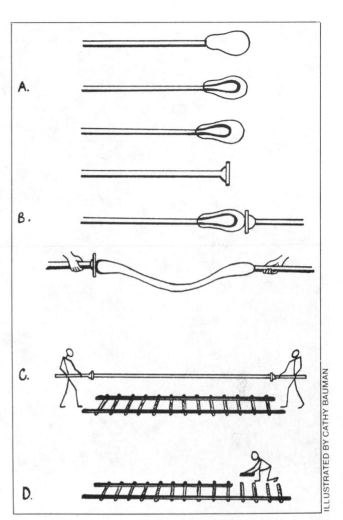

Steps in the drawn method: (A) Glassblower blows air into a "gather" of molten glass and creates a pear-shaped bubble. (B) Second worker attaches an iron plate to the bubble and begins the draw. (C) The drawn tube is laid on wood blocks to cool. (D) The tube is cut into workable lengths which will be further cut into tube and cane beads.

Cane or tube beads were the end results of the drawn method of manufacture. Used by the Egyptians and rediscovered by the Italians, it allowed the mass production of trade beads.

116

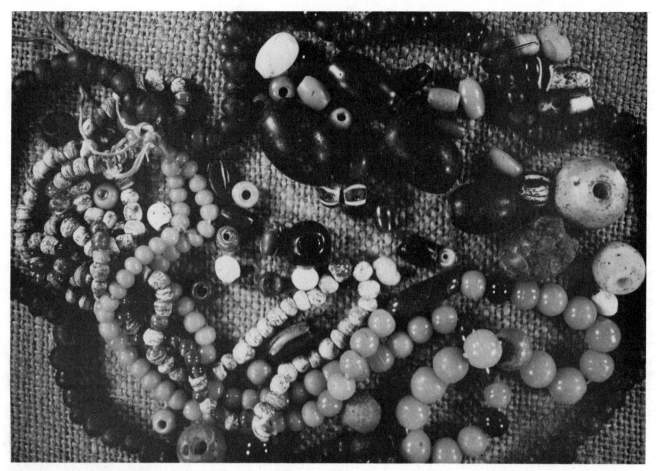

A cane bead could be rendered into an oval or rounded bead by filling their centers with a mixture of charcoal and clay, then reheating in a furnace.

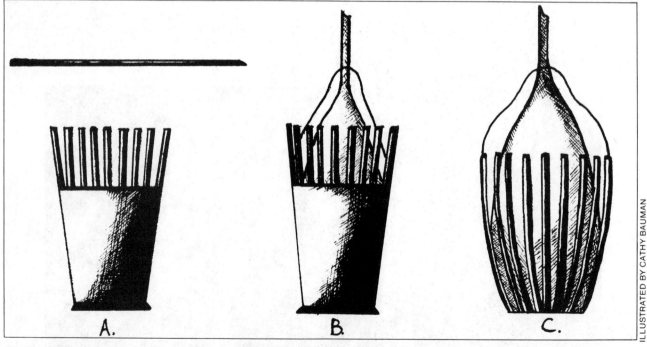

Steps in "inlaying" using the drawn method: (A) Solid glass rods are arranged around the inside of a bucket. (B) A pear-shaped bubble on the end of the glassblower's rod is inserted in the bucket. The bubble is then expanded with more air. (C) Bubble is withdrawn from the bucket with the rods infused in its surface. It is now reheated, then drawn. The results are striped tube or cane beads.

117

LAYERING

The "pear-shaped" bubble was sometimes re-dipped into its original pot of glass to build up more material, making a thicker tube. Or it might have been dipped into any number of pots, each with a different colored glass, and each adding a new layer of color. The bubble was then drawn as before, and the end product was multi-layered tube or cane beads.

INLAYING

The "pear-shaped" bubble was placed into a bucket of solid glass rods arranged upright around the edge of the bucket. Rods could be of different colors, single or pre-twisted into ribbons. Additional air expanded the bubble until it stuck to the rods. The glass blower withdrew the bubble, hopefully with the rods attached, and reheated it enough for them to sink into the surface without the rods losing their form. Sometimes a marver was used to roll the bubble and push the rods flush. Runners drew the bubble and ended up with striped tube or cane beads.

MARVING

A marver is a flat surface of polished iron or marble, though a corrugated marver with a surface of parallel ridges and grooves was often used. The glass blower took the "pear-shaped" bubble and, using the marver and hand tools, flattened, paddled, made triangular, square, or otherwise shaped the bubble. The tube was then drawn and, due to the "memory" properties of glass, it held its shape.

In the making of the chevron (Star or Rosetta bead), the beadmaker rolled the original bubble on a corrugated marver, pressing in the "star-shaped" pattern. The "star-shaped" bubble was dipped into a glass pot of another color, and this second layer was marved for the star pattern. This process was continued until the desired number of layers had been reached. The bubble was drawn into a chevron tube and cut into chevron beads.

TWISTING

Another technique performed by the runners was a simple twisting of the tube while stretching it.

Combining all the above procedures, a single bead could be layered, striped, twisted, and triangular in shape. Thousands of beads were made from one drawn tube.

FINISHING

Tube beads could be taken a step further and rendered into oval or rounded beads, depending on the length of the tube. The beads were placed in a pear-shaped drum of beaten iron filled with a mixture of charcoal and clay or sand. The drum was then set over a furnace and rotated by a worker. The charcoal mixture packed the bead holes, preventing them from collapsing. It also kept the beads from adhering to one another as the heat softened the extremities. This mixture, combined with the friction of beads hitting one another, rounded their forms. Beads were

In the early days gold foil was added to the surface of beads. In 1827 a technique was developed whereby gold foil or other metals could be secured by the slight running of the surface of the glass over the foil.

then washed, sorted into sizes, and for a higher polish, placed into sacks of bran and shaken.

Tube beads could also be faceted. In many cases the side facets had previously been marved, but it took workers using grinders to facet the ends. It was a tedious job and dangerous. The air in grinding shops was thick with glass dust.

WIRE WOUND METHOD

In this second method of manufacturing, a beadmaker gathered molten glass on the end of a pipe but induced no air into it. The "gather" was drawn by runners, leaving a solid rod. Cut into workable lengths, the tip of a rod was heated over a flame until softened and then applied to a revolving wire or mandril. The mandril was coated with clay or chalk to prevent the glass from adhering. The rotating motion of the mandril wound a thread of molten glass until the bead assumed the desired dimensions in length and thickness.

A bead could be a simple loop of glass wrapped around a wire, or it could be layered by applying a rod of a different color to the existing core and repeating the winding process. It could also be shaped on a marver as described with the drawn beads. But the mandril wound beads were most famous for their insets and overlays all done with rods of glass and the touch of an artist's hand. Heat kept beads and decorating rods in a malleable state while dots, squiggles of contrasting colors, geometrical patterns, leaves, or vines were created.

Designs were as numerous as the individual thoughts of the craftsmen who made them. Overlays would remain on the surface of the bead while insets or inlays would be impressed to the level of the surface.

Unlike drawn beads that were sold by the pound, mandril wound beads were sold by the bunch or string. A stringer would pick up a bead on the end of a long needle and allow it to slide down to a string. A skilled worker held eight to ten needles in each hand. Full strings were hung from poles to be delivered to warehouses and waiting traders.

OTHER METHODS OF MANUFACTURE

There were other methods of manufacture. Molded, pressed, and hollow blown beads created unusual shapes and designs, but the manufacture of the milliefiori or thousand-flower bead deserves special mention. The book *BEADAZZLED* states the following:

> *The pride of the beadmakers of Murano and Venice was the milliefiori, or thousand-flower bead, originated by the Egyptians but forgotten in Roman and medieval times.*

Simple mandril wound beads such as these came in virtually every color but the most popular was blue.

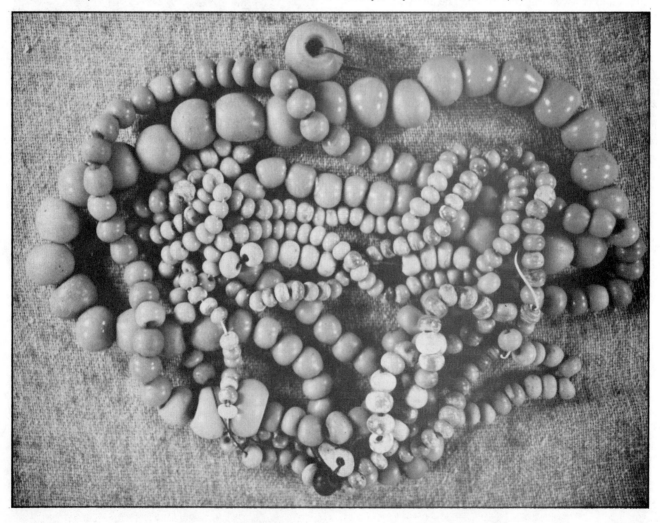

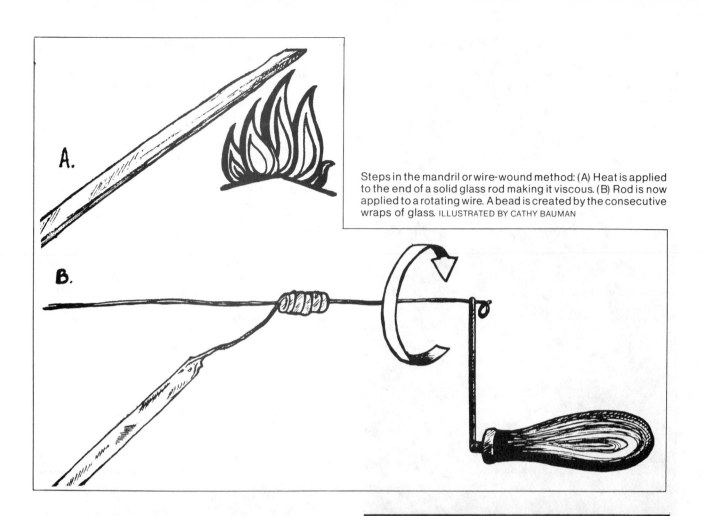

Steps in the mandril or wire-wound method: (A) Heat is applied to the end of a solid glass rod making it viscous. (B) Rod is now applied to a rotating wire. A bead is created by the consecutive wraps of glass. ILLUSTRATED BY CATHY BAUMAN

Starting with a gather of transparent glass, the worker shaped it into a cylinder and then dipped it into three or four different colors of glass. The beadmaker lowered the multilayered cylinder into a form whose inner walls were lined with canes of another color, often milky white. When the entire mass was heated in the reheating furnace, the beadmaker twisted the cylinder to make a complicated pattern. Then it was heated a final time and drawn by a runner. When this multilayered cane hardened, an assistant cut it into very thin disks, each with a cross section of the complicated color pattern of the multilayered cylinder. The master beadmaker reheated the disks and pressed them into large wire-wound beads. By making milliefiori beads in two steps — the first, making the elaborate cane that was cut into disks; the second, adding the disks to a wire-wound bead — the beadmaker produced true works of art. Flowers, honeycombs, and stars were the most popular patterns.

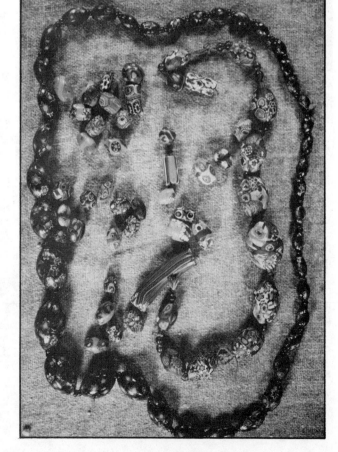

Older and scarcer millefiorie beads can be found in oval and tubular shapes. Most of them are cylinders and discs.

Venice, the bead production center, fought back. They wooed their glassmasters with wealth and status. When that failed, a series of stern "edicts" progressively tightened a dark veil of secrecy over industry and artisan alike. And, when they failed, suspected perpetrators were "eaten by the Salamander," an expression used by co-workers when a man failed to show up to work and was found knifed or strangled and floating in a local canal.

It was a futile effort. Holland, destined to become Italy's major competitor, built factories in Amsterdam and stocked them with Venetian glassworkers. A famous Dutch factory owner left Holland and set up beadworks in England. He did the same thing in Belgium. History does not mention whether he took Italian workers with him or not, but, feasibly, a Venetian might have made Dutch beads in a Belgian factory. Other countries were doing the same thing, and bead factories sprang up all over the known world. Even so, Venice had more business than it could handle. Drawn cane sections had to be sent to cheap labor markets in Bohemia, made into beads, and sent back.

Distorted by heat but still beautiful, these beads were washed out of the banks of the Columbia River. Pieces of sinew used to string the original necklaces can still be seen (with the aid of a magnifying glass) in the bead holes.

Bob Turner, a knowledgeable bead trader, wears his "Sunday best" on a stroll through camp.

OLD WORLD MANUFACTURERS

History records an Italian monopoly of trade bead production in the 13th century. It also records two events in the 14th century that would end it forever.

A Venetian glassworker rediscovered the drawn method for manufacturing beads; the Egyptians had used it. It immediately overlapped the slower process of mandril wrapping glass and allowed mass production. Simultaneously, European intelligence decided the world was not flat and started a five century race of exploring and exploiting new territories.

The demand for trade beads became immense along with the need to break the Italian stronghold on the bead industry. Super powers stole, lured, abducted and appropriated beadmakers and their secrets.

A wide selection of mandril or wire-wound beads showing designs from simple to complex.

If the pedigree of any given bead was in question, the fact that a lot of them were made was not. Beadmakers worked twelve hour shifts and furnaces made glass twenty-four hours a day. During the first decade of the 17th century, 150 furnaces were aglow on the Island of Murano. Across the water in Venice, a hundred bead-makers were mandril winding beads. The simple tools of their trade allowed them to work at home, thus the term "cottage industry." The combined effort produced a quarter million pounds of beads a year.

One tariff list of beads going to the New World described 562 different types and their countless variations. A late 19th century bead catalog stated ". . . that there are at least 5000 patterns of Venetian beads, but when it comes to stating the number of beads to be had of all kinds there are European commission houses that can easily show a collection of over 100,000, all different . . ." The numbers create a definite challenge to the individual bead collector.

NEW WORLD MANUFACTURING

The early settlers of Jamestown set up a second glass factory for the production of trade beads; the first factory was for bottles. Venetian glassworkers were imported from Murano by the London Company early in the year 1622. The workers were sent to Jamestown with a severe warning:

"The making of beads is one of Captain Morton's chief employments, which being the money you trade with the natives, we would by no means through too much abundance vilified or the Virginians at all permitted to see or understand the manufacture of them. We pray you therefore seriously consider what proportion of beads can be vented and their worth not abated."

The threat of economic over-indulgence was removed by an Indian uprising which destroyed Jamestown on March 2 of the same year.

In other reports about production, Lewis and Clark and the old west painter Catlin tell of Indians making or remaking glass beads. Cheyenne and tribes of the upper Missouri are mentioned. Somewhat confusing instructions describe the use of powdered glass from broken bottles or other beads and, in one case, the use of a bullet mold to form the bead. Other Indians used white quartz sand taken from ant hills and clay molds to make beads and animal effigies. More amazing was that this had taken place before European contact.

The only New World production of significant impact was a glass works in New Spain, in the present state of Puebla, Mexico. White, green, and blue beads and some crystal were imported to Guatemala and Peru. It would be

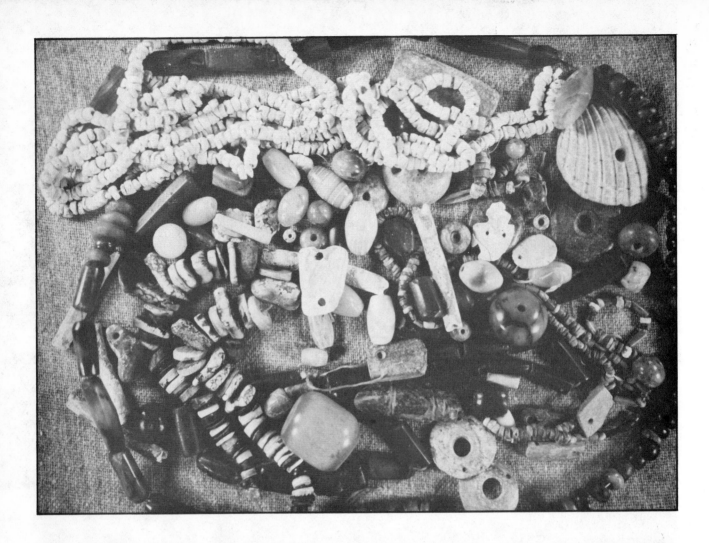

Top: Alternatives to glass beads were plentiful and used for thousands of years before their arrival. Bottom: A lot of Chevron trade beads. Most of these are simple, four layered, "tube" beads that were easy and cheap to make using the drawn method. Literally thousands of beads could be cut from one elongated tube.

Cathy Bauman and Leo Hakola reflect the look of a Southwestern mountain man and his woman. Cathy's dress is made from hand woven Taos linen. The dress is held in place by a wide tacked belt similar to those worn by Indian tribes of the Southwest. Her footwear is Kaibabs worn with tall Commanche leggings. One rebozo is tied sash-style around the hips and a large rebozo is typically worn around her shoulders. Leo wears leather pants, a white cotton shirt, a red wool vest, and a wide brim hat. His moccasins are of the style used by desert Indians of the Southwest.

2

3

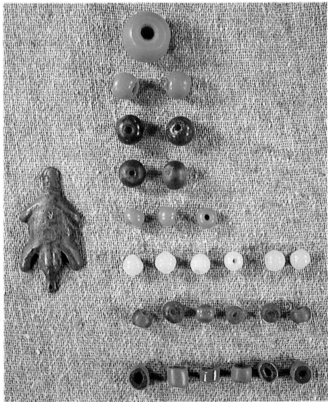

4

II

5

6

2 These early Chevron trade beads, circa 1450-1550, are the same type as those brought over with Columbus. They have seven layers, green cores or centers, and faceted ends. A rare bead by itself, a graduated strand like this is an incredible find. This necklace is owned by Ed and Blueberry Morgan.

3 Beads that convey a message like these "ghost" beads are extremely rare. The author has seen a similarly designed bead with "skull and crossbones."

4 The trade beaver represents "one made beaver" or a beaver hide that has been stretched, dried, and made ready for market. A "made beaver" became the Hudson Bay Company's standard of value for trading. The beads represent ones commonly traded in the northwest and their rate of exchange for a made beaver. See the "Trade Bead" chapter for detailed information.

5 Several different beads of unusual design and manufacture. Note the apparent file surface used on the yellow bead at the left.

6 Hundreds of thousands of melifiorie type beads like these were created through an intricate and complex manufacturing process.

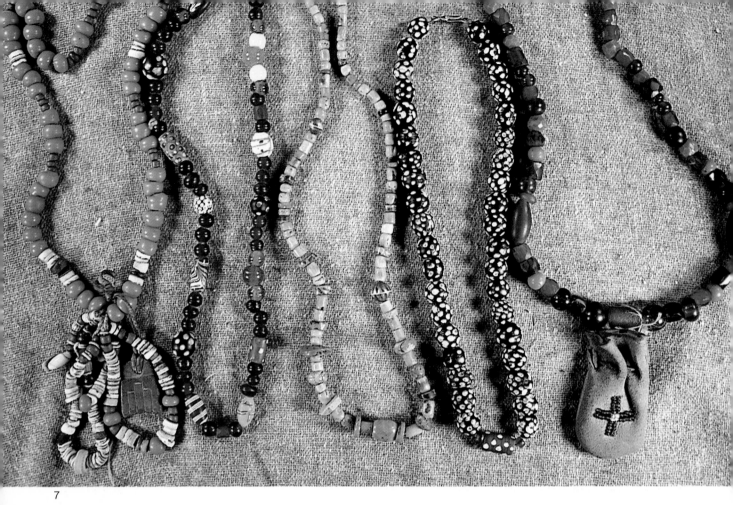

7

7 The necklace on the left is composed of beads traded in the southwest. Some are of European origin. The others, far older, were made of drilled shell by the Indians. The middle necklace is made of turquoise, shell, and other stones found in the southwest. The necklace on the right is made from beads found in the northwest.

8

8 A close-up of mandril wound beads shows designs created by the artist's touch. Each bead, unlike the drawn method, is individually made and decorated.

9 Beads known to have been traded by the Hudson Bay Company. Note the large round and cylindrical beads of two-layered, mandril wound construction. Some have white cores, others yellow. Note the bead in the middle with only the yellow core remaining.

9

IV

10   Chris Gilgun and Sandy Roosevelt dressed in colonial period clothing circa 1750 to 1760. Chris wears a white linen shirt with stock, a green wool sleeved waistcoat lined with linen, with cast pewter buttons, blue fustian (part linen, part cotton) breeches with cast pewter buttons and tie kneebands, brown cotton stockings and black leather shoes. Sandy wears a white cotton chemise, a printed cotton bodice or vest, a blue linen petticoat, a woven stripe linen apron and a low crown straw sun hat over a white mob cap.

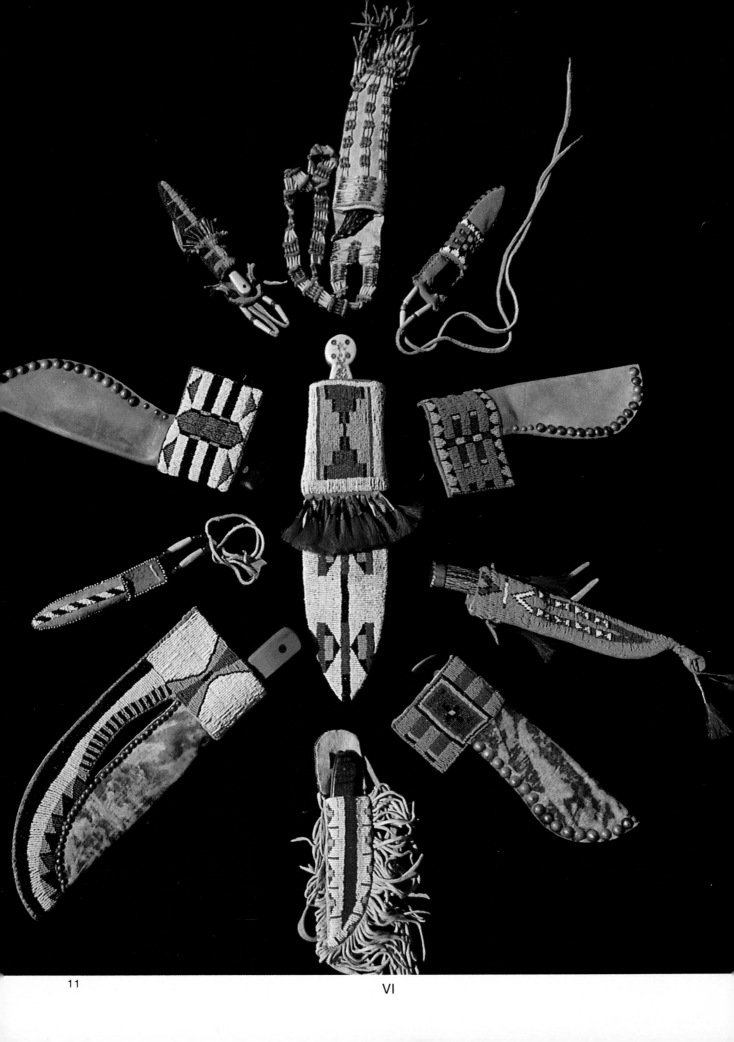

11 Clockwise from 12:00 o'clock: Northwest coast neck knife sheath of mid-1800s style; dentalium shells, old rose and greasy blue real beads with brain tanned spacers for necklace. Neck knife sheath beaded Cheyenne style with old seed beads. Old style belt sheath of rawhide with brass tacks; beaded in a Cheyenne design on brain tan which is sewn to the rawhide. Sioux belt sheath beaded with mustard yellow, red over white, dark navy blue and white; tin cones and red horsehair trim. Belt sheath of buffalo rawhide with Sioux design beadwork on brain tan. Fringed neck knife sheath of Sioux design with beaded brain tan covering over rawhide sheath. Old style rawhide and brass tack sheath with Sioux beaded design. Miniature neck knife sheath of brain tanned leather. Crow design old style rawhide and brass tack belt sheath. Small neck knife sheath. Center: Neck knife or over-the-shoulder sheath beaded in Sioux design using old colors; tin cones and red horsehair trim.

12 Charles Lamoreaux models a Northwest coast red and navy blue beaded trade wool shirt. The shirt is lined with calico and trimmed in yellow satin ribbon with white beaded edging. The style is of the Klukwan Frog Clan House from the 1870s.

13 Alton Safford wearing a brain tanned Mandan war shirt beaded with sky blue, white and red pony beads. The fringed shirt is trimmed with hair locks.

14 Kathryn McKibben dressed in a Northern Plains brain tanned beaded and quilled dress. The horse is finely outfitted in Crow style beaded trappings.

13

14

12

VII

15 Otter bow and quiver case with Crow/Nez Perce style beadwork made from beaver hides, red trade wool and old beads. 15

16 Tom and Gina Connin display the outfits of a French **Courier du Bois** (circa 1750) and an eastern Indian woman. Tom wears a white linen shirt, brown wool sleeved weskit, linen breeches with Indian leggings, finger woven sash, finger woven and quilled shot pouch and strap, and trade silver. The gun is a Kit Ravenshear French Fusil. Gina wears a blue wool (Ojibway) strap dress, wool leggings, necklace of wampum and fresh water pearls, finger woven sash, and her hair is wrapped with eel skin. The otter bag is beaded and trimmed with hawk bells.

17   Reproduction of an Assiniboin shirt, circa 1830. Rosette is made with natural dyed quills. (Made by Lance Grabowski and Blue Laslow)

18   Detail of original Arikara shirt showing multi-quill embroidered strips. (Collection of Denver Art Museum)

19   Central Plains pipebag and leggings from the 1830s period. (Made by Medicine Mountain Trading Co.)

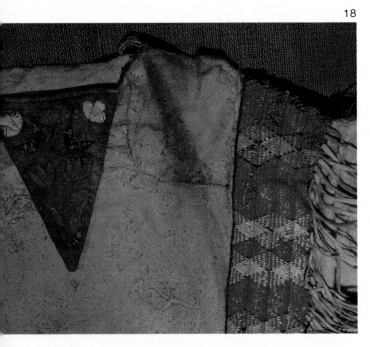

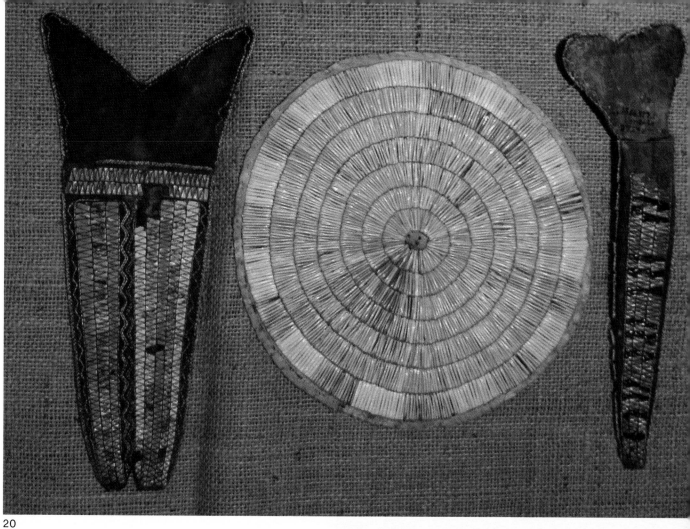

20

20 Left: Cree knife sheath, circa pre-1840. Quilled on black buckskin. Center: Blackfoot rosette, circa pre-1840. Right: Cree knife sheath, circa 1790. (Collection of Denver Art Museum)

21 Upper Missouri moccasins and porcupine tail hairbrush of the 1830s period. (Made by Medicine Mountain Trading Co.)

21

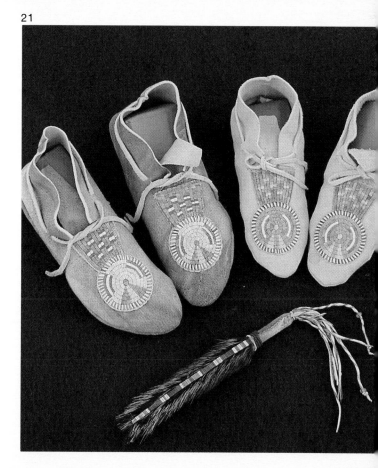

22   Stan Dolega and Kathryn McKibben show the trappings of a western mountain man and a Northern Plains Indian woman. Stan is clothed in a blanket coat, quilled buckskin leggings, breechclout, and Plains style moccasins. He's wearing a knife with beaded sheath, a quilled belt pouch, and is holding a Harper's Ferry rifle. Kathryn is outfitted in a quilled dress, leggings, and moccasins. A quilled knife sheath and belt bag hang from her wide, brass tacked belt. Their accoutrements include a painted buffalo robe and rawhide box.

The Star Chevron, King of trade beads (often known as the Star, Paternoster, Rosary, Rosette or Chevron) is the most sought after example of glass-art in the world today. The method of production is a secret art, jealously guarded over the centuries by the Venetian glass-makers. Each bead is hand made, and composed of 4, 5, or 6 individual layers of colored lead glass. When finished, the layers of glass form the characteristic 12-pointed star on each end. The color of the final and most prominent layer of glass is usually blue, and in some rare instances may be red, green, or black. Known history of the Chevron dates from the 13th century A.D..

1268- The Grand Council of Glassmakers decreed that the glass furnaces located on the banks of the Rialto river should be destroyed because of a mounting fire hazard. The furnaces were relocated on Murano, an island a short distance from Venice, part of the Venetian Republic. It was here that the first known production of Chevron beads began.

1300-1600- The Venetian glass industry flourished. Venice became the undisputed glassmaking capital of the world, and the Venetians were proud of their trade bead industry, particularly the Star Chevron. The years 1580 to 1700 were the Golden Age of Venetian glass, and during this period most of the trade beads were exported to Africa to be used as barter during exploration and colonization.

1613- A family of well known Venetian Master-glassmakers smuggled equipment into Amsterdam, Holland, and began producing large quantities of Chevron beads for export by The Dutch East Indies Company.

1673- The Senate of the Republic of Venice, enraged by the defection of several glassmakers to Holland and France, issued an uncompromising declaration:

"If any workman or artist transports his art into a foreign country to the detriment of the Republic, he shall be sent an order to return; if he does not obey, his nearest relatives shall be imprisoned, so as to reduce him to obedience by his interest in them; if he returns, the past will be pardoned and an establishment in Venice will be procured for him; and if, in spite of the imprisonment of his relatives, he is still determined to live abroad, an emissary will be charged to kill him, and after his death his relatives will be set at liberty."

1797- The collapse of the Venetian Republic.
1866- The Organization of Glassmakers was dissolved in Venice, and the glassmaking industry came to a virtual standstill.
1890- A revival of interest in the Chevron bead prompted renewed production, and world-wide acceptance lasting into the 20th Century.
                                                    - A.R. Conyers

This fact sheet about Chevrons was put out in 1971 by a private collector doing his own research. Continuing research has uncovered how the bead was made.

fairly safe to assume a few were delivered to southwest North America and beyond.

ARRIVAL OF BEADS IN NORTH AMERICA

History by its nature is obscure. Trade bead history suffers further. Craft secrecy, still in existence today, and the general illiteracy of the times provide serious barriers to knowledge.

Made with distinct characteristics, in changing styles, and in countless numbers, a trade bead can do its own talking. Found predominantly in graves at documented gravesites, beads are excavated with other artifacts that can be precisely dated.

The earliest traces of archeological evidence in America, (circa 1400s and before), point to trade with unknown sailors. Found in Indian burials are parts of ships — rigging metal and brass fittings. Found also are beads and earrings worn by sailors as talismen against misfortune. This exchange was honest barter for needed items. Primed with rumors from wayfaring sailors of vast unexplored continents, Europeans sailed west with serious intent and cargo holds full of trade beads.

The Spanish record the first exchange of beads with Columbus' debut on San Salvadore Island in 1492. These excellent seamen and hardy adventurers would sail north to the Gulf of St. Lawrence, and with a look at the snow covered reaches of land exclaim, *"CAPO DE NADA!"* (Cape Nothing!), and head for warmer waters.

In their wake came Dutch, French, and British settlements. To these coastal, colonial ports came Indians, powerful eastern tribes who, acting as middlemen, scoured the interior, trapping, buying, and murdering for fur. A lot of this fur was traded for beads.

Westward expansion turned these seaports into trailheads inland where, by foot, horse, and canoe, traders established posts among the Indians. Hudson Bay Company spread across Canada. Russia went down the Northwest coast and into California. The French followed the Mississippi to New Orleans. The United States went up the Missouri and across the Plains. Spanish conquistadors and padres traveled from the Florida Keys to California, through the Southwest, and north into Colorado, Utah, and Wyoming. Trade beads went the distance, smoothing the way, bribing Indians for their loyalty, food, lodging, and for a wealth of fur.

PHOTO BY PAUL DRAKE

Walt Sigfried wears a fine collection of Chevron trade beads at rendezvous.

Jean Senkow shows the old time way of displaying twenty feet of blue, faceted beads.

An opportunity to understand possible bead lamination of any given geographical area came as a result of Captain Cook's report of a Russian windfall of sea otter pelts off the coast of Alaska. In a mere forty year span (1780s-1820s) hundreds of ships from England, France, Spain, and a newly independent United States ranged up and down the Alaskan coast bartering for fur. And they bartered with beads.

Indians were not idle either. Alligator teeth were found in a cave in Arizona, parrot feathers in New Mexico, monkey mummies in Texas, and Northwest coast dentillian shells in Missouri. Remains of claws, stone beads, pearls, and bone give evidence of trade routes long established before canvas sails loomed on the horizon. Now trade beads moved through this ancient system as Indian traded with Indian, reshuffling the beads across America.

Century after century for 500 years trade beads poured into this country. Finally, in 1915, on the plains of northern Arizona, John Hubbell dispensed a European trade bead, made in Czechoslovakia and Venice to imitate turquoise, to use in trade with the Navaho Indians. The Hubbell trade bead was the last known bead specifically made to barter with Indians, thus closing a chapter in history.

COLOR AND VALUE

Coloring agents were added to the basic ingredients of glass. Cobalt, for instance, turned glass blue, various copper salts turned it green, tin turned glass milky white, and gold made it red. The simple act of adding a pinch of cobalt in a melting pot in Venice had far ranging effects on the misty shores of the Columbia River where Lewis and Clark bartered for badly needed supplies from Indians reluctant to trade for anything but blue beads.

Beyond the cost of transporting trade goods in and fur

125

pelts out of inaccessible places, the values set by traders on trade beads were in direct proportion to the preferences set by Indians. Size and decoration were important, but color appears to have been the deciding factor.

Records for rate of exchange for beads are rare. Prices for beaver and trade goods rose and fell like prices at the corner gas station. It is known the Hudson Bay Company's standard of value was "one made beaver." A "made beaver" is a skin that has been stretched, dried, and made ready for a shipment to the tannery.

Only fragments exist today of the old HBC trading complex. Found in the records of Ft. McPherson in the Canadian Northwest were the following values for a few glass beads:

Cornaline d' Aleppo or Hudson Bay beads, green or white centers, six/1 MB.

Pea sized transparent green and opaque yellow beads, six/1 MB.

Pea sized light blue beads, three/1 MB.

A bit larger amber, transparent blue, and opaque blue beads, two/1 MB.

One large blue bead of opaque blue glass, one/2 MB.

They were expensive beads, especially when the price of beaver rose to six and eight dollars a pelt. A penny was a penny in those days.

If any color held prestige among the Indians, it was the blue. As in the case with Lewis and Clark, southwestern Indians also wanted blue beads and blue beads only. The Pima and Papago Indians today treasure necklaces of blue beads given to their ancestors by the Spanish. Crow Indians would trade a horse for a handful of blue beads. A famous wife of a Seminole chief wore 200 or more strands of blue beads about her neck.

There are always exceptions to the rule. The Neutrals, a tribe of Canadian Indians (pre 1650) took color preference into their own hands. They had been in contact with the French and from them received the large "star" chevron bead. The royal blue exterior of most

Rumored to have preceded the "seed" bead into the Rocky Mountains, pony beads, somewhat larger in size, were put in casks and transported by horse.

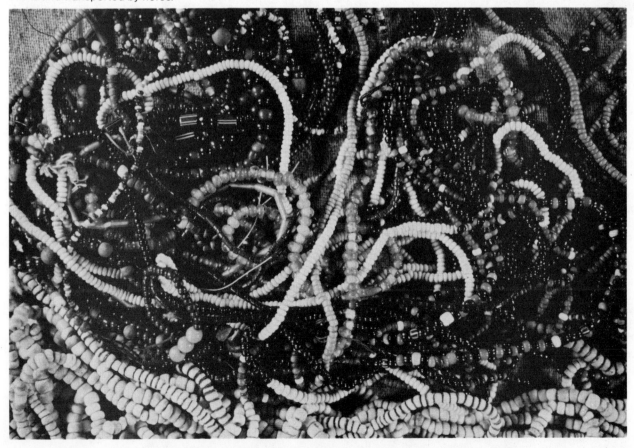

Bear claws, lion teeth, elk ivory, and leather provided the Indian with plenty of color and texture.

chevrons is held in esteem by many. For the Neutrals it clashed with a system of values in which red ochre and the red catlinite pipe were sacred. They carefully ground the offending layers against sandstone until they exposed one of brick red. The Neutrals were destroyed by the Iroquois in fierce trade battles to get fur to the coastal ports I described earlier.

Archeologists uncovered another insight of the value placed on beads by Indians. Working through gravesites of Seneca, Delaware, and Shawnee, they discovered that beads popular in the 1630s to 1690s were showing up in graves of the 1700 to 1750 period. On a hunch they went back to graves of the earlier sites and found that 25% to 90% of them had been looted but only for beads and wampum. Evidence was clear that as availability of beads declined, Indians were opening the graves of their grandfathers.

WAMPUM

Wampum, a pre-Columbian bead produced in America, caused a rare reversal of European influence over the Indians. The Indian accepted glass trade beads and more or less fit them into their system of value. Wampum, the shell bead of the Indian, became the European system of value, literally.

The Indians made beads by shaping and drilling fragments of shell. Cylindrical in shape, averaging a fourth inch in length and an eighth inch in diameter, they were made in two colors, white and purple. The quahog, or hard shell clam, furnished materials for both colors; the conch shell could only provide the white. Difficult and tedious to make, these beads were extremely valuable to the Indian.

This native state of production and value was soon obliterated by enterprising Dutch and English. Needing fur from the Indians and suffering a "coin money" shortage in the colonies, they made wampum a recognized medium of exchange. As the demand grew for wampum, metal tools were provided to upgrade primitive production. The colonists eventually set up their own factories. Wampum became so established that court judgments were made payable in shell money, and Harvard college accepted wampum for tuition. The Campbell brothers of New Jersey operated a wampum factory employing up to 100 people and produced 100,000 beads a year. They closed shop in 1905 after 170 years of business.

The Indians used wampum as personal adornment. When strung in a particular order as to color or woven into patterns in a multi-strand belt, it was used to convey inter-tribal messages or to record an event. Wampum was taken from the Algonquin word *wampumpeak,* meaning string of white beads.

THE AFRICAN CONNECTION

Almost as long as beads have been made and trade routes established, they have been taken to Africa and exchanged for gold, ivory, and precious stones. Beads from India, Mesopotamia, and Egypt lay among ruins 1000 years before Venice and Amsterdam made Africa a dumping ground for their wares.

Archaeologists have shed new light on European glass manufacturing and world commerce, discovering a "syncronization" between their finds and beads found in North and South America, Asia, and India. Apparently, similar beads arrived at similar times around the world, giving the common trade bead a "trans-world" status.

The English explorer Sir Richard Burton (1852), was heavily involved in the African trade. He comments, "Learn the prices of all beads before entering a strange village . . . a highly prized bead for one tribe may be worthless in another." There were also political problems in paying tribute to local chieftains: "Better this slight spending than chance a flight of arrows during the night."

He explains and complains about the amount and weight of beads the expeditions had to carry. Long bags of beads were slung between poles and most men carried an additional fifty pound bag on their shoulders. They could travel inland as far as half the beads would take them. The remainder was necessary for a safe return. There is an advantage to today's traveler's checks.

Africans have always loved beads as symbols of status and wealth. And they loved the old ones. Legends that beads grew in the ground were created because of the

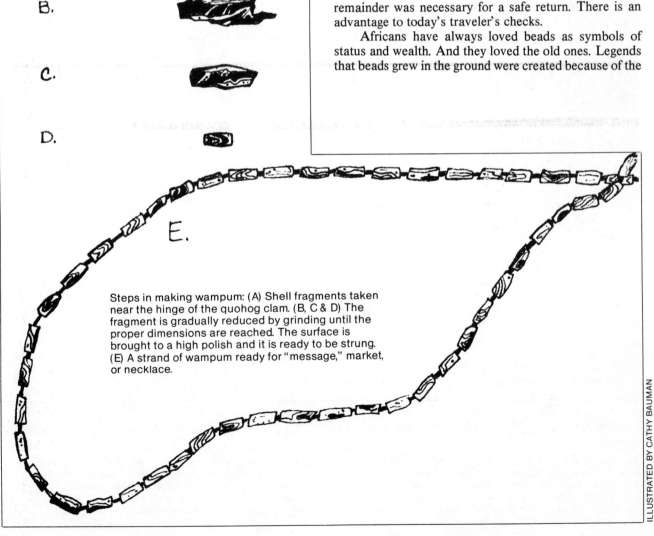

Steps in making wampum: (A) Shell fragments taken near the hinge of the quohog clam. (B, C & D) The fragment is gradually reduced by grinding until the proper dimensions are reached. The surface is brought to a high polish and it is ready to be strung. (E) A strand of wampum ready for "message," market, or necklace.

ILLUSTRATED BY CATHY BAUMAN

number of beads dug up around ruins. Africans also once believed beads carried the spirit or personality of their former owner. Reluctant to part with them, ancestors handed down beads through generations. The durability of beads and their cultural longevity have kept European trade beads above ground.

The massive influx of beads to the United States from Africa in the 1960s and 1970s should leave no question that the greater part of the beads available today came from Africa. Imports continue but they are mere shadows of the number of beads found and imported in the glory days a couple of decades ago. Africans have historically made beads; they still do. Interestingly, they do it in the same manner as the American Indian, with powdered glass and clay molds.

IDENTIFICATION

There have always been names for beads. "Pound" beads were so named because they were sold by the pound. "Pony" beads were brought in by horseback. "Russian blues" were blue and thought to have been traded by the Russians. "Cornaline d' Allepo" were named for the area in which they were made. "Cane" or "tube" beads looked their names.

Most names are insignificant, meaningful only to a handful of dealers and collectors. They are little help to the uninitiated and useless beyond regional influences. It is better to describe a manufacturing process and physical characteristics of shape, size, color, translucency, and opacity for identification purposes. For instance, a typical "Russian blue" bead offers the following information:

> Translucent royal blue, barrel shaped, of simple construction made from a hollow cane which is hexagonal in cross section. Hand cut facets on each end, leaving central facets around the bead.

Length, diameter, and size of hole aperture can be given if further description is necessary. Although this type of analysis may take longer, to do so removes a lot of responsibility from the Russians who may not have traded it.

I use colloquial bead names in this chapter; I'll continue to do so in life. They are comfortable and easier than the clinical descriptions. But if I want to make sense in describing a bead, I'll do it the hard way.

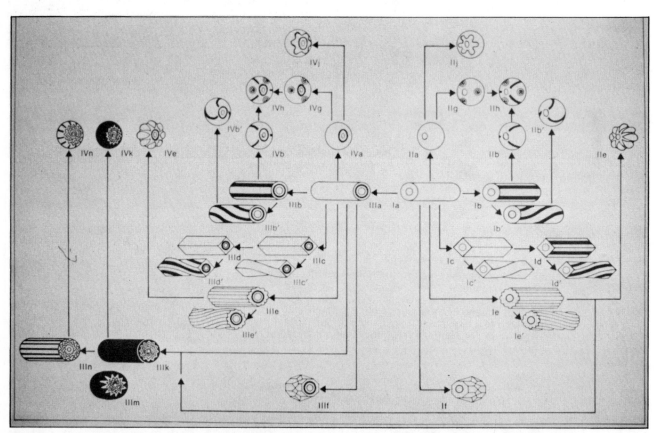

This cane bead chart proposed by Kenneth and Martha Ann Kidd offers classification and nomenclature which will permit exact descriptions and a reference base for all beads found in archaeological excavations. Starting with the **two tubes** in the middle of the chart, 1 aa, a "cane" bead and 1 1 1a, a layered "cane" bead, it is easy to see how all the beads are derived from the two basic forms. That is after they have been subjected to marving, layering, inlaying, reheating, faceting, and so forth. To best appreciate the Kidds' efforts, a complete description of their work can be found in the booklet, *Canadian Historical Sites,* included in the bibliography.

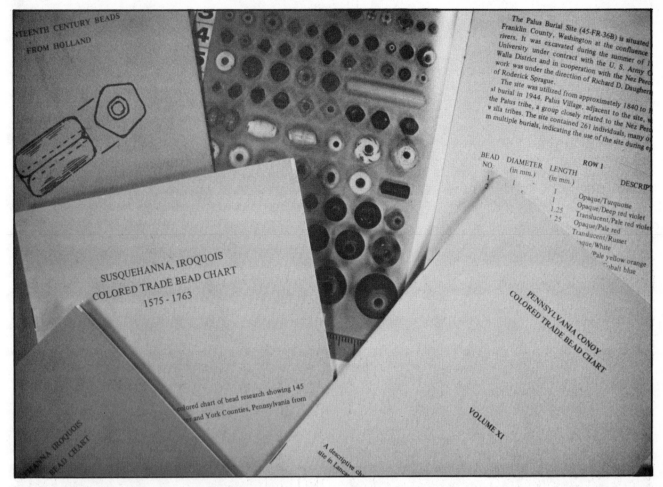

A collection of booklets by G. B. Fenstermaker. They provide archaelogical documentation of a selected geographical area and time period where trade beads were found.

DETERMINING THE AGE OF THE BEAD

All old beads have patina. It is best described as a film that forms on a surface, a mellowing with age. How it gets that way varies. The surface of glass reflects its use. Worn next to the skin, glass picks up oils and polishes to a high sheen. Glass also scratches. Over a period of time or under severe abuse, a surface becomes chipped and frosted. Glass resists damage because of its temper or hardness. Like metal, this property is acquired in the original heat treatment. (I just dropped, by accident, a 300 year old bead from table to concrete floor. It bounced like a marble.) Oxidation and leaching chemicals in the soil where a bead may have lain for years take a toll on appearances. Fragile or weak beads are usually removed from circulation because of their original condition.

Old glass differs from new glass. Regardless of the manufacturing process, the mixture of ingredients — sand, soda, and lime— of *any* batch of glass was dependent upon the discretion of the glass master. Variations are inherent when following recipes. They were also inherent in ingredients that were *rarely* chemically pure and this in-cluded the "coloring" minerals. Old beads show a soft rainbow of colors that yield to harsh, strident colors with the quality control standards of the 19th and 20th centuries.

When glass is "drawn" or "stretched," glass fibers are arranged side by side. Air bubbles, when present, are drawn into long thin shapes like the fibers. Mandril wound glass shows fibers in a helical fashion around the circumference of the bead. Bubbles were globular or oval, never elongated. Oftentimes glassmakers tried to remove these marks, so a look into the core with a magnifying glass may reveal tell-tale signs of manufacture. Other interesting things to look for are "marver" and "mold" marks and indications of other methods of construction. Machines are consistent in the manufacturing process; humans are not. Slight design and structural variations will be evident with older, handmade beads.

130

FINDING BEADS

There are far more beads under the ground than above, but that business is best left to the archaeologist. By happenstance, some beads will be found. A man I met used 16th century trade beads for gravel in a fish tank. They had been showing up in his sluice box while sifting for gold. Another person brought up handfuls of beads with a dredge on the Columbia River.

These stories are few and far between. Even the river bottom where I found blue beads as a boy has been destroyed by a sand and gravel company. Millions of trade beads have been brought into this country over the last three decades. Though they have been slow to resurface, they will do so through swapmeets, garage sales, and antique sales. The best bet for buckskinners are rendezvous. Perhaps the largest concentration of beads available are bought by traders, collectors, and people just interested in beads.

The next best thing to finding beads is finding information about them. Visit museums and reconstructed historic sites and look at the beads. Oftentimes a curator will allow a viewing of what is not on display. Ferret out books and pamphlets on beads. A bibliography usually provides leads to additional information.

G. B. Fenstermaker's archaeological research booklets, Van der Sleen's *A Handbook on Beads*, and *Arizona Highways'* article on trade beads are classics. Bead clubs and societies dedicated to finding information about all beads are showing up across the country. If there is not one in your area, start one.

TODAY'S VALUES

Any old bead is a valuable bead, a hardy survivor, a link to the past. Once again, they have been assigned values. Beads are still selected for shape, size, and color. The popular color, as with the Indians of old, is still blue.

A real find at rendezvous. Women sift through dirt laced with old beads.

Favorites are beads that are easily recognizable and available enough to create a market.

Prices are subject to supply and demand. Regardless of the temporary supply, supplies are always diminishing. Unlike precious metals, diamonds, or turquoise, beads are not renewable. Demand continues to grow, making trade beads a good investment. A rare strand of beads can still be purchased for less than an average gold chain (on sale) or a turquoise bracelet.

There are discerning collectors who are after the rare bead or a select strand of beads, but it helps to have a theme in any collecting. Record any information that comes with a bead.

Circa 1880s to 1920s, this unique piece of Chinese advertising was sent to America to promote their art glass. The same ad could literally have been used in 750 A.D. with their first recorded export of glass although the date was probably much earlier. As to the question of China's bead involvement in the American fur trade, it would be hard to believe otherwise. Most American beaver went to Moscow in the 17th century, and from there to unidentified Oriental markets. Indians loved beads and the Chinese had them. There is even some thought that the Chinese provided the Russians with cobalt blue, faceted cane beads used for barter on the northwest coast.

A Heaty Word To The Purchasers !— The imitations of Jade bracelet, bead, etc. are manufactured by Kwong Yick Co. of Canton, Kwongtung. They are one of the most famous industrial products in Kwongtung and the ones manufactured by Kwong Yick Co. are especially superior in quality. Our imitations are the most fashionable and are of any descriptions you like, In purchasing of these imitations of jade articles please adopt the Kwong Yick Co's branp.

KWONG YICK CO.
MAN KING LWE ST.
CANTON, CHINA.

A trapper and his "medicine" necklace.

Bead traders at rendezvous offer an extensive selection of beads. They can also offer a good deal of information to those interested. Collectively, traders have become a focal point in stimulating imports. They purchase in quantity, setting comparative and competitive values. The overall effect is a great bead at a good price. Determine if a bead is old, then determine what it is worth to you.

USES

Careful research has uncovered many ways Indians utilized trade beads. Even though the historic role of the bead has changed for the contemporary buckskinner, its use has not. A few documented ideas are listed below.

SPECIAL SECTION!

Turn to pages II, III and IV of the special color photo section for more on trade beads.

133

Indians placed strands of beads around a horse's neck. Men wore long strands of beads across their bodies from shoulders to hips. Large beads were worn on the tops of moccasins to signify rank. Beads were inlaid in rifle stocks, warclubs, and knives. They decorated pipes and sacred medicine pieces. Beads hung on strings from ears and nose. Hair was tied back, and the knot was decorated with beads. Beads were woven in bands and worn around the head like a crown. Long strands of beads, fifteen and twenty feet, were worn in wraps around the neck. Chains of beads were fastened to both hips and arranged in front in a slant over thighs or breech cloth. They were put on dolls and baskets and used to decorate clothing. Beads were hung from quivers and trigger guards. They were worn around arms, legs, and wrists. Beads were placed in medicine bundles and worn as magic around the neck. They were used as a medium of exchange and they were used to decorate the neck and chest.

A few words on necklaces. There are no rules. Everything and anything has been strung around the neck. There were tendencies toward symmetry, graduation, and texture; some things blend together better than others. A bright bead can be muted by a duller one. Color and shape of beads create contrasts. Beads were strung on leather, sinew, copper or brass wire, cotton and wool twine, twisted grass, bark, and cloth such as calico or part of a blanket.

CONCLUSION

If there was one item that kept pace with the frontier experience, it would be the trade bead. It fits every time period buckskinners express today. They are useable artifacts that bring us closer to the realities of a past we seek and enjoy. Glancing over a trade blanket filled with beads or seeing clothing or a necklace that displays old beads provides one with a visual experience lost long ago.

I once stopped an Indian going into a trading post with a jar of old beads he had found on his property. He glanced at me, then at the jar, and with a smile exclaimed, "Maybe we do better the second time around."

WORKS CONSULTED

Eridson, Joan Mowat. The Universal Bead. New York: Norton and Company, Inc., 1969.

Fenstermaker, G. B., and Alice T. Williams. The Chinese Bead. Lancaster, Penn: Fenstermaker Archaeological Research, 1979.

Filstrap, Chris, and Janie Filstrap. Beadazzled, The Story of Beads. New York: Fredrick Warne and Co., 1982.

Francis, Peter, Jr. The Story of Venetian Beads. Lake Placid, New York: Lapis Route Books, 1979.

Grand Rapids Public Museum Publication Number 3, Beads: Their Use by Upper Great Lakes Indians. Grand Rapids, Mich., 1977.

Kenyon, W. A. "Some Bones of Contention, The Neutral Indian Burial Site at Grimsby." Rotunda, 10 (Fall 1977), 4-13.

Kidd, Kenneth E., and Martha Ann Kidd. "A Classification System for Glass Beads for the Use of Field Archeaologist." Canadian Historic Sites: Occasional Papers in Archaeology and History, No. 1. Ottawa: 1970.

Liu, Robert K. "Early 20th Century Bead Catalogs." The Bead Journal, 2 (Fall 1975), 31-32.

Mille, Polly. "An Historical Explanation of Alaskan Trade Beads." The Bead Journal, 2 (Fall 1975), 20-25.

Orchard, William C. Beads and Beadwork of the American Indians. Museum of the American Indian, Heye Foundation, 1975.

Sorrenson. "Glass Indian Trade Beads." Arizona Highways, (July 1971), 10-37.

Van Der Sleen, W.G.W. A Handbook on Beads. York, Penn: George Shumway Publisher, 1967.

Whitthoff, John. "Archaeology as a Key to the Colonial Fur Trade." Aspects of the Fur Trade: Selected Papers of the 1965 North American Fur Trade Conference. St. Paul: Minnesota Historical Society, 1967.

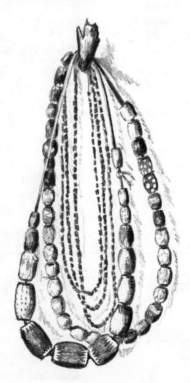

18TH & 19TH CENTURY COOKING

BY KARALEE TEARNEY

KARALEE TEARNEY ORIGINALLY PLANNED to be an art teacher, but when she met Pat Tearney 15 years ago, her life changed. She became a wife, a mother, and her husband's associate. In many ways though, she has become a teacher of history through the garments and accessories she makes and sells.

Karalee had been interested in history for a long time before she met Pat, but he introduced her to a history she was not aware of. Instead of just studying it from books or art works, they actually relived it by reproducing the clothing used 100, 200, and 250 years ago.

While she was a student at the School of the Art Institute of Chicago, Karalee studied the art works of George Caleb Bingham. Little did she realize that 15 years later she would be a resident of Bingham's hometown, Arrow Rock, Missouri. She lives among the buildings he painted 150 years ago on the cliffs of the Missouri River.

The Tearneys moved to Arrow Rock in the fall of 1983 because they felt it was the right place for what they wanted to do. That is, operate their mail order business in a small community and open a recreation of an 1840 merchantile (Joseph Huston Store which opened in May 1984) in a historic town.

Pat passed away on July 19, 1984 at their home in Arrow Rock. Karalee is still operating the store and the mail order business (La Pelleterie with the help of friends. La Pelleterie specializes in custom made garments and accessories of the 18th and 19th centuries.

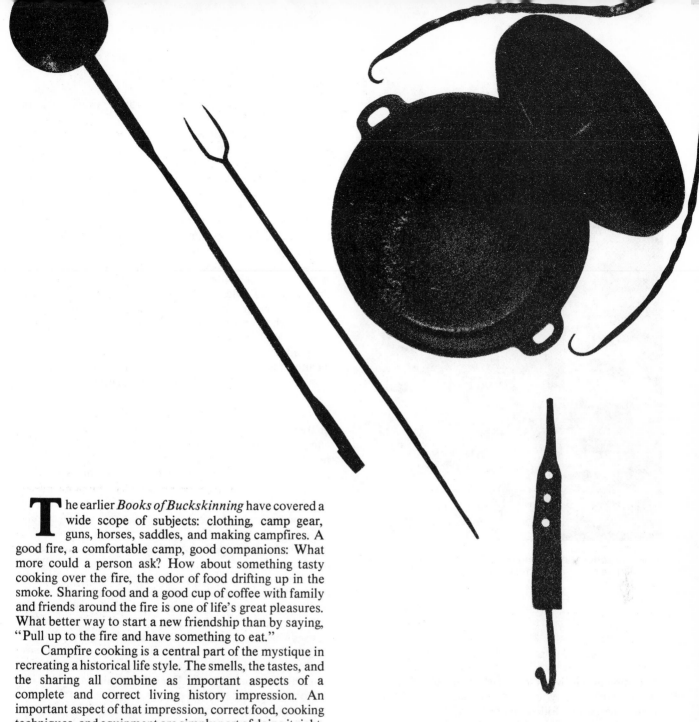

The earlier *Books of Buckskinning* have covered a wide scope of subjects: clothing, camp gear, guns, horses, saddles, and making campfires. A good fire, a comfortable camp, good companions: What more could a person ask? How about something tasty cooking over the fire, the odor of food drifting up in the smoke. Sharing food and a good cup of coffee with family and friends around the fire is one of life's great pleasures. What better way to start a new friendship than by saying, "Pull up to the fire and have something to eat."

Campfire cooking is a central part of the mystique in recreating a historical life style. The smells, the tastes, and the sharing all combine as important aspects of a complete and correct living history impression. An important aspect of that impression, correct food, cooking techniques, and equipment are simply part of doing it right. After spending time, money, and a good deal of personal effort on making your lodge, its furnishings, and your buckskins as correct as possible, doesn't it seem a waste to plop an aluminum sauce pan full of canned ravioli on the fire? A Rogers' Ranger in complete and authentic attire eating a cold cut sandwich on soggy Wonderbread just doesn't look right. Authentic cooking takes a little more effort — but those who take up our hobby are the kind who will make that effort (and it really does taste a lot better).

Cooking period foods well, and with the right techniques and equipment, is challenging. To do it right requires research and practice. It's a rewarding craft. It rounds out your historical impression, allows you to share knowledge with your friends, and it plain tastes good. It can be as simple or as complex as you wish — a basic stew or a full meal. You can practice at home, trying new recipes

136

Cooking period foods using authentic utensils is a great way to enhance your buckskinning image.

or combinations. Most mistakes are still edible, and if not, Rover will love you. The recipes, suggestions, and techniques which follow are ones which we've tried and enjoyed over the years. You will probably want to adjust the spices to suit your palate and may need to adapt some techniques (especially baking) to your region. Historical food and camp cooking can relate to any time period or place, and it can match any living history impression. So, pull up to the fire and let's get cooking.

Before we begin to talk about cooking, food and food preparation is a matter of personal taste. The recipes which follow are spiced and seasoned to my taste and you may wish to change them to suit yourself. Be sure to read through the recipe fully before you start. That way you can list the necessary ingredients.

Make sure you have everything before you begin so that you have some idea how long it will take to cook. Fifteen minutes before a bunch of hungry folks arrive is no time to find out that your baked beans will be ready in fifteen hours. If possible, practice the recipe at home before you spring it on unsuspecting palates in camp. An "at home try out" will allow you to adjust seasonings and practice techniques. Better to make any mistakes in private.

It's very popular to use the rather sweeping term "Early American" in describing everything from architecture to furniture. However, there is really no such thing as "Early American Cooking." Both food and cooking styles were influenced by your ethnic background, the region of the country in which you lived, and to a great extent by what you did for a living. The Eastern farmer, the long hunter, the Taos trader, and the mountain man all had differences in their diet (as well as similarities) which can be reflected in buckskinner cooking. A home place or settled camp provided an entirely different cooking situation from that of an overnight camp or a noon trail break. A party traveling with women would generally eat better than a party of solitary bachelors. How one traveled made a major difference in cooking. A man on foot was severely limited while those with a canoe or wagon could live in luxury. While there were those who starved to death or resorted to horrible methods to survive, there were also wealthy fur barons who camped with linen, crystal, and fine silver every night and English lords who traveled with French chefs and string quartets.

Like making clothes or deciding what type of character you are portraying you should also decide what camp type and what kind of foods you need to match your personna. This is especially true if you find yourself in a position to be demonstrating before spectators or visitors.

Having convinced you that camp cooking should be an important part of your overall skills rather than simply being fed, let's take a look at some historical examples. We are going to begin on the Eastern seaboard and, as did the frontier, move west.

Eastern seacoast cities had a wide variety of places one could eat outside the homes. There were street vendors offering "fast foods" (i.e. fruits, pies and cookies, meat pastries, cooked meat, bread, and beer). There were coffee houses where a gentlemen could stop for a cup of coffee and the latest in business or political news, while a lady might repair to a tea shop for a more genteel beverage and some not so genteel gossip. For a full meal, you could visit an "ordinary," where for a price you could share the owner's ordinary meal (hence the name) and even secure overnight lodgings. Those with more money would choose a tavern or inn where a choice of dishes and beverage would be available as well as sleeping rooms. Some taverns became so well known for setting a good table that they stopped letting rooms and became restaurants. Such establishments as the Queenshead in New York or the Green Dragon in Boston served extensive meals. A traveler, in 1746, wrote of a breakfast of "hashed and fricassed meats and venison pie and a choice of coffee, tea, chocolate, cider, beer and punch to drink." In 1780, General Washington listed a meal, at an unnamed inn, which was "composed of eight or ten main dishes, some of butcher's meat, some of poultry, accompanied by several kinds of vegetables followed by a second course of pastry all of which fell under two headings, puddings and pies." After spending two hours on this brief repast, the assembled officers broke out brandy, fruit, and walnuts. Of course, such dining out was expensive: In 1774 John

Adams ate a meal including "turtle and every other thing — flummery, jellies, sweetmeats of 20 sorts; trifles, whipped syllabubs, floating islands, fools, etc." and was outraged at the cost of almost nine shillings hard money — better than a week's wages for a common laborer.

Most city folks cooked at home — the wealthy had servants to do it — but bought their raw materials at shops or from street peddlers. By 1780 New York had butcher shops, fish houses, crab, turtle, and eel shops, bread bakeries, pastry and pie shops, an ice cream shop, coffee and tea sellers, brewers, green grocers, and fruit sellers. Farmers and street vendors went door to door with milk, butter, cheese, water (if you didn't like the city wells), and fresh fruits. Wharfside shops sold such rare imports as oranges, lemons, limes, coconuts, and pineapples. This last was so expensive it was often rented for use as a decoration rather then eaten. Space in cities was hard to come by. A small herb garden was all most people could afford.

Some cities became famous for certain types of food and these dishes can often be part of camp cooking. Boston, famous as the land of the bean and the cod, gave its name to **Boston Baked Beans.** This is an all time classic which bears little resemblance to the canned product. Dried beans keep well and have long been a mainstay of cooking. The small white pea bean we call a navy bean got its name because it was a big part of naval rations in the 18th century. The bean hole cooking was much used by

BOSTON BAKED BEANS

2 pounds White Pea (Navy) Beans
¾ pounds Salt Pork
1 tablespoon Salt
½ cup Maple Sugar (or syrup)

Soak the beans overnight in a pot covered by twice their volume of water. In the morning change the water (drain and add new). Add the salt, bring to a boil, then simmer until tender. (While beans are simmering, dig bean hole two to three feet deep and eighteen to twenty-four inches across and get a good hardwood fire going. Let it burn down to a good bed of coals.) Slice the salt pork, put in bean pot with beans. Add maple sugar, put on tight lid, and put into hole. Heap on more coals and cover the hole with dirt. Cook eight to ten hours. If you like, you can add one-half teaspoon dry mustard, some chopped onion, or an onion studded with cloves. If you dare to add catsup, the ghosts of one hundred Puritans will haunt your camp. If you are making this one at home, set your oven at 250°F for eight to ten hours.

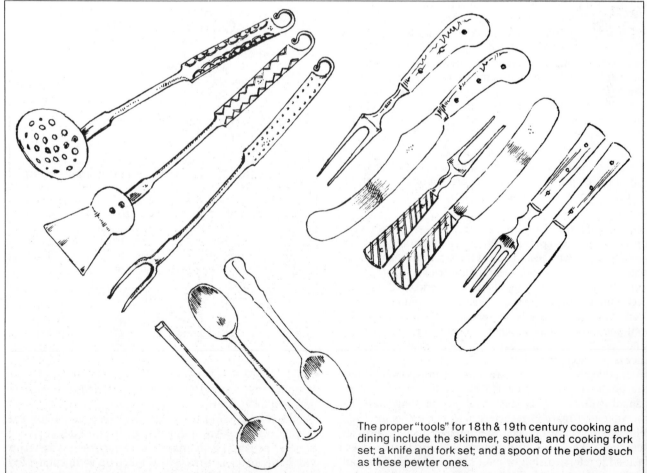

The proper "tools" for 18th & 19th century cooking and dining include the skimmer, spatula, and cooking fork set; a knife and fork set; and a spoon of the period such as these pewter ones.

DRAWING BY STEVE RAYNER

138

New England Puritans for whom Sunday cooking (and much else) was a sin and was to be avoided. The beans were originally made with maple sugar, a trick learned from the local Indians. As New Englanders began to import large quantities of molasses however, maple sugar gave way to blackstrap molasses. My recipe calls for maple sugar — if you wish to substitute molasses cut the amount by one half since molasses is twice as sweet and potent as maple sugar. A good beanpot is essential. It should be of sound stoneware to take the heat of the coals, round with a small neck, and have a tight lid. Several old cook books suggest sealing the lid with a flour and water dough to ensure the beans don't lose any juice.

Boston salt cod became both a major industry and a staple. Practically indestructible, salt cod was traded worldwide from the Mediteranean to the Caribbean where it was traded for molasses (which the New England Puritans made into rum), and to Africa where it was a major currency in the slave trade. Salt codfish can still be purchased at Italian food shops. After soaking overnight (change the water at least once), it can be pan fried with sliced onions for breakfast.

Philadelphia, the Quaker City, also made a famous contribution to American cooking and one which serves well in camp. **Pepper Pot Soup** reflects an early English willingness to use organs and innards. It was by legend, invented by a cook at Valley Forge who was able to forage several hundred pounds of tripe and some pepper corns from a local patriot. It was said to be so "belly comforting" that Washington's troops were able to brave the weather and win at Trenton and Princeton. The pepper used in the soup was an expensive item in the 18th century, but within the next thirty years, bold Yankee sailors had sailed to Ceylon and made the United States the world's pepper seller. Whole pepper corns, just as they were imported, are the best for camp use. The common man probably didn't own a pepper grinder, but put the corns into a small wood or tin cup and cracked them as much as possible. This gives a much fresher flavor than pre-ground pepper and a small poke of peppercorns is much easier to carry.

Philadelphia scrapple is another Quaker favorite and is made by boiling down a hog's head into a meat filled jelly. Pickled pig's feet were a favorite noon meal among Quaker farmers and lard cracklins were a children's treat.

Outside the Eastern seacoast cities, many New England Yankees combined farming and seafaring to earn a living. As fishermen and sailors they came to count on the ocean's bounty at mealtime. Clambakes and oyster stew were common from Maine to Long Island, with lobster becoming so commonplace it was considered poor folks' food. Yankee cooks adapted an old French soup into a well-known down east specialty — **chowder**. There are all kinds of chowders: clam, oyster, fish, lobster, corn, and cheese, just to name a few. It's as much a stew as a soup, often added to when there are more mouths to feed. Mrs. Murphy's chowder contained everything including red flannel drawers, or at least so says the song, and the chowder and marching society was the center of civic fellowship. Many old chowder recipes include broken "cracker." This isn't a reference to our modern cracker. Instead it refers to ship or pilot's crackers: what we call hardtack. You can still buy hardtack in hiking and

PHILADELPHIA PEPPER POT SOUP

3 pounds Honeycomb Tripe (ask your butcher)
1 Veal Knuckle (beef will work too)
2 chopped Onions
1 stalk Celery, chopped
2 Leeks, sliced
4 Potatoes, diced
Parsley
Thyme
1 tablespoon Salt
1 tablespoon fresh Ground Black Pepper
2 chopped dried Red Chilis
⅓ cup Flour
⅓ cup Butter

Wash the tripe, boil in salted water for twenty minutes, cut into small squares. Simmer veal, onions, celery, leeks, thyme, and parsley in four quarts water for two hours. Remove knuckle, cut meat off and chop. Return meat to pot along with tripe, salt, pepper and chilis. Simmer one and one-half hours covered. Add potatoes and cook another twenty minutes. Blend flour and butter into a paste, add a little hot broth from the kettle, mix and use to thicken soup. Serve with bread to sop up broth. My recipe makes a spicy soup; if your palate is more delicate, cut the chilis and black pepper in half. If you are using cracked peppercorns instead of ground pepper, use a little more.

CORN CHOWDER

⅓ pound Salt Pork, cubed
1 large Onion, sliced
4 Potatoes, sliced
2 cups Water
1 cup Milk
2 cups Corn, cut from the cob
1 teaspoon Salt

Fry up salt pork in bottom of iron pot until crisp. Add onion and cook until onion is golden brown. Add potatoes and water, cook until potatoes are tender. Add milk, corn, and salt. Simmer over low heat — do not boil — for ten to fifteen minutes. Season with fresh pepper and serve. You may wish to soak some crumbled hardtack, say six, in the milk and add to the chowder. Fish, clams, or scallops can also be added for a meaty dish.

mountaineering stores and it can be carried in a possible sack and lasts forever.

Hardtack is dry and crunchy; not even sailors eat them for gravy. According to legend, a Yankee sailor invented a new type of bread — not because he was fed up with hardtack, but because he was fed up with, but not fed well by, his wife. This unknown sailor, on being served

A nice cooking setup with everything handy. A meal is being prepared with fowls on the spit and bread baking in Dutch ovens.

ANADAMA BREAD

3 cups All Purpose Flour, sifted
1½ cups Yellow Corn Meal
2 packages Dry Active Yeast
5 tablespoons Butter
⅔ cup Molasses
1 tablespoon Salt
2 cups Hot Water

Combine the flour, cornmeal, dry yeast, and salt—mix well. Combine hot water, butter, and molasses. Beat mixture into flour for two hundred strokes with wood spoon. Place dough on a floured board, knead for ten to fifteen minutes. Place in buttered bowl, turn once to coat top, and let rise in a warm place (set it near the fire and turn bowl occasionally) until double in bulk. The rise should take one and one-half hours. Punch down, divide into thirds. Let rise again. Bake loaves separately in greased loaf pans or in Dutch Oven for forty-five to fifty-five minutes. When done, it is a deep brown and sounds sort of hollow when you tap it. Use 375°F in a home oven. Round loaves work best in a Dutch Oven.

PUMPKIN PIE

Crust
1 cup All Purpose Flour, sifted
Scant teaspoon Salt
½ cup Lard
¼ cup Cold Water

Filling
1 cup fresh Pumpkin Pulp
1½ cups Milk
1 cup Brown Sugar
      or
⅔ cup Molasses
2 Eggs
½ teaspoon Cinnamon
½ teaspoon Cloves
½ teaspoon Nutmeg

Crust: Sift flour and salt together, add lard and cut into flour with a fork until mixture is in pieces the size of small peas. Add water, drops at a time, until dough will form ball. Roll out and fit into pie pan, crimping edge.

Filling: Mix all filling ingredients together, mix well until smooth slurry results. Pour in pie shell and bake. It is done when a knife inserted into the center comes out clean.

If you are using a Dutch Oven, you can fit the crust directly to the oven. If you are doing it that way, raise the Dutch Oven up a little more than usual from the coals. An easier way (and a lot easier to clean up) is to put an ovenproof crockery pie pan inside the Dutch Oven. In this case, put more coals than usual under the oven since you must heat both metal and pottery.

cornmeal mush for the umpteenth time, mixed his mush with some flour and molasses, said "Anna damn her," and stuffed the results in the oven. **Anadama Bread** is typical of many early breads in that it combined expensive wheat flour with common, cheap, cornmeal. Many recipes use the term Indian, or Injun, to refer to cornmeal and items whose principal ingredient is cornmeal are listed as Indian dishes. Corn was the most important of the many food items to which the English colonists were introduced by the Indians. Corn became *the* principle crop. It was used as bread, vegetable, dessert, beverage, and animal food. Its dried kernels were used as checkers, its cobs as fuel in the smokehouse, and for other uses in other outbuildings. Kernels even could be popped as a snack or breakfast (popped corn and milk).

Corn was not the only food the colonists adopted. Almost equally important was the pumpkin. The pompion, as the pumpkin was first called, was eaten in puddings and custards, in soups and stews, cut crosswise into rings and dried, and even ground into a flour and used in baking. The best known use of pumpkin was in **Pumpkin Pie.**

The English loved pies and made many types: fruit, custard, meat, and game. Baking was done in ovens built

into the fireplace, but the same recipes can be used for baking in a Dutch oven or tin kitchen in camp. Baking in Dutch ovens requires care and practice, but once mastered, it is a skill which will allow you to turn out bread, biscuits, pies, and cakes. The ideal Dutch oven has three long legs which allow you to set the oven on uneven ground, and keep the bottom of the oven away from direct contact with the coals. It has a flat lid with a tall rim to hold coals. Place some coals beneath the oven and a greater number on the lid to insure even heating. Too much heat underneath will cause the bottom of your baked item to burn by the time the top is done. A friend of ours, Nancy Ann Selch (who is the best Dutch oven baker I know) puts bricks or flat rocks under her oven legs to give it more clearance and she then doesn't have to worry about a damp ground to draw her heat while cooking. Dutch oven cooking is a matter of trial and error. Different woods give off individual degrees of heat and the same recipe will bake differently on different days. Check often and don't get discouraged.

Not all the Northeastern farmers were of English descent. Many early settlers of New York and Eastern Pennsylvania were of Dutch or German origin. They made a number of distinctive contributions to American cooking, all of which can fit into camp cooking. Pennsylvania Dutch (who are really Palantine German) are often called Sauerkraut Yankees because of their fondness for cabbage, especially pickled. Few farms in the 18th century were without their kraut keg. Kraut is a good camp food as it keeps well and can be eaten either hot with salt pork, ham, or game, or cold with chicken or turkey. Try mixing it with green onions, vinegar, sugar, some dill and caraway seed for one of the few legitimate salads of the

CRULLERS

4 Eggs
⅔ cup Brown Sugar
3½ cups All Purpose Flour, sifted
⅓ cup Melted Butter
½ cake Yeast
2 tablespoons Warm Water
½ teaspoon Salt
⅓ cup Milk

Stir warm water and yeast in bowl, add sugar, mix and let stand ten minutes. Stir in eggs, milk, melted butter, and then flour. Stir well, set aside to rise (about one and one-half hours) until double in bulk. Heat a kettle of hot lard. Roll out the dough one-half inch thick, cut into one inch by two inch strips, give them a twist, and drop 'em into the hot lard. Do not overcrowd. When brown on one side, flip and brown on the other. Drain on a cloth. You can sprinkle these with a little sugar and cinnamon for an extra treat.

You can substitute honey for the sugar in this (or any baking recipe in equal proportion, but you need to lower the liquid to offset the honey's natural moisture).

The hole in the middle was said to have been invented in 1847, in Maine, by a boy who felt his mother's Crullers were never cooked in the middle.

DUTCH CABBAGE

1 large head of Red Cabbage
6 tablespoons Bacon Fat (save it from
    breakfast)
1 cup Red Wine
2 Apples, cored and diced — not peeled
2 tablespoons Brown Sugar
¼ cup Vinegar

Shred the cabbage and soak in salt water for ten minutes. Drain well. Melt fat in a Dutch Oven, add cabbage, and toss with a wooden spoon. When wilted, add wine and salt and pepper to taste. Simmer five minutes, add apples, brown sugar, and vinegar. Mix, cover and simmer about forty-five minutes — until cabbage and apple are tender. This goes well with pork, chicken, or turkey, but is truly superb with Canadian goose. This is tart and really satisfies the veggie craving I get after a couple of days in camp.

BRUNSWICK STEW

3 cups Chicken Broth
1 - 6 pound Chicken, cut into pieces
2 or 3 Squirrels, cut into pieces
2 large Onions, sliced
2 cups Okra, cut
2 cups Lima Beans
4 medium Potatoes, diced
4 cups Corn, cut from cob
3 stalks Celery, diced
1 head Cabbage, quartered and sliced
6 tablespoons Bacon Fat
1 teaspoon Rosemary
1 teaspoon Thyme
1 Bay Leaf
¾ cup Maderia
Flour
Salt and Pepper to taste
1 teaspoon Gumbo Filé

Mix flour, salt, pepper, thyme — flour chicken and squirrel parts well. Melt bacon fat in spyder, brown squirrel and chicken well, and put in cast iron stew pot. Put sliced onions in spyder, cook until golden, add to stew pot. Put some chicken broth in the spyder, bring to a boil, rinse scrapings into stew pot. Add all remaining ingredients, except gumbo filé, and add two quarts of water. Simmer stew for three to four hours. Stir in gumbo filé and simmer gently — DO NOT BOIL — for twenty minutes. It can be served at once, but many Southerners say it is better reheated the next day. Any other game can also be added, cut up and browned as with the chicken.

This is a stew in which you may add tomatoes and still be authentic. American blacks were using tomatoes late in the 1700s and by the 1820s they were commonly used in Southern cooking. So, if you like, add three cups of fresh tomatoes with the other vegetables.

period. Red cabbage, which as a head lasts a long while, makes a great side dish called **Dutch Cabbage.**

Pennsylvania Dutch and Yankees were both well-known for their love of fried pastries. The Germans called them **Crullers**; the English called them doughnuts, cannonballs, and sinkers; and the mountain men called them bear sign. They are easy to make and if you can make bear sign you'll be welcome in any camp. A good cup of hot tea and a couple of fresh doughnuts is a fine way to begin a day or to end one.

The Southern seaboard presented a much different picture than that of the North. There was broad contrast between the wealthy plantation owners and the smaller farmers who often had to scratch to get by. The plantation houses were the scenes of traditional Southern hospitality. made more noticeable since there were few inns in the region. Planters took pride in their ability to set a lavish table. One traveler noted his midday meal consisted of beef, veal, mutton, venison, turkeys, geese, (both wild and tame), fowl (boiled and roasted) pies, puddings, and assorted desserts. He then noted that supper was quite as copious. This was a simple family meal we must assume. Another planter served (all on silver mind you) "the finest Virginia ham and saddle of mutton, turkey, then canvasback duck, beef, oysters . . . Then comes the sparkling champagne. After that the dessert, plum pudding, tarts, ice cream (this was in the 1770s), peaches preserved in brandy . . . Then the table is cleared and on come the figs, almonds, and raisins and the richest Madeira, the best Port and the softest Malmwey wine." All the beverages were served in silver goblets.

Of course, plantation meals weren't always so extreme. The Southern heat made light meals necessary and simple foods were served for race picnics, elections, and hunt meetings. Whenever Southern hunters gathered. a perrennial favorite was **Brunswick Stew.** At least four states claim the honor of being the birthplace of this famous dish. It's a true hunter's meal, containing a mixture of game (probably originally dictated by the previous day's bag) and chicken — in case game was scarce. There is a wide range of recipes. One of the few common ingredients to all recipes is okra. Okra seeds came to America from Africa on the slave ships. Black cooks introduced okra, and the slow cooking techniques needed to prepare it. The slaves referred to okra in their native dialect as "gumbo" and the word came to mean a thick, slow cooked stew. Slave cooks also used a Southeastern Indian idea, powdered sassafras leaves, to thicken stews and make okra more palatable. Thus gumbo plus sassafras became gumbo filé.

Southern cooks also developed a wide variety of breads. One of them, a fine textured wheat bread was named after its creator **Sally Lunn.** Breads made with expensive wheat flours were eaten by the wealthy, but most folks ate some form of corn bread. One popular recipe was **Spoon Bread** which was a special bread for fancy company.

Corn was not the only grain raised in the South. Much of the Deep South had an abundant rice crop. Rice is an inexpensive, easily grown crop which can be used in a variety of ways. Southern cooks used rice in breads, as a main dish, and in desserts. A very common main dish was **Hoppin' John**; a combination of rice, peas and pork. This was a traditional New Year's Day meal, said to bring good luck and happiness to the home in which it was served. The rice used in the eighteenth and early nineteenth centuries was what we today call *brown rice*. Whole and unprocessed rice is a splendid camp food because it is easy to carry and cook. It's very useful in case of unexpected guests: a couple of handfuls of rice and some extra water will stretch a soup or stew to feed another mouth or two. Rice also works well to thicken a stew if you want a more solid meal. Rice sprinkled with sugar and cinnamon was an inexpensive dessert.

A much more elegant Southern dessert, although more difficult, is **Pecan Pie**. This pie is rather tricky to make in a Dutch oven, but is truly worth the effort.

Of course, a Dutch oven is not the only way to bake in camp. A very handy device, and a very correct one is the tin kitchen. This reflector type oven, in a half cylindrical shape came into use in the 1750s and was used by many who did not have an oven built into the fireplace. Our tin kitchen, a copy of a 1770s type, was built by John May, a

SALLY LUNN

1 cup Milk
½ cup Shortening
4 cups All Purpose Flour, sifted
½ cup Sugar
2 teaspoons salt
1 package Dry Yeast
3 Eggs

Heat milk, shortening, and one-fourth cup water until very warm — do not boil. In bowl, mix one and one-third cups flour, sugar, salt, and dry yeast. Add warm liquids and beat well with wooden spoon. Add two-thirds cup of flour and eggs, beat well, then mix in remaining flour. Cover dough and let rise until double in bulk (about one and one-half hours). Beat down and pour into pan — cover and allow to increase in bulk by one-half. Bake for forty-five minutes to an hour. Test for doneness using a thin straw. Thrust in center, if straw comes out dry, the bread is done.

This recipe is usually done in a bundt or ring style pan. If you have a ring pan that fits in your Dutch Oven, try it, if not — just bake in a Dutch Oven. Home oven temperature is 350°F.

SPOON BREAD

1½ cups Water
2 cups Milk
1½ cups Cornmeal
1 teaspoon Salt
2 teaspoons Sugar
2 tablespoons Butter
5 Eggs
1 tablespoon Baking Powder

Mix milk and water, heat to simmer. DO NOT BOIL. Add cornmeal, salt, sugar, and butter. Stir over heat until thick (about five minutes), then remove from heat. Beat eggs and baking powder with a whisk until eggs are fluffy, then mix in cornmeal. Pour into greased Dutch Oven, bake forty-five minutes to an hour.

Prior to the 1830s when baking powder became available, pearl ash was used. Pearl ash, a refined wood ash, is available from drug stores if you want to try it out.

HOPPIN' JOHN

2½ pounds Salt Pork, cut into ½" cubes
2 tablespoons Flour
½ pint Milk
2½ cups Dried Black-Eyed Peas
2½ cups Brown Rice
2 Dried Red Peppers

Pour boiling water over salt pork, drain, repeat (this removes excess salty taste). Fry two pounds salt pork in skillet, remove and reserve. Cook remaining one-half pound salt pork in three quarts water for one hour. Bring water to boil, add peas, remove from heat for one hour. Return to heat, add red peppers, and cook for thirty minutes. Add rice and cook until tender. While rice is cooking, reheat fat from frying in skillet, add flour and brown. Add milk and stir until gravy is thick. Add fried pork. Drain rice and peas, serve with gravy. Some cooks fried two chopped onions with the pork.

PECAN PIE

1 unbaked Pie Shell (same as Pumpkin Pie)
2 cups Pecans, use small pieces
2 Eggs
1 cup Light Molasses
½ cup Brown Sugar
2 tablespoons Rum
Salt, pinch
¾ cup Butter

Fill shell with nutmeats. Beat eggs in bowl, stir in molasses, sugar, rum, and salt. Pour in pie shell, cut butter into slices, and top filling. Bake in Dutch Oven for forty-five minutes. Keep checking this one, the top burns easily. Cut into small pieces, this is a rich pie.

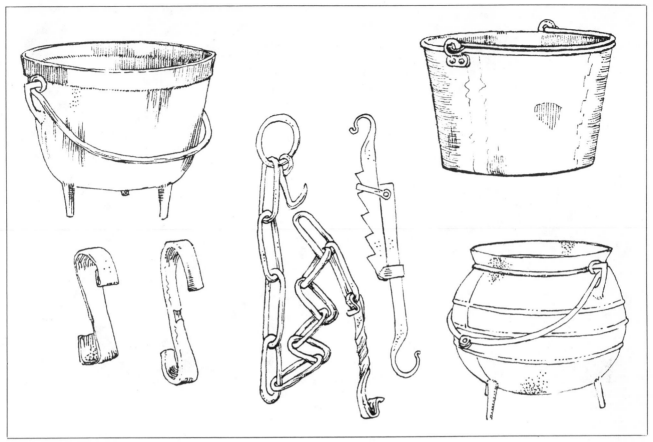

Cooking pots and the means to hang them over a fire. Clockwise from top left: A cast iron Dutch oven, a copper kettle, a cast iron kettle, a ratchet trammel, an adjustable chain hanger, and a pair of S-hooks.

local tinsmith and is a useful addition to a camp outfit. It bakes, broils or roasts meats and will keep foods warm without crowding your fire irons. Most tin kitchens have, as ours does, a small door in the hood, to check the food, and a spout for draining unwanted grease. Since they were originally designed for use with a hearth, most tin kitchens have legs: this means they need to be dug in slightly to work well at an outside fire. Since a tin kitchen works with reflected rather than direct heat, it cooks a bit slower, but it does a fine job. If you are roasting beef, you can slip a pan of Yorkshire pudding under the meat and catch the drippings.

As settlers moved westward, away from comfortable settled farms and onto the uncertainty of the frontier, living conditions changed drastically. Settlers on the frontiers were usually poorer folks, hardscrabble farmers who were trying to carve homes from the wilderness. There were fewer crops, mostly corn and beans grown in slash and burn fields. The few farm animals were pigs, dooryard chickens and a milch cow or so. Fewer available foods led to simpler meals; often everything was cooked in a single pot. Virtually every meal on the frontier was accompanied by **Corn Bread**.

Corn was the mainstay of the frontier farmer. In addition to its food value, corn was the pioneer's cash crop. Unable to transport raw corn, farmers cooked the corn and distilled it into raw and fire corn liquor which was easy to

CORN BREAD

2 cups Cornmeal
1 tablespoon Molasses
2 cups Milk
Salt, pinch
½ cup White Flour
2 teaspoons Baking Powder

Mix all dry ingredients, add molasses and milk, mix well, pour into a buttered Dutch Oven, bake one-half hour. This is a real old time style cornbread, hard and dry — good for soppin' in soup beans. If you want a lighter bread, beat three eggs in with the milk and molasses, then pour in one-third cup melted butter.

144

With practice you can make pies in a Dutch oven that come out as well as ones made at home. In this case the oven was placed on bricks to get it higher above the coals which were placed under it.

ship and considerably more valuable than corn. Although much about frontier life was crude, distilling was considered a fine art, and there was much competition to produce a good product. In Kentucky, a lucky combination of corn and pure water produced an especially good liquor. The discovery that shipping the liquor in charred oak kegs which mellowed and aged the alcohol led to the world famous Kentucky Bourbon.

Corn was also used as a feed for the farmer's hogs. Pork was the principal meat of the frontier and accounted for better than half of a frontiersman's diet. A common recipe combined pork with white beans. **Soup Beans and Salt Pork** was quite different from the baked beans of the East, requiring less time to cook and no special equipment. At times, home smoked ham, or the leftover bones from a ham, were substituted for cured pork.

Game was often found on the frontier menu. Unlike the settled Eastern areas where hunting was a sport, Western settlers hunted to expand their meager food supply. Small game such as **Fried Rabbit** was popular since it could be eaten at one sitting and did not present the warm weather storage problems a large animal such as a deer or bear would. The preference was to kill the larger animals in the fall or winter when cold weather allows

SOUP BEANS AND SALT PORK

3 cups White Beans — I like Navy
1 Onion, chopped
1 Bay Leaf
½ pound Salt Pork, cut into one inch strips

Pour boiling water over salt pork, drain. Repeat. Put beans in water to cover, bring to boil. Boil for three minutes. cover and set off fire for one hour. Add onion, bay leaf, and salt pork. Simmer until beans are soft and mushy. Season with salt and pepper. Crumble cornbread on plate, ladle beans over.

FRIED RABBIT

2 Rabbits, cut into serving chunks
1 cup Flour
Salt
Pepper
Sage

Put rabbit in boiling water, simmer twenty minutes. Drain and dry. Mix flour, salt, pepper, and sage. Roll rabbit in flour, fry in hot lard. If you would like gravy, drain most of lard off after all frying is done. Save about three tablespoons. Pour in one cup of buttermilk and simmer — do not boil — scraping the bottom of the spyder.

CHICKEN WITH CORNMEAL DUMPLINGS

1 Stewing Hen, 4 to 6 pounds, cut up
Salt
Pepper
2 Carrots, sliced
2 Onions, sliced
2 cups Cornmeal
1 teaspoon Salt
2 Eggs
2 teaspoons Baking Powder
⅔ cup Milk

Put chicken in Dutch Oven, including giblets. Add carrots, onions, salt, pepper. Cover well with boiling water. Simmer for one and one-half hours or until tender. Mix meal, salt, and baking powder. Beat eggs and milk together and add to meal mixture until dough is stiff. Add more meal if needed. Remove chicken to warm in tin kitchen, drop dough by spoonfuls into boiling broth. Cover tightly and simmer for fifteen minutes.

PERSIMMON PUDDING

1½ cups Buttermilk
½ pound Butter
2 cups Fine White Cornmeal
2 Eggs
2 cups Honey
Persimmons

Press persimmons through fine colander until you have two cups of smooth pulp. Mix eggs and milk, beat well, mix in honey and melted butter. Beat for one hundred strokes. Pour into well-greased Dutch Oven. Bake until done with top even brown.

CORN CAKES

2 cups Cornmeal
1 cup Buttermilk
½ cup Lard or Animal Fat
Salt

Mix all ingredients into stiff dough. Mold by hand into cakes and cook on griddle or in fry pan. This is a fancy corn cake recipe — in hard times water was substituted for the buttermilk. Cutting back on the lard makes for a tougher cake. If you are making them up ahead to carry with you, make them tough.

COOKING IN CLAY

To cook a bird in clay, first draw bird, cut off head, claws, remove tail and wings. Coat with one inch thick clay until bird is encased. Bury in coals until clay is baked brick hard. Crack clay; feathers will adhere to clay and bird will be moist and well cooked. When I tried this recipe, it did not work perfectly. I think if the bird were plucked, it would be much better. On the other hand, it works exactly as advertised on fish, even better if you can find some wild mint to put into the body cavity.

keeping the meat for a week or so less of a problem. On special occasions, one of the chickens would be made into a dinner, sometimes using a game recipe and sometimes stewing the **Chicken with Cornmeal Dumplings.**

The wilderness supplied the means to satisfy the frontier settler's sweet tooth. Since it takes many years for fruit trees to develop, wild berries and fruits were gathered and used. Molasses and sugar had to be imported from the east. Refined sugar's high cost put it out of reach for most pioneers and even molasses was expensive enough that it was a luxury. In areas where sugar maples grew, maple sugar was used, but most folks depended on wild honey for sweetening such foods as **Persimmon Pudding.** The honey bee is not native to North America and was imported by the first colonists. Bees quickly went wild and moved beyond the settlements. Indians called them "the white man's flies" and felt that the arrival of colonies of bees meant that settlers would be coming soon. Honey is a good sweetener to use in camp. It can be carried in a stoneware crock in the camp box and adds a special flavor, especially to tea.

For those men who moved westward beyond the frontier, cooking required a much different approach. Although longhunters, traders, mountain men, and wilderness travelers may have operated in different locales, they shared a common set of problems. Cooking facilities were much different on the trail. Instead of a fireplace and hearth, food was prepared over a campfire or without any fire at all. Transportation limited the amount of equipment available, especially for those traveling afoot and with no pack horse or mule. Cooking times were much shorter and the fire tended to be smaller. The food itself was different. Staples were dried and there was little fresh food. The only fresh vegetables were those which could be gathered at a campsite or along the trail. Game was the only fresh meat available, and often a need for speed or security made hunting difficult.

For most men on the trail baking was impossible. The need for bread was met by making **Corn Cakes.** Corn cakes were called hoe cakes because field hands were said to cook them on a hoe, or ash cakes because they were often cooked directly on ashes, or Johnny Cake. The name Johnny Cake is thought to be a corruption of either journey cake, the rations for a journey, or Shawnee cake because the Shawnee taught the white men how to make them. By whatever name, they are quick, easy, and taste good.

Often people traveling light cooked without utensils. Fish or game could be **Cooked in Clay** while corn or potatoes could be roasted in the ashes. The secret to ash roasting corn is to soak the corn, husks and all, for about half an hour. While the corn is soaking, dig a hole at the fire side. Put in a number of small live coals and cover them with cooler grey ash. Place the corn on the ashes, then cover with grey ash and a layer of live coals. It takes about twenty minutes for delicious corn. The same method works on potatoes, but instead of soaking, rub them well with lard or shortening. Potatoes take a good deal longer (depending on size) than the corn to cook.

At evening camp, a meal was often set in the pot with a banked fire to slow cook all night. In the morning, a hearty breakfast of **Slow-Cooked Jerky** filled a man up for the day. A cold Johnny cake, on the move, made do for a noon meal. Travelers used salt pork for overnite cooking if they had it. If not, beaver tail makes a fine substitute. To prepare beaver tail, hold over the fire with an iron fork (or a green stick) until the skin begins to char and blister. At this stage it is easy to skin and the fatty tissue inside is wonderful for cooking with peas, beans, or rice. Don't try to char and skin a beaver tail indoors—a friend of ours almost lost his happy home after doing that. UGH!

On the trail, sweets were limited to dried fruits and maple sugar unless the path led through a berry patch. Dried apples, pears, apricots, and plums carry a lot of sugar. A handful in a possibles bag will last a long while and keep your energy up.

Different national backgrounds brought new foods and cooking styles into the American diet. The frontier was a melting pot, with many cultures adding their part. A recipe would pass from campfire to campfire, often with a name change to fit English, until its original nationality had dissolved. A new spice or food would be spread far beyond those who originally introduced it. Camp cooking was truly international in flavor.

French Canadian voyaguers spread their cooking style all along the waterborne frontier. Some of their influences were subtle; the use of wild garlic, red wine sauces for meats and **Onion Soup** all came from canoe cooks. The voyageur is often referred to, with some contempt, as a "pork eater." This term refers to the French Canadian preference for salt pork instead of freshly taken game. Yet, when one considers the immense amount of caloric energy needed to paddle or cordelle a 34 foot freight canoe all day, the value of the richly fatty salt pork is obvious. **Habitant Pea Soup** is the best known voyageur meal and is still a favorite around the campfire.

French influence was also prevalent in the valley of the Mississippi, which was settled by the French in the early 1700s. French trappers and traders from Kaskaskia, St. Genevieve, St. Louis, and Cahokia traversed the Missouri country and traded into Santa Fe long before the mountain men. Lewis and Clark took ten Mississippi Valley boatmen on their trek and the Frenchmen did the camp chores. They took along almost two tons of salt pork, a ton and a half of flour, six hundred pounds of lard, rice, beans, and hardtack. I'm sure the Frenchmen made certain everyone ate well.

Many of the later fur brigades of St. Louis had a French or Cajun cook. A good cook is important in keeping spirits up and there could be few better morale boosters on a chilly day than a cup of hot tea and a fresh **Croquignole.** Cajun cooks also introduced some new uses of such staples as dried beans and rice. **Red Beans and Rice** was a traditional good luck dish said to help cure hangovers. We can't testify to either, but it tastes good enough to do both. This dish was often extended into an entire meal by adding frog or crayfish to it. Both are often overlooked as an easy source of camp food, yet they are easier to catch than fish and have fewer bones. A dozen boiled crayfish make a good quick meal.

SLOW-COOKED JERKY

½ pound Jerky
2 Onions, cut small
2 Carrots, cut small
4 Potatoes, cut small
3 quarts Water
3 cubes Bouillon
2 cups Barley

Break jerky into small chunks. Put all ingredients into sealed kettle. Hang low over strong, well banked fire. Simmer for seven to eight hours.
The idea of bouillon cubes is not out of character — it was called pocket soup and was recommended for travelers on land or sea. The onions, carrots, and potatoes could also be dried since both the British and American armies were using desicated (dried) vegetables by the 1830s. The troops called them "desecrated" vegetables and didn't think too highly of them.

FRENCH ONION SOUP

8 large Onions, peeled and sliced crosswise
2 pounds Beef, cut into cubes
3 cubes Bouillon
½ cup Lard
1 clove Garlic
½ teaspoon Rosemary
2 cups Red Wine
¼ cup Brown Sugar
2 quarts Water

Brown the meat in lard at the bottom of cooking pot. Add rosemary and garlic while browning. Remove meat and simmer onions in the same lard until onions are soft and transparent. Sprinkle with brown sugar and stir until onions are caramel colored. Return meat to pot, add wine and cook for two minutes. Add water and bouillon, cook for thirty to forty-five minutes. Serve with toasted bread and grated white cheese floating on top of soup. If you want to make the soup thicker, add half a cup of dried mushrooms when you add the wine.

HABITANT PEA SOUP

1½ pounds Split Peas
¾ pound Salt Pork, diced
1 Onion, with cloves in it
1 Carrot, diced
1 clove Garlic
1 Bay Leaf
1 teaspoon Thyme
½ cup Red Wine
3 quarts Water

Soak salt pork in boiling water, drain. Repeat. Brown salt pork in bottom of kettle. Add all other ingredients. Cover kettle tightly, simmer for three hours. Uncover and stir heavily with wooden spoon. Remove bay leaf and cloves.
This soup is often called Esau's pottage from the Biblical tale. If you cut down on the water a little, you will have pease porridge, from the nursery rhyme.

CROQUIGNOLES

2 cups Vanilla Sugar
1 teaspoon Salt
½ cup Lard
2 cups boiling Water
2 cups Flour, sifted
6 Eggs
1 teaspoon Cinnamon
¼ teaspoon Nutmeg
Lard for deep frying

Combine one-half cups sugar, salt, one-half cup lard, spices, and boiling water in pan. Mix and bring to rapid boil. Add flour all at once, mix and stir until thickened. Beat in eggs one at a time. Drop by spoonfuls into hot lard, fry until golden brown. Dust with remaining sugar.

Vanilla sugar was used to impart a vanilla flavor to baked goods prior to the late 19th century availability of vanilla extracts. Take several vanilla beans, break into pieces and put into a tightly sealed stoneware crock of fine sugar. Leave for several weeks before using. As it is used, replace sugar and reseal crock. Replace vanilla beans each full moon.

RED BEAN AND RICE

1 pound Red Beans - soaked overnight
¾ pound Salt Pork, diced
2 quarts Water
3 cups Onion, chopped
1 cup red Bell Pepper, chopped
2 cloves Garlic, crushed
1 teaspoon Cayenne
1 teaspoon Black Pepper
2 splashes Tabasco
1 pinch Oregano
1 pinch Thyme
1 pound Hard Sausage, sliced

Cover salt pork with boiling water, drain. Repeat. Cook salt pork and beans in two quarts water for one hour. Add all ingredients except sausage. Cook slowly additional hour. Add hard sausage — pepperoni works well — and simmer forty-five minutes to an hour. Let cool. Reheat while cooking four cups whole brown rice in eight cups of water — tightly sealed — until rice is tender. Serve beans over rice.

Since the French were early users of tomatoes, you may wish to chop four fresh tomatoes and add when you add the onions.

It's difficult to get away from all the modern packaging and cooking aids, but a wooden kitchen like this will allow you to keep a neat appearance in camp and still have the modern stuff handy.

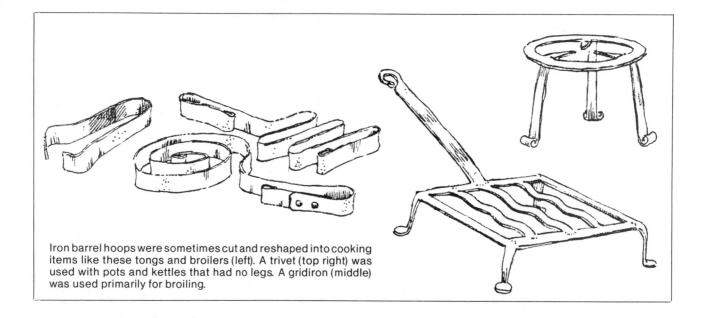

Iron barrel hoops were sometimes cut and reshaped into cooking items like these tongs and broilers (left). A trivet (top right) was used with pots and kettles that had no legs. A gridiron (middle) was used primarily for broiling.

The settlement of Texas and the expansion of trade along the Santa Fe trails added a spicy new flavor to American cooking. The earliest mountain men discovered senoritas, cigoullos, and chili all at once and decided Mexican territory was "good doin's." Most of the red hot reputation of Mexican cooking is based on the chili, a family of peppers ranging from mildly tingling to sulfuric acid. Traditional Mexican chili, such as **Green Chili Con Carne**, is a meat and spice dish: no beans and no tomatoes. Mexicans did use tomatoes in other ways, and helped introduce tomatoes to American cooking.

With the spicy base of so many Mexican foods, it was necessary to produce a soothing accompaniment. The pinto bean is a native of Mexico and was new to the Americans who found it as frijoles, refritos, **Refried Beans**. Camp cooks soon discovered that this recipe was equally tasty if other types of beans were used, and that it was a splendid use for leftover beans.

Mexicans ate thin fried corn cakes, tortillas, with all their meals but the idea never seems to have caught on with American camp cooks. The need for special flour, made from lye soaked corn, and a griddle on which to cook tortillas, made them impractical in camp. Cornbread, a familiar and well liked camp staple, was a good companion for searing Mexican dishes. Some cooks added chopped green chilis to their cornbread, which really livens it up.

After having scorched their taste buds on a meal, a sweet and mild dessert was a real treat to those not used to Mexican foods. A bread pudding, Capirotada, was a favorite of mountain men. Its name was somewhat difficult to pronounce, so they renamed it **"Spotted Dog"** because of the raisins. It's similar to a sailors' duff, and first cousin to the bread pudding served back east.

Just as those who ventured into the Southwest were introduced to new taste by the Mexicans those who went north and west were given a taste of Old England from the Hudson's Bay Company. Although the Company, as it was called, employed a wide variety of nationalities in menial capacities, all of its factors were English or Scottish gentlemen. They brought upperclass living to the wil-

GREEN CHILI CON CARNE

5 pounds Beef, cut into 1" cubes
Lard
3 large Onions, diced
3 cloves Garlic
3 tablespoons dried ground Red Chili
1 tablespoon Salt
1 tablespoon Oregano
1 tablespoon Cumin
½ cup Flour
1 cup Green Chilis, cut into strips

Brown beef in lard, a few at a time, until all are browned. Remove beef, cook onions and garlic in drippings until onions are tender. Add red chili, salt, oregano and cumin, stir for one minute. Add beef and three cups water, heat to boil, then simmer for two hours. In small bowl, mix flour and one cup water. Add flour mixture to chili, stir until thickened. Add green chili strips, cook five minutes.

REFRIED BEANS

1 pound Pinto Beans
½ cup Lard

Soak beans overnight. Drain. Cover with water, simmer for three to four hours or until beans are tender. Let beans cool. Heat lard in spyder, add beans a few at a time and mash with wooden spoon. Mix mashed beans and lard, cook gently for several hours.

This dish works well with any other type of dried bean, and you can cut preparation time if you use leftovers. If your leftover beans have diced salt pork or onion in them, so much the better.

149

SPOTTED DOG

6 slices Stale Dry Bread
4 Eggs
2 cups Milk
1 cup Raisins
½ pound Brown Sugar
2 tablespoons Cinnamon
1 teaspoon Nutmeg
1 small Onion, chopped
½ pound Butter
2 Apples, chopped

Break bread into bite-sized pieces. Beat eggs well and mix with milk. Add raisins, sugar, and apples. Mix well. Add onion and spices. Melt butter in two cups of water, mix with bread pieces, and add all to milk mixture. Pour into well greased Dutch Oven and bake until solid, about one hour.

Some recipes add shredded cheddar cheese, some add one-half cup of brandy or rum and some omit the onion. They are all worth trying.

MULLIGATAWNY SOUP

1 Stewing Chicken, cut into pieces
½ cup Lard
1 Onion, diced
1 Green Pepper, diced
2 stalks Celery, diced
2 Apples, cored and diced
1 tablespoon Curry Powder
1 tablespoon Flour
1 quart Water
4 cups White Rice

Dust chicken with salt and pepper. Brown chicken in lard. Remove chicken, fry vegetables and apple in browning lard until tender. Add curry powder and stir well. Add chicken and water, simmer until tender — about two hours. Remove chicken, debone and chop meat. Return to kettle, add rice and cook until tender.

There are numerous curry powders available; I like madras curry the best. If you want a spicier soup, add some cracked peppercorns with the vegetables.

derness. Fine wines, silver and crystal table settings, and imported foods were commonplace on Hudson's Bay posts. Cooks were chosen who could prepare the dishes from the old country and at least one factor had a bag piper to play at meals. We can't really recommend bagpipes as an aid to digestion, but many of the imported recipes became popular in camps throughout the West.

Many of the recipes introduced by factors reflect British interests throughout the world. Spices from India, fine teas from China, strange condiments from the West Indies — all were to be found on "Company" tables. Curries from India were popular with factors, especially a curry soup, **Mulligatawny**. Spicy meat sauces from India were being bottled in England and appeared at factors' meals. Worchestershire sauce, A-1 meat sauce, and House of Parliament sauce all date from the early 1800s and were in North America by 1840. Ketchups of all kinds — mushroom, walnut, oyster, and tomato — were patterned from the Far Eastern kechap and became common at wilderness posts.

Hudson's Bay posts usually had extensive gardens, herds of cattle and sheep, and droves of swine. The "gentlemen" got the best of all produce and the finest of cuts from the butchering. Roasted beef or **Boiled Beef** was served at most meals. Traditional British dishes, such as steak and kidney pie, and sirloin with Yorkshire pudding, kept up the spirits of Britons far from home, while Scottish factors, it is recorded, enjoyed **Haggis**, that fine sausage of sheep's innards and oatmeal. Hudson's Bay men had a greater variety of vegetables than many less settled frontiersmen, and their recipes can be used to authentically add vegetables to camp cooking. Carrots, parsnips, turnips, potatoes, and cabbage were all popular, and dishes such as **Colcannon** and champ added variety to camp menus.

BOILED BEEF

1 Beef Roast, rump is best
1 large Onion, chopped
2 medium Turnips, peeled and diced
1 stalk Celery, chopped
3 large Carrots, chopped
2 teaspoons Salt
1 teaspoon Pepper
3 cups mushrooms, sliced-Morells are great
1 tablespoon Flour
¼ cup Lemon Juice
1 Egg Yolk
2 Anchovies, crushed
1 tablespoon Capers
Lard for browning
2 tablespoons Butter

Melt lard in large Dutch Oven, brown roast on all sides. Add two and one-half quarts of water, onions, turnips. celery, carrots, one teaspoon of salt and pepper. Heat to boil, then simmer covered until tender, about three and one-half hours. Remove meat to platter, allow to rest ten minutes. Remove vegetables. Reserve two cups of broth. Melt butter in spyder, saute mushrooms. Add flour and stir for two minutes. Add one cup reserved broth. Whip egg yolk, capers, and anchovies into remaining broth, add to mushrooms. Slice beef, pour sauce over meat and vegetables.

HAGGIS

1 Cleaned Sheep's Stomach Bag (you read right)
1 pound Suet
1 pound Sheep's Liver, boiled and diced fine
1 Sheep's Heart, boiled and diced fine
1 set Sheep's Lungs, boiled and diced fine
2 Sheep's Kidneys, boiled twice and diced
2 pounds Dry Steel Cut Scots Oats
1 large Onion, chopped
1 teaspoon Salt
1 teaspoon Pepper
1 cup Ale

Toast the oatmeal in a dry spyder until it is crisp, then mix all ingredients except stomach together and moisten with one cup water and one cup ale. Fill bag just over half full, press out the air and sew up and secure, leaving some room to expand. Prick in several places with a large needle or it will burst. Place in large pot of boiling water and boil four hours.

Haggis is said to be even better if a deer's parts are substituted for sheep's. Traditionally served to the skirl of the pipes and washed down with malt whisky. The Scots love haggis; but then they liked bagpipes, wearing kilts, and King George III, too.

CHRISTMAS PUDDING

6 cups Flour
2 cups fine shredded Suet
2 teaspoons Baking Powder
1 cup Brown Sugar
2 teaspoons Ginger
1 teaspoon Nutmeg
½ cup Raisins
½ cup Candied Peel
½ cup Currants
½ cup dried Figs, diced
pinch Salt
3 Eggs
grated rind and juice of one Lemon and one Orange
½ cup Brandy
½ cup Water

Mix flour, suet, baking powder, sugar, salt, and spices. Add fruit, peel and rind. Mix well, beat eggs and add to juice, brandy, and water. Mix with wooden spoon into smooth firm paste. Add more flour if too moist. Form into solid ball. Dampen a heavy cloth, coat one side with flour. Wrap ball loosely — it swells during cooking — and tie top. Lower into large kettle, cover with boiling water and simmer for three and one-half hours. Unwrap, slice, and serve.

If you wish good luck tokens, make sure they are silver and that you warn your guests. Swallowing a piece of trade silver does not constitute good luck.

The Hudson's Bay posts made great celebrations of the holidays, partly to keep morale high and partly to emphasize the power and status which made the Company a legend. Both Christmas and New Year's (the Scots called it Hogmony) were occasions of great festivity with feasting, drinking, games, and presents. A traditional holiday sweet is **Christmas Pudding**, a boiled suet pudding served with a brandy sauce. Such puddings were decorated with holly and often had silver trinkets inside which were said to bring good luck to the finder. Boiled puddings require some effort, but make a truly special dessert for a camp celebration. They are served sliced and if you really have a sweet tooth, you can top a slice with fruit jam.

Dundee Orange Marmalade has been made and sold by James Keller and Sons since the 1760s. The Hudson's Bay Company carried Dundee Marmalade as an expensive retail item, packed in white stoneware jars. Spread this tart fruit jam on toast and wash it down with Irish breakfast tea and you will have the early morning repast of a Hudson's Bay gentleman.

Of all the different cultures which have made contributions to camp cooking, certainly the most romantic and mentally appealing to the buckskinner (although probably not the most palatable) is that of the American Indian. Their foods and cooking methods were used from the days of the earliest colonist onward and many of the items discussed earlier, such as corn, pumpkins, and maple sugar, were taken from the red man's cuisine. Different tribes developed different levels of

COLCANNON

8 Irish Potatoes
1 head Cabbage
¼ pound Butter

Peel and boil potatoes. Boil cabbage separately. Drain and chop cabbage. Drain and mash potatoes. Mix — there should be twice as much potatoes as cabbage. Add butter, salt, and pepper to taste. Mix well.

If you add in some turnips mashed, in place of two of the potatoes, you have champ. Some recipes call for milk to make it creamy, some for chopped onions. Colcannon is a traditional dish on All Hallow's Eve (Halloween). In London, the mixed potatoes and cabbage are fried gently in lard. The frying causes the mixture to make some odd noises, hence its nickname — "Bubble and Squeak" cooking. The Eastern Woodlands peoples, having game, settled gardens, and seafood, presented a mixed and interesting menu while subsistence level groups such as the Diggers lived on a cuisine of vermin and insects. Both can be duplicated in camp cooking, but I rather question the popularity of Yellow Jacket Soup or Fried Locust. On the other hand, few camp foods can match the popularity, or utility of Indian trail foods. Foremost is **Jerky,** sun and air dried meat. There are all sorts of jerky including deer, elk, buffalo, bear, domestic meats such as beef or mutton, and even turkey. Some jerky is plain, other is well seasoned. Jerky was a staple for travelers in the old days and many commercial establishments did a brisk trade in jerky.

Jerky was eaten both in its plain state and used as a base for other foods. Jerky was often shredded and mixed with high grade suet (ask your butcher for kidney fat) and dried berries to make pemmican. Jerky can also be soaked in water and used in stews and soups.

Not all Indian trail rations were meat. Eastern Indians also used **Parched Corn**. This dry cooked grain can be eaten as is or crushed and put into boiling water (often with jerky) to make a thick and filling porridge. Eastern Indians also carried uncooked popcorn on journeys, popping it at night in a small kettle. Although Indians grew corn, the making of flour was a long and laborious process for them. Two stones, used like a mortar and pestle, were used to pound and grind corn into meal, but fine flour was much more difficult. Most Indian breads were of the corn Johnny cake variety. When wheaten flour became available, Indians began to make other kinds of

bread. **Fry Bread** is now considered a traditional "Indian" food item, but it is unclear how far back it goes. Since it requires both white flour, and lard for frying, fried bread (as we know it) probably was not made with great regularity before the "reservation period."

Indian cooking methods in general changed after contact with the European culture. Iron and copper pots made cooking easier; iron pans and implements allowed new cooking methods. For example, **Succotash** was a traditional Woodland Indian dish. Using corn and beans, it was a slow cooked vegetable stew. Originally it was prepared in clay pots; post contact it was made in trade kettles. Many Indian women used animal stomachs to boil the meat in. Rocks were heated, then placed in the stomachs which were hung from a tripod of sticks. Water and the meat were already in the "stomach kettles,"

PARCHED CORN

4 cups Dried Corn, shelled from ears
1 cup Lard

Heat small amount of lard in a spyder until it smokes. Then add one-half cup corn and shake until the kernels swell. Repeat. Just like popcorn.

FRY BREAD

1 cup Flour
1 teaspoon Sugar, heaping
Salt to taste
2 teaspoons Baking Powder, rounded

Mix in bowl and add enough water to make a stiff dough. Form into small flat pieces one-half inch thick and four inches across. Put into very hot deep frying grease. When it floats and the bottom is golden, flip it over.

You can substitute one-half cup of sourdough starter for half the flour (don't forget to feed the mother).

SUCCOTASH

3 cups Sweet Corn, just cut from cob
3 cups Fresh Lima Beans or String Beans or Butter Beans
1 cup Milk
6 tablespoons Butter

Cover beans with the least possible amount of boiling water and cook until tender. Drain and add the corn and milk. Cook slowly until corn is tender. Add butter. Salt and pepper to taste.

The Indians used bear grease in place of milk and butter. Corn and beans were the base for a vegetable stew which might also include squash, pumpkin, or seafood and which might be sweetened with maple sugar. Succotash is Narragansett for fragments.

JERKY

5 pounds any Lean Meat

Cut meat into six inch strips about one-half inch wide and one-quarter inch thick. Be sure to cut the strips lengthwise with the grain of the meat. Trim away all the fat — otherwise you'll get rancid jerky. Thread wood skewers through one end of the strips and let hang. Fix a rack to hang skewers in the hot sun — let dry for two or three days — don't let any two pieces touch and watch out for Rover. If flies seem to be a problem, cover with cheesecloth.

I like to soak my meat in garlic, salt, pepper, Worcestershire sauce, and a little honey for a day before drying. Some folks like a little soy sauce.

You can dry meat in the oven overnight by setting at lowest oven temperature, rigging skewers on oven racks and propping oven door open slightly to allow moisture to escape.

A friend of ours claims you can jerk turkey as easily as anything else. I've eaten beef, mutton, deer, elk, moose, sheep, antelope, and buffalo jerky. You can make jerky out of everything but pork and Englishmen. If you have access to a smokehouse, hang your meat in there for two or three days to jerk.

and when one set of rocks cooled, those were removed and replaced with another set. However, with the availability of spyders (frying pans with legs) as a trade item, succotash began to be served as a **Fried Vegetable** dish. The stewing of pumpkins and squash was made easier in iron kettles. Flavoring of dishes changed as the traders' big iron kettles made the evaporation of salt easier. Large iron pots also made the boiling of maple sap for sugar easier for the Indian.

Maple sugar was one of the few sweets used by the American Indian. It was used in meat dishes, such as racoon or bear, and in vegetable mixtures such as **Mohawk Corn** and walnuts. The Indians made use of natural wild fruits, such as peaches, berries, and persimmons. They were also quick to plant European fruits such as apples. Fruits were eaten fresh, stewed, or dried.

Hopefully, these brief historic sketches will give you some ideas about period foods in camp. Authentic cooking can be a blend of different cultures and different styles. People two hundred years ago had individual tastes just as you and I. Catering to everyone's palate while serving meals which match and complement both you and your camp's character, elevates camp cooking to the height of fine craftsmanship.

Part of the craft of good camp cooking is having the correct tools. Although good food can be prepared with a minimum of gear, or in an emergency situation with none at all, having the right equipment makes cooking easier and allows a camp cook to offer a wider variety of foods. Everyone cooks differently, so the choice of cooking gear can be as individualized as your gun or clothing. You should try and match your cooking tools to your character and that of your camp.

Cooking equipment in a permanent camp differs from that used on the trail. The size of the group for which you will be cooking also affects your choice of equipment. If you plan your meals ahead, you'll have an idea of what items you need to take, and *what you can leave at home*. Cooking gear is heavy and bulky, and transporting more than is essential can be a lot of trouble.

If you will be in camp three or four days or longer, you'll want enough equipment to do some baking as well as different kinds of cooking. For camp baking, the heavy Dutch oven is the best choice. This is an item on which you shouldn't scrimp. The inexpensive imported ovens aren't heavy enough and their thin walls don't radiate heat the way an American built oven does. Make certain your Dutch oven has legs — the longer the better. Without legs, you will need a trivet to keep the oven bottom away from the coals. Your Dutch oven should also have a flat lid with a high lip on it for holding coals. Make certain that the lid has a good solid handle in the center — one you can slip a pot hook thru to lift and check without spilling great quantities of ash on your baking. A good glazed stoneware pie plate is helpful. Not only does it bake better but it's helpful in serving. Our favorite is from Bastine Pottery in Indiana.

For frying over a campfire, nothing beats a good three legged spyder. These come in two styles; sheet iron or cast iron. Sheet iron ones have a sheet iron body, three forged legs, and handle. Several of the smiths we see at rendezvous and shoots are building them. Since they are

FRIED VEGETABLES

1 pound Salt Pork, diced
1 pound Fresh Corn, cut from cob
1 pound Fresh green beans
2 large Onions, chopped
1 pound Mushrooms, sliced

Soak salt pork in boiling water, drain, and soak again. Fry salt pork until crisp. Remove salt pork, retain grease. Snap beans into pieces. Add all vegetables to grease and stir while frying. Add cooked pork.

MOHAWK CORN

4 cups Corn, freshly cut from cob
2 tablespoons Lard
½ cup shelled Black Walnuts
¼ cup Maple sugar

Cook corn gently in a small amount of water until tender. Drain most of liquid, add remaining ingredients and stir until lard melts and sugar coats corn.

custom done, you can pick a size which fits your needs. Make certain the legs are wide spread to sit level in the coals, and that the legs are solidly riveted onto the body. The forged handle should be long enough to stay cool and must be tightly attached. A pan full of bacon grease wobbling around on a long handle is a real danger around a fire. If you want a cast iron spyder, you'll need to hunt at flea markets or antique shops, since there are no reproductions currently available. Although cast iron spyders are thicker, and thus less likely to burn food than a sheet steel one, their shorter legs and handles — designed

These longhunters are cooking at a trail camp. Note the small skillet and miniature fire irons. When you have to pack the stuff in, cooking becomes more elementary and your utensils can be smaller and lighter.

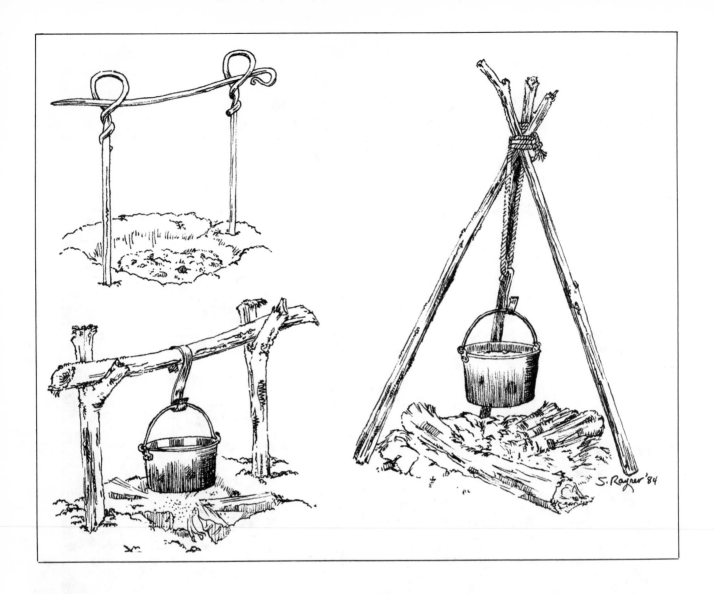

for use on a hearth — aren't as easy to use around a campfire. You may come across a cast iron griddle with legs in your wandering — they are splendid for flapjacks and corncakes and well worth picking up.

If you prefer to grill your meat (and in the eighteenth century frying meat was considered unhealthy and an idea to be avoided) then a hand forged grill, or gridiron, is a good addition to your camp gear. Many of them have attached legs at each corner while others have legs you drive into the ground with a lift off grill frame. Both work well; the one with separate legs packs flat but if you misplace a leg you're in trouble and you need to make a smaller fire pit for them rather than using the main fire as you can with a legged grill.

Several smiths are now building braziers and they are very handy. A brazier is a small iron box with a floor, raised up on legs and intended to serve as a table top stove. Those who camp in a tent, rather than a lodge, and don't have an inside fire can use them for small cooking chores such as morning coffee. Military officers and traders used them in marquees to both cook and heat the tent. Either charcoal or small kindling work well in a brazier, many of which were also fitted with a grill top. An authentic answer to the Coleman stove!

Probably the most used items in your camp will be your kettles. Cast iron kettles come in a variety of sizes and shapes. The round bellied types with exterior seams from a multi-pieced mold are older in style than the flat sided seamless ones. There are numerous new made cast iron kettles available and old ones can be found by haunting the local yard sales and junk shops. Beware the ones which have been used as planters as the bottoms are often rusted badly enough to be weakened and the extensive pitting makes them hard to keep clean. Make sure the bail is sound (although many people have new bails forged for all their cookware to get rid of the thin wire handles), and if you find one with a lid, you are well ahead of the game. Some cast iron kettles come with legs and, as in Dutch ovens, the longer the better.

Many early period kettles including great numbers of Indian trade kettles were copper. Copper kettles are good camp cooking kettles as long as you are aware of their limitations. You need to be careful about what you cook in a copper kettle: High acid content foods such as tomatoes, lemons, vinegar, or tea can cause a harmful chemical reaction. Modern copper pots have a tin lining, but if your pot doesn't, then cook carefully. Foods left overnight in copper kettles take on a strange taste and odor. Copper

157

I've tried, through the historical narrative, to lay out a wide variety of recipes, but there were a few that just wouldn't fit. Most of these are tried and true old favorites of mine that we've served in camp through the years. I think they'll be as popular around your fire as they have been around ours.

BOSTON BROWN BREAD

1 cup All Purpose Flour
1 cup Rye Flour or Whole Wheat Flour
1 cup Cornmeal
2 teaspoons Baking Soda
1 teaspoon Salt
2 cups Sour Milk
1 cup Molasses
2 tablespoons Melted Butter

Sift flours with soda and salt. Add meal and stir. Add milk, molasses, and butter, blend well. Pour into three well greased stoneware molds and tightly seal with heavy cheesecloth. Set in a steamer of boiling water to a depth of one-half of the molds. Cover and steam three hours. Let cool fifteen minutes and remove from molds.

If, like us, you don't happen to have stoneware molds, a one pound vegetable can will substitute well. A big Dutch Oven makes a good steamer. Serve this bread warm, with butter and jelly, as a side dish to Boston baked beans.

TEXICAN CHILI

1 cup dried Pinto Beans
4 cups Stewed Tomatoes, chopped
3 pounds Lean Beef, chopped ½ inch cubes
½ cup Lard
1 Bay Leaf
4 tablespoons Chili Powder
1 tablespoon Salt
1 teaspoon Cumin
1 teaspoon Oregano
3 tablespoons Paprika
2 teaspoons Crushed Red Pepper
2 teaspoons Tabasco
3 tablespoons Cornmeal
2 cups Beer

Cover beans with water, bring to boil. Let boil two minutes. Cover pan and remove from heat for one hour, then cook until beans are tender. Brown meat in hot lard. Add beer and five cups bean liquid to meat, cover and simmer one hour. Add tomatoes, all spices, and simmer for thirty minutes. Blend cornmeal and water into paste — stir into simmering chili to thicken. Add beans and simmer ten minutes.

This is for those who cannot imagine chili without beans, tomatoes and the taste of sulfuric acid. This is **hot** stuff. Beware — will make strong men weep and weak men faint. Not to be eaten by women or children. Leftovers make a great paint stripper.

SOURDOUGH BREAD

Starter (Mother)
2 cups Lukewarm Water
1 Yeast Cake
2 cups Flour
½ teaspoon Salt

Mix all ingredients in a <u>stoneware</u> crock. Cover loosely with a cloth and keep in a warm spot. Every day for four days, add one-half cup lukewarm water and one-half cup flour to feed the starter. In four to six days it should smell slightly sour. Feed it once a week. When using, replace starter with equal amounts lukewarm water and flour. Store in warm area.

1 cup Lukewarm Water
1 tablespoon Sugar
2 tablespoons Melted Lard
1 tablespoon Salt
1 cup Starter
¼ teaspoon Baking Soda
5 cups All Purpose Flour
Melted Butter

Mix water, sugar, lard, and salt. Mix starter (don't forget to feed the mother) and soda. Mix into water. Beat in flour until dough is very stiff. Turn onto floured board and knead in another one-half cup flour. Put in bowl, brush top with melted butter, cover with cloth and let stand in warm place until it rises — double in bulk. Turn out onto floured board and shape into two loaves. Let stand in warm place until it rises — double in bulk. Turn out onto floured board and shape into two loaves. Let stand in warm place until loaves double in bulk. Bake about forty minutes in Dutch Oven. That's 350°F in your home oven.

This is the oldtime miners' and drovers' recipe. If you want to take your starter with you into camp, hollow out a hole in the middle of your flour, put a lump of starter in and cover with flour. Dig it out when you need it.

SNOW ICE CREAM

1 bucket <u>Clean</u> Snow (use as needed)
1 cup Vanilla Flavoring
2 cans Evaporated Milk
OR
2 pints Cream
Sugar to taste

Combine all ingredients and stir until mixed thoroughly. Serve at once. This is a favorite with kids and a sure cure for cabin fever.

GERMAN RYE BREAD

3 cups Rye Flour
2 cups Boiling Water
¾ cup Molasses
⅓ cup Butter
1 tablespoon Salt
1 Yeast Cake
5¼ cups Unbleached Flour

Mix rye flour, boiling water, molasses, butter, and salt. Let cool. Dissolve yeast in one-half cup warm water. Gradually add unbleached flour until dough is stiff. Turn out on a floured board and knead until no longer sticky. Place in a buttered bowl and let rise until doubled in bulk. Punch down and let rise again — about thirty minutes. Turn out on floured board and knead five minutes. Make into three loaves. Sprinkle with cornmeal. Bake 45 minutes to an hour — until dark brown and hollow sounding when thumped. That's 350° F in a home oven.

IRISH CORNED BEEF AND CABBAGE

4 pounds Corned Beef Brisket
1 teaspoon Thyme
1 Onion stuck with cloves
3 Onions
6 Carrots
2 two pound Cabbages

Fill a large pot with cold water. Add beef and spices. Bring to a boil. Add onions and carrots and return to a boil. Then simmer gently for three hours. Remove the cloved onion. Quarter the cabbages, add to pot and simmer half an hour — until cabbage is tender. Drain and serve, dotted with butter and well peppered. Boiled potatoes are often eaten with this.

This is for the true sons of the old sod who suffered through reading the Haggis recipe.

IRISH SODA BREAD

4 cups White Flour
1 tablespoon Butter
1 teaspoon Salt
1 teaspoon Baking Soda
1 cup Buttermilk (sweet milk will do)

Rub the butter into the flour. Add salt and soda, mix well. Add buttermilk and stir into a soft dough with wooden spoon. Knead lightly into a ball and then flatten into a circle one and one-half inches thick. Cut a cross in center with well-floured knife. Bake for forty-five minutes until brown.

You can also cook in a thick cast iron spyder by making the circle one inch thick, cutting it in quarters and placing the quarters on a hot floured spyder. After about fifteen minutes at a low heat, flip over and cook other side for same length of time.

STEAK AND KIDNEY PIE

2 cups Unbleached Flour
1 teaspoon Salt
¾ cup Butter
1 pound Veal or Beef Kidney
¼ cup Suet (substitute butter if needed)
1 Onion, chopped
1½ pounds Round Steak, cut into ½" cubes
6 cubes Bouillon
1 tablespoon Lea & Perrins Worcestershire Sauce
3 tablespoons Flour
3 cups Water

Remove outside membrane from kidneys, split lengthwise, and remove white core and center fat. Soak covered in milk for one hour. Chop into one-half inch cubes. Heat suet in spyder until melted, add onion and saute until golden, add steak and brown. Add three cups water, bouillon, Worcestershire sauce. Salt and pepper to taste. Simmer one hour. While meat is simmering, combine two cups flour and one teaspoon salt. Cut in butter with fork until grainy. Sprinkle with cold water until flour is moistened. Mix well. Divide into two-thirds and one-third. Form into balls and roll balls out one-eighth inch thick. When meat is tender, add kidneys. Thicken juices by sifting in three tablespoons flour while stirring vigorously. Allow to cool until quite cool. Line buttered Dutch Oven with larger pastry, add filling, cover with smaller pastry, and crimp to seal edges. Bake an hour and fifteen minutes — until crust is golden.

If you dislike kidneys, you can substitute two dozen shelled oysters for the kidneys. Sliced mushrooms make a nice addition in either case. For real luxury, add both along with a quarter cup of port wine.

BRAMBLE DUNFILLAN

1 cup Flour
¼ cup Butter
¼ cup Sugar
1 Egg
¼ teaspoon Baking Powder
2 tablespoons Milk
1 teaspoon grated Lemon Rind

Cut butter into flour until crumbly, mix in sugar. Beat egg and combine with milk and baking powder. Blend with flour thoroughly. Mix in grated lemon rind.

1 pound fresh Brambles (blackberries)
½ cup Sugar

Stew the berries with the sugar and water to cover, in a Dutch Oven. When berries are tender, spoon batter over them. Bake for twenty minutes.

You can substitute sweet stewed apples with cinnamon and nutmeg for the berries — then it's called Eve's Pudding.

VENISON SADDLE-SPIT ROASTED

Marinade
- 1½ cups Olive Oil
- 2 Carrots — cut thin
- 1 Onion, diced
- 1 stalk Celery, diced
- 2 Garlic cloves, crushed
- 2 teaspoons Rosemary, well rubbed
- 1 teaspoon Thyme
- 10 Juniper berries
- 1 teaspoon Pepper
- 1 bottle Red Wine - Port is best

Marinate venison saddle for five days, turning twice a day. Remove from marinade. Make small cuts in meat and insert pieces of fat salt pork in the saddle (since venison is not well marbled, the pork will keep the venison tender). Balance the saddle on your spit and secure with skewers. Roast over live coals, use a flavorsome wood such as apple, hickory, or mesquite if possible until well done. While venison is roasting, strain marinade and cook down until only four cups are left. Combine with one-half cup of currant jelly and simmer until meat is done. Serve over meat slices. Be sure meat is hot when served — it tastes tallowy when cool.

This marinade works well with all venison and makes the wild flavor more subtle.

CHICKEN STOVIES

- 1 Stewing Hen (three pounds)
- 1½ pounds Peeled Potatoes, sliced
- 2 large Onions, peeled, sliced
- 6 tablespoons Butter

Joint chicken by removing legs, thighs, wings, and breast meat. This gives eight pieces. Crush carcass and simmer with giblets and four cups water. Brown chicken in Dutch Oven with two tablespoons butter. Remove chicken, place a layer of potato slices, then chicken, then onion then a few shavings of butter, repeat until all ingredients are gone, ending with a layer of potatoes. Salt and pepper to taste. After carcass has cooked for two hours, take two and one-half cups of the stock and pour over layers in Dutch Oven. Salt and pepper to taste. Cover and simmer for one and one-half hours.

kettles weren't made with legs. Occasionally you may see a cast bronze saucepan with legs, known as a posnet. They were also made in cast iron and are useful in camp.

Once you have chosen your major cooking pots, you need to consider small items and utensils. This is the area in which imaginations run wild, especially those of blacksmiths. For example, look at fire irons. Every camp has at least one set and sometimes more. They're often elaborately curled and decorated — but how authentic are they? Other than the chuck wagon and cowboy period, I've never seen one depicted in a drawing or painting nor mentioned in a period description. Have you? The oldtimers used green sticks cut on the spot and left them there. That's often impractical today. Then too, scalds from a spilled pot when the cross bar burned through may be authentic, but no fun. We use a sturdy, simple set of fire irons.

Once your fire irons are in place, you need a way to hang pots from the cross bar. The simplest answer is the "S" hook. These come in all sizes and weights and a good assortment will allow you to hang pots, kettles, or whatever at different heights over the fire. The same result can be achieved by using a trammel; in effect an adjustable "S" hook. Some trammels operate with a notched slide and dog, others with a chain to lengthen or shorten.

If you have a matched pair of "S" hooks, or better yet two pairs, you can use them to raise or lower your spit or skewer. Skewers are small rods used for roasting little birds or game over an open fire; spits are larger versions and usually include some form of prongs to further secure a large roast or poultry. Often skewers are used to aid in holding meat on a spit. An iron toasting fork, with its own legs at the base of the tines, is useful in roasting a small chunk of meat, piece of bread or (very British) an English muffin for breakfast.

A very useful cooking item, although one might not think of it as one, is the poker. You can use it for moving logs, spreading coals and generally adjusting the fire to give you a precise cooking temperature. A poker will also double as a lid lifter, allowing you to check contents without moving a pot from the fire or risking a painful burn. A poker can be used, if you don't have a proper flip iron, to make hot drinks. A flip iron, or loggerhead, looks like a poker with a thick ingot replacing the point. The ingot is heated red hot and used to quickly heat a mug of flip, hot buttered rum, or mulled cider.

Beyond fireside equipment, a good camp cooking setup should include items to prepare and serve food. A good knife, or knives, bear the same importance to a camp cook that they do to a buckskinner. You'll need a good knife for peeling and chopping, one for cutting through bone. Green River knives are good butcher items and they have a variety of shapes and sizes. A couple of wooden spoons for mixing and a forged iron one for working around hot pots are worthwhile investments, and a good ladle, either wooden or iron makes serving easier. A wooden or forged spatula is very necessary for cooking or frying in a spyder and a sturdy work fork is helpful for many chores.

A couple of mixing bowls — wood are easier to transport, stoneware easier to clean — a rolling pin and a whisk or beating stick are necessary if you want to bake to any extent. Find and mark cups or spoons with exact capacity so you can measure in camp. A tin cup is as good a measuring cup as the fancy kind and you can scratch marks for graduations. A reproduction horn or pewter spoon can be filed down until it gives you an exact measure. For all the old time cooks talked of a pinch of this or a dab of that, dependable measurements are an important part of the craft of campfire cooking.

By this time, you will have decided that anyone with one of everything I've mentioned goes to rendezvous in a semi-truck. How do you pare all that down to a reasonable load? Try to plan out menus and numbers being served ahead of time. If you know what you won't be needing, you can cut your baggage considerably. Baking bread ahead of time, for example, may allow you to leave your baking tools at home. Deciding not to feed the whole brigade may mean you can get by with a smaller stew pot.

No matter how much gear you end up carrying, a good camp box makes it a lot easier. A working camp box should hold your cooking equipment, eating utensils and some camp staples. An important thing to remember is that you must be able to lift and move the camp box once it is packed. If you have a large amount of cook gear, consider dividing it into two boxes. Not only will you have more room and an easier moving chore, you'll also be able to use your chests as benches or work tables. A flat topped camp chest is an extremely useful item of camp furniture.

Your camp chest should also be packed with a steady supply of staples: flour, sugar, spices, bouillon, dried fruit, jerky, some dried vegetables, condiments, a sealed container of lard, items you can use to stretch a meal for extra guests, or whip up something special on the spur of the moment. If you've got a good camp chest design, build a spare and line it with inch and a half styrofoam to use as a cooler.

It's difficult to write a closing paragraph to such a chapter, because cooking and then sitting around a glowing campfire and sharing food and friendship is so close to the heart of our hobby. The best words are those of the great Robert Burns:

"Some hae meat and cannot eat
And some would eat that want it
But we hae meat and we can eat
Sae let the Lord be thankit."

THE HUNTING POUCH

BY MADISON GRANT

MADISON GRANT HAS ALWAYS BEEN interested in every phase of our early history. From the time his parents took him, at the age of seven, to the site of the first permanent English settlement in America at Jamestown, Virginia, the impact of that visit and its accompanying story never left him.

Although a native Virginian, Madison now lives in Chester County, Pennsylvania in an eighteenth century stone farmhouse.

Being interested in every area of pioneer life, the muzzle loading rifle and its accoutrements seem to have become his favorites. An intensive study of this field resulted in the authorship of two books: *THE KENTUCKY RIFLE HUNTING POUCH* and *THE KNIFE IN HOMESPUN AMERICA.*

Both of these efforts were the result of not only the willingness, but the desire to share the knowledge of authenticity with friends and fellow admirers of our heritage. As Madison says, "We learn from each other. Every step in this process is one more tie in the never-ending search for the truth."

PRIOR to the second quarter of the 19th century almost everything was handmade. Generally, each man made his own hunting pouch or had the local harness maker contrive one for him. In either case, there was no such thing as uniformity in workmanship. Individual expression was the "hallmark" of every article. I would suggest that this feeling of pride in personal accomplishment be the attitude of every buckskinner.

The explanations, drawings, and specific instructions are offered as a basic reference that does not exclude other treatment that may be more fitting for some outfits. In addition, this chapter leans heavily upon photographs of original pouches. There is no substitute for visual representation.

Having mastered the use of needle and thread, there remains but the choice of style, the desire to achieve results, and the labor of bringing the pouch into being. Don't be afraid to undo, revise, or even start all over. Experience indicates that first attempts should be confined to a simple or plain pattern. More elaborate designs can follow with practice.

One must keep in mind the ultimate use of the pouch, which is to assist in the operation of the gun. The hunting pouch is not a catchall. There were also coat pockets and possible bags for odds and ends. Another point to consider is how the pouch fits into the entire scheme of the period of dress. The pouch should be harmonious with the rest of the clothing and not stand out as an extraneous article. The frontiersman's or hunter's most precious possessions were his rifle and hunting pouch. They became a part of him.

The hunting pouch has an ancestry almost equal to man's existence. With the development of weapons to assist him in either hunting or combat, the need arose to always have with him the tools he required. These items

This pouch made of pigskin (circa 1750-80) is of one piece construction with the flap being an integral part of the skin which is simply folded over. The sinew stitching is limited to the bottom and one side of the pouch. When found, only a segment of the shoulder strap remained. The balance of the strap is a restoration as are the horn thongs. The powder horn is of French & Indian War construction and decoration. The butt plug is maple with a wrought iron staple for the thong. The entire surface of the horn is covered with scenes of the forts in New York State and Canada.

could best be kept in a container which was easy to fashion, durable in nature, and immediately accessible. Thus, an animal skin attached by a thong to his waist or shoulder became almost a part of him. He dared not be without it.

Stones for a sling, spare arrow heads, sinews for binding, or materials for fire-making were his most precious possessions, and were ever within working position. Curiously enough, the chief elements of a bag or pouch have remained unchanged through milleniums of time.

The need for this type of receptacle was heightened by the fact that man had to fortify himself against the rigors of nature by the use of skins, smocks, robes, cloaks, and sundry coverings, none of which had pockets. A pouch or bag was essential.

Even until the Middle Ages, which is comparatively late in the chronology of the human race, pants or voluminous leg coverings were practically unknown. Dutch paintings of the 16th century show both men and women with leather or cloth pouches suspended by thongs from the belt. These were usually of the purse variety so that the weight of the contents would make an automatic closure. Also, during the early days of America, the Indian had no pockets, but depended upon pouch, backpack, and travios to hold and carry his tools and trinkets.

Inevitably then, with the coming of firearms, the hunting pouch came into its own. However, the significance and necessity of the pouch has been subordinate to the glory of the gun. This is unfortunate, since without the means of care and loading, the gun becomes merely a club in the hands of either hunter or soldier.

Leather was the natural material from which to make a pouch. It was easy to work, obtainable on every hand, relatively inexpensive, and accommodated itself to this particular purpose better than any textile could have done. Whether crude or fancy, made by a backwoodsman or city harness maker, its indispensability as an auxiliary to the

A heart shaped, black cowhide pouch of two piece construction. It is laced with leather strips. Dimensions are 9½ inches wide and 8½ inches deep. The powder horn is 10½ inches across the curve and has a flat pine butt plug held in place by hand wrought tacks. The priming horn has similar details in every respect. Seemingly, a plantation made outfit, circa 1830-40.

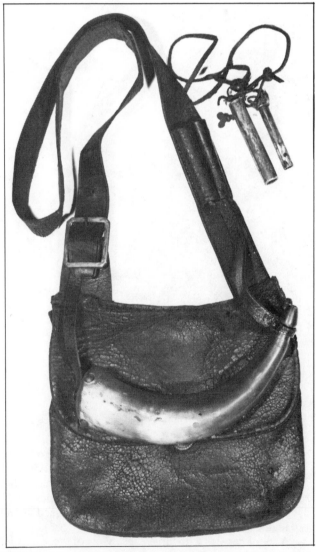

This black cowhide pouch from central Pennsylvania measures 8½ inches wide and 7½ inches deep. The flap has a bound edge and a button closure. The wide shoulder strap has a double scabbard to receive one variable iron measure and one of tin. Circa 1830-40.

rifleman has never been equalled. One of the appeals of the hunting pouch is its individuality.

While Kentucky rifles may be readily assigned to given schools or individual makers because of their style or workmanship, the absence of identifying characteristics makes it difficult to pinpoint the exact origin of a pouch unless it is accompanied by the rifle for which it was made. Even then, the chances that the pouch was made by the gunsmith are exceedingly remote.

The construction of the pouch is not really complicated. It consists of an enclosed area produced by sewing together pre-patterned pieces of leather. It may be a simple single pouch or it can be a double pouch, having two separate sections held together as a unit. The contents are protected and secured by a flap which acts as a closure. The pouch is suspended by a shoulder strap which, in most cases, has an adjustable buckle. Two thongs, attached to the shoulder strap, hold the powder horn which should rest about half-way between the top and bottom of the pouch. It is usually customary to hang the powder measure, vent pick, and pan brush from the shoulder strap. Many riflemen like to have a small patch knife snugly fitted into a scabbard sewn to the shoulder strap; however, some

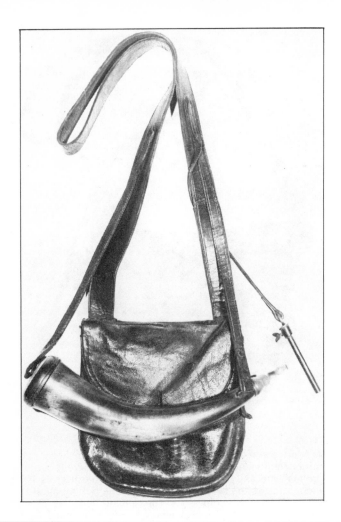

A very nice, typical Pennsylvania outfit, circa 1835-50. The well-proportioned pouch is made of calfskin, and the bound flap has a button closure. There are tooling lines on the shoulder strap and horn thongs. Rivets are used to fasten the thongs to the powder horn which has a screw tip and turned butt plug. The entire arrangement seems to be completely original.

This brown calfskin commerical pouch (tanned with the hair on) was machine stitched. The shoulder strap is attached by leather loops. The powder horn has a pine butt plug with a turned finial and is held in place by brass tacks. Brass tacks were added to the butt plug as ornamentation. This type of pouch was very popular and could be obtained at almost any store that sold hunting supplies. Circa 1840-50.

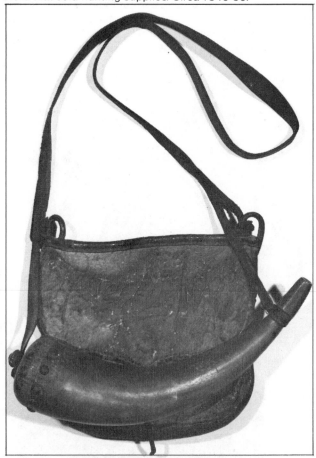

knives were affixed to the pouch itself.

Such simple elements enabled men of limited skill to make a pouch that was as practical as those made by more sophisticated workmen. Like all other man-made objects, the hunting pouch can be judged on the basis of quality and good lines, but we should accept them as they are; just as we do the facial architecture of our friends, namely each one is sufficient unto itself.

Since the advent of the firearm, the hunting pouch has faithfully and in an unheralded manner carried the necessities and whims of the frontiersman and woodsman. Combining the esthetic with the practical, and using the materials at hand, the rifleman fashioned the tools of his trade in a way unmatched for simplicity and workability. Moreover, incorporated in each implement was a mixture of experience and personal expression that permitted no duplication. Each man left his own mark. Perhaps these objects, more than anything else, bespeak the adaptability of these men. Who can deny that adaptability and intelligence are one, and the basis for all accomplishment?

TOOLS USED IN MAKING A HUNTING POUCH

1) Punch board. Preferably of soft wood that the awl can penetrate without breaking the point or requiring too much effort. The ends of the board should be rounded to prevent the thread from catching on the ends. The board itself should be at least two feet long, ten inches wide, and three quarters of an inch in thickness.
2) Standard type of awl. These can be purchased at any leather-work shop.
3) A set of needles with large eyes. Most of these needles will be straight, but the set should contain some that are curved.
4) A sharp knife for cutting out patterns. A large pair of shears may also come in handy.
5) Two pairs of pliers. One should be normal size but you should also have a pair of needle nose pliers.

A hunting pouch from Berks County, Pennsylvania (circa 1835-50) measuring 9½ inches in width and 10 inches deep. This machine stitched pouch is made of brown calfskin and was the work of a professional leather worker. The gusset is quite wide, permitting folds which have a bellows effect. The powder horn is one usually associated with Berks County and is 14 inches across the curve. The butt plug is well turned walnut terminating in a pointed button finial.

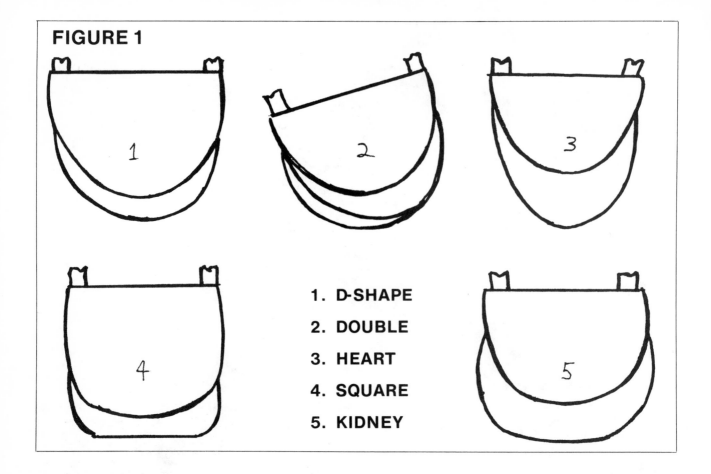

FIGURE 1

1. **D-SHAPE**
2. **DOUBLE**
3. **HEART**
4. **SQUARE**
5. **KIDNEY**

6) A marking wheel (if desired). Otherwise use a rule to mark off the stitching points.
7) A yard stick. This is indispensable for layout work and measuring for shoulder straps.

MATERIALS USED IN POUCH MAKING

1) Linen shoemaker's thread.
2) Leather. Select the type you think is appropriate for the job. Calfskin, buffalo, cowhide, and buckskin are usually appropriate and available at a leather shop. The leather should range between four and six ounces in weight.

THE SHAPE OF THE HUNTING POUCH

Since the pouch is essentially a bag, it can be of almost any shape as long as it performs the function of a receptacle. However, there can be quite a difference in size and style.

As with many other items, trial and error usually provides a product that conforms to the wishes of its maker. Thus, the hunting pouch evolved as the most practical container for the rifleman's accoutrements. When worn between armpit and hip it is protected, readily accessible, does not impede movement, and assists the powder horn as a working companion piece.

The average pouch appears to fall within the dimensions of an eight inch square, although many individual examples are larger and some are smaller. Earlier pouches tended to be smaller in size, accompanied by a quite larger horn, while later pouches seemed to become larger and were used with smaller horns. Undoubtedly, the earlier use of large bore muskets and rifles required bigger charges of powder in contrast to later reduction in bore size and less demand for heavy loads.

Observation of a great number of pouches indicates that there are five basic styles in profile and construction. Needless to say, there are untold numbers of variations. The basic types are the D-shape, the double pouch, the heart shape, the square shape, and the kidney shape. These can be seen in *Figure 1*.

FLAP DESIGNS AND DECORATION

The flap is one of the most important parts of the pouch. It secures the contents as well as acting as the doorway to the interior. Moreover, it should be in harmony with the architecture of the pouch, thus lending a sense of completeness as well as an artistic expression of the owner's individuality. Practicality and beauty have always been good companions.

Always use paper or cardboard patterns to insure balanced designs. Lay out the pattern on leather and mark with a scriber or other sharp point. Do not use a pen or any

FIGURE 2

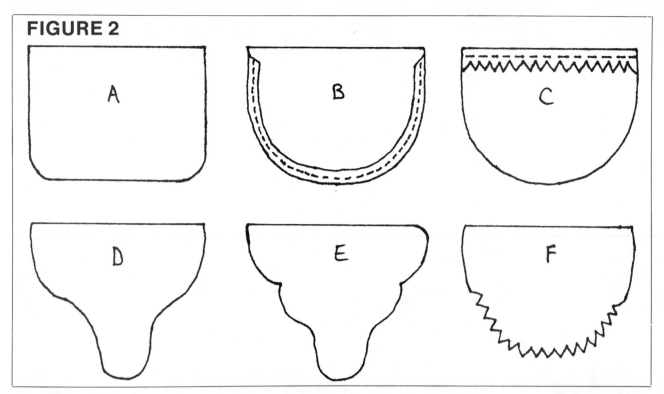

Figure 2: (A) Either square or rectangular with bottom edges rounded. (B) Plain D-shape with bound edge. (C) Regular D-shape with pinked or serrated spine. (D) Plain beaver tail. (E) Scalloped beaver tail. (F) Regular D-shape with serrated bottom half.

Figure 3: (A) D-shape with bottom fringe and button closure. (B) Overlay type. Beaver tail with hearts and bound edge. (C) Overlay type. D-shape with tulip and stars. (D) Modified beaver tail with pinwheel designs done by engraving or by impressing while wet. (E) Chippendale design, reminiscent of flaps on 18th century cartridge boxes. (F) D-shape with beaded decorations. Note: All flaps can be fitted with buttons if desired. Dotted lines indicate stitching.

FIGURE 3

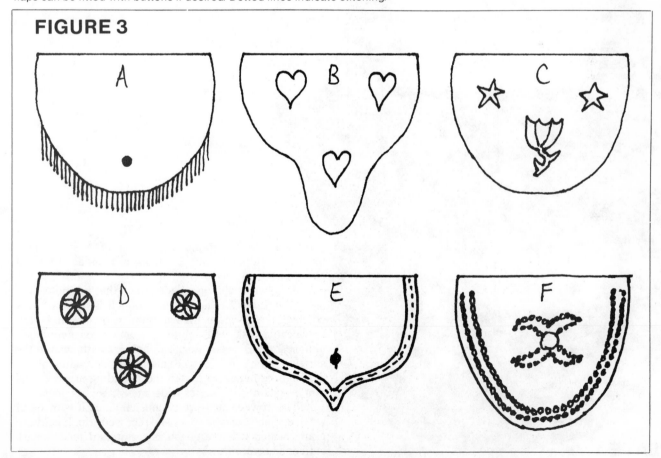

other marker that will stain the leather. Then, cut slowly, checking to make sure you are not straying from the lines.

Figure 2 and *Figure 3* show some designs selected from original pouches which were made during the first half of the nineteenth century. Some of them are simply variations of the basic shapes shown in Figure 1. Each modern day maker has the privilege of enjoying his own creation.

THE ONE-PIECE SINGLE POUCH

This terminology refers to the main body of the pouch and does not take into account the small pieces such as the welt, shoulder straps, and thongs for the powder horn.

Plate 1 shows a single pouch made of cowhide. There is no pocket or interior compartment. This type was by far the simplest form of construction, yet very sturdy. It was made in 1864 and came with a rifle from Somerset County, Pennsylvania. The outfit was a birthday present and was in use until 1910. The plainness of the pouch is relieved by the serrations on the flap. The dimensions are 7 inches wide and 8 inches deep.

The horn has a convex butt plug which is well turned. A circle of rope carving is centered with an iron staple and

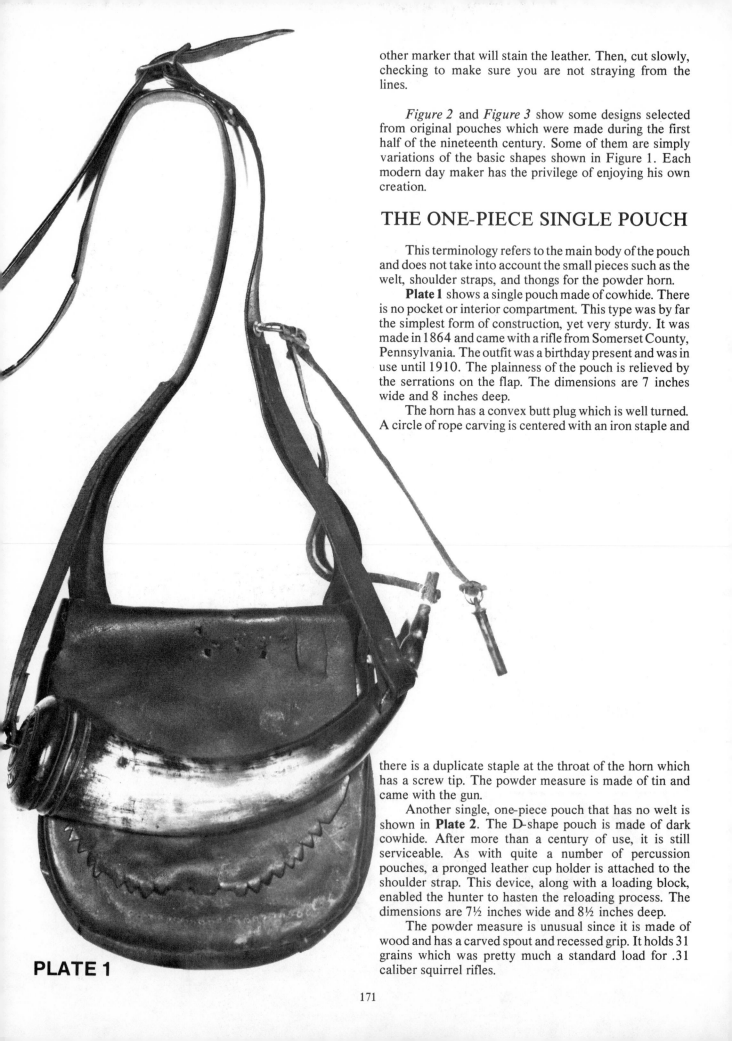

PLATE 1

there is a duplicate staple at the throat of the horn which has a screw tip. The powder measure is made of tin and came with the gun.

Another single, one-piece pouch that has no welt is shown in **Plate 2**. The D-shape pouch is made of dark cowhide. After more than a century of use, it is still serviceable. As with quite a number of percussion pouches, a pronged leather cup holder is attached to the shoulder strap. This device, along with a loading block, enabled the hunter to hasten the reloading process. The dimensions are 7½ inches wide and 8½ inches deep.

The powder measure is unusual since it is made of wood and has a carved spout and recessed grip. It holds 31 grains which was pretty much a standard load for .31 caliber squirrel rifles.

PLATE 2

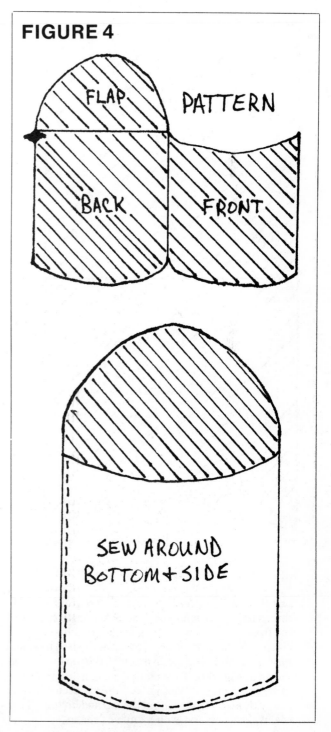

FIGURE 4

MAKING THE ONE-PIECE SINGLE POUCH

The earliest, simplest, and perhaps the crudest example of an 18th century single pouch can be made of one piece of leather. See *Figure 4*. The procedures for making this pouch are as follows:
1) Lay out pattern on leather and trace it off.
2) Cut out pattern (one piece).
3) Fold front to back (right sides together).
4) Sew front to back on two sides only.
5) Turn pouch right side out.
6) Add shoulder straps and powder horn thongs.
Note: This pouch contains no welts. The dimensions are seven inches by seven inches. Earlier pouches were quite small.

Another one piece pouch (*Figure 5*) is a single pouch of the first half of the 19th century. Parts to be used are the main body with attached flap, a small inner pocket, welts, shoulder straps, and powder horn thongs. Determine the desired final size of the pouch by the back section. Add equal size sections for the front and flap. Don't forget the seam allowances. Flap shape can be chosen after the pouch is sewn. Pocket optional.
1) Make pattern, transfer to the leather, and cut out.
2) Cut welts wide enough to be sewn between front and back. The excess can be trimmed after the pouch is turned right side out.

FIGURE 5

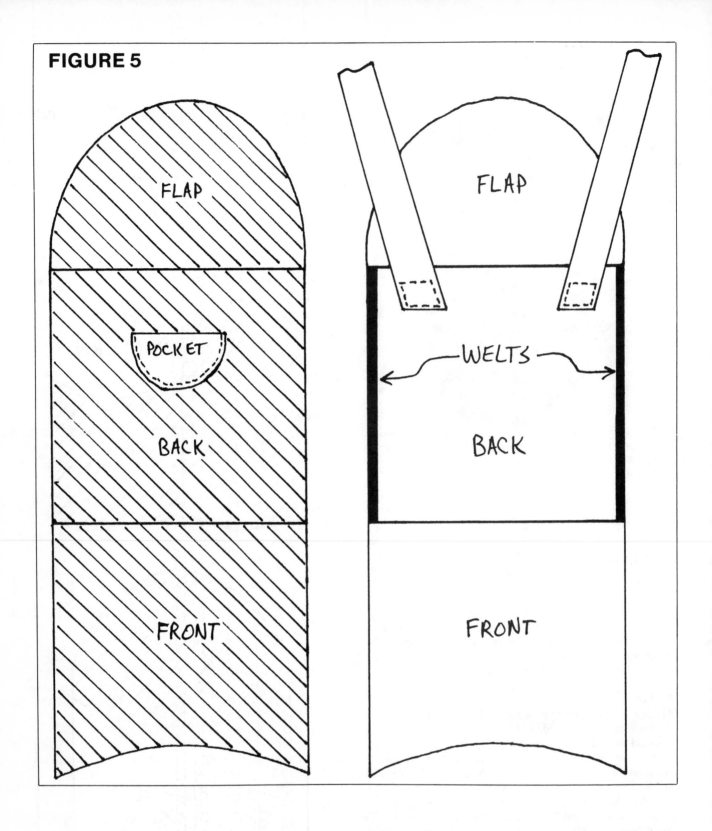

3) Lay the welts in place with glue or secure them with thread to prevent slippage. You may want to reenforce the front top edge with extra leather or stitching.

4) Place right sides together, creased at the fold line, and turn up the front section in line with the top fold line as shown in *Figure 6*. Then mark the stitch line and holes to be pre-punched with an awl. Stitch securely with heavy thread, reenforcing at the top and bottom. Trim seams, if necessary, with a knife or shears.

5) Turn the pouch right side out, wetting the leather if necessary. Fold flap down and decorate or shape it to your liking.

6) Finish the straps for closure and length. Remember that when in use, the pouch should hang high enough to be covered by the bent elbow.

7) Attach the thongs which hold the powder horn. The horn should hang half way between the top and bottom of the pouch.

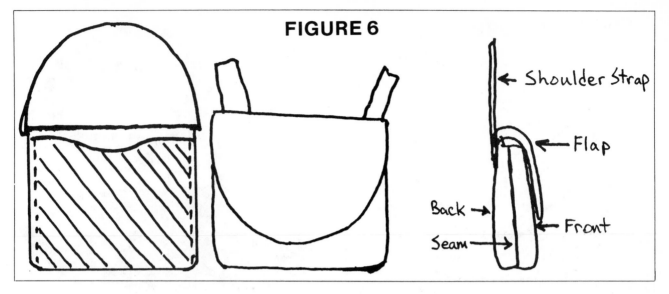

FIGURE 6

Shoulder Strap

Flap

Back

Front

Seam

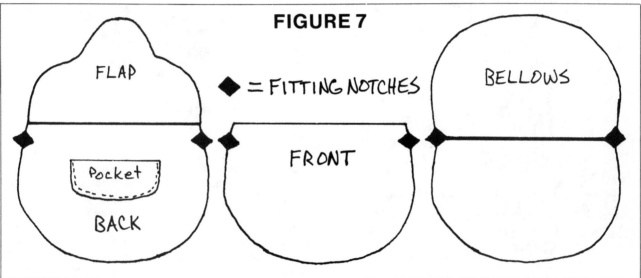

FIGURE 7

FLAP

◆ = FITTING NOTCHES

BELLOWS

Pocket

FRONT

BACK

THE DOUBLE POUCH

Double pouch means that the finished pouch will have two separate compartments. A double pouch is composed of the following parts: A) The back which also includes the flap; B) the front; C) The bellows which lies between the front and back; and D) the straps, welts, and optional inside pocket. The back, front, and bellows can be seen in *Figure 7*.

1) Cut pattern to the desired size making sure to add enough for seam allowances. Make middle bellows approximately one or two inches shorter than the front piece (notice the fitting notches). After laying out the pattern on the leather and marking or scoring your outline, cut out the pieces. You may want to reenforce the front opening and sew in a small back pocket now.

2) Glue welts in place along the front and back to the fold line. Then line up the bellows with the front section to the fitting notches. Do this with the right sides together. If you don't have glue to hold the pieces in place, use your awl to punch holes from top to bottom and use some thread to temporarily tack the pieces in place. Space your stitching holes and punch with the awl. Stitch from notch to notch.

3) Repeat procedure 2 on the back section.

4) After the front and back sections are sewn to the bellows, continue sewing the front to the back above the notches. Secure the top stitches so they won't pull out with use.

5) Turn the pouch right side out. If necessary, wet the leather to aid in turning it. Be careful not to tear the leather in the process. Finish the flap to your liking.

6) Sew on the shoulder straps. If you do not especially like the shoulder straps sewn to the back of the pouch, here is a suggested variation. After the pouch has been completed, cut a slit the width of the strap on each side of the top of the pouch, where the flap folds over. Insert the strap ends at least an inch and a half into the pouch, punch holes with the awl, and stitch securely as shown in *Figure 8*. Place the straps at a slight angle so that they will more easily follow the body contour.

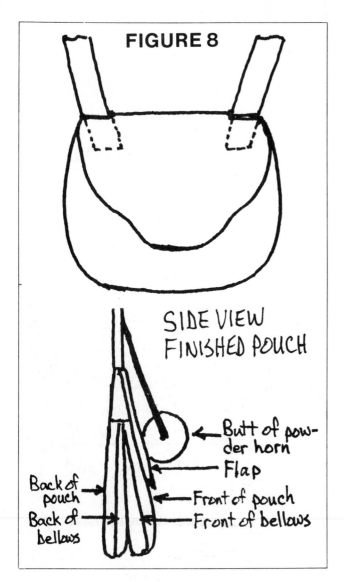

FIGURE 8

SIDE VIEW
FINISHED POUCH

Butt of pow-
der horn

Flap

Back of
pouch

Back of
bellows

Front of pouch

Front of bellows

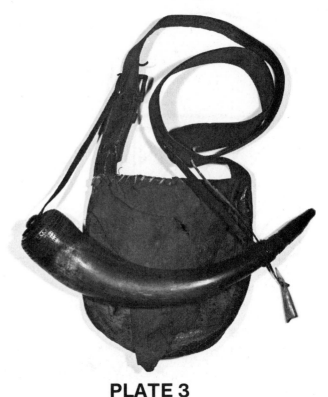

PLATE 3

VARIATIONS OF THE
CLASSIC D-SHAPE POUCH

Plate 3 shows a handsewn single pouch with long flap. Dimensions are 7½ by 7½ inches. There is a 2 inch wide gusset present to permit a bellows effect allowing the pouch to hold more items. The shoulder strap has stamped designs and evidently came from a harness shop, but the pouch was made by the owner. The antler tip measure holds 38 grains. A bullet mold, cap box, turkey call, and bone handled, patch cutting, folding knife are still in the pouch.

The powder horn is an example of fine folk art having a large convex walnut butt plug that is elaborately carved. The extra long spout is highly decorated and carries the name Elijah Peague and the date 1844. The outfit came from Bedford County, Virginia.

The single pouch in **Plate 4** is of black calfskin and machine sewn. Dimensions are 7 inches wide and 6 inches deep. The elongated flap is covered with a design of stars and leaf scrolls. The shoulder strap is cotton listing with an adjustable buckle. Original items still in the pouch are a bullet mold, cap box, worm and tow for cleaning, and cloth patching material.

The horn is pale yellow with a pine butt plug held by iron tacks. There is no flange at the throat. An iron staple at the spout and a screw in the flat butt plug serve as thong attachments. A bone measure of 35 grains is used for a .38 caliber bullet. Found in Rockingham County, Virginia.

Plate 5 displays a dark brown calfskin single pouch of fine proportions and sturdy construction. Deep D-shape with contoured beaver tail flap backed with homespun. The shoulder strap is made of either girth material from a harness shop or the webbing from an older chair. Such use of this type of material was quite commonplace. The pouch is 7 inches wide and 8 inches deep.

The dark brown powder horn is 12 inches across the curve. The pine butt plug contains a screw type thong finial. It should be noticed that in most cases the powder horn is large enough to extend for at least an inch and a half beyond each side of the pouch. This size lends an air of good proportions to the outfit.

A calfskin variation of the kidney shape exhibited in **Plate 6** is 7 inches wide at the top and 8½ inches wide at the bottom. The depth is 9 inches. Long beavertail flap. Handsewn throughout. Shoulder strap is 1½ inches in width.

The fine, large, main powder horn has a carved throat flange and a flat pine butt plug with a wrought iron staple. The priming horn is 6½ inches long with almost identical features of the big horn. A tin powder measure of 50 grains accompanies a vent pick on a double jack chain. An excellent example of a complete flintlock arrangement. Found in the Valley of Virginia.

175

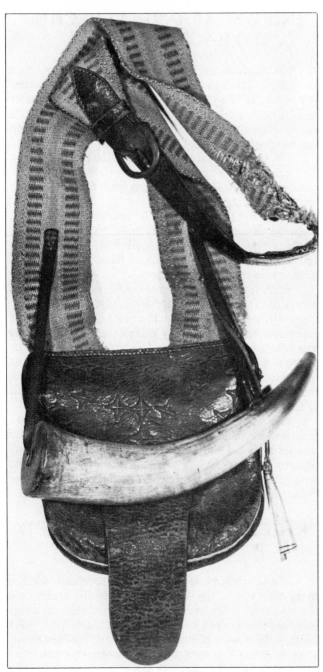

PLATE 4

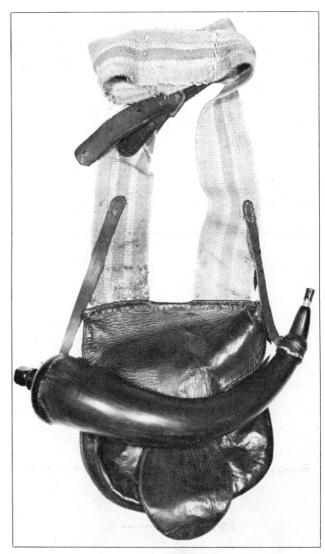

PLATE 5

PLATE 6

176

KNIFE SCABBARD ATTACHED
TO BACK OF POUCH

The fine original outfit in **Plate 7** is hand stitched throughout. The pouch is calfskin with a 1½ inch gusset. The beaver tail flap has a bound edge. The wide shoulder strap is made of treated fabric. The powder horn is 10½ inches across the curve. Incised geometric designs and carved spout are nice touches on the powder measure.

The knife scabbard is attached to the central area on the back side of the pouch by hand stitching. The antler handle of the knife is 3½ inches long while the wrought iron blade is 6½ inches in length.

The usual necessities for the operation of a gun are present and include the bullet mold, worm, linen tow, patching material, and turkey call. This pouch is characteristic of the average hunter who did not put extraneous items where they did not belong.

Very few pouches remain which were made of bearskin. The one in **Plate 8** exemplifies that type. Originally used with a flintlock, it saw later service with a percussion rifle. It is slightly kidney shaped. Most of the hair is still intact on this single pouch. The width of the pouch is 8 inches and the depth is 6 inches. Patches and repairs indicate hard usage. The chief feature of this pouch is the antler handled knife which is also attached to the rear of the pouch.

The visible accessories include a wire vent pick and a bone powder measure. The somewhat homely but efficient powder horn is harmonious with its companion of many trips to the woods. The flat butt plug is held by hand wrought iron tacks. A real veteran from the mountains of Pennsylvania.

KNIFE SCABBARD ATTACHED
TO SHOULDER STRAP

The pouch in **Plate 9** has the knife scabbard attached to the outer edge of the shoulder strap which contains a cut down butcher knife made by I. Ames, a Massachusetts company that worked during the second quarter of the 19th century. They were prolific sword makers. Butcher knives were modified and used by many hunters because they could serve as either patch or skinning knives.

The outboard face of the pouch, which is 7 inches in width and 8 inches deep, is made up of four pieces. The shaped flap is scalloped and is held down by a figured brass button.

The powder horn is 9½ inches across the curve and the convex butt plug of pine is fastened with brass tacks.

Plate 10 shows a typical hunting pouch from central Pennsylvania. Somewhat deeper than usual (9 inches), it is 8 inches in width. The flap is backed by ticking material for stiffening and has a fully bound edge. The shoulder strap is wide enough to carry the hand stitched scabbard and the bone handled hunting knife is an exceptionally fine one. The powder measure is iron with adjustable load markings.

The powder horn has a screw tip and a turned butt plug and is representative of those found in the York County area. However, horns, like their owners, were used to traveling.

PLATE 7

177

PLATE 8

PLATE 9

CONTRAST IN POUCH STYLES

The possible variations in the construction of hunting pouches are almost infinite. Both individual owners and harness makers gave personal touches to their work which set them apart from their fellows. This is to be encouraged in modern pouch making. One of the appealing aspects of pouches in general is their lack of uniformity. Pride in one's own work is far more desirable than regimentation.

But, a word of caution on this score. Be sure that the pouch you make is in keeping with the period you wish to portray and certainly the pouch should blend with, or be coordinated with the costume you wear. A pouch that is blatantly different can destroy the harmony of your outfit.

Plate 11 exhibits a very good variation of the square type of pouch with an overlay flap. It was made in the vicinity of Mt. Eaton, Ohio. An old hand written note contains the date 1837. It is made of brown calfskin with an interior compartment. The flap has tool work of geometrical designs and carries the initials of the owner, Isaac Tharpe. These letters are of red leather.

A few remaining shreds indicate that three quarters of the pouch was encircled by fringe. The width of the pouch is 9 inches and the depth is 8 inches. Two powder measures are present, one of bone and the other of tin. This combination frequently indicates the use of a smooth bore.

The black cowhide pouch in **Plate 12** is from central

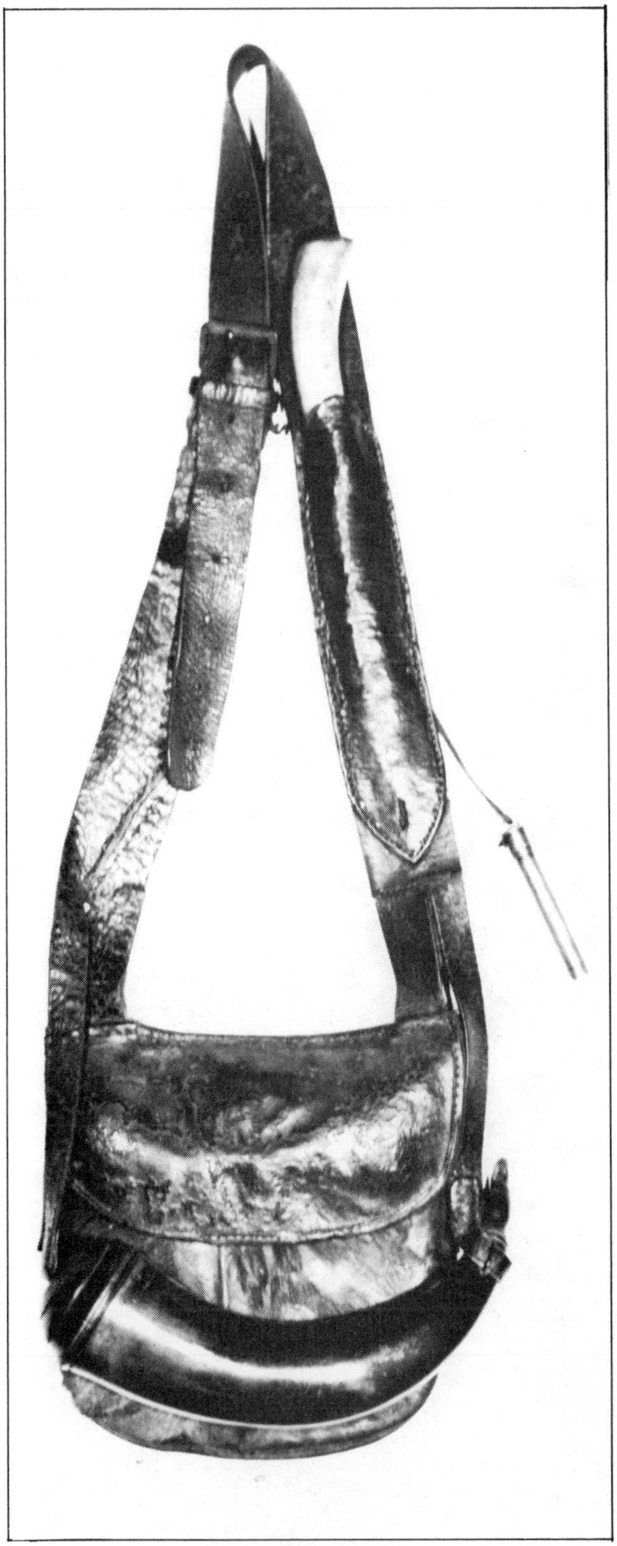

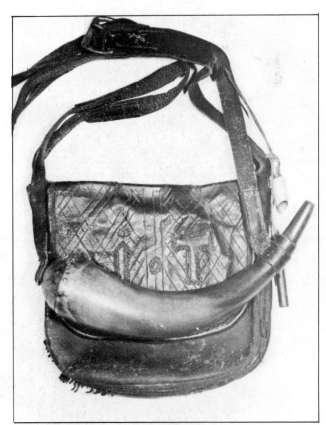

PLATE 10

PLATE 11

Pennsylvania. This pouch is typical of the nice work done by a professional harness maker. The pouch is machine sewn with the fringe work being part of the welt and encircling the entire perimeter of the face. A scabbard is attached to the left side of the pouch to hold the turned brass powder measure.

PLATE 12

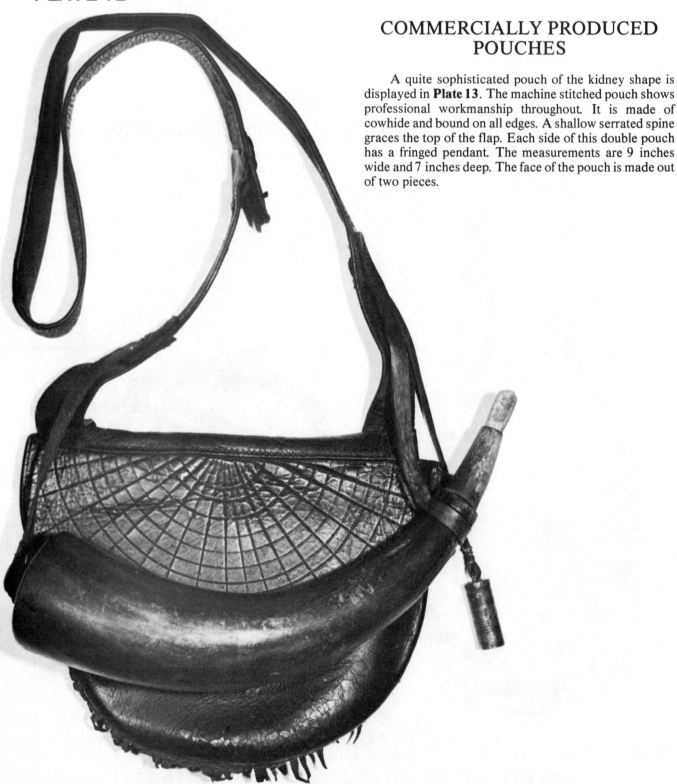

The feature of the pouch is the flap which has a unique design in the form of a spider's web. A plain dark green powder horn has a brass thong attachment which screws into the flat pine butt plug.

Although the pouch is quite formal in appearance, it was used with a flintlock rifle. This is not unusual since many flint rifles were made long after the percussion type of ignition was introduced.

COMMERCIALLY PRODUCED POUCHES

A quite sophisticated pouch of the kidney shape is displayed in **Plate 13**. The machine stitched pouch shows professional workmanship throughout. It is made of cowhide and bound on all edges. A shallow serrated spine graces the top of the flap. Each side of this double pouch has a fringed pendant. The measurements are 9 inches wide and 7 inches deep. The face of the pouch is made out of two pieces.

PLATE 13

PLATE 14

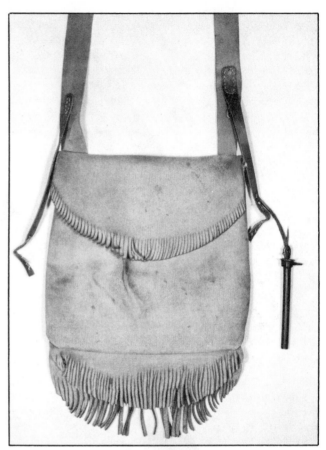

PLATE 15

holder. This pouch was used with a rifle made by Henry Gibbs of Lancaster, Pennsylvania.

The powder horn is 13 inches long with a flat pine butt plug and a screw for thong attachment. The paneling on the spout is somewhat long. A variable measure permits a charge of 80 grains. Altogether a superb outfit. Pouches like this often accompanied rifles made by big city gunsmiths.

The double pouch in **Plate 14** shows very good proportions and quality construction. Coming from central Pennsylvania, it has a modified kidney shape and is 7½ inches wide and 6½ inches deep. The calfskin surface of the face and beaver tail flap retain a major portion of light brown hair. It is machine stitched with the exception of the flap which is bound and hand sewn. There are many instances in which the pouch was sewn by machine and the flap by hand. Note also the wide spine and shoulder strap.

The bone measure has a turned tip and slotted thong

MODERN POUCHES COPIED FROM ORIGINALS

The somewhat large pouch in **Plate 15** was made for use with a double barreled percussion shotgun. Made of mule hide over forty years ago, it is still in use. Measurements are 9 inches wide and 10 inches deep, excluding the two layers of fringe on the bottom. The pouch itself was constructed by two pieces. The bottom fringes were sewn to the main section and then the face added. As usual, the pouch was sewn inside out and then reversed.

An adjustable iron measure of Pennsylvania origin carries marks up to 100 grains, but only 75 grains is used with the shotgun as a safe and efficient load. The Berks County screw tip powder horn has been removed to show the pouch by itself.

Plate 16 shows a small squirrel hunter's pouch. The dimensions are 6½ by 6½ inches. It is made of six ounce latigo leather. Most leather shops today carry leather of good quality and give the prospective pouch maker a good selection to choose from.

This is a three piece pouch with serrated spine which serves to hold the flap and pouch together. The spine is slotted to receive the ends of the shoulder strap which are

183

countersunk and sewn to the back of the pouch. There is an inner pocket for either flint holder or cap box.

The pouch of split cowhide in **Plate 17** is tan in color. I made this pouch with the suede side out because it tends to be less noisy. It is of the classic D-shape and is 8 inches wide and 8 inches deep. There is a one inch gusset that permits considerable expansion. In addition, the spine is scalloped. The shoulder strap is one and a quarter inches wide and made with two pieces joined with lacing instead of a buckle adjustment.

The scabbard was made for a converted bone handled table knife of English manufacture. A tin gunsmith's measure holds 32 grains of powder. The powder horn has been removed.

An out of the ordinary arrangement in an old pouch almost demanded that it be copied. The pouch in **Plate 18** was obviously made for a short stay in the woods such as a morning's squirrel hunt. It is only 6 inches wide and 4 inches deep. There is no interior pocket although there is room for a small one. The shoulder strap is exactly one inch in width and has a scabbard for a patch knife.

In this instance, the pouch nestles into the curvature

PLATE 17

PLATE 16

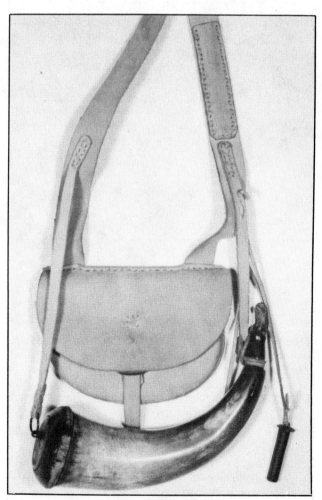

PLATE 18

184

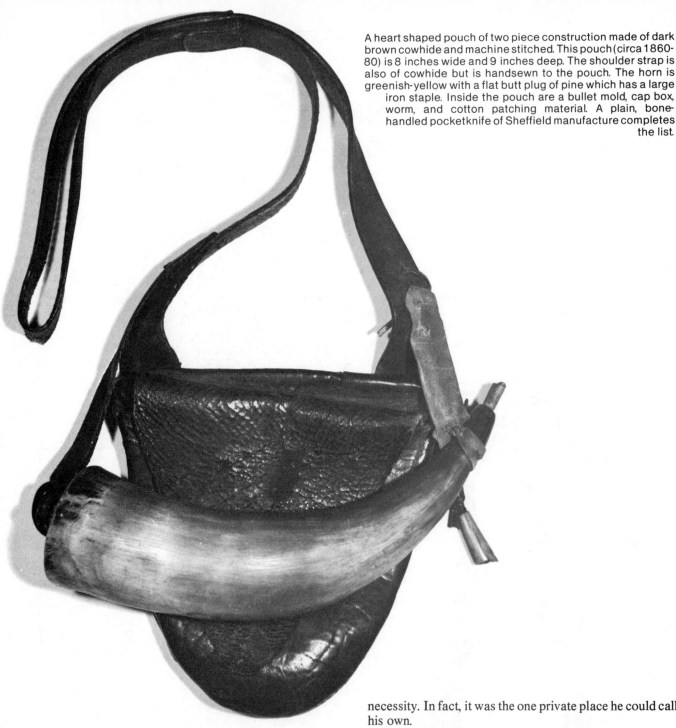

A heart shaped pouch of two piece construction made of dark brown cowhide and machine stitched. This pouch (circa 1860-80) is 8 inches wide and 9 inches deep. The shoulder strap is also of cowhide but is handsewn to the pouch. The horn is greenish-yellow with a flat butt plug of pine which has a large iron staple. Inside the pouch are a bullet mold, cap box, worm, and cotton patching material. A plain, bone-handled pocketknife of Sheffield manufacture completes the list.

of the horn. There is a buckle arrangement under the flap. Actually, this outfit is really a powder horn with a bullet pouch suspended above it. The horn is 7½ inches across the curve and is the commercial kind advertised by the Edward K. Tryon Sporting Goods Company of Philadelphia.

THE GAME BAG

The game bag is a first cousin of the knapsack. Soldiers have been carrying knapsacks since time immemorial. It held rations, personal articles too bulky for pockets, and whimsical objects not required by military necessity. In fact, it was the one private place he could call his own.

This carry-all, by its very size and nature, became the indispensable companion of every old-time hunter. Keep in mind that the bob-tailed canvas hunting coat with its commodious pockets did not come into being until the latter part of the 19th century.

Seventeenth century Spanish and French ceramic tiles show figures of hunters shooting either birds or rabbits. In every case, the hunter is shown carrying a game bag which was either suspended in the middle of his back or hanging from his belt. We are all familiar with the folklore expression, "It's in the bag," meaning it is a foregone conclusion or an accomplished fact. In addition, we say even today that we "bagged" several rabbits or quail.

Certainly, a game bag was a necessity during the heyday of the passenger pigeon and the time when shore birds and reed birds were taken in countless numbers.

PLATE 19

Think of the problem also of the fellow who long ago was responsible for the nursery rhyme, "Four and twenty blackbirds baked in a pie."

One of the sorrows of my life occurred many years ago when I rummaged through the loft of an old barn at a public sale in Lancaster County, Pennsylvania. Heaped in a pile of broken and rusted parts were the pitiful remains of what was once a grand firearm. Through the grime, dirt, and pigeon droppings, the butt showed masterful raised carving back of the cheekpiece. The lid to the patchbox was missing, but the panels demonstrated equal ability with the engraving tool. The wrist area was not even present, but another small portion of the stock contained the lock plate and one silver escutcheon. Scratching through the rust on the top flat of the barrel, I could faintly see the name J. P. Beck.

Lying next to the remnants of the gun was a shoulder strap and top part of a hunting pouch joined in disarray with a worm-eaten powder horn that was missing the screw tip. The final blow was the homespun game bag that hung from a peg just above the gun and pouch as if presiding over a gathering engaged in self-bereavement. Two-thirds of the bottom part of the bag had been destroyed by rodents. Obviously, they had sought to make a meal of the old cloth that had been saturated with the dried blood of birds and animals.

I was so distressed by the sight of these infirm comrades of the hunt that I later dared to make a replica of the game bag, as though to rectify the inroads of time and neglect. **Plate 19** shows the result of my labor. I used heavy "feedsack" homespun and made the bag 15 inches wide and 13 inches deep. I shaped and bound the flap with deerskin from which the hair had been shaved. The 18th century style buttons are one inch in diameter. The width of the shoulder strap is 1½ inches. Linen shoemaker's thread was used throughout for sewing.

THE POSSIBLE BAG

The possible bag is actually self-explanatory. At the risk of repetition, let me say once more that the hunting pouch is NOT a possible bag. The possible bag is an all-around "workhorse" that carries the extra hunting paraphernalia, small camp articles, and small objects for gun care with a few personal items thrown in. It may even contain lines and hooks or a miniature survival kit. It is a haven of almost limitless "possibilities."

For ease in carrying and yet of ample proportions, the bag should be around twelve inches wide and ten to twelve inches deep. Since it will contain some weighty objects, it

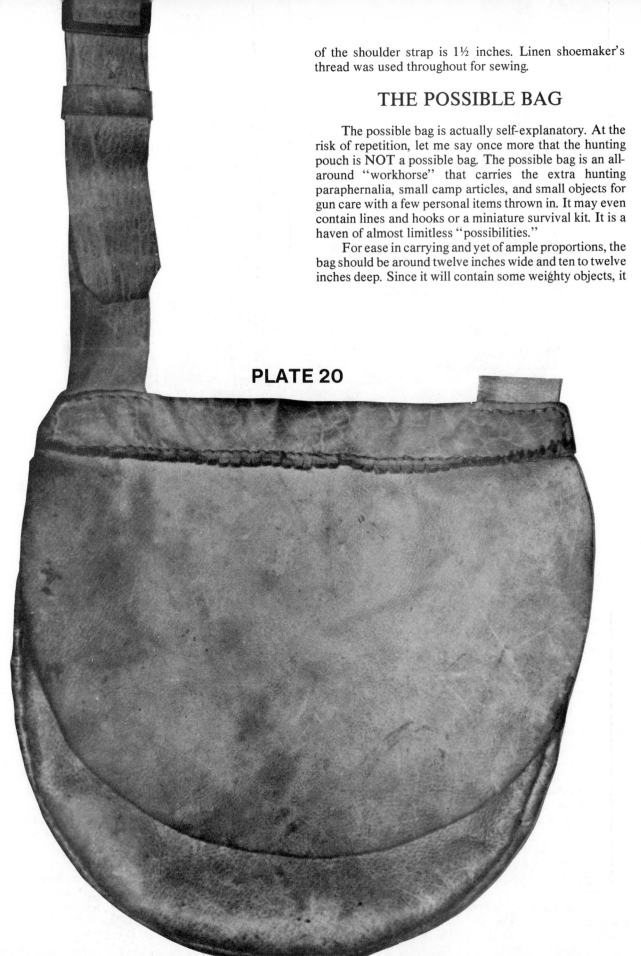

PLATE 20

should be constructed of sturdy material such as pliable leather. It can be of any particular style or shape that pleases the maker. In fact, it can be patterned after an oversized hunting pouch. But, here the similarity comes to an end because of the function. Perhaps a choice should be made between the D-shape and the square shape. In either case, a gusset should be used to permit a bellows effect. In addition, the shoulder strap has to be at least 1¾ inches in width to be comfortable. Do not forget to make a two part shoulder strap with a buckle in order to permit alternate lengths for changes in clothing layers with the seasons.

Plate 20 displays a possible bag made of buffalo leather. The D-shape bag is 12 by 12 inches and has a two inch gusset with welts. The two part flap is serrated near the top and the shoulder strap is two inches wide.

CONCLUSION

If a chapter needs a dedication, surely the hunting pouch should pay homage to the countless men who carried the long rifle. The gun and the pouch are inseparable. Through the generations, the pouch has received personal treatment that reflected the character and wishes of its owner. The modern resurgence of interest in the pouch has followed a pattern within the bounds of precedence. Although there is no exacting standard, the principles remain unaltered.

There are many of today's craftsmen who have brought tremendous ability to their work. In particular, I would like to express my appreciation to Chris Chapman and Gary Birch for their counsel.

BEADWORKING

BY DIANE CHAMBERS

DIANE CHAMBERS, A LANGUAGE ARTS teacher for the past 22 years, started primitive camping and buckskinning in the late 1960s. She tried her hand at sewing her husband, David's, shirts and capotes, making dresses for herself and shirts for their son, and knitting voyager hats for the whole family. Later she went into painting leather Indian tipi bags, parfleches, and possible bags. She began beading around 1978 and her enthusiasm for researching and doing authentic work has increased with each year.

She and her husband, David, make an excellent match. He does all the leather work, cutting and making patterns, sewing most finished items, and adding additional embellishments to make the beaded item complete.

Both Diane and her husband find this an exciting and rewarding hobby. Learning through traveling, visiting the archives of museums, and attending many rendezvous makes an exciting summer vacation.

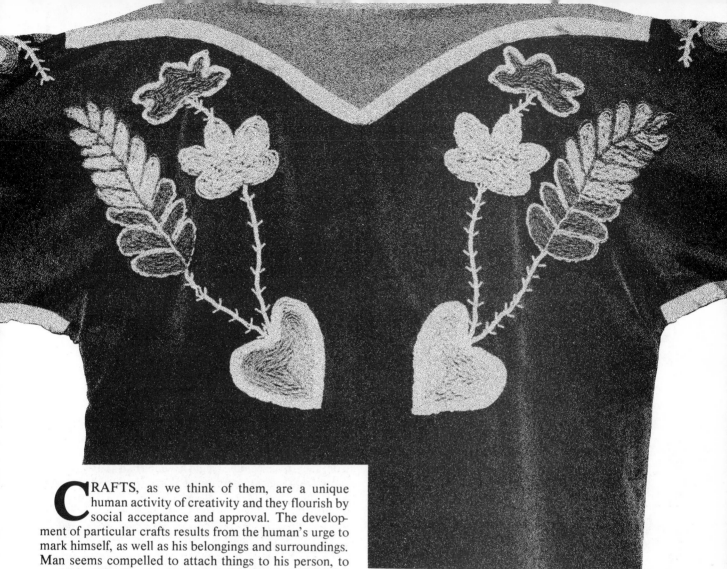

CRAFTS, as we think of them, are a unique human activity of creativity and they flourish by social acceptance and approval. The development of particular crafts results from the human's urge to mark himself, as well as his belongings and surroundings. Man seems compelled to attach things to his person, to mark his skin, pierce body parts and decorate the clothing that covers his body. The American Indian took pleasure in decorating himself and his world. The productivity of his hands and mind that has come to us through research and collected artifacts is magnificent and sometimes overwhelming. This chapter will take one small segment of our Native American's talent, beadwork, from the earliest recorded beginnings to the present.

Indians, especially the Plains Indians, valued fine beadwork. Beadwork was held in such high esteem that certain women who were highly skilled belonged to a sorority as we would say. The Indians called this special group a guild. The head woman of the guild admitted women on their previous merit and desire, then instruction and training began. The tipi, dew cloth, inner partitions, and bed articles were made by women and belonged to the women. Later, taboos were lifted on the sacred items and other articles were included. The fine work done on the sacred items carried over to all other types of beadwork produced including pipebags, moccasins, cradleboards, etc.

We think of the trader, the trapper, and guns like the Colt and Winchester as opening the West. Maybe we should consider the bead as the factor in winning the West. Not only were beads traded for prime beaver hides but also horses, provisions, and in some instances, slaves. One Indian tribe would trade a good horse for 30 sky blue "padre" beads. It has also been stated that the U.S. Army once paid the Mohave Indians six pounds of white beads plus other items for a captured woman.

Beadwork was primarily a woman's art. In the course of a relatively short time, it developed, flourished, reached its peak, and then faded. Some of the finest work was completed before the turn of this century, but it is a craft worth reviving for its wonderful and unique decorative appeal.

The status of beadwork as we look to museum design and craftsmanship seems to be low at this time among our Native Americans, but is picking up among certain interest groups such as buckskinners. It seems that beadwork will continue in museums of the past, scout troops, and our buckskinners, but not in the vital work of those whose ancestors brought it to a culmination. Hope for the future persists that some craftsmen continue to make beautifully designed pieces for personal, family, and ceremonial use. Another positive sign may be the interested, informed white buyers and beaders who are being educated to appreciate the traditional designs and who are willing to make and pay an honest price for a timeless craft.

BEAD TYPES

Most people do not stop to consider that a large percentage of our everyday words had their origin someplace else. We have very few words that began in America. The word bead is an example. The original word bede, came from Middle English, which had as its meaning prayer. For ageless years man has used beads of all kinds; shell, bone, pottery, metal, and glass for decoration and ornamentation.

In Egypt the earliest known glass factory existed in the 18th Dynasty. There is a glass factory still active today that was making beads 7,000 years ago in Lebanon. A glass works was found in Egypt that had been thriving in 1365 B.C. Other evidence has been written that glass beads were made in Russia about a thousand years before those in Egypt. It is overwhelming to believe that glass beads have been in production for so long.

Lots of confusion exists today over bead classification, color, and size. This is due to the lack of a standard reference guide. One example of this is the "pony" bead which is usually considered to be a simple, sometimes crude, monochrome glass bead about the size of a corn kernel or one-eighth inch in diameter. These were first brought into the western United States by the pony pack trains of the traders, thus the name. This bead was twice as large as the beads used later. The most common early pony bead colors were white and medium sky blue. A few black, red, and dark blue beads also have appeared on old pieces.

Then there is the "Crow" bead not unique to the Crow Indians but nevertheless with that name. These are quite large, over ¼ inch in diameter. These beads are sold today in fewer colors than pony beads, and are not much used by today's craftsmen. They are mostly used for necklaces and other colorful accents. These beads were not normally used for weaving or stitching on buckskin designs.

The first recorded introduction of glass beads to America was by Columbus in 1492. It is recorded that on Oct. 12, 1492, he gave the natives of San Salvador Island strings of red glass beads which they wore around their

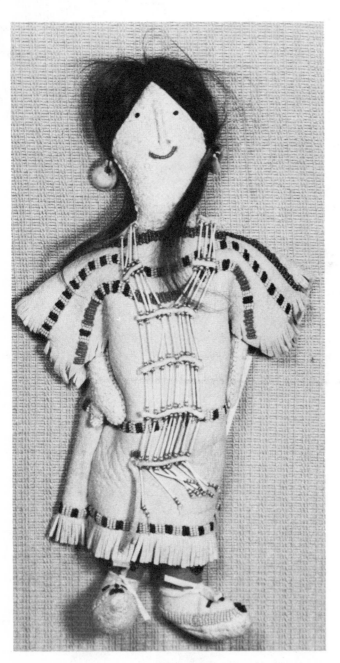

Sioux doll made of brain tanned buckskin with breast plate necklace. The hair is horse hair.

191

Kiowa style man's purse decorated with a double row of tin cones.

necks.

From earliest journals the first recorded exchanges of glass beads in what is now the United States was done by Coronado in 1540. He reached the Buffalo Plains (now Kansas) by 1541. From Coronado's time until the late 1600s a good part of the glass beads traded in the Americas were probably made in glass factories in Murano, Venice. The Venetians passed laws to protect their industry. These laws required imprisonment of the nearest relative of any skilled glass worker who defected to another country. Upon refusal to return, a contract was placed on his life and that of his relatives. The death decree did not stop all defecting workers, however. There were early glass factories in France, Holland, Sweden, Spain, England, and in America at Jamestown. Later, beads were, and still are, produced in Czechoslovakia. The Czech beads of today are considered by some the best produced in qualities of even sizes, colors, and centered holes.

The 300 year old Hudson's Bay Company chartered by the British Crown in 1670 traded untold billions of beads throughout the Northwest. They still trade and sell beads to the Indians. The names of beads change with different manufacturers, wholesalers, and retailers, and even different terms were used by traders and various tribes. That is why colors and exact sizes of beads can be so confusing. The pony bead is about ⅛ inch in diameter or the size of a corn kernel. The Crow bead is larger than the pony. The seed bead came in various sizes from Italian 4/0 and 5/0 to the seed beads of size 10/0 to 15/0 or 16/0. The smaller the bead, the closer and more even the bead-work.

The old records of the Hudson's Bay Company, of colors, sizes, and amounts did not survive in their archives. Today the only samples we have are a few found in European warehouses that bring exorbitant prices when and if you can find some to buy, and those preserved on examples of beadwork that have been collected by museums and/or passed through private collectors and Indian families. Many of our very finest pieces are housed in museums all over Europe. One example would be the Linden Museum in Stuttgart, West Germany, where many items collected by two Germans, Prince Maximilian and Paul Wilhelm in the years 1832-1839, are housed.

The seed bead first appeared with the French in the eastern United States in the late 1600s to early 1700s, but it was not until the mid 1800s that this bead saw any extensive use in the Western states. One of the earliest known pieces of beadwork surviving in the U.S. today is a worn and fragile woven beadwork sash attached to a powder horn dating 1760. The beads are black and white and are woven with spun buffalo wool.

By 1775 all the Indians in the Mississippi River Valley and eastward to the Atlantic had had some contact with Europeans; explorers, missionaries, fur traders, or settlers.

In 1808 the first American owned fur company, the Missouri Fur Company, was established, and Astor organized the American Fur Company in the same year. The trappers left countless millions of glass beads exchanged for vast fortunes in furs. At that time one hank or string of beads 4-8 inches long could bring a prime beaver hide.

When the early traders introduced the glass seed beads and they became readily accessible in the 1700s in the East and mid 1800s in the West, the traditional quillwork began to disappear. Unlike quills, which had to be dyed, the shiny beads came brightly colored and were much easier to work with than quills.

The seed bead was a much smaller, round opaque Venetian bead which became prevalent around 1840 on the Plains. The seed bead was traded in bunches of five or six strings, the strings varying in length from four to six inches long. There were four or five bunches to the pound. The beads came in three sizes varying from one-sixteenth to three-sixteenths of an inch in diameter. The most common sizes were 4/0 and 5/0. Today most of our beads are imported from Czechoslovakia and range from 10/0 to 13/0. These are not the only sizes available but seem to be the most popular. Beads today are available in transparent colors, white, or opaque. The earliest colors appear to have been opaque white and a medium blue.

Because the old beads were made by hand they were somewhat irregular in shape and old beadworkers found it necessary to search for beads of equal size. Commercial beads today generally do not have such variations in size, and are sold on the basis of evenness of length and diameter. The colors of the older beads were richer and softer than the modern colors of today.

The worker should consider the evenness in size when purchasing beads whether by the hank, pound, or kilo. Many colors are available in different sizes. One should take care that all beads purchased for a project should be of a particular size and color or a peculiar irregularity will result when mixing sizes and colors over a large surface. When buying colors, even white, you should buy in quantity enough for the entire project, for colors do vary in dye lots just as yarn does.

Around 1870 translucent beads became available and around 1885 glass colored silver or gold and faceted beads became available plus the metal and glass angular beads. Instead of being rounded they were cut or faceted, which gives a flashing or sparkling quality like a diamond.

Early beads varied considerably in size. Some early work shows this unevenness, as it appears quite crude and irregular in pattern and texture. Finer quality work required the beader to select even sizes, a process which resulted in a quantity of leftover odd sizes and shaped beads, which had to be used later.

Not only did the size of the bead fluctuate with the

Cheyenne design braintan covered rawhide sheath beaded using Cheyenne lazy stitch technique. Tin cone and horse hair decoration.

193

Top left: Cheyenne style beaded buckskin mittens with bear fur cuffs. Lazy stitch technique.

Right: Strike-a-light, ration ticket, or men's dice pouch.

Below: Sioux rosettes made using the lazy stitch technique.

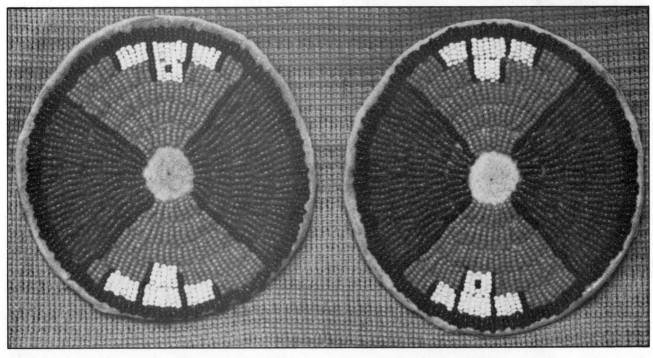

Buffalo rawhide knife sheath
of Cheyenne style with brass tack decoration.

area, trader, and availability, but the colors did also. Backgrounds were usually white or light blue because these colors were the easiest to obtain. Red was the most prized because of its rarity.

In sizing beads today, the Italian and Czech are not exactly compatible. The Czech 12/0 roughly corresponds to the Italian 4/0 and 13/0 roughly to the 5/0.

Just as the sizes differ and change so do the colors. Today many of the old colors such as greasy yellow, blue Cord d' Aleppo, and very recently mustard yellow are very rare and dear. Now we have new colors and types such as Japanese cuts and aurora borealis. Some bead workers have been quick to pick up on these new colors which give a modern look to beadwork.

Remember, to produce an article of beadwork and have it conform to tribal style and period which inspired it, you must use the proper colors, bead size, design technique, and base material of that period in time.

TRIBAL DIFFERENCES

Color symbolism and preference were very strong with many of the tribes, but because they varied with each tribe, sometimes from year to year and often with each individual, it is difficult to state any definite conclusions. Sometimes a certain color they wanted could not be obtained. In the earlier days of trading, red glass beads were very expensive because of a gold compound that was necessary as a pigment. Careful temperature control was also required, making red a difficult color to produce. Bright yellow and orange beads were very rare and almost impossible to obtain until the middle 1800s.

Beginning first with the simple geometric patterns used on old quill work and parfleches, using a few basic colors, the fine art of Indian beadwork developed into the highly complicated and colorful designs in both loom weaving and hand beaded skins and clothing, continuing in some areas into modern times.

The Metis were a mixture of European and Indian heritage and were sometimes called the flower beadwork people. They were influenced by the Ursuline Sisters, who taught French embroidery to the Native American girls at the convents in Quebec City in the early 1600s. However, the Northeastern people already had developed a simpler kind of curvy design which they combined with the more realistic French style to create the resulting naturalistic floral beadwork which became predominant in eastern Canada and the Great Lakes area of the United States and spread westward across the continent into the northeastern corner of the Plains by the late 1700s.

Long before the arrival of the Europeans, the Great Lakes Indians were masters of decoration. In the 1600s the French had introduced beads, silk ribbon, and cloth as well as European designs. Floral beadwork, according to some authors, is from this European influence. From observing museum collections we can see that these patterns gradually spread from the Eastern Indians to the Western tribes. Two main reasons for this influence could have been the expanding 18th and 19th century fur trade and the use and sale or trade of Indian materials made in the East by these Metis to fur traders and Iroquois voyagers in the Northwest. Long before the turn of this century floral beaded materials had been collected from most Western tribes except from the Southwest (Pueblos, Apache, Ute, and Navajo), California, and the Northwest Coast.

Floral beadwork seems to fall into two main styles and from there it is a mixture of individual and tribal differences. The realistic beadwork makes the flowers and leaves look alive. Shading is done on both flowers and leaves and the beads tend to flow along the natural lines, hence, naturalistic style.

The geometric style has evenly made flowers and leaves that can follow a squared grid pattern, with each element of the flower the same size and shape. The leaves are evenly made also, and can fit into a grid pattern. Beading usually does not follow the natural lines, but can go according to individual choice with all petals being beaded in one direction or going in the opposite directions. Usually the design element is spaced so that a repeat mirror image is seen on opposite ends or sides of the piece being beaded.

The Southern Ojibwa, Woods Cree, and Canadian Santee seem to favor smaller and sometimes isolated floral units. The flowers are often multicolored and rarely are the veins of the flowers traced internally. In many cases the stems have little barbs two to four beads long which come off the stem at a 45 degree angle.

The earlier realistic floral beadwork of the Blackfoot and Plains Ojibwa was angular and symmetrical in style, but when you look at Crow, Nez Perce, or other Plateau groups you see highly realistic and multi-colored beads with a cloth background often left plain. Today the background is usually filled in with white, light blue, or light green.

Flathead Indians in Montana were influenced by Eastern Indian men who accompanied Canadian fur traders as boatmen and servants. A strong Ojibwa presence pervades the Flathead floral designs.

The Eastern Sioux were a marginal tribe sandwiched between the Great Lakes and the Plains. They had stylized floral designs which greatly influenced the Northern Plains Indians as floral designs gained popularity. They preferred fine cut sparkling beads. Their main method was the applique technique with occasional lazy stitch.

The Southern style realistic is a fill-in bead design with an outline of one or two rows of beads of a sharply contrasting color which forms the contours of each design element. Usually the floral elements are beaded on blue tradecloth.

The Northern style is to follow the contour of the flowers with a complete fill-in of the floral design. Sometimes they made one-half of a leaf or flower one color and the other half another color. Occasionally some floral beadwork combines both styles.

A minor style of floral work was one in which the floral designs were executed in the lazy stitch with an allover beaded design as seen in Sioux or Cheyenne work.

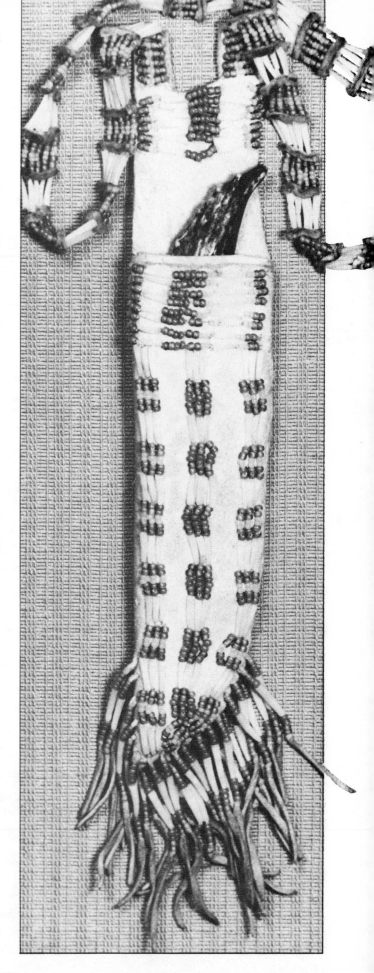

Northwest coast dentalium shell and pony bead neck knife sheath. Rawhide liner covered with brain tanned buckskin.

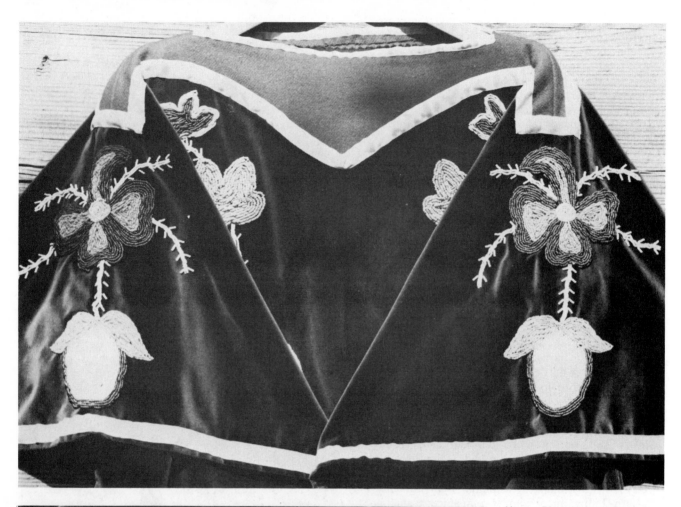

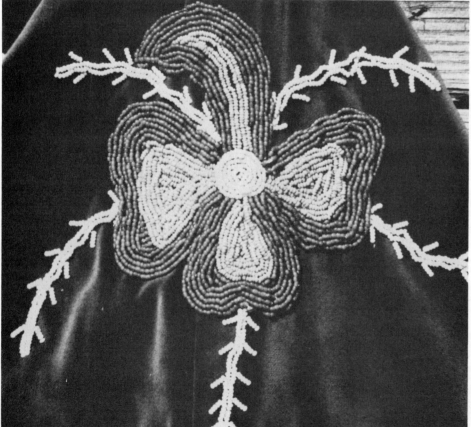

Above: Blackfoot applique technique on velvet dress. Geometric floral designs. Red wool and satin ribbon trim.

Left: Detail of Blackfoot dress with geometric floral designs.

Some floral patterns were used by the Ojibwa, Southern Winnebago, and Menomini in loomed beadwork particularly bandolier bags and garters. This effect was angular rather than the rounded floral style produced by the applique method.

Many controversies arise from this type of beadwork because it is so hard to distinguish different styles, pattern types, and the mixtures of bead application. In no way do I pretend to be an authority on any style or technique. Like so many others, I am a product of all I've read, seen, and tried to produce. The more I read and study, the more I believe that "no one" is an absolute authority on every style, technique, and tribe that produced said work.

The Iroquois use a heavy floral design which came into being about 1860 and continues to the present day. This type of beading is raised above the cloth by one or two methods. First, padding can be used under the beads or the beads can be humped by putting in more beads for the space than you need. Pull the thread tight and the beads will hump up, rising above the cloth. The beads used here were larger and coarser than the beads used in the previous 150 years. This beadwork also included a varying color scheme which created a more naturalistic floral design. Their color scheme was a process of shading.

In the early days the Iroquois had no written language so they communicated their ideas and messages through curving, flowing lines, which created a lacy look. They used bead colors to convey meanings: white expressed peace, health, and harmony; dark purple or black represented sorrow, death, mourning, and hostility; red beads were used to make a declaration of war or an offer to join a war party. The scroll design is the most distinct feature of Iroquois beadwork.

The Iroquois and Mohawk in the mid-19th century devised a new style of bead embroidery that seems to reflect Victorian design concepts. Usually referred to as "embossed beading" because heavy application of beads in an applique technique creates a bas-relief effect, the new style was a departure in both technique and esthetic concept. In addition to a wider color range, which included more dark and medium tones, embossed beading designs became fuller and more florid, often covering most of the background. Muted, transparent beads were generally used for tourist pieces while strong opaque shades were applied to objects intended for tribal use.

Some of the oldest Iroquois designs included diagonal, geometric, and curving lines. Elaborate border patterns with white beads on a dark background were seen mainly between 1750-1850. They often added extra color by running silk ribbon (light blue or rose) along the edge of the item between the border and the white beadwork. Sometimes a floral design was added to the corners for a striking effect. The Iroquois pieces show much evidence of clear glass beads, especially those pieces made for non-tribal members.

Most Plains Indian work was done with opaque beads. The Crow seem most famous for their beautifully beaded horse trappings. They used white beaded lines against blue, yellow, red, and green hour glass and triangular figures. The Crow had their own method of beading commonly called the "Crow stitch" which was an elongated method of the overlaid stitch. They would sew long rows two or more inches in length attached to the

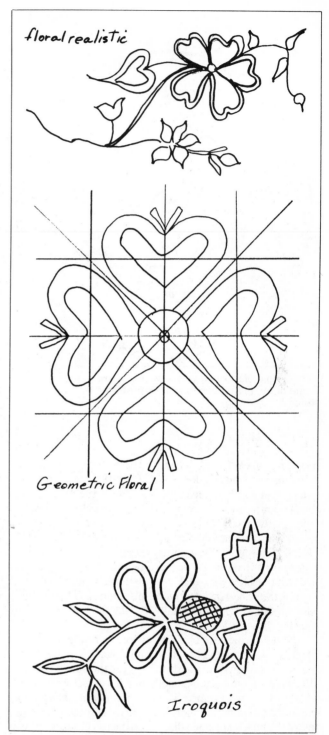

Three drawings of different floral beadwork designs used by different tribes. Some variations will occur within these designs.

198

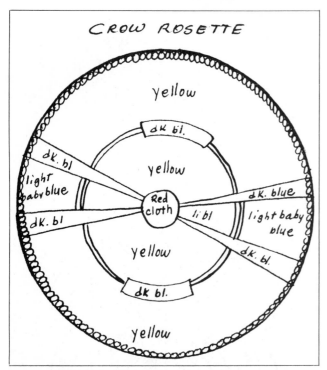

An example of a common design on a Crow rosette and some of the more common colors preferred by the Crow Indians.

material at each end. Then to prevent these rows from sagging and hanging loose in the center, another thread was run at a right angle to the rows under the first row and back over it, under the second row and back in a series of stitches until all rows were tacked down. This was a combination beading technique which suited their needs. These lines of back stitching are placed irregularly at intervals of from 6-12 or more beads. In a row of beads three inches long, six tack down stitches would be used to fasten the long rows to the base material. They usually sewed their beads vertically to the long axis of any piece.

The Crow used a lot of red wool and flannel background areas. The background was actually pieces cut to fit and sewed to the skins between the beaded figures. Very few examples are actually beaded directly on the red cloth. The appearance is misleading unless you can actually examine the work carefully. In some very early work the beads are sewn directly to the red cloth, but this is the exception rather than the rule.

One trait of the Crow was the use of several color schemes in one design. Light blue background was common and sometimes lavender was used but not white.

Typical Crow colors would be blues, red, yellow, green, and white used to outline large darker areas of the design. They generally used only seven colors in their work. Their technique was primarily the overlaid stitch with the lazy stitch used for narrow bands or bordering. Black or orange beads were very rarely used on their work. The designs came from quill and parfleche designs.

The Cheyenne seemed to specialize in borders with feather patterns such as pipe bags decorated with borders

of blue, black, and white bars. Their lazy stitch has a flat look. Painstaking care was given to lining up the rows one above the other. Their beadwork was so flat that from a distance it looked like overlaid stitch instead of lazy stitch, which they mainly used. Their designs can be divided into three categories: (1) geometric (squares, triangles); (2) realistic (birds, horses, people, animals); and (3) stripes or contrasting lanes of color. Older Cheyenne work was done in the preferred Italian bead sizes of 5/0 and 6/0. These old Italian beads were very uneven but the colors were rich with a good selection.

The 1890s brought definite color and bead changes. This work was done in Czech bead sizes 12/0 and 13/0. They primarily used ten colors: (1) flat chalk white (old beads were almost transparent with a slight bluish cast, (2) dark blue (old blue had a purplish hue). (3) turquoise blue (old color was a light turquoise), (4) dark transparent green (old color was an opaque dark green), (5) black for sacred items, (6) transparent rose (old rose with white opaque centers, lots of color shades), (7) pink (old dull pink with a lavender tint), (8) yellow (old dull color, pale, referred to as greasy yellow), (9) orange (old dull pumpkin color), (10) medium green (old dull mint green color). The Cheyenne are among the few Plains tribes using black in their beadwork. Black is mostly used on sacred beadwork or now as a substitute for dark navy blue.

The Kiowa and Comanche stressed border beading with bands of green, yellow, and red, with the overall color a particular mustard yellow.

The Sioux technique is the lazy stitch, but not flat like the Cheyenne. Their rows of beads humped. They did not hook one row on to the other. Each loop was sewed to the material independently of any other of the loops. The early Sioux style was simple and they used few colors which was reminiscent of early quillwork and parfleche designs. They mainly had two types of figures: (1) early, simple blocks and crosses worked with pony beads, (2) later, delicate

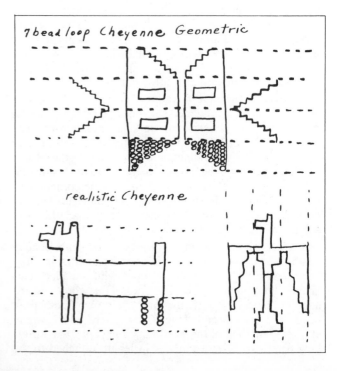

Above: Crow mirror bag beaded using the overlaid stitch. Trimmed in red wool stroud cloth and tin cones.

Right: A Cheyenne style awl case with tin cones and a brass shoe button.

spidery designs with forks, lines, and terraces worked with seed beads. White beads were by far the most common background color, with medium or light blue next, and the other colors used for design accents. These accent colors were usually red and blue with green and yellow less common, and other colors scarcely appeared at all.

Since 1875 the Sioux trend has been toward increasing elaboration. The strong simple quality of forms of early work in small beads has given way to overcrowded

Sioux lazy stitch blanket strip with lazy stitch rosettes. Braintan streamers with hawk bells in rosette centers.

Sioux belt bag beaded using lazy stitch technique. Ermine and tin cone decoration.

Capote epaulettes of Sioux design beaded with the lazy stitch.

patterns. About 1900 the traditional old geometric style gave way to animals, horses, and swastikas which had no connection with their traditional designs.

There was no general beadwork language with the Sioux. Each woman named her design as she saw it. What might have been spears for one became feathers or tipis for another. As with the quillwork the beadwork often served to cover seams and the form of the design was thus dictated.

The Sioux, who resisted domination so long and so well, ironically became the leaders in the use of patriotic symbols in their beadwork. From 1880-1900 the traditional life style of the Sioux underwent a traumatic change. Their way of life was vanishing. The buffalo herds were gone, and deer, elk, and moose had become scarce. They were no longer the nomadic warriors of the Plains. Confined within boundaries established by the government, the old ways and values disintegrated under reservation life, disease, and poverty. However, the enforced idleness of reservation life allowed the artists plenty of time to produce the beaded, quilled, and painted objects they so much admired. Beginning with the early reservation days through the turn of the century, tremendous quantities of beadwork were produced. Good glass beads from Venice were readily available along with domestic cattle skins. Although cowhide does not make good Indian tan, it did provide a firm beading surface. A survey of museums and private collections supports the conclusion that a huge amount of this beadwork was done by the Sioux.

In the 1800s they were the most populous tribe on the Plains. Few other tribes had developed a beadwork tradition as strong and as widespread as theirs. Sioux women were wonderfully skilled and ambitious beadworkers. Family pride was a dominant factor as evidenced by their efforts. Lavish clothing decorations and suitable presents to give to visiting friends or to take on travels to other friends was a necessity. The Sioux's attitude was typical of most Indians: A person was judged by his generosity, not by the amount of possessions he owned. Also a need for income prompted a surge of beadwork. The dealers and collectors surrounded the Sioux wanting to purchase all they could.

This was also the time when completely beading an object became the rule instead of the exception. Moccasins often were beaded on the uppers and the soles. These were showy when riding a horse or sitting visiting with friends. These completely beaded moccasins have often been called burial or wedding moccasins. But, when you see a child's completely beaded moccasin then you can see how the label wedding moccasin is erroneous. Also, you are not going to bead a pair of moccasins in anticipation of a loved one dying in order to wear them. The completely beaded items could have been either their pride of workmanship or an attempt to use idle time to improve on the beaded article's artistic appeal.

Keep in mind that beadwork is frequently not well identified. One of the problems stems from the manner in which pieces were collected. By the fourth quarter of the 19th century many non-Indians were buying mementoes from reservations. Items were picked up at celebrations which were attended by a number of tribes. A tribe would trade something taken in battle, given as a gift, or traded, and later no one knew where the pieces originated.

The best sources are the items accompanied by a history, such as ones taken early to Europe and those in United States Army post collections which were gathered during the Indian Wars of the 1860s-1880s. So keep this in mind when you look at beadwork. Look for materials, shapes, techniques, and decorations of the basic material of the item. Most of the Plains art was done on a base material of animal skin of elk, deer, antelope, buffalo, mountain sheep, moose, cougar, and later after 1882 cow hide was used. Beads were distributed at different periods in various sizes and shapes. Native preferences in color and size can help identify some tribes or a section of the country.

The peyote stitch, sometimes called the gourd stitch, brickwork, or Commanche stitch, has at its base a religious significance for ritual items. This stitch reached the Western Sioux from the Omaha and Winnebago around the turn of the century. This work coming to the Sioux was done in 13/0 beads and the Sioux, preferring 16/0, would tear the beadwork apart and redo it to suit themselves. This beadwork was done on sacred fans, staffs, drumsticks, and rattles. This is a laborious type of beading: one bead applied at a time and tightly drawn into the others. Geometric and rainbow patterns dominate the peyote beadwork using the gradual shading of reds, oranges, and yellows as the main theme colors. This was men's work for men. It would have been almost unheard of for a woman to make a sacred peyote item.

A second religious movement of the late 19th century, one which preceded the Ghost Dance on the Southern Plains, spread far beyond the prairies and still exists today. It is known today by the name of the Native American Church. Their system of worship is based on the beneficial healing qualities of the peyote plant. Attributing to the plant the power to serve as an intermediary with the supernatural, they established a system of worship based on its use.

The ceremonies connected with this movement led to the creation of ceremonial utensils. Implements of worship such as fans, rattles, and birds came into being. The passion for color reached its apex in the beadwork and the use of feathers. Contrasting colors seem to be very important for beadwork to be called outstanding or exceptional.

When studying museum pieces it is quite evident that one important aspect is shading. In other words, colors are thought of as light, medium, and dark as opposed to red, pink, green, yellow, etc.

There are two schools of thought when doing beadwork: (1) Don't be afraid to copy designs or color schemes. Remember you can't improve on the way it was done. Don't substitute your ideas for the old Indian craftsman's designs. After all aren't we trying to emulate the way of life of the pre-1840s in our mode of living, clothing decorations, etc.? (2) Use your imagination, bring your life experiences to your work and create unique and personal designs by combining all these ingredients. Consider producing your own designs and when you do, you will become a true craftsman and you'll not see a copy of your work on several other people or their blankets.

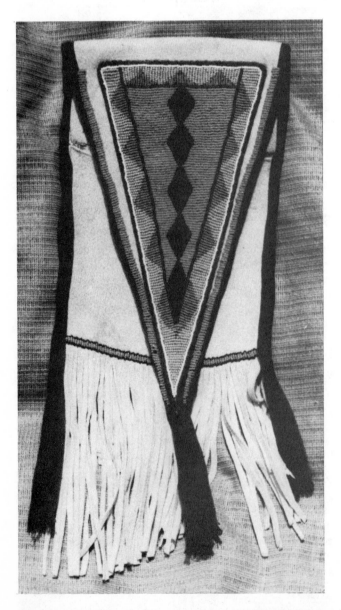

The overlaid stitch technique was used on this Blackfoot style belt bag. It's trimmed in foxbraid.

203

TECHNIQUES

There are two basic techniques which have been practiced by Indians since they began beadwork. How they started these techniques and developed them no one seems to exactly know. It could have been some traders' teaching or perhaps native ingenuity but they are still used today and with older and newer innovations added. The first technique is the woven beadwork and the second is the embroidery method stitched on a foundation.

Bead weaving which may or may not be worked on a loom was practiced by Woodland Indians and occasionally, by the Eastern Sioux. Weaving without a loom consists of tying threads or hair in a clump to a branch or tree and tying the other ends to the beader's waist, keeping the warp threads taut. You pick beads and thread them on the shorter weft threads as you introduce them and weave the thread in and out adding beads at random; a very primitive and less definite pattern than most other types of beadwork.

The weaving frame used by some early bead workers was a bow with a number of warp strings strung on it in the position of the bowstring and with perforated pieces of birchbark used as spreaders. In time, an oblong wooden frame took the place of the bow and this frame found its way to the Western Sioux. Bead weaving by this method is an easier and quicker process than any method of sewing (embroidery) beadwork and is well adapted to the geometrical style. Strong cotton threads forming the warp are wrapped around the frame to the desired width. Some people use a comb, others notch the frame the width of the beads. Beads are then strung with a fine needle on a thread the size of the bead and held under the warp threads. The needle and thread cross over the end warp thread and pass through all of the beads as they are pushed up in between the warp threads from the bottom. Over and under with each row of beads securely fastening each bead between the warp threads with two threads. This is one technique that has been practiced many, many years.

The most commonly used beading techniques are the overlaid (spot stitch) and the lazy stitch with the applique stitch following.

The *overlaid* technique uses two threaded needles, one to string the beads, and the other to sew the lines of beads to the material. This stitch produces long flat lines

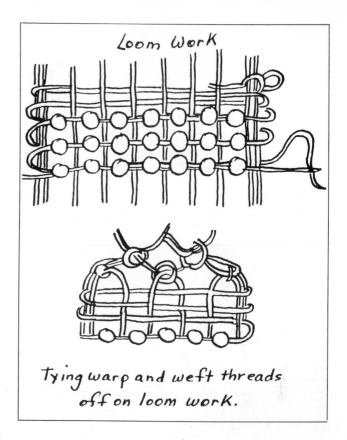

which are held very tightly against the base material. This is a very versatile stitch as it also permits you to execute elaborate circular designs. This technique is substantially the same as that of quillwork.

The thread used for stringing the beads should be as thick as possible. The thicker the thread the more even the line of the pattern to be obtained. Thoroughly wax the bead thread. A single spiralling stitch is used to fasten the beaded thread between every two or three beads. I like to sew from right to left so I can hold the strung beads in my left hand and keep the beads taut and in place with my fingers while I stitch with the right hand. You'll devise your own comfortable way as you practice. Usually the design is outlined first, then the inside of the area is completely covered. Rosettes use this technique with two threaded needles and a stiff base material. Irregular beads can be

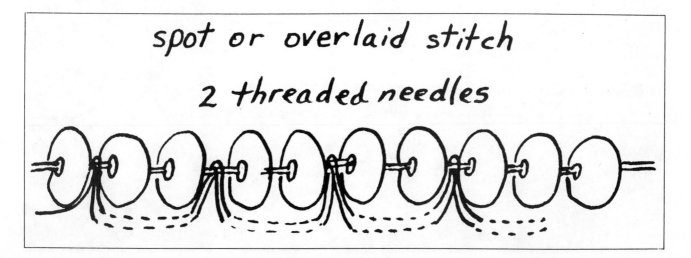

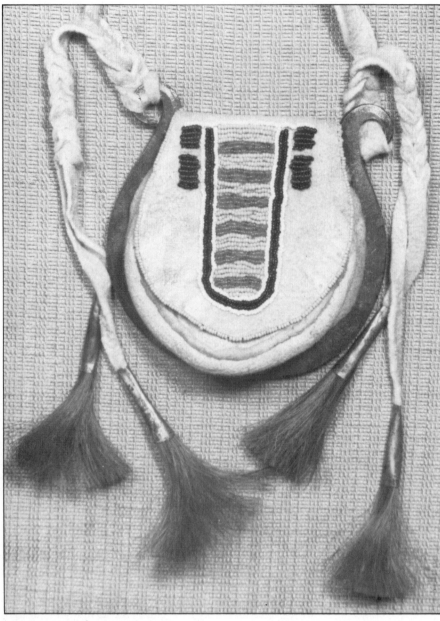

Above: The overlaid technique on a striker bag with tin cone and horse hair decoration.

Right: Nez Perce design knife sheath beaded using the overlaid technique.

Below: Sioux beaded belt. Combination of overlaid stitch and lazy stitch.

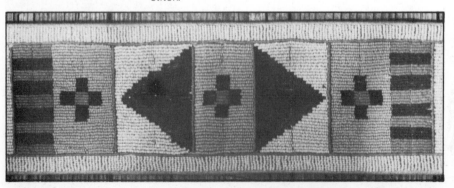

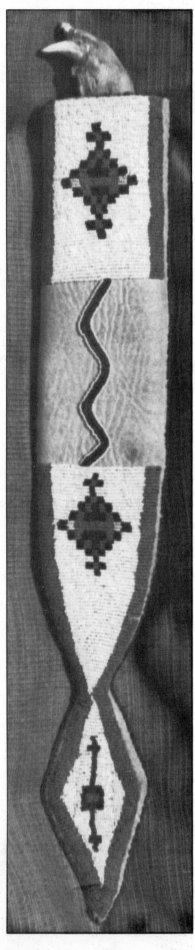

205

utilized in a rosette to fill in or cut down space size as needed to complete the circle.

Use the following steps to make a rosette by this technique. (1) Draw your design on your material. You need to mark the exact center of the circle. You will be beading directly on your drawing, so be sure it is legible and exact. A compass is a good tool for a perfect circle, with an exact center point. (2) Some beginners use an embroidery hoop to keep the fabric tension perfect so their rosette will not buckle or pucker. (3) Sew one bead in the very center of the circle. (4) Bring both needles up near the center and string enough beads on one needle to fit around the center bead. The number may be as few as four or as many as eight. (5) Sew these beads to the material with the second needle. (6) Continue putting beads on the thread for the next row and fitting the pattern and number of beads as you thread them. (7) Sew each row in place with the second needle every third bead. If you want to vary this technique, start the center bead at the edge of the circle and make concentric rows over the center bead. You can also start a rosette around a concho or a button.

The *lazy stitch* was one of the earliest methods used on the Plains to attach beads to articles of clothing. This is perhaps one of the most widespread of the beading techniques. Some people have said the name reflects the ease and speed at which the work progresses in comparison to the overlaid or applique stitch. It is true that the lazy stitch requires a smaller number of stitches in the base material than does the overlaid stitch, but anyone that does beadwork knows it is not a lazy man's craft, regardless of the technique employed.

In the lazy stitch the beads usually are applied in a series of loops or bands each composed of transverse strings of beads. The number of beads on a loop varies according to the type of beads used and the design employed. The bead loops will usually vary in height from ¼ to ⅜ inch, with an average height of 5/16 of an inch. The smaller the bead, the more you can use in a loop. The thread is passed through just the surface of the leather. If cloth is used, then the stitches go through the fabric from front to back.

Loops with odd numbers of beads can be centered to form points without crowding. Crowding happens when you use loops with even numbers of beads and try to form points. Some geometric and most floral designs however, use even numbered bead loops (2, 4, 6, 8, 10, etc.). Odd bead loops (3, 5, 7, 9, etc.) are good for any pointed triangular design or single center point designs. If there is a triangle in the design you should be able to put a straight-edge along the side of the triangle. To make sure the design stays this straight, make your corrections in either the background or in the body of the triangle.

The number of beads in a loop is not absolute. Due to irregularities in the size, it may be necessary to put either more or fewer beads in a particular loop. That is why you mark your row width because this helps keep the design even on both sides.

As either a beginner or an experienced person with an intricate design, you can use graph paper, which can be purchased with small squares approximately corresponding to size 10/0 beads.

When using graph paper line off your bead rows with a dark pencil. Using colored pencils, color in the design

Brain tanned buckskin covered rawhide knife sheath of Sioux design. Beaded using lazy stitch. Horse hair and tin cone decoration.

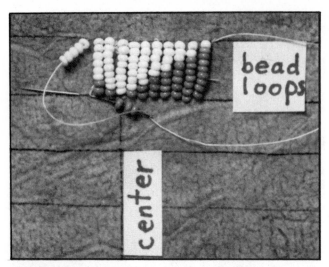

Mark the leather for center line and bead rows. The photo also shows the proper spacing for putting down bead loops.

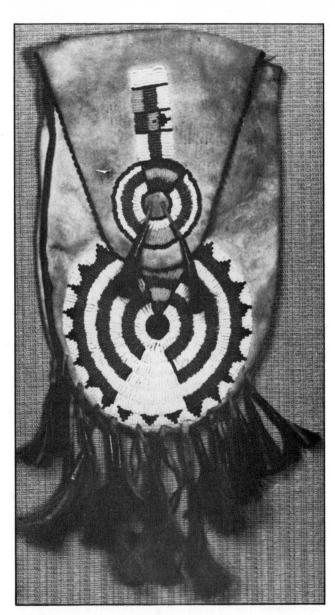

Cheyenne keyhole design using lazy stitch technique. Tin cone and horse hair decoration.

according to the number of beads in each loop. When you are beading you can keep up with your design by counting the squares in each part of the design and using that many corresponding beads of a particular color. This will not give an exact design size because the beads will not exactly conform to any graph paper, but it will show you approximately the size and shape of your design. Size 10/0 beads will be approximately ten loops per inch. Size 11/0 beads will estimate at eleven loops per inch and etc. The Italian 4/0 beads usually give four loops per centimeter, etc. Remember this is loops we're talking about not individual beads in a loop.

When you lay out the center lines, give some extra space between the design elements to let the background fill in for the actual size of the design. Experience will be the best teacher. (1) To get the width of the beading row I start by stringing six to twelve beads on the needle, push them tightly together and lay the needle on a card, marking the first and last bead. Then string four times the number of beads first put on the needle to get an average distance. (2) Next divide the total number by four, which gives you the width of one row. I do this to offset the effect

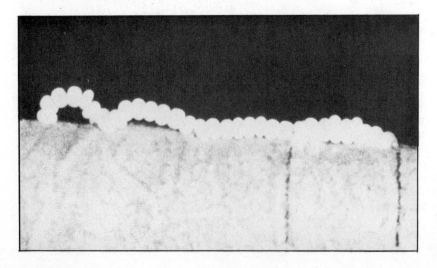

A line of lazy stitch bead loops showing various results. Starting on the left, the first loop is incorrect because it has too much hump. The second loop is the Sioux loop. A little hump is correct. The third loop is Cheyenne and should be as flat as you can get it. Loop four shows how a bead loop fits inside the marked rows.

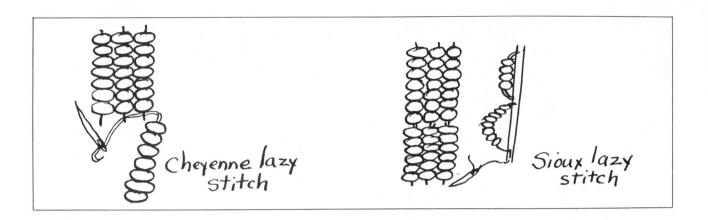

Cheyenne lazy stitch

Sioux lazy stitch

of irregular beads in getting a bead row. (3) Third, mark the width of your rows on the beading side of the base material with a #2 lead *pencil*. Do *not* use ball point or ink, which can smear or show through the beading loops. Lay out the center line of your area to be worked. (4) Tie your knot on top of the leather or on the bottom of cloth. Your design should be started at the center. Put the beads on your needle for the first loop, take a stitch just through the top surface of the leather following the grid line you marked on your material. The length of the stitch should be about one and a half the bead width. Stitches that are too small will cause the beads to bunch together resulting in cramped rows. If the stitches are too far apart the leather will show between the bead loops. Remember, Cheyenne lazy stitch is a flatter loop, while the Sioux style has a slight hump in the bead loop. Bead toward one end of the design from the center. Next bead the other half of that row. Once you have the first row finished you may start at either end and bead completely across the entire design and background. Starting at the center of the design in the center of your article will ensure even spacing of all your elements.

In doing geometric work be careful that your bead loops are vertical with your center line. This is crucial so that your design will not lean to one side or the other.

A lazy stitch can also be used to make rosettes. You do not use a center bead as a starting point as a rule. Draw your circle with a compass, cup, or other round object. In the center, using another small object like a thimble, draw another round circle. Your lazy bead loops start fanning out from the smaller circle like the spokes on a wheel. As you make each row of beads, you will add more loops to fill in the area. Be careful to keep each loop pointed in a straight line to the edge of the circle. You must change the width of the stitch when beading a rosette with this stitch. Wider stitches may be needed on the outside of each row to keep the loops going in a straight line to the edge of the circle. For very tight curves it may be necessary to put in a partial loop. (Example: A five bead loop in an eight bead row to fill out the outer edge of the curve.)

Below: Lazy stitched rosettes.

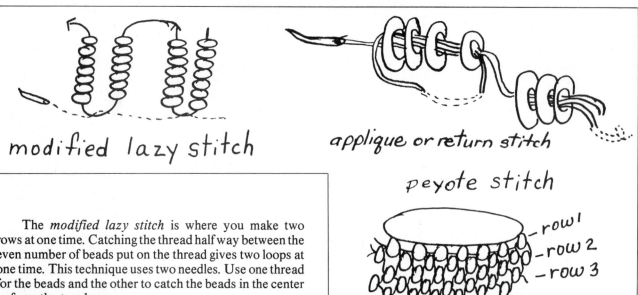

modified lazy stitch

applique or return stitch

peyote stitch

—row 1
—row 2
—row 3

The *modified lazy stitch* is where you make two rows at one time. Catching the thread half way between the even number of beads put on the thread gives two loops at one time. This technique uses two needles. Use one thread for the beads and the other to catch the beads in the center to form the two loops.

The *applique* or return stitch is a system of sewing down beads and retracing through the last half, one third, etc., before adding more beads to the thread. String two to six beads, stitch these to the backing then bring the needle back, coming up behind the middle bead or chosen one. Now go through the last few beads again before adding any new beads to the needle. The amount of beads you go back through can be your selection. Only one needle is used and the beads are held tightly to the backing with this double stitching method. Many floral designs are beaded with this technique.

Peyote, gourd, Mohawk, or Ute stitch is named for the location from which it comes. This technique is good for cylindrical objects or small rosettes. With a wooden handled object wrapped with a leather covering (or without the covering) wind the thread tightly around the handle several times. The wound thread provides a surface for beginning and ending stitches.

For a leather or fabric covered cylinder: (1) Knot the thread in the material near the top edge. (2) String the thread with enough beads to go *half* way around the handle. (3) Wrap the thread once around and knot. (4) Move the beads and space them equally around the complete circle, one bead space apart along the wrapped thread. (5) Now starts the slow process of adding the beads one at a time by stitching each bead on your first row. Add a new bead, go through the next bead in line spaced on the handle. Each new bead is pulled half way into the space between the strung beads on the first row. (6) When the second row is finished, add the third row, which will be in direct line, vertically with the first row. (7) Add the fourth row, which will line up with the second row in the same manner and so on.

You pull each new bead up into the space provided by the preceding row with the thread running a zig-zag course through both the old and the new beads. Thus, the thread passes through each bead twice. If you want to put all the beads on the first row at the beginning you are actually putting on two rows at once. You will add the third row by adding a new bead *every other* bead. The original number of beads for the total circumference (distance completely around the object) at the beginning should be an even number. If the thread is pulled tight with each new

bead added, this produces a firm, strong, tight beadwork on the foundation that will not move easily.

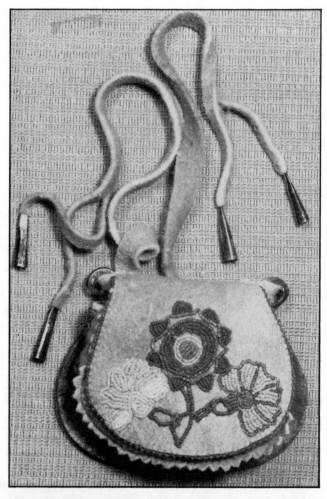

This neck or belt pouch is beaded using the applique (floral naturalistic) technique on brain tanned buckskin.

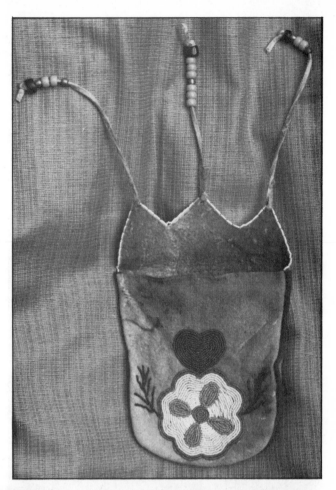

Above: Northwest Coast Tinglet shirt made of red and navy blue wool and lined with calico. Beaded using the applique technique and trimmed in silk ribbon.

Right: Applique technique on a geometric floral pouch.

Below: Detail of Northwest Coast Tinglet shirt beaded with the applique technique.

Edging can be done in several ways. The most common seems to be to pass from the edge through two beads and back through the edge, back through the last bead, thread two more beads, leave one free and go back through the lower bead and back through the last bead. Thread two more beads and repeat until the edge is finished. This can be varied by the number of beads used along the edge in the outer loop. An edging adds a finishing touch to set off a fine piece of beadwork.

A *lazy stitch covered edge* is a good technique for

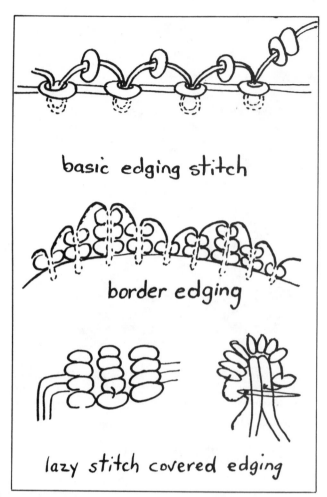

basic edging stitch

border edging

lazy stitch covered edging

Geometric style beadwork using applique technique. Scatter beadwork around the edges.

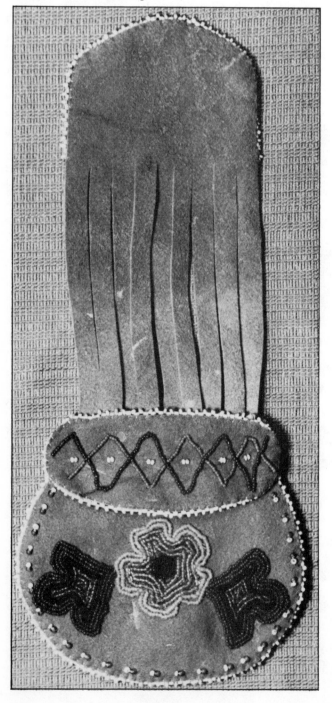

covering several edges sewn together. Use enough beads to cover the edges and stitches that were used to sew the edges together. A lazy stitch is started on one side close to the edge using four or more beads, drape them over to the opposite side and stitch down. Pick up the same number of beads and stitch back on the original side. Go back and forth in this manner until the desired edge is covered.

Scatter beading, as the name suggests, is a method of sewing beads individually to the material in either simple figures or an open polka-dot pattern. The technique was used by a few plateau tribes such as the Nez Perce and Spokane. Obviously, this style was limited in its design potential. Scatter beading was primarily used as a subtle means of varying texture or mottling a surface.

Oblique beading can be done in interesting geometric designs. Tie a row of beads loosely to the edge of the material. Each bead must be tied. At the end of the run the needle is passed through the first bead, through a loose bead, through the second bead, through a loose bead and so on to the end. If the return run must pass through the last bead a loose bead is strung to hold the thread. This process is repeated and different colors are added as desired.

Bead fringe uses are as diversified as bead edgings for borders. Good beads to use for fringe besides the round seed, pony, or Crow beads are the bugle or tube beads. You can also finish a rosette, a sash, the bottom of a possible bag, or ties. End the fringe with beads, shells, claws, cones,

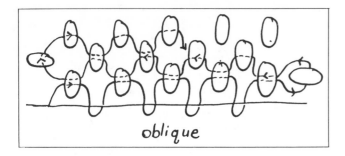

oblique

or teeth.

Oglala butterfly beadwork is beadwork independent of a base. You can make necklaces and bracelets by stringing a single strand of beads on heavy waxed thread the length desired, and then tie in a circle, or tie a bone button on one end and a loop on the other for the fastener. Use waxed thread for the rest of the necklace or bracelet. The second row will go through every third bead, adding three new beads in between. The third row will have the five beads attached through the center of every third bead in the second row. The fourth row has seven new beads attached through the center of beads in the third row. The shape will ruffle like lace as you add more rows. You can continue to use seven beads on each additional row going through the center bead on the previous row or if you want a wide bead collar add two extra beads to each new row until the desired size is reached. Colors and pattern are up to the individual beader.

The techniques of beadwork you have been given are by no means all inclusive or the final word in this craft area. Visit museums, Indian artifact shows, trading posts, galleries and powwows, any place beadwork or Indian work might be shown. Inspect the work closely and learn from other artisans. Ask respectful, intelligent questions. Most beadworkers will gladly share information with you and hopefully you will learn something from each other.

BEADING MATERIALS AND TOOLS

Your materials, like the tools of a carpenter, make you the best you can be with experience. You need to be organized, so start with a beading or tool box. A homemade or purchased box with dividers or compartments is fine. Make sure the box is primitive looking because you don't want to go to rendezvous without your equipment. In this box you will want the following items: (1) needles, (2) threads, (3) scissors, (4) pliers, (5) awl, (6) beeswax, (7) thimble, (8) beads, (9) leather scraps and base material, and (10) a small 6 inch ruler.

NEEDLES — Use a Sharps (short) needle for embroidery beading. I prefer the English or German needles as opposed to the Japanese. I find the quality of the steel and the strength of the eye much superior to that of the Japanese. Just like beads, the larger the number the smaller the needle. A number 10 needle can be used with a 10/0 bead, but it is best to get needles one size smaller than the beads to allow for the thickness of the thread passing through the bead. The following is a good guide for English and German needles: 10/0 beads = size 11 needle, 11/0

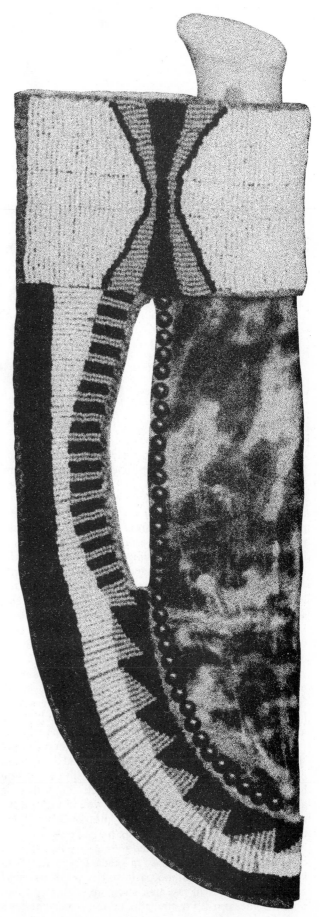

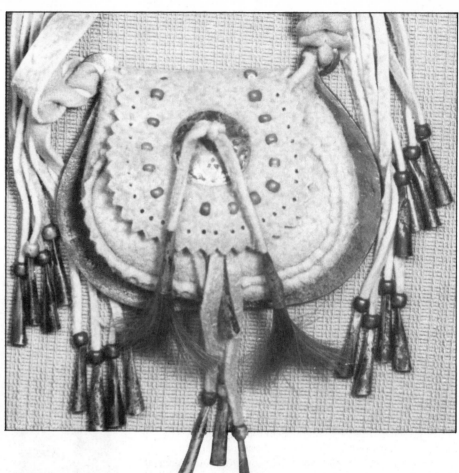

Brain tanned buckskin striker bag with pony bead and tin cone decoration. A sterling silver concho acts as a closure.

beads = size 12 needle, etc. Japanese needles come in only two sizes, size 14, which corresponds to a 10/0 bead and size 16 which corresponds to a 12/0 bead. The thinner the needle the easier it is to break, so have a good supply on hand. Keep your needles sharp. Using a seamstress pincushion helps keep them from rusting and keeps the points sharp. You have to experiment with the needles to find the kind you prefer. Beading needles used primarily for loom work are long, thin, and flexible. These are not satisfactory for embroidery beading because they are too limber and the extra length is unnecessary and bothersome.

Glover's needles are triangular shaped for easy puncture of leather and fabrics. These are best for sewing items and articles of clothing together. Size 9 is the smallest I have used and it makes small holes for sewing most items. Split sinew works extremely well with size 9. Size 7 seems to be the most common size as it is so versatile for small and large projects. Your holes will be quite large and you need to use thicker thread to fill the space.

THREAD — This is also a personal preference but I shall list several kinds with their good and bad qualities to help you choose one to begin with or for possible use, if you had not thought of it before. (1) Waxed dental floss is already waxed to some degree, but as you use it, it frays easily and is hard to thread on a needle. (2) Silk or linen thread is extremely strong and silk has superior strength even when the thread is twisted into a very fine thread, making it good for the smallest of beads. I have used both kinds for everything but moccasin soles. At this writing I cannot find either in my area anymore, but if you can obtain some, test it for strength and use either one with your next project. (3) Sinew, the most authentic sewing thread, can be purchased at most trading stores. It is the most trouble to work with as you have to separate the fibers and keep them moist to make them flexible to work with. The sinew I've purchased has been from 12 to 18 inches long, which means a lot of starting and stopping with the short strands. The sinew does a fine job of giving stability to the beads, because of its tackiness. The end of each strand can be cut into a sharp point and when dry it is stiff enough to follow an awl hole through leather and is fine for threading a needle. Sinew sewed buckskin is remarkably sturdy. Pieces made with this can be fairly serviceable, even up to a hundred years. (4) Artificial sinew, or harness lacing, can be used full strength or split in strands fine enough for a 13/0 bead. Some brands split more times than others. Your needle can separate the fibers and split them until you cannot separate any more. (5) Cotton thread is used by some beaders in a single or double strand. If you have no other thread use a polyester covered cotton instead of just cotton. Neither one is very strong and is a poor choice to use in such a time consuming craft. (6) The most popular thread today is "nymo" nylon, which is very strong, but does have a tendency to stretch. Another drawback of nylon is that the knots seem to work their way loose quite often. When tying the knot weave the thread back and forth several times making several flat knots going in different directions. Be sure and wax your thread

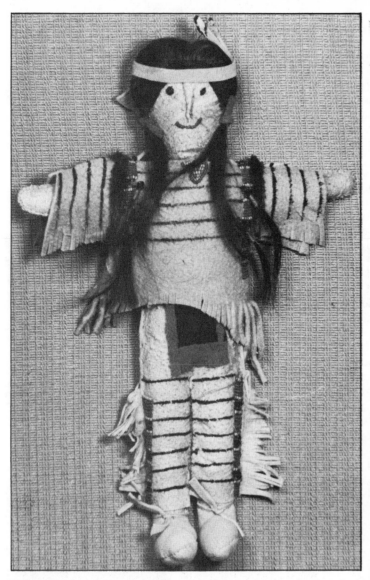

Mandan male doll complete with
war shirt, leggings, loin cloth the
human hair. Beaded legging and
arm strips.

Plains awl case with tin cone
and silver button decoration.

because this tackiness helps hold the knots in place. Nylon
is best used on a base material that has a little give. The
sizes of nylon thread differ from the beads or needles. The
larger the letter the thicker the thread. Sizes 000,00,0 to A
are the finest to fine. Sizes B, D, and F being thick, thicker,
and thickest. F is mainly used for stringing beads and warp
threads on a loom. The thicker the thread, the stronger it is.
The thread size depends on the bead and the needle size.
You want the thread to fill the hole in the bead so the beads
will easily follow your pattern and stay firm without
wiggling around. If you are using a 10/0 bead and a 10 or
11 needle you would use size D thread. Keep on hand the
fine size A thread for 12/0 or 13/0 beads considering you
are using size 12, 13, or 15 needles. Very, very fine 000 to

214

0 thread is for the very small 16, 18, and 24 size beads, not used by a lot of beaders.

SCISSORS — Your first pair of scissors for strictly beading purposes should be small (3-4" long) with very pointed sharp blades for cutting in small areas and snipping unwanted threads. The second pair for your sewing box is a good sharp pair with the ability to cut through leather without force on your part. Cutting fringe with bad scissors can produce blisters on your fingers almost immediately.

Not necessary, but very useful for seams on clothing and decorative edgings on leather, would be a pair of pinking shears. Get good scissors that can be sharpened when needed. Cheap throw away shears will not perform satisfactorily and in the long run you will have spent more money on several pairs of cheap scissors than investing in one good pair.

PLIERS — One of your most useful tools is a small pair of needle nose pliers with small pointed ends. If they are not tapered enough, file the points so they are narrow enough to get in between the smallest beads to break the unwanted one, but not disturb the beads on the opposite sides. They also help pull a needle through a piece of leather without breaking it.

AWL — I prefer a three-sided, tapered awl which helps me adjust the size of the hole I need. Round awls do not seem to pass through the leather with as much ease. The awl is not awkward to use in beading. Once mastered you can go twice as fast and the hole makes it much easier on the needle and the thread.

BEESWAX — Use beeswax on any thread you choose. Even artificial sinew needs rewaxing as you continually pull it in and out of the base material. Beeswax helps make the thread easier to manage by helping to eliminate tangles and knots, plus holding the beads tighter in position and also protecting the thread from being cut by some beads with sharp edges. I prefer to use beeswax candles cut into 3-4 inch lengths, which are easier to hold and roll the thread over the cylinder. Do not confuse candle wax with beeswax, which has a definite smell and a tacky feeling. Wax your thread before trying to thread the needle and the stiff point will help make the job easier. I wax the thread between each bead loop when doing the lazy stitch. The wax not only helps hold the position of the beads tighter but a small amount of wax will show around the beads creating the slightly used look as it collects dust and other elements.

THIMBLE — A thimble on your middle finger will become an essential tool, once you get the feel of using it or you find your fingers are so sore you cannot bead for several days while they heal from all the puncture wounds. Experiment with sizes until you find the one that fits snugly.

BEADS are of your own choosing. If you are a new beader, start with 10/0 Czechoslovakia beads and save the smaller or older, more irregular shaped beads until you have gained experience. A few small containers of beads are useful for repair and if room is available in your box, take along a small project to work on as you sit and while away the hours with friends. You may also need extra beads for practicing a new stitch a fellow beader shows you. I use small, clear, screw-together plastic cylinders for my samples of beads. These can be purchased in two sizes

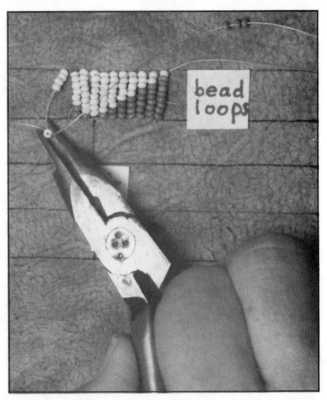

Above: The incorrect way to break beads. A bead broken this way can cut the thread.

Below: The correct way to break seed beads using needle nose pliers.

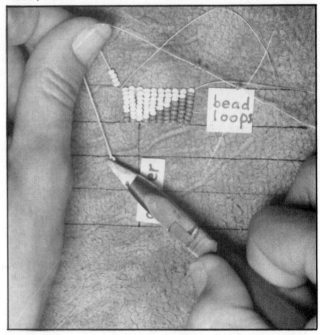

in the sports department of local discount stores.

LEATHER SCRAPS AND BASE MATERIAL — The scraps of leather will be useful as thongs or for stringing beads. Cut in a circle and you can strip out a very long thong.

Beaver tooth medicine bag. Real bead size beads on brain tanned leather. Brass shoe button closure.

Your base material or foundation is one of your most important considerations, next to your choice of beads. Wool is one type of base material. Historically called strouding or stroud cloth, the most prominent colors are navy blue or deep red. Be careful and do not let the wool get wet and make sure it does not stretch.

Good work can be done on canvas, which a lot of people use because of its price, but I feel that for the most part it is inferior to work done on leather. You can thicken your canvas by making a sandwich of brown paper sacks, or dressmaker's pellon in the middle. This sandwich provides a stiff, thicker foundation for items like bag flaps, cuffs, collars, etc. You can also use the sandwich for wool, which lessens the stretching tendency.

Commercial leather such as buckskin provides a good background, but be sure and bead on the rough side of the leather. The needle will have a tendency to tear through the smooth side, and the rough side has a richer look and in some cases the texture from a distance resembles brain tanned leather.

The ultimate in base materials is smoked, brain tanned deer, elk, or moose. Buckskin would be considered the best of the three because of the suppleness, flexibility, and fluffiness of the skin plus the ease with which the needle passes through the top layer of the skin. All of your stitches may be hidden by going only part way through the leather. Unsmoked or white brain tan is fine except it gets awfully dirty as you work on it, and if the item gets wet, the leather stiffens and loses shape, and the beauty of your work is lost. If you can buy or trade for white hides, learn to smoke them yourself. You'll save quite a bit of money or better still, learn to brain tan. There are several good books on the market and a chapter in this book that will take you step by step through the whole process.

You now have all the materials you need, and when at home, you should have a well lighted flat surface to work on. How you keep your beads depends on your own choosing. Some beaders separate colors in shallow dishes, some keep them on strings taking one, or several, at a time from the hank knotted on the end. Others pick up each individual bead as needed. Put a piece of flannel, wool, or leather on your working surface. Beads are more easily picked up and roll less on a fabric surface. You want to use the best, most convenient method to suit your needs.

Graph paper is one tool that is very useful for the beginner and for a very intricate design, for advanced beaders. Graph paper is ideal for geometric designs, but much harder to lay out for other designs such as floral. You can even use a special graph paper for the peyote beadwork. Colored pencils work well in filling in your design, which will give you an approximate picture of what you will have in the final product.

Photographs help the mind to refresh itself on an idea or get new ideas of exactly what an item looked like and the little added decorations to finish it off. Photographs may be obtained from museums, books or in some cases another beadworker willing to have his work photographed. ASK! Don't just snap a picture of their work, or they may snap at you!

ACCESSORIES ON BEADED ITEMS

Accessories are not essential in themselves but they do add to the beauty or effectiveness of the finished article. Here are a few of the many final touches you may add to complete your finished article: hawk bells, dentalium shells, brass thimbles, flattened coins, buttons, hair pipe, tin cones, brass hawk bells, and brass shoe buttons. Tin cones are very effective when used with colored horse hair or you can yarn wrap the fringe several inches from the bottom of the article. Pinking shears make a finished saw tooth edge.

Look closely at museum pieces, and other work that attracts you to see what final embellishments were added to each piece. A friend just recently noted a piece of Crow beadwork decorated with spoons in the Field Museum in Chicago. She took photographs so she could have a refresher after she had obtained all her materials and was ready to start the project.

Observation and experience will let you know whether the finished item "lacks" something. You can use native materials that would be correct for the time and tribe of the piece you are doing. Deer toes, elk teeth, and quill wrapped fringe are a few of the many ideas.

TIPS AND RECOMMENDATIONS

If you buy tin cones, age them by taking the shiny finish off. Making your own cones would add more authenticity to your work. Making cones is a tedious and time consuming job. You need tin in strips cut to the width of the cones you need for each special project. When you look at old pieces you will note that not all the cones were the same length and diameter. This depends on the size of the beaded item. Don't worry about making perfectly shaped cones. No two handmade cones would ever look exactly alike, and you want them to have the flair of looking handmade.

Make several copies of the different kinds of graph paper (see page 267) and use colored pens or pencils for your design. Remember the small graph paper will almost correspond to a 10/0 bead so you'll have a fair idea of the size and shape of your design.

Fabric carbon, which dressmakers use for marking darts, can also be used to mark geometric designs on your base material. This does not rub off and make a mess like regular carbon paper. I like to use a #2 lead pencil to mark the starting point and the first line for geometric designs. The pencil will eventually rub off and does not leave any telltale smudges or lines on your fabric. Ball point or ink pens are as bad as carbon paper. They smear and leave a glaring dark line to peek at you from the edges of your design.

Dye your own horse hair with Rit dye. Hang the hair outside in nice weather to drip dry. Buying a tail or clump of blond hair is much cheaper than buying colored hair and you can dye in the quantities you need for a long time.

Don't use glue to fasten beadwork to the background material. Sew your beadwork as you do it, or sew the beaded piece to the background or base material when it's

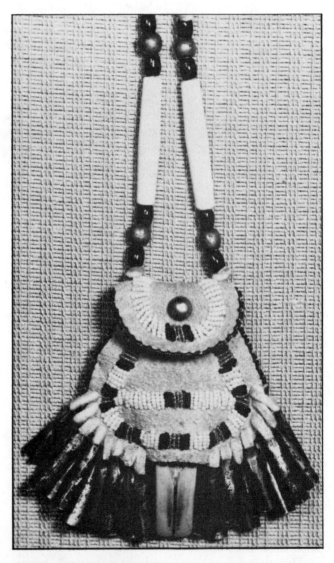

Beaver tooth medicine bag. Tine cone, brass bead, and cobalt blue pony bead decoration.

217

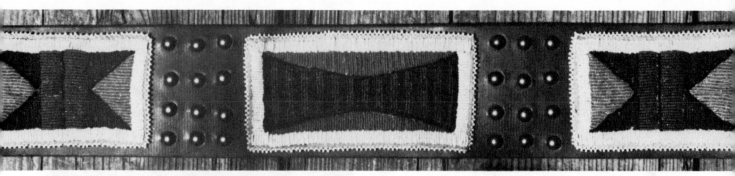

Above: Gros Ventre beaded tack belt. Beaded by using a combination of the lazy stitch and overlaid stitch.

Left: Teton Sioux comb and mirror case with tin cone decoration. Beaded with lazy stitch technique.

finished. You can use rubber cement to hold the beaded piece to the background in position while you sew, but don't use a glue like Elmer's because it becomes hard and stiffens your base material. If it dries before you've had a chance to sew, you'll be trying to bead through a piece of leather as stiff as a board.

Rawhide is expensive and buying a side may be more than you would use in a year. If you need a small piece for a knife sheath, awl case, or even moccasin soles, buy a rawhide dog chew bone. Soak the chew bone in a pan of water until it becomes soft and pliable, then untie the twist at each end, flatten the piece and let it partially dry. Then you're ready for your project. You don't want the rawhide soaking wet when you're getting ready to use it, but just wet enough to be easily molded into the shape you need. Remember, rawhide shrinks when it dries and can twist into odd shapes. Knife sheaths and awl cases can be wrapped and sewn damp. Grease your knife, fashion damp rawhide around the knife, sew, let dry, sew your buckskin around the rawhide sheath and you are ready to bead. Or draw the sheath pattern on leather, bead, then sew beaded leather around rawhide case. Thin rawhide is good for awl cases, medium to thick for knife sheaths, moccasin soles, and trunks. Have a project in mind before you buy your rawhide.

"Bead your project before you sew it together," is the rule with a few exceptions. I like to bead awl cases and knife sheaths after they are stitched on the rawhide base. In most cases beading before sewing the item together will save you time and frustration.

SPECIAL SECTION!
Turn to pages VI, VII and VIII of the special color photo section for more on beadwork.

218

Sioux doll made of brain tanned buckskin with ermine wrapped
horse hair braids. Beaded belt set includes a knife sheath, awl
case, and strike-a-light bag.

To be traditional and bead the old way, do not stitch completely through the leather. Catch the top half of your leather with the needle and thread. This helps prevent the thread from wearing in two which is caused by friction with other objects if left exposed.

Most contemporary beaders of today do stitch all the way through the base material. When working on fabric, unless you make a "sandwich" you have no choice, but always back the beadwork to protect the exposed threads. You can tie a flat knot on the top of the beadwork, bead over the knot and the underside is completely clear of any threads at all.

CONCLUSION

I am not an expert, nor do I pretend to be, and there are many things I've yet to learn, ideas to absorb, and others to discard. I only hope someone has been helped over the hurdle or become more enthusiastic in a hobby that is rich in heritage, and rewarding in terms of personal achievement. A few words worth remembering: If you want to produce an article of craftwork and have it conform to a certain tribal style and period from whence it came, you must use the proper bead color, size, design, and base material of that era!

A beaded item is appreciated for the overall effect, the pattern, and the hues (light, medium, and dark). Don't look for the little mistakes, because only you the beader will know where they are. You must do careful work and be willing to take apart and do over a large error, but don't get upset with a small irregularity. As you progress and refine your technique, your mistakes will become fewer, but almost impossible to do away with completely.

There are some Indians who believe only the Creator or Maker of the earth is perfect. Sometimes they will intentionally make a mistake to demonstrate the imperfection of the beader. So if someone ever starts pointing out a mistake you've made, tell him that only the Creator makes things perfect.

You've been given some basic knowledge of beadwork and now you need hours of practice necessary to build your skills. Remember, there is one final catch. Being an expert technician will not be enough. You will have to study colors, designs, and techniques at every opportunity. You have arrived when you can execute exemplary beadwork. Following is a list of sources I give credit to for factual information and dates used in this chapter. There is one source that I feel is extraordinary and you should have a copy in your library of beadwork books, and it is Monte Smith's *Technique of North American Indian Beadwork*, the best book I've seen on the market recently.

WORKS CONSULTED

Bugelski, Peter. "Lazy Stitch Beadwork." Whispering Wind, Vol. 10, No. 8 (May 1977), 5-13.

Cameron, Agnes. "Metis Artisans." The Beaver, Outfit, Vol. 36:2, 52-59.

Conn, Richard. "Cheyenne Style Beadwork." American Indian Hobbyist, Vol. 7, No. 2 (1968), 4-18.

----------. Circles of the World. Denver Art Museum. Seattle: University of Washington Press, 1982, 4-40.

----------. Native American Art. Denver Art Museum. Seattle: University of Washington Press, 1979.

Douglas, F. H. Plains Beads and Beadwork Leaflet, 73-74. Denver Art Museum (Dec. 1936), 90-95.

Ewers, John C. "Blackfeet Crafts." In Indian Handicraft Series, 9. Lawrence, Kan.: U.S. Indian Service, 1945.

Hail, Barbara A. Hau, Kola. Bristol: Haffenreffer Museum of Anthropology, Brown University, 1980.

Hungry Wolf, Adolf and Beverly. Blackfoot Craftworker's Book. Ivermere, British Columbia: Adolf Hungry Wolf Good Medicine Books, 1977, 4-7.

Johnson, Mike. "Notes on Algonkin Beadwork." American Indian Crafts and Culture, Vol. 6, No. 8 (Oct. 1972), 2-5.

Lyford, Carrie A. "Iroquois Crafts." Indian Handicraft Pamphlet No. 6. Lawrence, Kan.: Bureau of Indian Affairs, Haskell Institute, 1945.

Martin, Susan K. "Ablaze with Color: Native American Indian Crafts." Woman's Day. No. 1 (1975), 44-46.

McGreevy, Susan. "The Dyer Collection." American Indian Art Magazine, Special Plains Issue, Vol. 3, No. 4 (Autumn 1978), 69-73.

Scheider, Richard C. Crafts of the North American Indians. Libby, Mont: Old Way-Today.

Smith, Jerry. "Southern Women's Buckskin Bags." American Indian Crafts and Culture, Vol. 5, No. 7 (Sept. 1971), 2-5.

Smith, Monte. The Techniques of North American Indian Beadwork. Ogden, Utah: Eagle's View Publishing, 1984.

The Art of Native American Beadwork. Denver: Morning Flower Press, 1980.

The Crow Indians. New York: Holt, Rinehart and Winston, 1955.

"The Enduring Intrigue of the Glass Trade Bead." Arizona Highways, Vol. 42 (July 1971), 10-37.

TECHNIQUES FOR MAKING FOOTWEAR

BY GREGORY J. GEIGER

GREG HAS BEEN ACTIVE in the muzzleloading and buckskinning field for twenty years, and is currently the Captain of Boat 17, a Rogers' Rangers re-enactment and buckskinning outfit from central New York state.

Geiger's interest in early American life began as a small boy when a family vacation brought him to the excavations at Fort William Henry, New York, in the early fifties. He was an apprentice shoemaker at Bethpage Village Restoration, located on Long Island, where he grew up. His articles on leatherwork, shoemaking, and Rogers' Rangers have appeared repeatedly in muzzleloading periodicals over the last ten years.

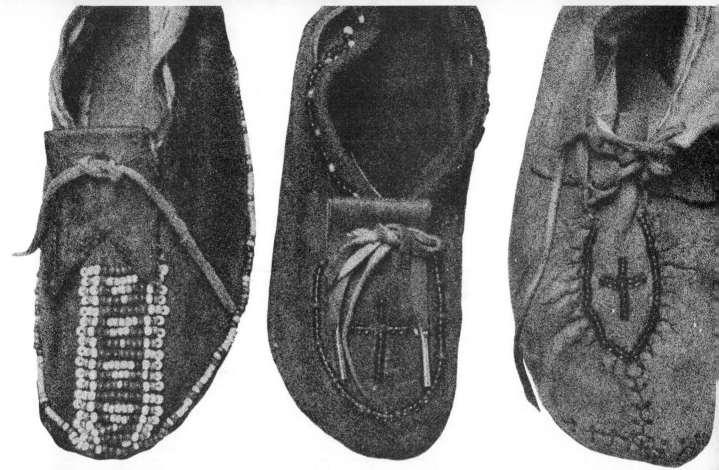

THIS chapter will try to state working techniques for the making of primitive footwear at a level of detail deeper than most current instructional literature. For example, if the *Craft Manual of North American Footwear* instructs its user to measure, cut, and stitch, our chapter will demonstrate working techniques showing *how* to measure, *how* to cut, and *how* to make stitches. Their achievement has been in showing the steps in making a variety of moccasins, whereas our achievement hopes to be showing the steps in performing the steps. Additionally, for complicated footwear such as shoes and boots, advice and tips for purchase and modification will be offered. It is felt that this will be of greater value to the buckskinner because shoemaking is a skill which requires training and time on a scale greater than can be conveyed in one chapter.

I'd rather not bury you with complicated, wordy, or flowery language. No assumptions regarding skill will be made. The format will be that of illustrated, step-by-step procedures with caution notes inserted as needed. Reading level at these procedures will be low, with sentences not exceeding two phrases and definition of terms as needed; this to be consistent with the approach of a working manual. Ideally, you'll be able to read some of these procedures while working on a project rather than before undertaking it.

THE FOOT: STRUCTURAL NOTES

The foot is actually a complicated part of your body, in that it combines a lot of functions which all imply wear and tear. You stand on it, requiring endurance. You move about on it, implying shock and stress as well as demanding flexibility and precision of balance. Try walking around without bending at the ball of your foot or without pivoting

WHAT TO AVOID

and bending at the ankles. That is almost impossible and imposes a great deal of stress, caused by the inflexibility of the foot, which gets converted to stress on the knees or shins. That's an important idea; discomfort caused by the feet is almost always felt somewhere else in addition to sore feet. We're talking a lot of bones and joints which can all be overstressed by pressure points caused by improper footwear, or age, or both.

Realize that the age factor and the condition of your foot will override any notes we make here. Nothing in authentic footwear is going to help the fallen arch, for example, and your wear time in a pair of moccasins prior to total collapse won't be helped by any of our construction techniques. Look for a moment at Figure 1, which shows the stress points on the human foot.

Hollywood and the publishing business have done an outstanding job of convincing us that the frontiersman had incredible stealth to the point that he could glide effortlessly in complete silence over any terrain at any time with the advantage of complete surprise of an adversary who fails to notice him coming. In the movies they turn off the sound track. In even the best of books the hero... "pads silently" ... and ... "slips noiselessly." When this image takes hold in our minds, especially at the beginning of our buckskinning career, we tend to want our moccasins or shoes to be our handcrafted pals, being so neat as to facilitate our doing just what the books and movies suggested we could do. In reality, few have complained more about the moccasin than the woodsmen who had to wear them, and the "honest" craft of shoemaking let so many people down that the term "shoemaker," when applied among tradesmen, is a form of insult. This is the heart of the reasoning behind writing a chapter such as this, because most of these techniques are designed to alleviate the overwhelmingly common reason for discomfort caused by footwear — the poor fit.

Rather than devote space to the history of the shoe or the variety of moccasin styles, we'd rather devote this

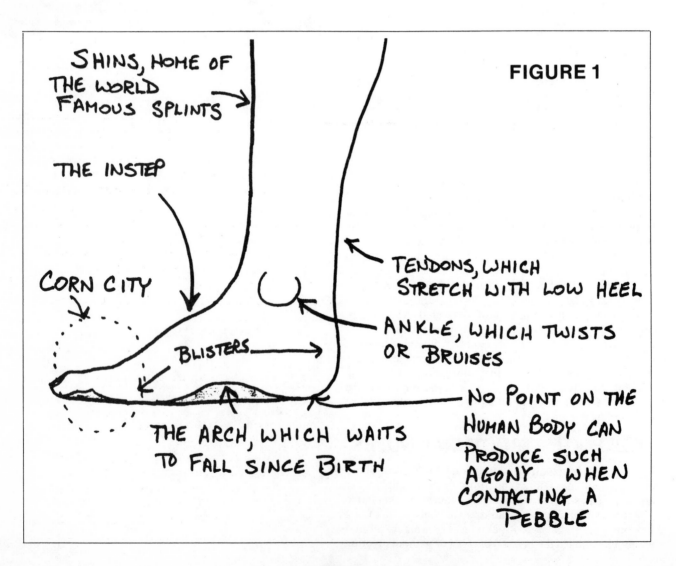

FIGURE 1

SHINS, HOME OF THE WORLD FAMOUS SPLINTS

THE INSTEP

CORN CITY

BLISTERS

TENDONS, WHICH STRETCH WITH LOW HEEL

ANKLE, WHICH TWISTS OR BRUISES

THE ARCH, WHICH WAITS TO FALL SINCE BIRTH

NO POINT ON THE HUMAN BODY CAN PRODUCE SUCH AGONY WHEN CONTACTING A PEBBLE

section to taking care of your foot. Some of the general rules are as follows:

(1) Too loose is sometimes worse than too tight. A shoe that allows your foot to slip and slide around will throw your foot's stress points off the support platform that the sole implies. In that event, your own body weight becomes your foot's enemy. A baggy moccasin flops around to the point where it actually catches on things or stresses your foot in wilderness terrain. For example, going uphill and fighting against imbalance because your foot is sliding downhill within the baggy moccasin.

(2) Unless you're used to going barefoot, and have a thicker sole on your foot, you ought to plan on putting some form of inner sole in your moccasin.

(3) Leather always stretches. If you take it off wet, it will want to dry in the same form and shape you left it in.

(4) Look where you're going, especially when wearing moccasins. This point is almost as important as a proper fit. Try to keep your feet pointed straight when you walk, with a slight curl in the toes when you have your moccasins on. If your toe is curled a little, it won't jam as easily if you stub it. Try not to clump down on your heel when you walk. A shorter stride which distributes the shock along the outside of your foot will do wonders for you in the office on Monday after rendezvous.

Look at Figure 2. It shows the most common footwear deficiencies to avoid when selecting or making footwear, and their correspondence to the stress areas of the foot.

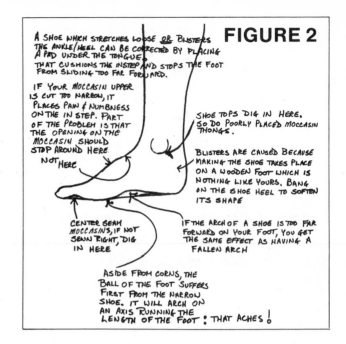

FIGURE 2

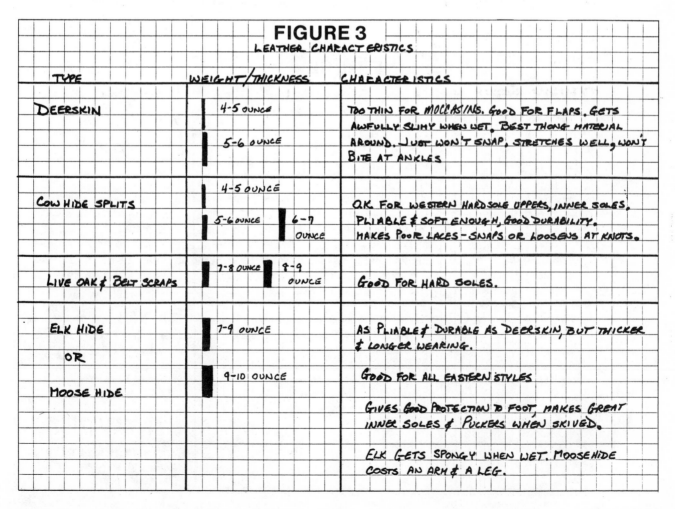

FIGURE 3
LEATHER CHARACTERISTICS

TYPE	WEIGHT/THICKNESS		CHARACTERISTICS
DEERSKIN	4-5 OUNCE		TOO THIN FOR MOCCASINS. GOOD FOR FLAPS. GETS AWFULLY SLIMY WHEN WET. BEST THONG MATERIAL AROUND. JUST WON'T SNAP, STRETCHES WELL, WON'T
	5-6 OUNCE		BITE AT ANKLES
COW HIDE SPLITS	4-5 OUNCE		O.K. FOR WESTERN HARDSOLE UPPERS, INNER SOLES.
	5-6 OUNCE	6-7 OUNCE	PLIABLE & SOFT ENOUGH, GOOD DURABILITY. MAKES POOR LACES - SNAPS OR LOOSENS AT KNOTS.
LIVE OAK & BELT SCRAPS	7-8 OUNCE	8-9 OUNCE	GOOD FOR HARD SOLES.
ELK HIDE	7-9 OUNCE		AS PLIABLE & DURABLE AS DEERSKIN, BUT THICKER & LONGER WEARING.
OR			
	9-10 OUNCE		GOOD FOR ALL EASTERN STYLES
MOOSE HIDE			GIVES GOOD PROTECTION TO FOOT, MAKES GREAT INNER SOLES & PUCKERS WHEN SKIVED.
			ELK GETS SPONGY WHEN WET. MOOSEHIDE COSTS AN ARM & A LEG.

224

TOOLS AND MATERIALS

Hides and Leather for Footwear

For the purposes of purchase, consider leather as a tool rather than a material. The reason for this is that the leather is going to be converted into something functional, and its final criterion is its performance. In effect, you're looking for good leather in a moccasin the same way you'd look for a file made of good steel. The hide which looks great on a shelf may not, in fact, be what you need for your footwear. There's an overwhelming temptation to buy the cheaper leather when shopping, and that almost never works. With footwear, in a special sense, there is a very limited set of characteristics to look for. On the one hand, if you want your sheath leather to be stiff and dense, the only part of a moccasin which should be like that is a hard sole. Hides billed as chap or apron leather might also say "moccasin", but that's only because many retail kits are made from it . . . not because it is the desirable or authentic material.

If leather for leggings should be as thin as possible, there are minimum thicknesses needed for moccasin leather, just as there is such a thing as too thick to be workable. If the grain on the unfinished side seems to be peeling or shedding to any extent, then a shorter period of wear is implied. Although the occasional hole in the middle of the hide may be all right, two or three weak or thin spots ought to be enough to put the leather back on the shelf.

Figure 3 shows characteristics of leather and its uses.

One feature to note is that suede, or cowhide with both sides rough, is a mite controversial for those seeking museum quality in their work. Although footwear made from suede dated to the early days of colonization documentation seems to support that Eastern style footwear made from it implies white rather that Indian origin. Western style footwear implies reservation period. Both Eastern and Western wear made of suede should be used in an outfit for a period in which the people, red or white, had access to cows. That implies closer proximity to civilization. Moreover, it occasionally occurs to the prospective buyer that a calfskin suede of the right color will make a good substitute for deerskin. That is only correct until it gets wet and stiffens or until it prematurely tears along a seam. The only substitute for deerskin is deerskin.

Measuring, Drawing, and Cutting

More so than any operation you will perform while making footwear, measuring and cutting will reflect your efficiency. If you do these tasks incorrectly, then you will waste materials or your finished product will look poorly. Before we go through the practice procedure, there are a few general rules concerning the measuring/drawing/cutting process.

You can almost never see your measuring error until after you try the moccasin on. Therefore, the first pair you make should be done one moccasin at a time, from start to finish. That way, the other pattern can be modified as you pick up mistakes.

You're going to make mistakes. Figure 4 shows the

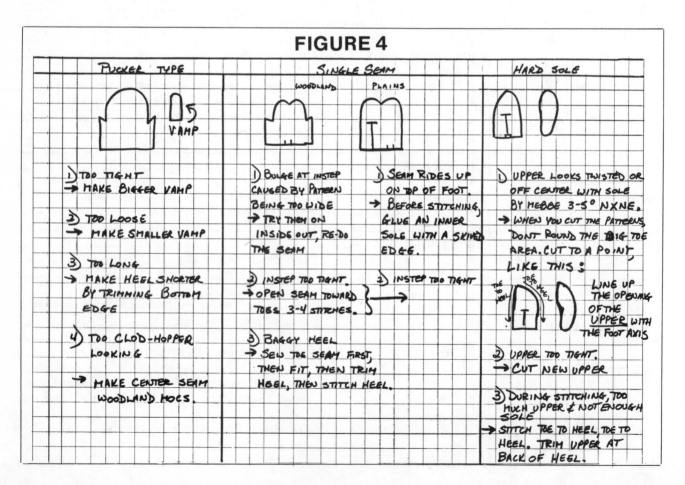

FIGURE 4

PUCKER TYPE

1) TOO TIGHT
→ MAKE BIGGER VAMP

2) TOO LOOSE
→ MAKE SMALLER VAMP

3) TOO LONG
→ MAKE HEEL SHORTER BY TRIMMING BOTTOM EDGE

4) TOO CLOD-HOPPER LOOKING
→ MAKE CENTER SEAM WOODLAND MOCS.

SINGLE SEAM

WOODLAND

1) BULGE AT INSTEP CAUSED BY PATTERN BEING TOO WIDE
→ TRY THEM ON INSIDE OUT, RE-DO THE SEAM

2) INSTEP TOO TIGHT.
→ OPEN SEAM TOWARD TOES 3-4 STITCHES.

3) BAGGY HEEL
→ SEW TOE SEAM FIRST, THEN FIT, THEN TRIM HEEL, THEN STITCH HEEL.

PLAINS

1) SEAM RIDES UP ON TOP OF FOOT.
→ BEFORE STITCHING, GLUE AN INNER SOLE WITH A SKIVED EDGE.

2) INSTEP TOO TIGHT

HARD SOLE

1) UPPER LOOKS TWISTED OR OFF CENTER WITH SOLE BY MEBBE 3-5° NXNE.
→ WHEN YOU CUT THE PATTERNS, DONT ROUND THE BIG TOE AREA. CUT TO A POINT, LIKE THIS:

TOE TO HEEL / TOE TO HEEL
LINE UP THE OPENING OF THE UPPER WITH THE FOOT AXIS

2) UPPER TOO TIGHT.
→ CUT NEW UPPER

3) DURING STITCHING, TOO MUCH UPPER & NOT ENOUGH SOLE
→ STITCH TOE TO HEEL, TOE TO HEEL. TRIM UPPER AT BACK OF HEEL.

three moccasin types with the most common errors and what to do about them before getting frustrated. The chart is cryptic, but the procedures cover the needed detail.

Resist the temptation to reserve an actual moccasin for a future pattern. After you've hopped around rendezvous for a few years, that pattern is going to shrink and stretch in some areas, and will not even fit flatly on the next piece of leather. To retain a pattern, revise the paper or cardboard copy after you've tailored the fit, before you begin the second moccasin. If your feet are different, be prepared to make and modify two patterns as you go along.

Sizes increase by the half inch. A pattern for a size eight moccasin will be about a half inch bigger all around than that of a size seven. That's a decent rule of thumb if you intend to do some trading; however, it is unreliable beyond two or three sizes. I'm not talented enough to explain why.

Pattern material should be of a minimum of paper bag weight and a maximum of masonite thickness. Using metal for patterns runs the risk of dulling your cutting blades. Paper patterns need pencil or markers to be transformed to the leather; however, cardboard or masonite patterns can be placed and cut in one operation.

Forget about the fact that old-timey Indian women didn't use patterns and measurements. They did this for a living.

Use scissors to cut paper. Use a knife to cut leather. We'll describe making the knife at a later section. To use a knife, you'll need a lapboard, made of masonite or a hardwood, which measures about 14" by 20". The idea is to sit with your thighs parallel to the floor. Although this might sound inconvenient, you will see the working advantage of this arrangement in upcoming procedures.

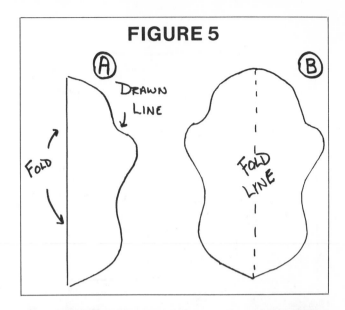

HOW TO DRAW AND CUT PATTERNS

Materials: pencil, felt pen, paper bag, knife, cutting board, scissors, scrap leather

Purpose: To work with pattern and knife in techniques useful for any pair of moccasins. This is a practice procedure.

Procedure:

(1) Cut the bottom out of a large paper bag. Throw the bottom away. Let the bag lay flat and folded on your lapboard. **NOTE:** *Drawing and cutting should always be done while sitting. The lapboard, resting on the thighs, acts as a small table. Footwear patterns are small enough to enable all work to be done in a small controlled area.*

(2) At a folded edge, draw a line such as shown in Figure 5 A. Draw the line with a pencil. Draw the pencil point by moving the heel of your hand. Keep the wrist straight. Pivot the paper, not the wrist.

(3) Using scissors, cut out the pattern and unfold it, as shown in Figure 5 B.

(4) Put the rest of the paper aside. Using the felt pen, mark the unfolded pattern shape onto the scrap leather. Save the pattern for use in the cementing procedure later on.

(5) Hold the knife the same way you held your pencil back

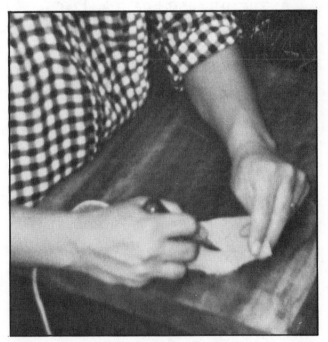

The left hand pins and parts the leather along the cut. The right hand pulls the knife and makes the cut.

at step two. Cut along the line as if you were tracing the line with another pencil. **CAUTION:** *Keep your wrist stiff and straight. Drag the knife. Don't try to cut so hard that you force the knife. You can always retrace the cut to keep it clean. When the angle of the curves makes your cutting uncomfortable, stop and pivot the leather. If your blade is not sharp enough, you will be forcing the cut and will lose control. This will ensure that you suddenly jump off the line and botch the job.*

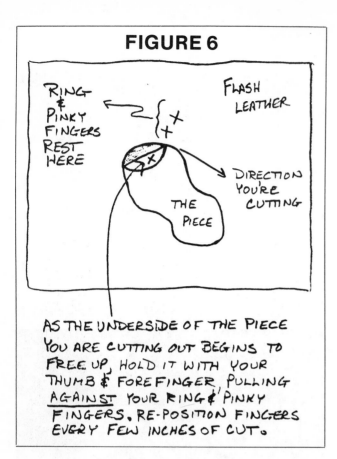

FIGURE 6

RING & PINKY FINGERS REST HERE

FLASH LEATHER

THE PIECE

DIRECTION YOU'RE CUTTING

AS THE UNDERSIDE OF THE PIECE YOU ARE CUTTING OUT BEGINS TO FREE UP, HOLD IT WITH YOUR THUMB & FOREFINGER, PULLING AGAINST YOUR RING & PINKY FINGERS. RE-POSITION FINGERS EVERY FEW INCHES OF CUT.

(6) While cutting, allow the heel of your knife hand to drag the blade along the line. This will also pin the piece of leather to the board. Look at Figure 6. With the thumb and index finger of your free hand, pull the part labeled "the piece". Use the middle, ring, and pinky fingers of the hand to pin the part labeled "flash leather." You will have to adjust the position of your hand as the blade travels every few inches.

(7) Reread step six, because it takes longer to describe this process than it does to do it. The point of doing it this way is that it helps the blade cut by separating the leather and prevents mistakes.

When you're through cutting, you should have two pieces; the plug you just cut out and the leftover "flash" with a hole in the middle. The purpose of cutting a wavy circle like this is to let you practice control.

The procedure is ended when you have the plug correctly cut out. If you goofed it a couple of times before getting the hang of it, realize that no moccasin has a cut this wavy or troublesome. If your fingers hurt, and the board has a deep impression of the knife cut, then you were applying too much force. A good technique implies using just enough pressure to cut through. Thicker leathers, such as sole leather, may require soaking and two passes with the blade.

HOW TO TRIM EDGES (SKIVE)

Definitions:
    skive — to use the length of your knife blade to taper the edge of your leather.
    skin side — the finished side of a piece of leather.
Materials: thick piece of leather (as in sole piece or moosehide), knife, board, and patience.
Purpose: You skive the edges of hard soled moccasins to prevent the stitching from coming into contact with the ground. You skive the edge of leather where it is supposed to pucker, to help it shape to the pucker and make it easier to hold while working.
Condition: You've already cut your pattern. If your leather has a skin side, you've made a decision as to

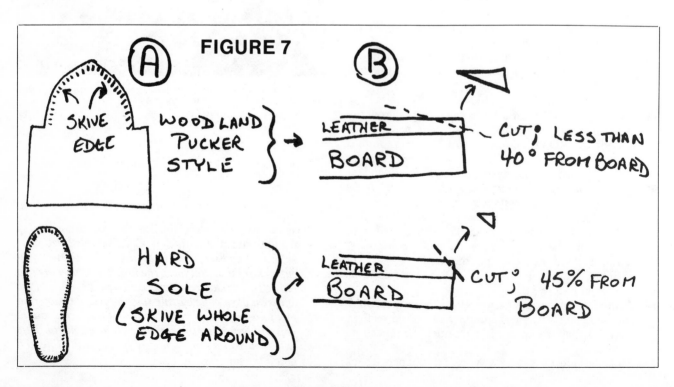

FIGURE 7

(A) SKIVE EDGE

WOODLAND PUCKER STYLE

LEATHER
BOARD

CUT; LESS THAN 40° FROM BOARD

(B)

HARD SOLE (SKIVE WHOLE EDGE AROUND)

LEATHER
BOARD

CUT; 45% FROM BOARD

Skiving. You shave the edge of the leather by trimming the corner.

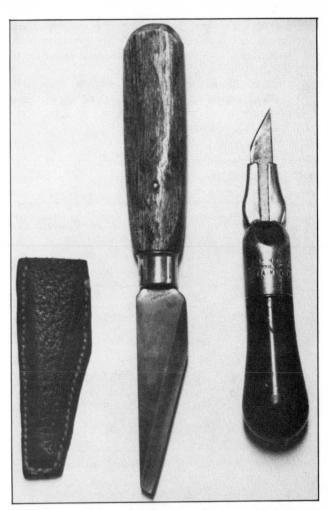

Two useful types of knives. The one on the left can be purchased at a hardware store. It will come with a rounded file handle. Feel free to shape the handle to fit your hand. The hobby knife on the right is a very precise cutter because the steel is high quality and the point makes it maneuverable.

whether it will be on the outside or inside of your moccasin.

Procedure:

(1) See Figure 7A. Note the areas we're talking about skiving.

(2) Line up the edge of your leather with the edge of the lapboard. Your blade is going to slice along that edge, **AWAY FROM** your body. Look at 7B. It shows a cross section of the leather positioned on the board, and the angle of cuts you will make.

CAUTION

NOTE: *That's SLICE, not hack. That's AWAY, not toward. To avoid hacking, you will have to be sure your blade is sharp (per the knife maintenance procedure) and you will have to strop it while doing this. Strop it along the edge of the cutting board, across the grain.*

(3) Soak your leather, and let it air out the excess water. This helps your cutting process and is a must with sole leather.

(4) Make your cut, trying to keep the piece you're cutting off in one piece. If you can do that, then your cut will be uniform and even. Slice slowly and patiently. If you have to push and grunt, then your blade needs maintenance. If you're missing a piece of your finger, then you should have maintained your blade when you noticed yourself pushing and grunting. Even the best of knives needs constant maintenance.

The procedure is ended when you have two pieces of leather, the flash left over from the taper, and the moccasin part with a neatly trimmed edge. This may seem tedious. Its value shows up when you have to punch holes to do your stitching, when you have to use pressure to make a pucker, or when you're walking around safe in the knowledge that your seams are not touching the ground.

KNIFE CONSTRUCTION AND MAINTENANCE

A picture is worth a thousand words, so look at Figure 8.

Keeping Your Edge

Materials: stone, knife, cutting board

Purpose: To keep a working edge on your blade while you work.

Condition: You're cutting or skiving away merrily and you notice that you are now forcing your cut.

Procedure:

(1) Put your work aside. Strop your knife along the edge of the board across the grain of the wood. Make your stroke firm and smooth, and do it evenly over both sides of the blade. Feel each side of the blade with your thumb for burrs or rough edges.

(2) If these burrs don't go away with stropping, then it is time to sharpen. Put the stone on the board, which is

still resting on your lap. Notice the bevel your blade forms, and try to keep this bevel. Sharpen in smooth, firm strokes as if you were trying to take a slice out of the stone with each stroke.

(3) Strop the blade, as in step one, after you sharpen it.
NOTE: *Don't be a maniac. Work slowly and patiently, as if you stood a chance of hurting the blade or the stone.*

(4) Feel the blade again with your thumb across each bevel. The procedure is ended when you can't feel a burr and your knife cuts smoothly again.

FIGURE 8

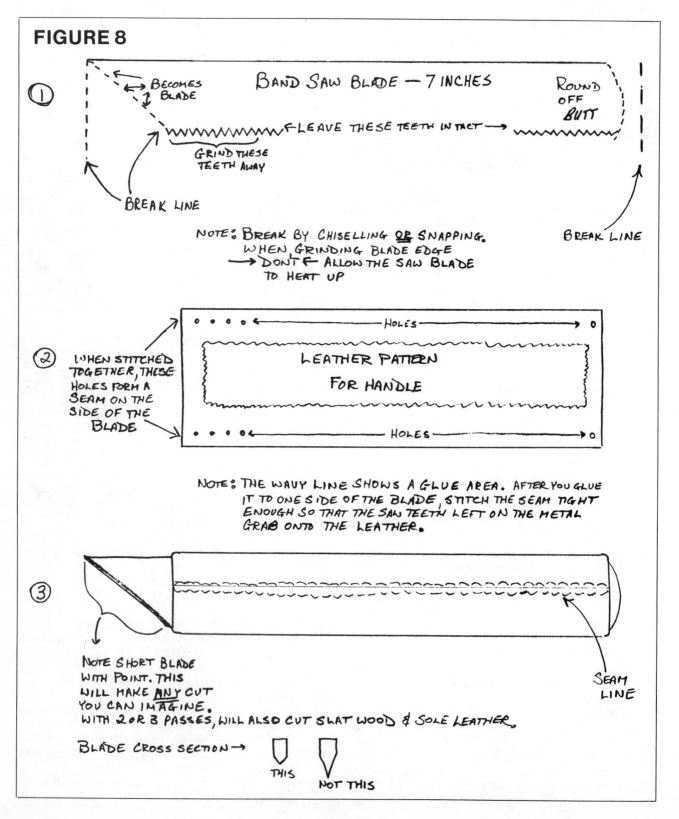

AWL CONSTRUCTION AND USE

A picture is still worth a thousand words, so look at Figure 9.

Punching Holes the Right Way

Materials: your new awl, a piece or two of scrap leather

Purpose: We're not insulting you here. Believe it or not there is a technique for punching uniform holes which resist tearing.

Procedure:

(1) Note the thickness of your leather (or both pieces of the leather together if you're imaginative enough to glue two pieces together to simulate a real piece of work). It's probably around an eighth to a quarter of an inch thick.

(2) Note your awl shape. Its cross section is an elongated diamond.

(3) Note Figure 10. The distance between each hole and from each hole to the edge is the same as the thickness of the leather. If the thickness is ¼" or greater, then the distance to the edge is ⅛" and the distance between each hole is the same as the thickness of the leather. The length of the diamond shape made by the awl hole points to the edge. This helps keep the

Strop the blade across the grain at the end of the cutting board.

Left to right: A scratch awl with the blade ground down, a handle and blade which is sold in leather stores, and an awl made per Figure 9.

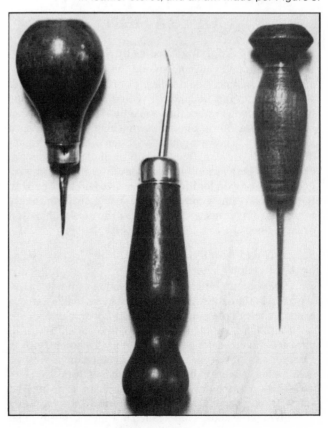

FIGURE 9

STEEL

WOOD HANDLE

GRIND 4 FLATS

DIAMOND SHAPED

LATHE OR FILE OFF SHADED AREAS OF WOOD

VERY GRADUAL TAPER THE BLADE SHOULD BE BRITTLE, AND BE ABLE TO PUSH GENTLY THROUGH A PIECE OF SUEDE. TO PROTECT IT WHEN NOT IN USE, CAP IT WITH A CORK

HANDLE SHAPES

GOOD   BAD

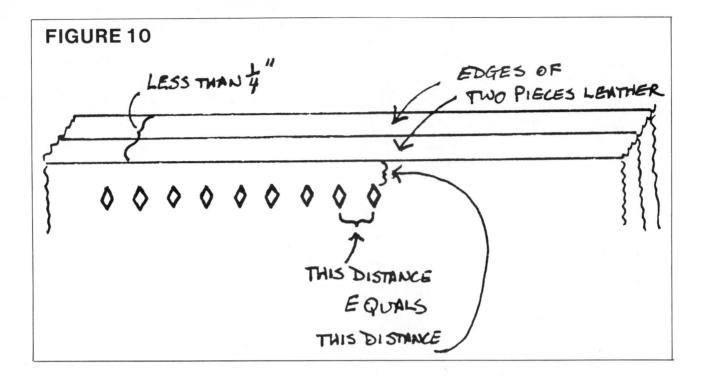

FIGURE 10

LESS THAN ¼"

EDGES OF TWO PIECES LEATHER

THIS DISTANCE EQUALS THIS DISTANCE

stitches from ripping through the holes.

The procedure is ended after you've punched a neat, uniform row of holes.

NEEDLE AND THREAD OPERATION

Selecting and Applying Needles by Size and Type

All stitching can, and should, be done with harness needles, or ball pointed needles. For one thing, you don't stab yourself, and for another, you should be punching holes with an awl rather than a needle. These needles can be found in a fabric or sewing machine store, or via a leather outlet. They are gauged with zeroes through higher digits to indicate size. It will be sufficient to state here that you need a package of large and package of medium size needles to last you for life. The large size will be used with the artificial sinew product you can get from many muzzleloading firms, and medium will be used with cotton or flax (linen) thread.

Selecting and Modifying Thread by Application Criteria

The most common misconception among buckskinners is that the waxed thread sold in leather stores needs a rotary hole puncher and a big fat lacing needle to get it through a gaping hole made by the punch. In truth, punched holes were generally slammed home with a hammer and chisel-like tool which was used on harness or belt leather, never on footwear unless by a total clod.

What we would like to discuss here is using the sinew product, and taking the waxed thread and separating its individual strands. That's called unwinding the ply. The strands are referred to as plies, and most of the leather working thread, waxed or unwaxed, comes in five or seven ply. The idea is to unwind the thread and use it in combination with smaller needles and correctly punched awl holes. When working this way, strength is not at all sacrificed, you increase the mileage of the thread five or sevenfold, and it will perform every task from sewing a seam to beading (on any size bead greater than seed).

There are general rules of thumb to preparing and working with thread or sinew, and before we show some procedures it would be a good idea to cover them.

Try not to stitch with thread lengths longer than two feet. The temptation is to make a long thread and needle set up because the seam is long, but you're better off with short lengths and knots. For one thing, if the thread gives out the whole seam won't go with it, and for another thing you can lose a lot of time trying to untangle long lengths of thread.

Don't dig your awl in too deeply. Get the feel of pushing it just deep enough to let the needle and thread pass snugly through. You should never have to use pliers. Rather, back the needle out and use the awl to make the hole a mite larger.

In the hole punching procedure we showed you how to position the diamond shaped hole. The line of the stitching should run across the diamond. Look at Figure 11. If you are making a line of stitches which runs parallel to the edge, or along it, then the diamond shaped hole should be punched as shown in the procedure. This is most often called a harness stitch, and is mostly used with stiff leather products such as holsters and sheaths. The loop, or whip stitch, which goes round and round the edge up the length of the seam, needs an awl hole which has its length run parallel to the edge. Read that again if it sounds confusing. The idea is to get the thread to pull across the width of the awl hole because it gets to grab more leather.

The whip stitch would be used on center seam Eastern or one piece Plains style moccasins, and when it stretches out each stitch seems to run across the line described by the seam. The harness stitch, in which the thread runs the length of the seam, and is most often turned inside out, works best on hard soled moccasins. You should not see the thread if the stitch is done right and turned inside out.

Don't be a puritan about pre-waxed thread. Although you should try to stay away from synthetics, the symmetrical, rope-like look created by pre-waxed thread goes away when you unwind it. Also, don't feel bad about using cotton thread sold in fabric stores. Just get the heaviest gauge available. We're going to show you how to work with it and strengthen it.

How to Unravel Waxed or Unwaxed Thread

Materials: a vise, a length of five or seven ply thread cut to four feet.

Purpose: We can't show you how to stitch neat little holes unless we've shown you how to work with smaller units of needle and thread. Avoid bulk.

Procedure:

(1) Clamp one end of the thread in the vise. Let it rest.
(2) Make "amen" with your hands, fingers pointing to heaven. Rub your palms so that the left hand goes down and the right hand goes up. This is the friction motion that you will use to unwrap or unravel or unwind the thread.
(3) Now take the thread end between your palms, and step away from the vise until the thread is taut.
(4) Using the motion described above, unwind the thread. At a distance of four feet or so, you should be able to

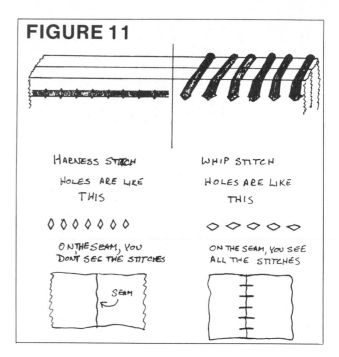

FIGURE 11

HARNESS STITCH
HOLES ARE LIKE THIS

0 0 0 0 0 0 0

ON THE SEAM, YOU DON'T SEE THE STITCHES

WHIP STITCH
HOLES ARE LIKE THIS

◇ ◇ ◇ ◇ ◇

ON THE SEAM, YOU SEE ALL THE STITCHES

SEAM

Unwinding the thread to isolate each strand or ply. The right hand travels up and the left goes down. This action unwraps the thread.

start separating the thread after the twentieth motion or so. **NOTE:** *There's only one hitch to this whole process. The thread wants to kink up in the worst way. You can partially stop this by holding onto the end of the thread with one hand, and then running your thumb and forefinger back and forth along the thread. Use a lot of pressure when you pin the thread between your thumb and forefinger.*

(5) After a short time you will see the plies of the thread begin to unwind all the way down the length. If you unwind too far it is as bad as unwinding not far enough.

(6) Take one ply at a time and pull it away from the pack. It should pull away all the way down to the vise. Lay it aside, maybe pinning it on the workbench with something. Repeat this until all the thread plies are separated.

(7) Hold onto the end at the vise, and open the vise. Finish the job by unwinding the part of the thread that was in the vise.

The procedure is ended when you have five or seven separated pieces of thread, all four feet long, each wrapped around a pencil for storage.

How to Thread Your Needle

Materials: Some of the thread you just unwound, a medium harness needle, the vise and maybe a little beeswax if your thread doesn't have it already. You can also use fabric store type cotton thread for this procedure.

Condition: You have taken a four foot length of thread and run it through the eye of your needle. The thread is doubled over so that it is now two feet long.

Purpose: We want to rewind and wax the thread. This is immensely helpful when stitching because the thread won't tangle too much.

Procedure:

(1) Put the needle in the vise, point down, and seat it so that only the eye sticks up from the vise. This will keep the brittle steel from breaking.

(2) Step back until the two lengths of thread are taut AND EQUAL IN LENGTH.

(3) Wrap one end around an index finger and keep it there.

(4) Using the now world famous amen-like motion from the last procedure, unwind the other piece of thread about fifteen strokes worth. This creates a spring-like pressure within the thread fibre. It wants to spring back in the other direction. We won't let it until we have unwound the other piece of thread.

(5) Repeat steps 3 and 4 on the other piece of thread, being careful to keep the piece you have already worked on from getting loose and tangled.

Rewinding the thread. The right hand travels down while the left travels up. The friction action of your palm wraps the thread plies or strands around each other.

(6) When both pieces are unwound and nice and tense, place them firmly between your palms. When you make the motion this time, let the left hand travel up and the right hand travel down. This uses the spring tension to wind the pieces of thread together. Repeat the motion about four or five times.

The procedure is ended after you have waxed the thread and taken the needle out of the vise.

How to Thread Artificial Sinew

Materials: A large harness needle, artificial sinew about two to three feet long, knife and board.

Purpose: Since the fastest known way to waste sinew is to double it, we'd like to show you how to lock the sinew in the eye of the needle and use only one piece to stitch with.

Procedure:

(1) Lay the end of the sinew on your lapboard.

(2) Place your knife blade about a half inch from the sinew end, so that it straddles the piece of sinew.

(3) You're going to taper and shave the end so it fits through the smaller needle eye. The whole blade should rest across the sinew and on the board. Tilt it so that the back of the blade rises about a half inch above the board.

(4) Hold it there firmly, and draw the sinew so that the blade shaves it to a point.

233

FIGURE 12

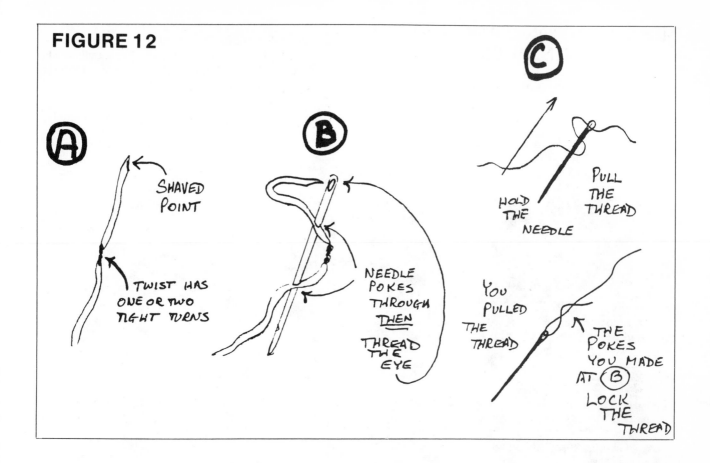

A — SHAVED POINT — TWIST HAS ONE OR TWO TIGHT TURNS

B — NEEDLE POKES THROUGH <u>THEN</u> THREAD THE EYE

C — HOLD THE NEEDLE — PULL THE THREAD — YOU PULLED THE THREAD — THE POKES YOU MADE AT Ⓑ LOCK THE THREAD

(5) Put the knife down.

(6) About an inch and a half from the point on the end, twist the sinew twice, making a tight twist. Use a little pressure in this, so that there is a tight twist.

(7) Look at Figure 12. Poke the needle through the sinew twice, on either side of the twist. This is shown at 12A.

(8) Thread the needle, as shown at 12B.

(9) Pull the thread over itself and the eye of the needle as shown at 12C.

The procedure is ended when the needle is threaded and the thread locked in place.

USING CEMENTS

Try not to rely on rubber cement for anything related to leather, because it smells and won't hold up with time. In fact, the only reason you ought to be using cement at all is to glue a sole inside your moccasin. Use a contact cement, because it will last forever, and because stitching in an inner sole detracts from the appearance of the moccasin, whereas gluing it will hide it from view. You might also want to add a thin strip of glue to both edges of two pieces which will form a seam. This allows you to get frustrated when stitching the seam for reasons other than the two pieces of leather not staying together whilst you try to stitch. In either case the technique is simple but deceptive.

Take the piece you cut out during the cutting practice procedure. Trace its outline on another piece of scrap leather. You're going to glue it in the same way you'd glue an inner sole to a moccasin pattern. With contact cement,

the idea is to spread around the only type of glue in the world which smells worse than rubber cement on both surfaces. Let them dry. If your leather was wet, or you put the pieces together when the glue was still wet, then the bond won't hold. If you let both pieces dry, then the bond will hold for the life of the moccasin.

The only problem is that once the two surfaces contact each other, they bind. Therefore great care is required to glue properly. Once they touch, they're stuck fast. When gluing an inner sole to a moccasin pattern, lay them together from heel to toe. By working lengthwise it is easier to control both pieces. On the practice piece lay them together lengthwise. If the ink won't show, then it is a good idea to trace the inner sole pattern onto the leather to which it will be glued.

If you really have tender feet, and give in to the urge to put a really thick inner sole into your moccasins, be sure to skive the edge of the sole as shown in the procedure a few pages back. When you make your cut, the width of your slice should be at least a half inch, and the edge of the inner sole should be quite thin. This will not only allow your moccasins to shape correctly to your foot, but will also prevent an unnatural look at the sole of the moccasin when you're through.

MOCCASIN CONSTRUCTION TECHNIQUES

The following procedures are more than just practice techniques for working with leather. They are for use during the construction of your pair of moccasins. The only idea that is assumed is that you have already followed instructions from whatever source you are using to make

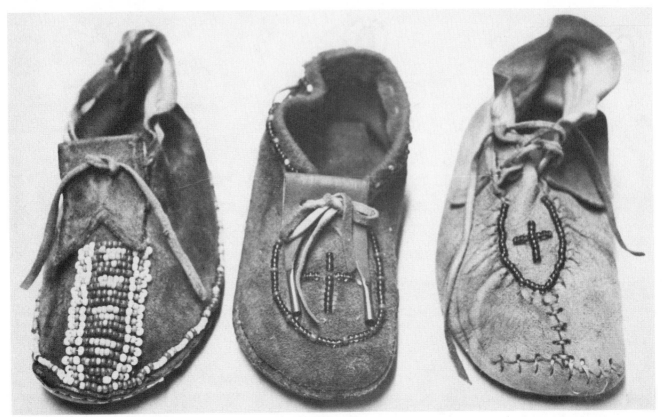

Three basic types of moccasins. Left to right: The hard sole Plains, the one-piece (in this photo a Plains style), and the Eastern pucker toe.

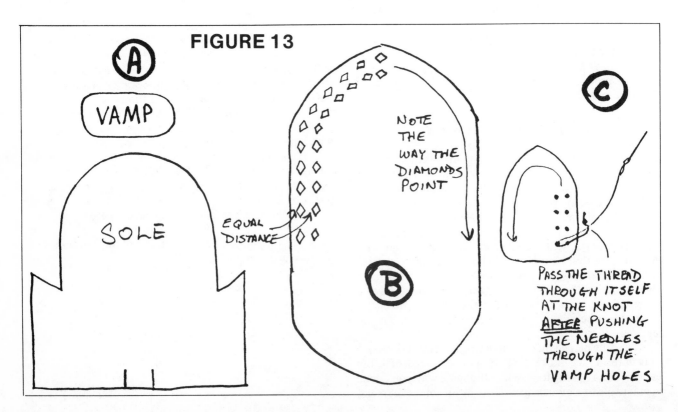

FIGURE 13

Ⓐ

VAMP

SOLE

EQUAL DISTANCE

NOTE THE WAY THE DIAMONDS POINT

Ⓑ

Ⓒ

PASS THE THREAD THROUGH ITSELF AT THE KNOT ~~AFTER~~ AFTER PUSHING THE NEEDLES THROUGH THE VAMP HOLES

235

the footwear. Since none of these procedures interferes with those instructions, it is important that the instructions be followed closely from measuring through assembly. All we really want to do here is enhance both the finished product and the workflow of making it. These five procedures were picked because they represent the most common and frustrating problems found when making footwear. The differences in both wear and looks they make is quite dramatic.

CONSTRUCTING PUCKERS FOR EASTERN STYLE MOCCASINS

Condition: You have measured and cut out the patterns for pucker soled style moccasins and are ready to begin putting them together. It does not matter whether you have glued an inner sole.

Purpose: If you cannot get the leather to pucker evenly, your moccasins will neither look right nor wear comfortably. This procedure will show you how to stitch even puckers.

Definitions: **vamp** — the smaller part which sits on top of the foot. Look at Figure 13A.

sole — The larger piece which will be puckered when stitched to the vamp.

Procedure:

(1) If you are working with thick elk or moose or cowhide, skive the edge. The thicker leathers are almost impossible to work with otherwise. When you are done skiving, the tapered edge should be half the original thickness of the leather. The slice you just cut off should be about one half to three quarter inch wide.

(2) Look at Figure 13B. Punch an inner row of holes on

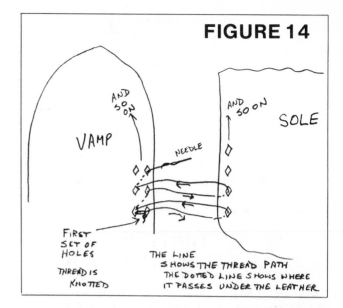

the vamp. There must be one inner hole for each outer hole. The distance between the inner and outer row of holes must be the same as the distance between the hole and the edge of the sole, just the way 13B shows.

(3) When you are ready to stitch the sole and vamp together, knot the thread as shown at 13C. Your stitching is only going to make one pass, and will not retrace itself.

(4) Okay, here's the concept. The stitch is going to come up through the outer row hole on the vamp, up through the hole in the sole, and down through the inner hole in the vamp. Look at Figure 14. By doing this, you have pinned the sole to the vamp. The thread is now in the

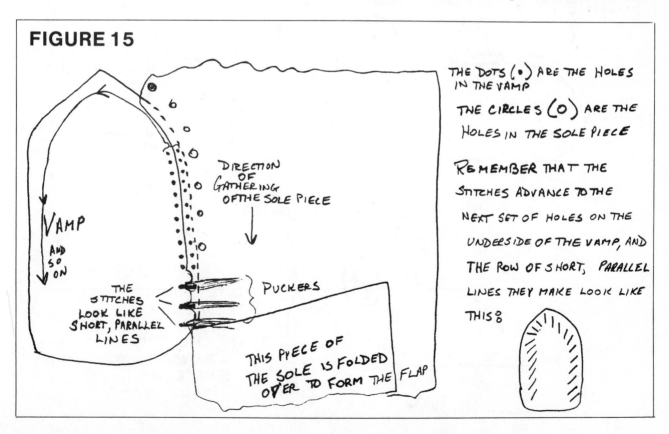

236

little valley that will be made by the pucker when you gather it and go on to the next stitch.

(5) Gather the leather of the sole. At this point, in order to line up the holes in the sole and the vamp, the pucker is actually made. Bring the needle and thread to the next set of inner-outer holes on the vamp. Stitch up through the outer hole in the vamp, up through the hole in the sole, and down through the inner hole in the vamp. Now the thread is going to advance to the next set of holes, and you will repeat this stitch again and again until you're done. Look at Figure 15.

The procedure is finished when you have stitched the entire pucker seam like this. All the neat and uniform puckers set you apart as a craftsman.

PREVENTING HEEL SAG IN SOFT SOLED MOCCASINS

Condition: You are making Plains one piece, woodland, or any other type of soft soled moccasins. You have followed directions and have cut out the pattern. At the back of where the heel will be, there is a little square cut out called a flap. Look at Figure 16. Don't cut the flap! Just draw where it is supposed to be!

Purpose: Heels sag and look sloppy because the cut was either too baggy, or because gravity pulls the moccasin down at the heel, or because the flap was not cut right. We're going to avoid all of that.

Procedure:
(1) Bring the lines which show where to cut the flap to within one eighth of an inch of the line of your foot's

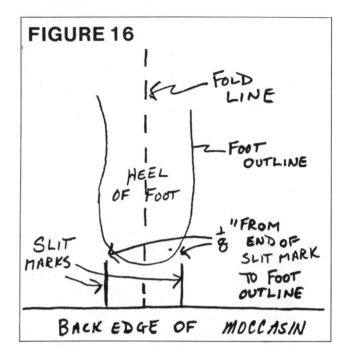

FIGURE 16

heel.
(2) Now cut the flap.
(3) Fold the moccasin over so that the fold line runs down the middle of the flap. Look at Figure 17A.
(4) Cut the pattern as shown at 17B. Don't cut too much, and be sure you cut through both layers of the folded leather. This is where the knifework you did in the

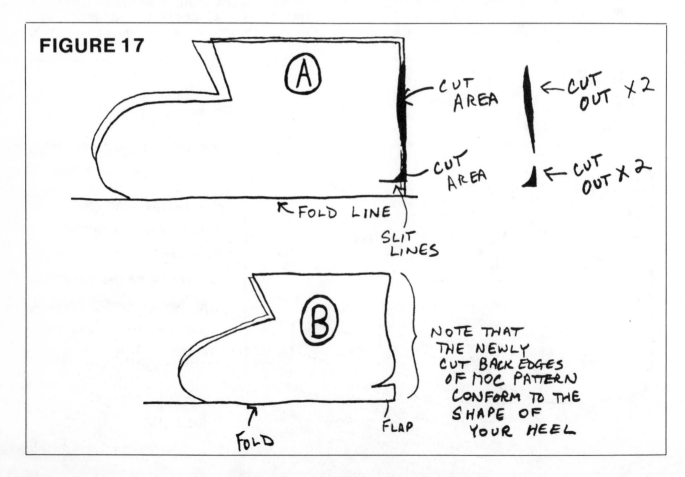

FIGURE 17

237

practice procedure pays off. **NOTE:** *By cutting the corner by the flap, you have tailored away excess leather which is there because the moccasin pattern is straight and your heel bottom is round. By cutting the sliver along the back edge you have tailored the moccasin to fit up against your ankle. This counters gravity. It also ends the procedure.*

STITCHING AND WORKING WITH THE HARD SOLE

Condition: You have cut out the pieces for hard-soled moccasins. You have skived the edge of the soles.

Purpose: This whole procedure is here to help you deal with the three biggest problems faced when making the hard-soled moccasin: Lining up the sole and the upper so that they are not off center, stitching the pieces together so that your work space is not cramped as the seam closes, and fitting the heel.

General: Most patterns call for you to trace your foot, with a little extra, to be converted into the sole. The upper part gets a slit where it will open up for your foot, and a forked tongue piece to be attached separately. Some patterns call for you to soak the sole, stitch the moccasin inside out and turn it to get it right side out. This is not necessary because we will show you a more efficient stitching technique.

PART ONE — Lining up the two pieces

(1) On the inside of the foot pattern which will be the sole, draw a pencil line which runs the length of the foot. It should start at the center of the heel and run up through the middle of the second toe. Draw the same line on the inside of the upper. It should run on the slit. Look at Figure 18.

(2) When you start to stitch, the first hole in the sole and the first hole in the upper will each be on these lines up by the toe.

PART TWO — Stitching

(1) If you're the compulsive organizer type, then punch all your holes at once on both the sole and the upper. If you're the "que sera'-sera'" type, then you can punch holes as you go along. In either case the distance between the holes should always be the same. Check the awl use procedure. Don't worry if the number of holes punched in the sole does not equal the number of holes punched in the upper.

(2) Look at Figure 19. You're going to make a stitch line which runs parallel to the sole edge. The upper is going to fold over the stitch, hiding it from view. The skive side of the sole will be down, and the stitches won't touch the ground.

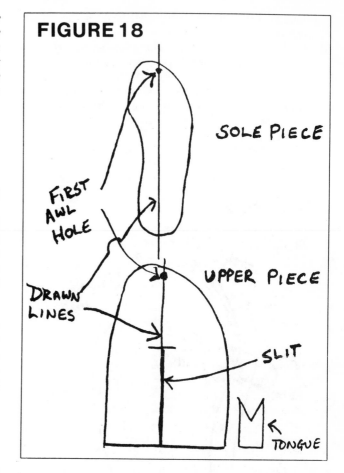

FIGURE 18

SOLE PIECE

FIRST AWL HOLE

DRAWN LINES

UPPER PIECE

SLIT

TONGUE

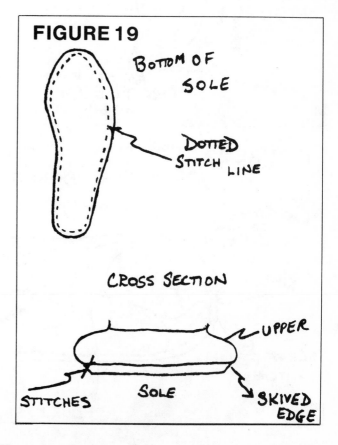

FIGURE 19

BOTTOM OF SOLE

DOTTED STITCH LINE

CROSS SECTION

UPPER

STITCHES

SOLE

SKIVED EDGE

(3) Thread TWO needles as shown back at the thread section.

(4) Look at Figure 20. Start stitching with both needles up by the toe. Each needle goes through the same hole from opposite directions. You fold the upper as you go along. Sew along the inside of the foot first, and stop about an inch from where the line you drew on the sole runs through the heel. Leave the needles on the thread. Don't cut.

(5) Thread two more needles, and stitch the outside of the foot the same way. The reason you started at the toe and worked toward the heel is because, as the toe part gets finished, you get cramped for hand space. By putting all the knots down by the heel, you not only can

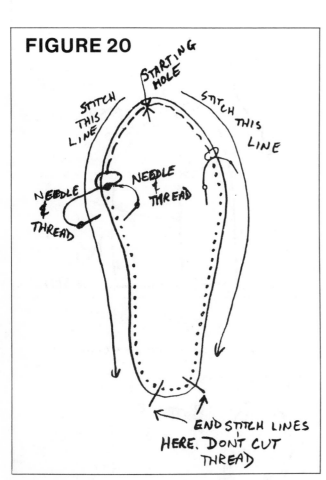

FIGURE 20

STARTING HOLE

STITCH THIS LINE

STITCH THIS LINE

NEEDLE & THREAD

NEEDLE & THREAD

NEEDLE & THREAD

END STITCH LINES HERE. DON'T CUT THREAD

FIGURE 21

Ⓐ OVERLAPPING PARTS

ALL FOUR NEEDLES ARE ON THE INSIDE OF THE MOC

SOLE

Ⓑ GLUE OVERLAPPING AREAS. THIS GLUE LINE IS ABOUT ½" WIDE

STITCH LINE

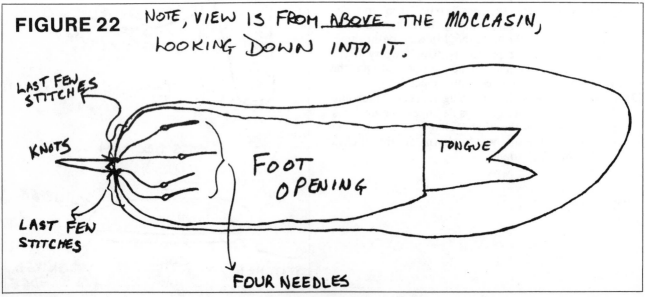

FIGURE 22 NOTE, VIEW IS FROM ABOVE THE MOCCASIN, LOOKING DOWN INTO IT.

LAST FEW STITCHES

KNOTS

FOOT OPENING

TONGUE

LAST FEW STITCHES

FOUR NEEDLES

FIGURE 23

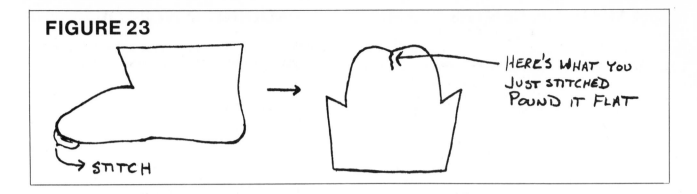

STITCH

HERE'S WHAT YOU JUST STITCHED POUND IT FLAT

have more room because of the space formed by the slit in the upper, but can also trim the heel.

PART THREE — Trimming the heel

(1) Look at Figure 21 A. Your moccasin is just about all stitched, with a gap at the heel. Using both hands, and working with both ends of the upper, pin them to where they will be stitched on the sole. The parts of the upper overlap. If this overlap is more than one half inch, then trim with the knife until they overlap by one half inch.

(2) Look at 21 B. Glue the edges as shown. Keep the curve of the heel of the sole in mind while you are doing this, because you still have to stitch it up. Don't try to glue

the upper to the sole.

(3) Look at Figure 22. Finish stitching so that all four needles are in the inside of the moccasin at the very back of the heel. Make two knots.

(4) Stitch up the back of the heel as shown, and maybe trim the top of the sides of the moccasin so they match.

(5) If you are into kink, a little crazy glue on each of the knots will ensure that they don't come unknotted. So much for this procedure.

FIGURE 24

STITCH ABOUT ONE INCH

ALREADY STITCHED

POUNDED

FIGURE 25

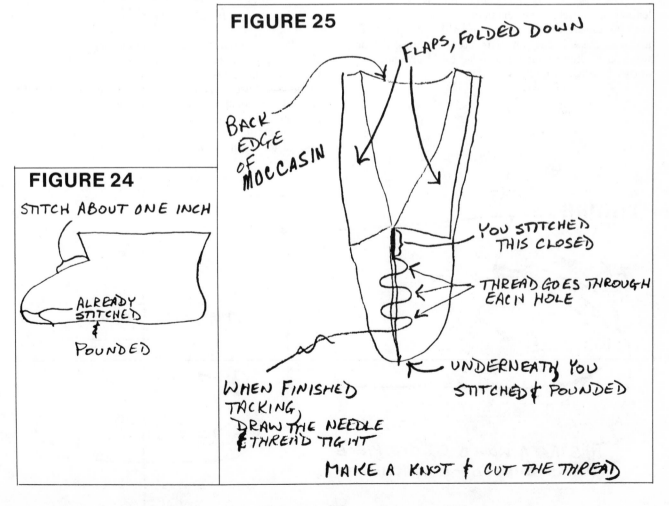

FLAPS, FOLDED DOWN

BACK EDGE OF MOCCASIN

YOU STITCHED THIS CLOSED

THREAD GOES THROUGH EACH HOLE

WHEN FINISHED TACKING, DRAW THE NEEDLE & THREAD TIGHT

UNDERNEATH YOU STITCHED & POUNDED

MAKE A KNOT & CUT THE THREAD

240

TAILORING CENTER SEAM CONSTRUCTION

Condition: You have cut out your patterns for a pair of Iroquois style, center seam moccasins. The seam starts under the toes and runs up over the center of the top of the foot before ending at the hole where you put your foot into the moccasin.

Purpose: If you have cut these like the rest of us, then you will have a moccasin which will have ridges and bulges at the seam just over the instep. This is unsightly, hellatious on bead work, and makes for a bad fit. Since you won't know until you try them on, you get stuck with this problem. This procedure tries to prevent it.

Procedure:
(1) Stitch the part of the seam shown in Figure 23. It's the part that goes under the toes. Lay the moccasin as flat as it will go and pound the seam with a hammer. this will help keep it from bothering your toes.
(2) Stitch the part of the seam shown in Figure 24, only about an inch or so down the instep.
(3) Tack the rest of the seam. A tack is a temporary substitute for a stitch. You pass the needle and thread in and out of the holes as shown in Figure 25.
(4) Now poke your foot in as far as it will go. Remember that this pattern is inside out. Stand up, with your foot in the toe of the moccasin. Take heed of where the bulge is. Mark it and trim it as shown in Figure 26.

The procedure is ended after you have trimmed the leather and stitched the remainder of the new seam that your cut describes. When you finish stitching the backs, and turn these inside out, thus hiding stitches, the only way you will know your handiwork is by the absence of any unsightly bulges above your instep.

ADDING INNER SOLES

Condition: You're about to cut the patterns for your soft-soled moccasins. The instructions you use will call for you to place your foot on the paper to do this.

Purpose: Since we've already shown you how to glue the sole, we ought to show you how to position it the right way.

Procedure:
(1) Just after you draw your foot and draw the pattern, make sure that everything you did follows the instructions.
(2) When you cut out your pattern also cut out the foot print.
(3) The cut out becomes the pattern for your inner sole. The foot shaped hole in the moccasin pattern shows where the inner sole will be placed.
(4) When you cut out your patterns, draw the outline of the foot. Make sure you trace your pattern on the inside of the future moccasin. You don't want the line of your foot to be on the outside sole of the new moccasin.
(5) Before you trace the second moccasin on the leather, flip the paper pattern over. That's how you avoid two left feet.

The procedure is ended when you have a left and a right moccasin drawn on the leather, with the outline of the foot showing where the inner sole will go.

MAKING PATTERNS AND MOCCASINS

The next three procedures will summarize the process of making the hard-sole, center-seam, and pucker-toe styles of moccasins. It is important to remember that whether you use these three procedures or another book, the first attempt should follow the directions as closely as you can. All craft work is a sequence of organized steps, and the person who wrote them had a system of working. The master taught his apprentice the way his master taught

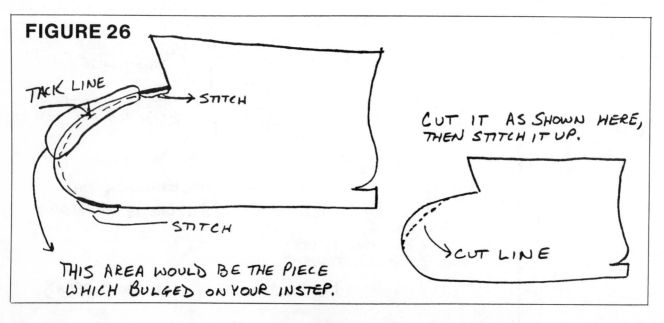

FIGURE 26

TACK LINE

STITCH

STITCH

THIS AREA WOULD BE THE PIECE WHICH BULGED ON YOUR INSTEP.

CUT IT AS SHOWN HERE, THEN STITCH IT UP.

CUT LINE

him, and if he thought to get creative at all it was only after he had learned the trade.

All footwear requires that you measure your foot before thinking about your pattern. For these procedures you will use only three measurements. Use a tape measure, and you'll probably be better off using metric measurements.

Measure the length of your foot from heel to the tip of the big toe.

Measure the circumference of your foot. Step on the tape measure so that the ball of your foot is resting on the tape. Use your right foot, with the end of the tape on the left side of your foot. Measure around so that the tape runs around the ball of the foot and covers the ball behind the big toe and the ball behind the pinky toe.

Draw the pattern of your foot, keeping the pen or pencil straight up and down. Press tightly against the flesh of your foot. When you get to the heel part, trace your line so that it shows where the bottom of your heel meets the paper. That's the only way to ensure a good pattern.

Now you're ready to begin the procedure of your choice. Good luck and work carefully.

MAKING THE HARD-SOLED MOCCASIN

Condition: You have two types of leather, a hard and stiffened piece of anything except rawhide. It is about 7-8 ounce thickness, and will be the sole. The other piece is anything pliable, such as cowhide or deerskin.

Materials: knife and board, paper and shears, medium size harness needle, artificial sinew or flax thread, and awl. If you made your awl point with a fine, thin taper, then be careful not to force it to the point where it snaps.

Procedure:

(1) Draw, cut out, and trace your pattern as shown in Figure 27.

(2) Use the skiving procedure to take the corner off the bottom edge of the sole piece.

(3) In the area you just skived, use the hole punching procedure to punch awl holes about one half a centimeter or one quarter inch apart. Work your way all around the sole edge in one shot.

(4) On the upper piece, punch holes all around the edge as you did in step three. Look at the marks you made per the instruction on the figure.

(5) Reread "Stitching and Working with the Hard Sole." Thread your needle with a length of about three times the length of your foot. Stitch from toe mark to heel center. Note that each stitch goes through both holes in the upper and "mate" hole in the sole. Stop stitching when you reach the center of the heel. There will probably be a lot of upper left over.

(6) Repeat this process from toe to heel on the other side of the moccasin. Trim the extra leather at the heel of the upper so that you can stitch up the back.

(7) Attach the tongue piece and run a deerskin lace through the lace holes on the top edge of the upper.

(8) Repeat the procedure for the other moccasin. Make sure that you have one right and one left moccasin. If you have two right or two left, make another pair once again forgetting to turn the pattern over when you do your tracing. If you end up with four right or four left, then have someone else make your moccasins.

FIGURE 27

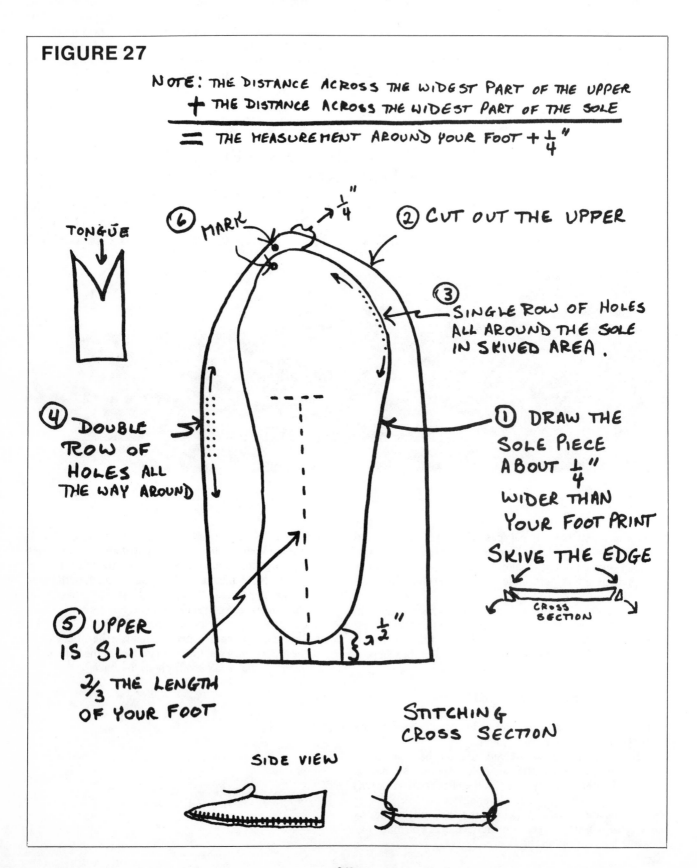

NOTE: THE DISTANCE ACROSS THE WIDEST PART OF THE UPPER
+ THE DISTANCE ACROSS THE WIDEST PART OF THE SOLE
$$= \text{THE MEASUREMENT AROUND YOUR FOOT} + \frac{1}{4}\text{"}$$

TONGUE

⑥ MARK → $\frac{1}{4}$"

② CUT OUT THE UPPER

③ SINGLE ROW OF HOLES ALL AROUND THE SOLE IN SKIVED AREA.

④ DOUBLE ROW OF HOLES ALL THE WAY AROUND

① DRAW THE SOLE PIECE ABOUT $\frac{1}{4}$" WIDER THAN YOUR FOOT PRINT

SKIVE THE EDGE

CROSS SECTION

⑤ UPPER IS SLIT

$\frac{2}{3}$ THE LENGTH OF YOUR FOOT

$2\frac{1}{2}$"

SIDE VIEW

STITCHING CROSS SECTION

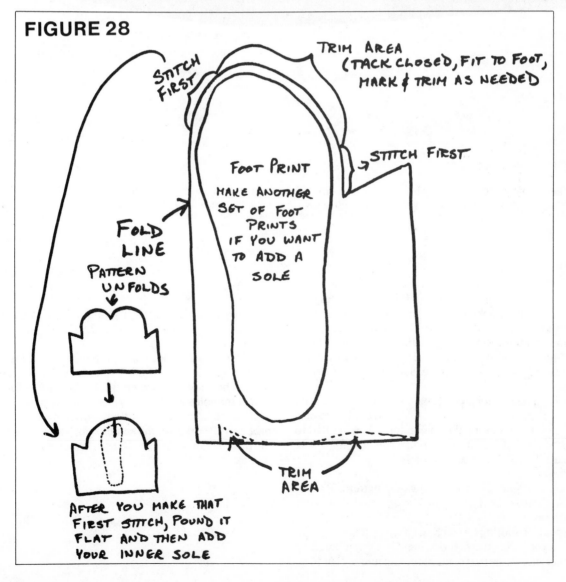

FIGURE 28

STITCH FIRST

TRIM AREA
(TACK CLOSED, FIT TO FOOT, MARK & TRIM AS NEEDED

FOOT PRINT

MAKE ANOTHER SET OF FOOT PRINTS IF YOU WANT TO ADD A SOLE

STITCH FIRST

FOLD LINE

PATTERN UNFOLDS

AFTER YOU MAKE THAT FIRST STITCH, POUND IT FLAT AND THEN ADD YOUR INNER SOLE

TRIM AREA

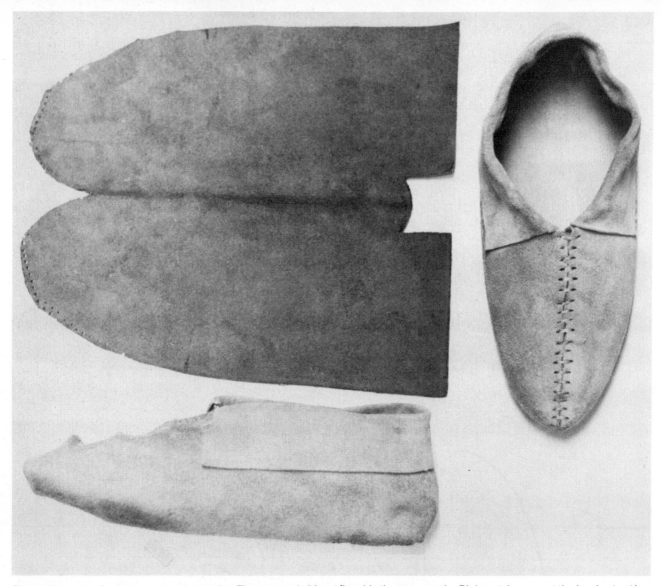

Three elements of center seam construction. The pattern (without flaps) is the same as the Plains style, except the heel cutout has been moved to the center of the back edge. The moc shown on its side shows a poor fit in the toe where irregular bulges in the seam are visible. The moc on the right has been trimmed and is plainly shaped to the foot.

Condition: You've gone Eastern, and believe that real men don't wear puckered toe moccasins. You also swallowed the garbage from the movies that said a good frontiersman could tell the tribe of an Indian instantly by looking at his moccasins. The Iroquois must have been real men because they wore center seam style.

Materials: a thick but limp and pliable leather such as elk, deer or moose-belly. Try not to use cowhide because it tends to be unforgiving in comfort when applied to this style. You might want to use cowhide for a sole insert if you're a semi-real man.

Procedure:
(1) Look at Figure 28 which shows the pattern. Reread "Adding Inner Soles" and mark and cut your patterns.
(2) Reread "Tailoring Center Seam Construction." Right after you make the first one inch section of stitching which closes the part of the moccasin under your toes, add the inner sole. Now finish the tailoring procedure, thus stitching up the front part of the moccasin.
(3) Reread "Preventing Heel Sag" and stitch up the heel.

This style moccasin, particularly because of the leather we advise, should fit snugly to the point of being tight. They always stretch after being worn for awhile. When the soles wear out, you can cut the part where your foot made a print and attach a separate sole. That's probably the origin of the center seam style you always see in the sketchbooks as the rifleman or ranger style pumps.

MAKING THE PUCKER TOE
MOCCASIN

Condition: You either like the comfort of a moccasin which doesn't allow a seam to touch your foot, or you want to make a pair of winter moccasins. Use this pattern, about two sizes too big, with a lot of wool socks for the latter.

Materials: Same as center seam pattern.

Procedure:
(1) Look at Figure 29. Make your cuts and mark off where you will want the inner sole.
(2) Use "Adding Inner Soles" to add the inner sole before you start anything else.
(3) Use "Constructing Puckers for Eastern Style Moccasins" to finish the front of the moccasins.
(4) Use "Preventing Heel Sag" to finish the back of the moccasin.

These moccasins should be snug to the point of being tight because they are going to stretch. For winter moccasins you may consider a sheepskin lining. That results in a heavy glue job after you have traced the pattern on the wool lined sheepskin. Don't forget to waterproof. Your problem in the woods is less the cold than the water.

FIGURE 29

NOTE: THE DISTANCE ACROSS THE PATTERN
+ THE DISTANCE ACROSS THE VAMP
= THE MEASUREMENT AROUND YOUR FOOT + ½".

SINGLE ROW OF HOLES

KEEP THE DISTANCE BETWEEN THE FOOT & BONE UNIFORM

DOUBLE ROW OF HOLES

VAMP

FOOT PRINT DRAW IT ON THE PATTERN AND ON THE INSIDE OF THE LEATHER FOR THE SOLE POSITION.

⅔ THE LENGTH OF THE FOOT

ABOUT ½"

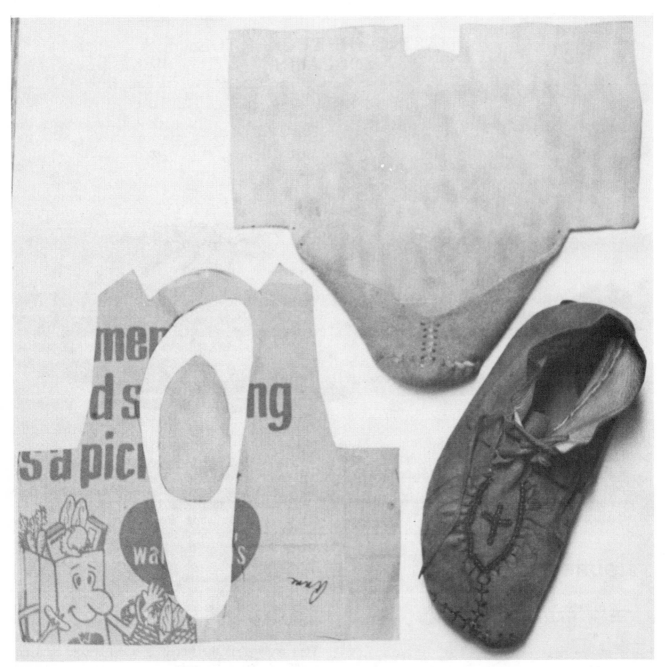

Pucker toe construction. This is a Seneca style and features a short seam in front of the vamp. Note the outline of the sole as a foot shaped hole in the pattern (left). The vamp piece is positioned about where it covers the foot. The moc in the upper right is already under construction. The toe and center seam have been stitched.

WINTERIZING AND WATERPROOFING

Short of stuffing your moccasins with a pair of totes, there really is no way to waterproof them. One thing to avoid is silicon if you're a hunter, because game will smell you miles away even over the lures you have bathed yourself in. Another is to avoid Crisco-like cooking fats because they wash away and leave the leather stiff and brittle. You can make an inner moccasin of sheepskin if you desire, but the best solution to the cold is in two or three pair of good wool socks on your feet and another two or three in your pack. Sorry.

SELECTING AND AUTHENTICIZING SHOES AND BOOTS

Unless you are buying a period shoe stay simple and black. Women should restrict themselves to a flat pump which can be of colors other than black or brown. If your women's shoe has a heel that you know is not leather wrapped plastic, then use a bastard file to trim it as shown in Figure 30. Dye it black when you're through.

Both men and women should avoid the following,

FIGURE 30

FILE AREA

BE SURE THE HEEL IS SOLID LEATHER OR WOOD, NOT THE HOLLOWED OUT INDUSTRIAL KIND!

AFTER FILING, THE HEEL NOW HAS A CONCAVE WAIST. DYE IT BLACK

especially on shoes or boots which were factory made to be as those in the 18th or 19th century:

    *Glue marks where the upper joins the sole
    *Eyelets
    *Light spots in the dye

    *Spots where the machined loop stitching didn't take right. These will come undone within the first two or three times you wear the shoe.
    *Synthetic material for the sole, even if dyed. The dye comes off and it sticks out like a sore toe.

CONCLUSION

This marks the end of these construction procedures. If you had the feeling of, "Why didn't I think of that," as you were reading them, the reason is simply because someone else just taught you the way someone else had taught me. The big difference is that you got the information all at once, whereas I had to waste a couple of pairs of moccasins through hard knocks.

If the procedures in this chapter seemed like much ado about nothing, then this chapter has done its job well. Although they are simple, they are often overlooked, and the maker has to live with lesser results for the life of the moccasin. Right down to the last one, they will cost you more time, but in the long run they'll make for more comfortable and longer wearing footwear.

PERIOD SHELTERS

BY GEORGE GLENN

GEORGE GLENN IS a Professor of Theatre History at the University of Northern Iowa, where, in 1974, he originated and taught the first college-level course in muzzleloading. He has been an avid black powder enthusiast for thirty-five years, becoming involved with buckskinning after moving west across the Mississippi in 1966. Recently he has been participating in Revolutionary War reenactment activities.

Glenn began writing for *Muzzleloader* magazine in 1975 and has been a member of *Muzzleloader's* editorial staff since 1976. His chapter on "The Lodge" was included in the first *Book of Buckskinning*, and his chapter on "Making Camp Gear" was in *The Book of Buckskinning II*. He is a member of the NRA, the NMLRA, and Cap. Hawkens Boone's Company, Morgan's Rifle Corps, of the North West Territorial Alliance.

On March 5, 1864, 25 year old Private James L. Vanlieu of Company D, 1st Regiment New York Veteran Cavalry, wrote home to his family in Illinois:

My Dear Father, Mother, Brothers & Sisters all,

> *Now don't get scared to hear your Jimmy is in a hospital, for here I am but doing well. We left camp four weeks ago last Tuesday. I had a bad cold at that time, & was on guard the night before we left. We were ready to march at 6 o'clock, & was in our saddles until night, except for a short stop at noon. Stopped that night & lay on the ground with our blankets for beds. We each man had a piece of canvas for a tent, 5 feet by 6. I was too tired to pitch mine, consequently I got wet as it rained in the night. I took more cold but I kept up pluck. . . . I haven't done any duty since. The Doc says I have got the bronchitas. I have been in the hospital since a week last Wednesday. . . This is the first day I have been able or felt able to write. . . . My sheet is full and I am tired so I guess I will have to stop — my love to all. How I want to see you all. Good bye for this time. Jimmy.*

The entry for Vanlieu in the company muster roll for March and April, 1864, contains the following laconic line in the space for "Remarks": "Died of disease at Martinsburg, Va., April 27, 1864."

These two documents — the letter and the muster roll — graphically illustrate the importance of having and using a shelter, whether on the march in the military, or in camp. As far as Vanlieu's letters reveal he was never in battle, but he was as much a casualty of the war as if he'd been shot out of his saddle at the height of the hottest action. Whether he would have lived if he'd taken the few minutes necessary to pitch his tent is, of course, an unanswerable question, but it is undeniable that *not* pitching it certainly hastened his eventual death.

The need for shelter has not diminished over the years. Today, outdoor recreation still creates a demand for temporary shelters. Camping is a widespread and popular activity and many people still camp in tents, either because of preference or economic convenience. Sporting-goods stores and catalogs display a bewildering variety of styles, models, and types of tents.

The buckskinner, too, has need of suitable shelter, and although some of the buckskinner's requirements are the same as a modern camper's, some are different. Like the camper, the buckskinner is concerned about such things as portability, stability, comfort, and style. Unlike the modern camper, however, the buckskinner or the muzzleloader involved in military re-enactment, is in addition concerned with authenticity or historical accuracy in style and materials.

This chapter will discuss the main kinds of primitive and authentic shelters that are available to the modern buckskinner and re-enactor. For the most part we will stick to four main periods: the French and Indian War; the Revolutionary War; the era of the Fur Trade (roughly 1800-1840); and the Civil War. We will not attempt to examine the many varieties of Native American shelters, except for the tipi, since, with the exception of the tipi, few of them were adopted for use by the military, mountain men, or miners.

After a brief survey of the history of tents, we will look at the typical tents from each period. Finally, we will discuss some styles of tents and shelters that have become common in modern buckskinning even though they are not historically accurate.

The tent obviously has a long history; I suspect it can be traced back to the time when the first primitive man threw a skin over a framework of poles in front of the fire and crawled in under it. References to tents and other kinds of shelters can be traced back thousands of years; references to tents abound in the Bible, and most people have heard of the Greek hero Achilles sulking in his tent outside the walls of Troy some 3000 years ago. The Romans used tents on their campaigns, and a mosaic of a Roman hunting scene shows the hunters' camp equipped with a tent that resembles a modern cabin tent from Sears (see Illustration 1).

Private James VanLieu, posed in front of a photographer's painted backdrop showing a typical Civil War camp scene. (From the author's collection.)

Illustration 1: Roman tent taken from a mosaic depicting a wild animal hunt in North Africa. (From Moses Hadas, *Imperial Rome.*)

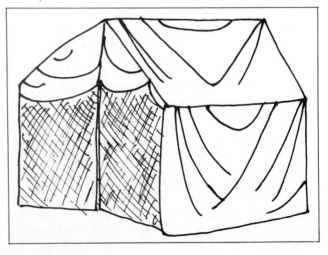

Illustration 2: Muslim tents from a 13th century illustration. Strips of Persian carpet circle the tops. The interiors were also hung and carpeted with Persian rugs. (From Desmond Stewart, *Early Islam.*)

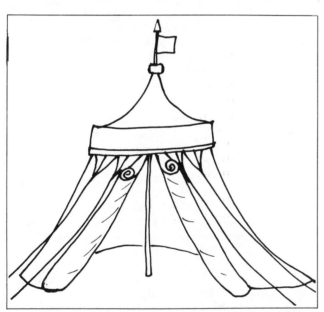

Illustration 3: Crusaders' tent from a 1455 painting of the siege of Constantinople. (From Philip Sherrard, *Byzantium.*)

Various tents were used during the Middle Ages and the Renaissance, according to pictorial evidence and other documentation. The Crusaders carried tents and pavilions with them, and encountered the Muslims with their tents (Illustration 2). The tournaments of the Middle Ages used tents for the knights to array themselves in, and pavilions from which the lords and ladies watched the jousts (Illustration 3). Tents have been an indispensable item of equipment for the military for literally thousands of years.

In all that time, probably every size and shape of tent known today has been used, but this does not necessarily mean that any style of tent is suitable for a historically accurate camp. If your interest is in creating an authentic camp — regardless of the historic period — you must not fall into the fallacy of "if they'd have had it they'd have used it," or its corollary, "if it was used once, it's accurate for every subsequent period." As Kyle McGonigle, captain of the recreated 1st Iowa Regiment of 1843, points out, styles go out of fashion in tents as well as in clothes and uniforms, and what was correct for, say, the Revolutionary War period may or may not be correct for the Army of 1843.

Fabrics for tent materials seem not to have changed too much over the years. A suitable fabric for tentage would be any strong, closely-woven, light-weight fabric. Linen has been around for thousands of years, and linen canvas was probably the standard common tent material. Other fabrics were used, of course, from light-weight wools in those societies where sheep and goats were common, to silk in the tents of the Far East. Cotton, although a very ancient fabric, did not become a common tent fabric until the industrialization of the cotton industry around the turn of the nineteenth century. Today, our most

Illustration 4: Typical wedge tents from the Revolutionary War period.

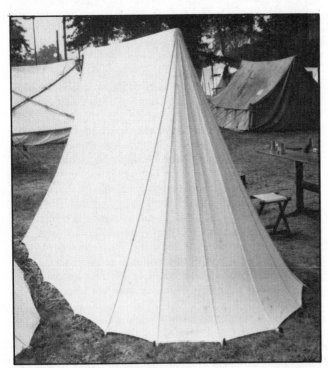

Illustration 5: The back of a wedge tent showing the belled-out end.

common, relatively authentic fabric is cotton canvas. Linen canvas is the most authentic fabric for most reproductions, but it is virtually unobtainable.

The most common tent in use throughout the entire period from the 1750s through the 1860s was the *wedge* or "A" tent. In essence the wedge is a simple rectangle of canvas thrown over a ridge pole held up in front and back with upright poles. The back is closed and the front has a center-opening doorway. The whole is staked down around the perimeter (see Illustration 4).

The wedge was the tent of the common soldier (although it was used by civilians) and was meant to hold four to six men. Today the wedge is usually considered to be a two-man tent. About the only changes in the wedge through the years was in size, but there were also some minor variations in shape. During the Revolution, the standard British Infantry tent, according to the Patternmaster of the Brigade of the American Revolution, was six feet wide by eight feet six inches long by six feet high at the ridgepole. The ridgepole was seven feet long: the remaining foot and a half of length was a belled-out extension at the rear of the tent (Illustration 5). Neumann and Kravic, in *The Collectors' Illustrated Encyclopedia of the American Revolution*, list the dimensions of the American privates' wedge tent as six feet six inches square by five feet high. Wedges were made of linen canvas, with the seams beeswaxed or painted for waterproofing (Illustration 6).

Wedges were erected with three two inch by two inch poles: the two upright end poles had three inch metal pins

Illustration 6: Revolutionary War wedge tents with painted seams.

Illustration 7: Typical U.S. Army wedge, ca. 1840. Note that these wedges have a narrower base and a steeper pitch than Revolutionary War wedges.

in them which fit into corresponding holes in the ridgepole. The pins sometimes extended through grommeted holes in the tent, and were then sometimes capped with wooden balls painted in the regiment's uniform facing color.

The wedge continued in popularity into the nineteenth century, remaining the shelter of the common soldier. By the 1840s the standard size was about six feet two inches square and six feet two inches high, with a squared-off back (Illustration 7). The Civil War wedge remained in the six to seven foot square size range, but according to Francis Lord in *The Civil War Collectors' Encyclopedia*, began to fall out of use after the first couple of years of the war because wedges required too much wagon transportation to take along on campaigns. Consequently they, and other larger tents tended to be relegated to more permanent military encampments. But the wedge was popular: almost every photograph and contemporary illustration of large Civil War camps — both Union and Confederate — show large numbers of wedges in use. (See, for example, *The American Heritage Picture History of the Civil War.*)

The second "standard" military tent of the eighteenth century was the *marquee*, whose origins can be seen

Above: Illustration 9: Marquee with the sides removed, converting it into a shade canopy.

Top right: Illustration 10: Rectangular marquee. Note that both styles of marquee have the typical scalloped roof edges.

Below right: Engraving after John Trumbull's painting of Burgoyne's surrender. Burgoyne is offering his sword to Gates. Notice the marquee tent at the right.

Illustration 8: Oval Revolutionary War period marquee. Here a side has been left partially down for ventilation.

Illustration 11: French and Indian War period officer's pavilion tent. The sketch is from an engraving of Sir William Johnson's camp at Lake George which was under attack by Baron Dieskau's forces in 1755. (From *The American Heritage Book of the Pioneer Spirit.*)

in the tents and pavilions of the Renaissance, and whose descendants can be seen today in the circus tent or exhibition tent. During the period of its use, the marquee was an officer's tent. Basically, the marquee is an oval or rectangular side-walled tent, with a peaked roof supported by two center poles with a ridge pole between them. The ridgepole is shorter than the overall length of the tent. The sides, which are not attached permanently to the roof, are supported by a number of shorter poles. The tent is further supported by guy ropes and pegs (Illustrations 8 and 10). Characteristic of the marquee is the scalloped roof edge around the eaves.

The marquee was a large tent: An average size was about ten feet by fourteen feet by eight feet high at the peak; the side walls were around five feet high. It was dependent on wagon transportation, so tended to be used only by high-ranking officers. The interior could be subdivided into small rooms so that an officer could have a bedroom and perhaps a dining room as well as an office. In hot weather the side walls could be allowed to gap open or could be removed entirely, converting the tent to a fly or canopy (Illustration 9). Two or more marquees could be pitched and attached together, creating a large, multi-roomed tent.

Allied to the marquee, but becoming uncommon by the time of the Revolution, was the *pavilion,* a center pole, wide-walled, circular tent (Illustration 11). Most of the tents depicted in medieval and Renaissance illustrations are of this type, and they continue to be observed in illustrations of seventeenth and early eighteenth century military camps.

Not only men were sheltered by tents: Small conical tents known as *bell of arms* tents were used to protect the stacked muskets of the troops. The upright center pole had a crossbar which supported the muzzles of the muskets.

Illustration 12: A bell of arms.

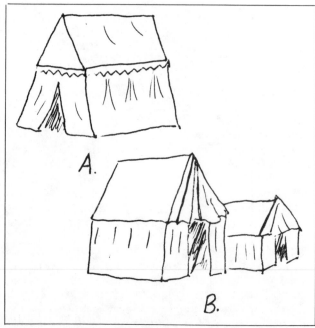

Illustration 13: French and Indian War period wall tents. (A) From an engraving of Sir William Johnson's 1755 camp at Lake George. (B) From an engraving of Henry Bouquet's camp on the Muskingum River. (From *The American Heritage Book of the Pioneer Spirit.*)

Illustration 14: An officer's wall tent from the 1840's U.S. Army.

The exterior was decorated with the regimental coat of arms (Illustration 12).

A popular nineteenth century tent — the *wall-tent* — began to be seen in military camps as early as the 1750s. A 1756 English engraving depicting Baron Dieskau's 1755 attack on Sir William Johnson's camp at Lake George clearly shows wall tents as well as wedges and circular pavilions or marquees (Illustration 13A). An engraving of Henry Bouquet's 1764 council with the Seneca, Delaware, and Shawnee tribes on the Muskingum River also shows wall tents in use (Illustration 13B). The wall tent's popularity really begins in the nineteenth century. In the 1840s, for example, the standard officers' tent was basically a large wedge, ten feet by seven feet, with three foot high side walls permanently attached, making the whole a wall tent about eight feet high at the peak (Illustration 14). The pitch of the roof was the same as that of the common soldiers' wedge or "dog tent," even though the officers' tent was larger and taller. The interior could be subdivided into a small sleeping section, usually just large enough for a cot and perhaps a foot locker, and an office section. What distinguishes this style of tent from the marquee was the flat ends set perpendicular to the ridgepole. The ridgepole of the marquee was shorter than

the tent's long dimension, whereas the wall tent's ridgepole is the same length as the long dimension.

As in the past, tents were also used for functions other than housing personnel: Tents were used as kitchens and bakeries, hospitals, and the stores of the various suttlers and traders attached to the army. It is possible that the suttlers' and civilian tents took different shapes and forms from the "standard" military models.

The wedge maintained its primacy during the era of the fur trade, according to Charles Hanson, Jr., in "Some Notes on Tents in the Western Fur Trade," in *The Museum of the Fur Trade Quarterly* for Spring, 1980. According to Hanson the wedge had become popular as a utility tent, being used not only by the military wherever they went in the west, but also by explorers, travellers, traders, and trappers. Alfred Jacob Miller painted wedges as part of Sublette's caravan to the Rendezvous of 1837, and the wedge was standard with the Hudson's Bay Company in the mid-nineteenth century. Wedges of six feet by seven feet by six feet high and nine by fourteen by eight feet high were still being advertised and sold only fifty years ago.

Wall tents were certainly in use by civilians during the period of the western fur trade, although the only reference

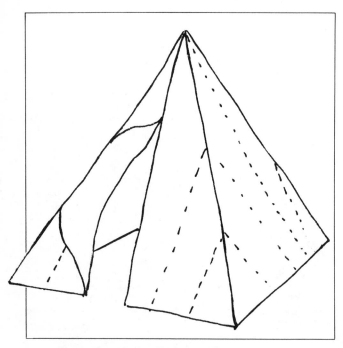

Illustration 15: A mid-19th century pyramid or miner's tent. (From Charles Hanson's "Some Notes on Tents in the Western Fur Trade.")

found by Hanson is a report that Old Bill Williams and George Perkins carried one in 1842 to use as a store when trading with the Indians.

A third type of tent whose use was documented during the 1840s was the simple *pyramid* or *miner's* tent. It was set up with only a center pole and a small tent might use only four pegs to hold it down. Sizes apparently ranged from seven feet six inches square and seven feet six inches high to fifteen feet square and nine and a half feet high. A pyramid tent was apparently the type carried by Francis Parkman in 1846 (Illustration 15).

Lean-tos were obviously used in great numbers, and undoubtedly appeared in a great variety of styles, although such twentieth-century styles as the "Whelan" and the "baker" cannot apparently be documented for any earlier than the beginning of this century (more on these two styles later). What appeared to be the most common lean-to was a simple strip of canvas or other fabric thrown over a ridgepole or a rope and staked to the ground. Hanson reports a mid-nineteenth-century account of gold miners using lean-tos, and fastening the ends together with ties or wooden skewers to form an enclosed shelter. Lean-tos were also constructed of blankets thrown over poles, and indeed, could easily be made from any number of materials such as hides, interwoven branches and grasses, etc.

Then there was the tipi. This excellent shelter is still the preferred home-away-from-home of the modern buckskinner, although its use by the mountain men was probably not as extensive as many of us would like to believe. The tipi is well-enough known to need no extensive description here (see *The Book of Buckskinning I*). Its manifest advantages as a shelter are its stability in storm, its relative coolness in summer and warmth in winter, and the fact that a fire can be built inside for cooking and warmth (Illustration 16).

The original Indian tipi that the explorers and trappers encountered as they moved west was made of buffalo hides, and was relatively small — probably not exceeding twelve to fourteen feet in diameter. (Larger "medicine lodges" were built, but were not used as dwellings.) The size restriction was due to the weight of the hide cover—anything larger was simply too heavy to manage. Only when canvas was introduced did tipi sizes start to expand, but the mountain man era was pretty much over by then. Hanson points out that any canvas tipis of the mountain man era would have been made of linen canvas.

As in earlier periods, the typical material for tents during the fur trade was linen canvas, but there are some accounts of tents being made of striped bed-ticking, probably linen, although cotton ticking was available by the mid 1840s.

The era of the Civil War saw some new tent designs. The wedge for the common soldier was replaced by the French *tente d'Arbi*, known in this country as the *shelter tent,* or "dog" or "pup" tent. As used by the French army, the *tente d'Arbi* was supposed to accommodate six men, according to the 9th edition of *The Encyclopaedia Britannica* (1889). The *tente d'Arbi* was pitched by stretching a rope across the top of three low poles set in a line, and pegging the rope to the ground at each end. Over this rope was thrown four squares of canvas buttoned together and pegged to the ground. The ends were formed by two more squares of canvas, one thrown over the sloping support rope at each end and buttoned to the main cover. Each of the six men who were to use the tent carried a square of the canvas and a portion of the rope, poles, and pegs.

As introduced into the U.S. Army in the early 1860s, the tents were constructed of two shelter halves, made of cotton drilling, cotton duck, or rubberized fabric, according to Lord. The shelter halves were buttoned together and thrown over a guy rope stretched between two uprights. Shelter tents used by artillerymen utilized a ridgepole instead of a rope. Over 300,000 of these pup tents were used by the Union Army in the first year of the war. The dimensions at this time were five feet two inches long by four feet eight inches wide. By 1864, according to General Order No. 60 from the Quartermaster General's Office (as reported by Lord), the dimensions were five feet six inches long by five feet five inches wide. They were made of cotton duck with nine metallic top buttons and seven metallic end buttons. Each half had 23 buttonholes along the upper and side edges, and three loops for pegs along the bottom edge. A six foot ten inch manila guy line was specified (Illustration 17).

Lord reports that the pup tent was pitched by driving two muskets with fixed bayonets into the ground (bayonet

Illustration 16: Tipis are by far the most popular shelter at western rendezvous.

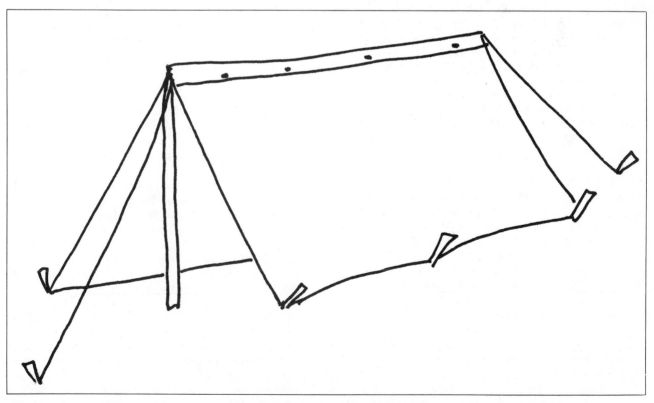

Illustration 17: A Civil War shelter tent.

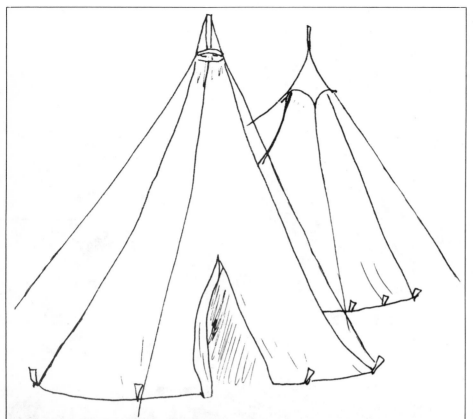

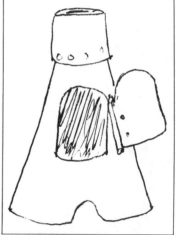

Illustration 18: Sibley tents. The tent in the background has its "rain cap" in place. Drawing from a chromolithograph after a Chapman painting of a confederate camp at Corinth, Mississippi, in 1862. (From *The American Heritage Picture History of the Civil War.*)

Illustration 19: The Sibley stove. (From Jack Coggins' *Arms and Equipment of the Civil War.*)

first), and then stretching the guy rope between the trigger guards of the muskets. With all due respect, this sounds to me like a very silly method, although it may have been used in emergencies. Not only would it expose the muskets to the elements, but it would render them inaccessible in case of sudden attack. None of the contemporary paintings and drawings and photographs of camp scenes that I have examined show shelter halves pitched with muskets. Indeed, Winslow Homer's painting "Home, Sweet Home" shows a pup tent pitched with standard poles for uprights.

In any case, for a man more than five feet tall, the shelter tent must have been an inadequate shelter, for either one's head or feet would extend past the limits of the tent. But as a campaign tent, meant to be quickly and easily pitched and struck, and easily portable, the shelter tent was certainly better than nothing, as Private Vanlieu could have attested.

The other major new tent design of the Civil War was the *Sibley,* or *bell* tent, invented in 1857 by Henry H. Sibley. Sibley had accompanied Fremont on one of his Western expeditions, and had been inspired by the tipi. The Sibley was a conical tent eighteen feet in diameter and twelve feet high (Illustration 18). It was held up by a single center pole which rested on an iron tripod, so the pole could be raised and lowered to adjust tension. At the top was an opening about a foot in diameter for ventilation, or for the pipe from the Sibley stove (Illustration 19). A canvas cap,

attached to two long guy ropes, could cover the top opening in stormy weather. The Sibley could also be "stockaded"; that is, pitched on permanent side walls, thus raising the whole tent up two or three feet, and increasing the effective floor space. When stockaded, the Sibley could hold twenty men.

Because of the difficulty in transporting the Sibley it was taken out of field use in 1862, but it continued to be used in more permanent rear echelon camps as many photographs and illustrations from the period can attest.

The wall tent or hospital tent continued to be popular and in the Civil War served the same function for officers that the marquee had during the Revolution. Wall tents were prescribed by General McClellan in 1862 for general, field, and staff officers (line officers each had a single shelter tent).

When used as field hospital tents, the wall tents could handle six to twenty patients. Often two tents were joined back-to-back to form a single double-length tent. The most common size hospital tent was fourteen feet six inches by fourteen feet, and eleven feet high in the center, with four feet six inch side walls. They had a supplemental fly twenty-one feet six inches by fourteen feet that provided additional protection from sun and rain (Illustration 20).

The choice of a particular style of tent for the modern buckskinner or reenactor depends on which style is most appropriate for the particular period of choice. As we have seen, the wedge in its variety of forms seems to be the most

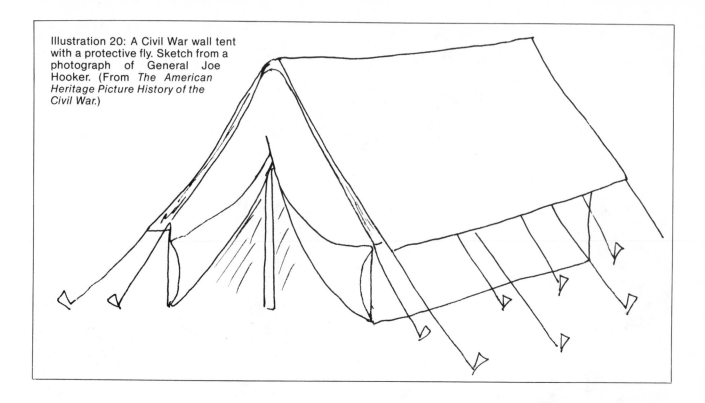

Illustration 20: A Civil War wall tent with a protective fly. Sketch from a photograph of General Joe Hooker. (From *The American Heritage Picture History of the Civil War.*)

universal style for almost two hundred years. The problem with the wedge is that even in its larger sizes there isn't as much usable area in it as there is in the various side-wall tents or in the tipi. Nor can you conveniently have a fire or a stove in a wedge, although it had been done (Illustration 21). If family accommodation is a question, then only the marquee, the wall tent, or the tipi are possibilities (I'm not considering the Sibley, although it certainly would have the room). The decision may be taken out of your hands by the nature of your participation and the degree of authenticity it requires. If you're engaged in military re-enactment, then the size, style, and material required for your shelter will be determined by the specifications laid down by the controlling organization. The guiding rule in most cases is: If it can't be authenticated, it can't be used.

For non-military activities — buckskinning — the guidelines are less stringent, but authenticity should still be the goal. It's fairly clear what shelters are authentic for any given period, but there is another consideration for the modern buckskinner: There is a pseudo-authenticity that has been granted by current usage. That is to say, there are shelters in use that are not authentic but have been accepted for so long that there is probably no hope of eliminating them from the rendezvous scene. I'm not convinced that it is so awful to allow non-authentic shelters in a rendezvous camp, as long as they *look* authentic. After all, as much as some dislike it, we often put up with primitive-looking but non-authentic camp furniture, cooking utensils, clothing, and weapons, so why not shelters?

If there's nothing in the authentic list of shelters that will serve your turn, let's look at some of the "accepted" non-authentic types. Two have already been mentioned: the baker and the Whelan lean-tos. The baker is basically a wall-tent cut in half front to back, and gets its name from its

function in WWI when it housed company bakers in the field (Illustration 22). Bakers come in numerous sizes. from small, one-man versions to large, family-sized editions. The baker usually comes with a front flap or awning that can be let down to completely cover the front opening (Illustration 23).

The Whelan lean-to, invented by the late Col. Whelan, is shaped somewhat like a reflector oven, and was designed to serve somewhat the same purpose; that is,

Illustration 21: A curiosity. A wedge tent with an inside stove.

(Above) Illustration 22: A baker lean-to. (Below) Illustration 23: A baker with the front flap lowered.

reflect the heat of the campfire into its interior (Illustration 24). Again, Whelans come in a number of sizes to suit most needs.

Recently we have seen some new additions to the primitive family of shelters; oddly-shaped tents or lean-tos called *lean-tis* or *ti-tos*. These designs are a cross between the lean-to and the tipi. Some are supported by a number of interior poles, similar to the tipi (Illustration 25), while other versions are held up by a single pole (Illustration 26). As regards to the former, I see no advantage over a small tipi. Indeed, the tipi is infinitely preferable in a number of ways, including the advantage of the interior fire. The one-pole versions, however, have the same rapid set-up facility of the pyramid tent, and are fairly spacious as well. They also have some claim to authenticity — perhaps even more than the baker and Whelan — according to one manufacturer. The reference to this style was found in a 1930s Boy Scout Manual, which referred to this style as an 1848 "forester's tent." The only difference between that and the new version is that the forester's tent was supported by a rope thrown over a bough and then pegged down while the new version uses the single interior pole. It has been reported that the one-pole lean-ti has been accepted as an authentic "scouts' tent" by certain Revolutionary War reenactment

Illustration 24: A Whelan lean-to.

Illustration 25: A multi-pole lean-ti or ti-to.

societies, but I have had no confirmation of that claim.

Given the choices available, which is the right shelter for you? As suggested, that choice will be determined in part by the role authenticity plays in your decision-making. Further, give some consideration to such practical matters as ease of set-up, ease of transportation, and comfort. One advantage of such shelters as wall tents is that they can be easily equipped with small wood-burning stoves. Care must be taken that the hole for the stovepipe be lined with a non-flammable substance such as asbestos, or, more traditionally, tin, to prevent or reduce the risk of fire. Actually, a stove in a wall tent or marquee will keep the interior warmer longer and with less effort (and less expenditure of fuel) than an open fire will a tipi. For a winter rendezvous, or even in the spring and fall, warmth is a serious consideration. The stove can be used for cooking, also, but is rather limited in this regard.

The tipi fire, while less efficient than the stove, has advantages in atmosphere and cooking. Its disadvantages are that it requires constant tending if it is to be kept burning through the night, and there is always the danger of sparks. I have seen stoves used in tipis, with a tall stovepipe extended through the smoke flaps (and with a spark arrestor on the stove pipe), and, while not strictly in keeping with the atmosphere of the traditional lodge, a stove in a tipi has its advantages. At the last rendezvous I attended, I saw a neighbor sneak a kerosene heater into his lodge. I'd never thought of that, but he reported that it worked pretty well, if you don't mind substituting the smell of kerosene for wood smoke.

Another advantage that wall tents, marquees, and the larger baker lean-tos have over the tipi, wedge, pyramid, lean-ti, and the smaller lean-to is that the upright walls allow the use of cots. Cots are impractical in a tipi or other sloping-wall tent but work well in any side-wall tent. I confess that as I grow older, the thought of keeping my

Illustration 26: A multi-pole lean-ti or ti-to.

body off the cold, hard ground has a powerful attraction for me.

In summary, the selection of a primitive shelter will be determined by the requirements of authenticity weighed against such personal considerations as family need and comfort. If you are representing a Continental or British private, your choice is the wedge; if a Yank or Johnny Reb, it is a shelter tent. If you're officer material, or are participating with your entire family, then the larger marquee or wall tent is for you. The lone mountain man will pick a wedge, a pyramid tent, a small tipi, or a simple lean-to. If he's a family man or has a lot of possibles he'll go to a large tipi, wall tent, or a large lean-to. Suttlers and traders also tend to use marquees, wall tents, and large lean-tos. The variety is there — the choice is yours.

WORKS CONSULTED

Blitzer, Charles. Age of Kings. New York: Time Inc., 1967.

Coggins, Jack, Arms and Equipment of the Civil War. Garden City: Doubleday and Co., 1962.

Encyclopedia Britannica. 9th Edition (1889).

Farrow, Edward S. Farrow's Military Encyclopedia. 3 vols. New York: Military-Naval Publishing Co., 1885.

Hadas, Moses. Imperial Rome. New York: Time Inc., 1965.

Hanson, Charles Jr. "Some Notes on Tents in the Western Fur Trade." The Museum of the Fur Trade Quarterly. 16 (Spring 1980).

Ketchum, Richard M. (Ed.) The American Heritage Book of the Pioneer Spirit. New York: American Heritage Publishing Co., Inc., 1959.

The American Heritage Book of the Revolution. New York: The American Heritage Publishing Co., Inc., 1958.

The American Heritage Picture History of the Civil War. New York: The American Heritage Publishing Co., Inc., 1960.

Lord, Francis A. Civil War Collector's Encyclopedia. New York: Castle Books, 1965.

Neumann, George C., and Frank J. Kravic. Collector's Illustrated Encyclopedia of the American Revolution. Harrisburg: Stackpole Books, 1975.

Sherrard, Philip. Byzantium. New York: Time Inc., 1966.

Stewart, Desmond. Early Islam. New York: Time Inc., 1967.

Peyote graph paper

Rows ... Rows

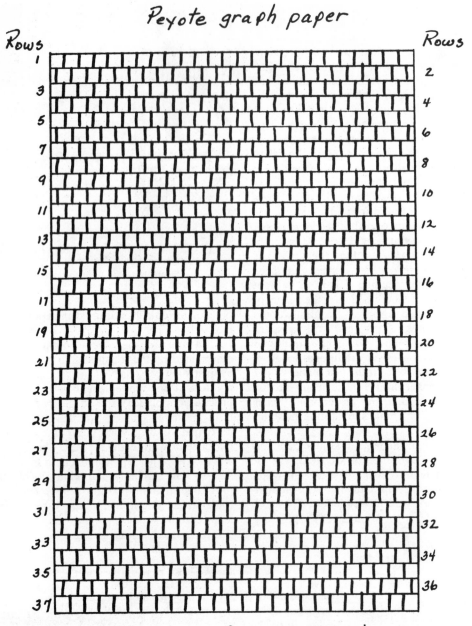

Graph paper for 10/0 beads

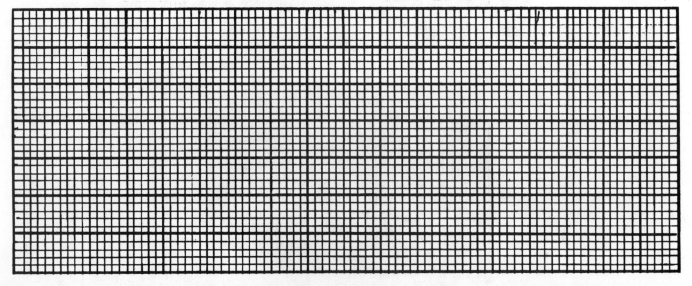